Sustainability in Art, Fashion and Wine

Sustainability in Art, Fashion and Wine

Critical Perspectives

Edited by
Annamma Joy

DE GRUYTER

ISBN 978-3-11-078389-6
e-ISBN (PDF) 978-3-11-078393-3
e-ISBN (EPUB) 978-3-11-078397-1

Library of Congress Control Number: 2023951741

Bibliographic information published by the Deutsche Nationalbibliothek
The Deutsche Nationalbibliothek lists this publication in the Deutsche Nationalbibliografie;
detailed bibliographic data are available on the internet at http://dnb.dnb.de.

© 2024 Walter de Gruyter GmbH, Berlin/Boston
Cover image: Hybert Design
Typesetting: Integra Software Services Pvt. Ltd.
Printing and binding: CPI books GmbH, Leck

www.degruyter.com

Acknowledgements

I am very grateful to all the people at De Gruyter who have encouraged and supported me through the entire process of editing this book, including
- John Stewart, Commissioning Editor, and Steve Hardman, Acquisitions Editor (Business and Economics), who believed in my endeavor to bring together a group of scholars who provide great insight on these topics.
- Jaya Dalal, Content Editor (Social Sciences), who was the contact person for my first book and who continued to be the contact person on this book. In your quiet and efficient manner, you managed to keep in touch with me through the long process of reviewing and editing 16 manuscripts.
- Other members of the team at De Gruyter, such as the cover page designer and copy editors, who offered creative ideas and helped me keep a schedule.

This collection could not have come together without the help of the brilliant contributors from many parts of the world. I thank you all for your hard work, your patience, and your sense of humor.

I have to thank my friends at UBC who believed in me and offered guidance and support.

I am grateful to the UBC publication fund, who provided a $2,000 grant to see this book in print, and to the Social Science and Humanities Research Council of Canada (SSHRC), who over the years have supported me with numerous grants to study art, fashion, and wine. The most recent grant was for the study of marketing and consumption of wine (grant #435-2017-0958).

My thanks to my editor, Letitia Henville, who patiently worked through several iterations of the book.

My long-suffering siblings, Jolly, Joecha, and Kochu (and their respective spouses Kantha and B.J.) who have humored me through this entire process and who believe in everything I do. Without the almost daily conversations I have had with each of you, I would not be so energized and enthusiastic about what I do. Without your love, I would not accomplish the things I do. Thank you.

The subsequent generations of the Joy family – Anita, Toto, Anna, Annika, Yeshwant, Nihal, Nesa, Talia, Lana, and Abby – I love you all very much!

Thank you Babs (Baba Vishwanath, past Dean, De Groote School of Business, McMaster University) for championing me in all my endeavors. You have always been there for me through good times and bad. You are my source of inspiration and sustenance.

My mentor and role model, Dr. Brenda E.F. Beck—I thank you for your unfailing trust in me, right from the start.

When I spoke to my daughter Annika about this book, she was very enthusiastic to share some of her thoughts on the subject. I was amazed that she had written a poem about the ideas with which I was grappling. With her permission, I would like to share it with this book's readers.

Thanks so much, darling, for being there—you are the reason there is a spring in my step and hope for the future. This book is dedicated to you. . .

TURTLE ISLAND

By

Annika Joy (2022)

There once were good people.
Who shared Turtle Island.
They lived on the land. With the land.
How to define these people?
Perhaps we should not.
For they come from many groups
With many traditions.
Each individual, unique.
They all shared the beautiful land
Where the spirits played amongst the trees.
Where the animals shared their wisdom
Where all were one child.

Then, a change came.
A tsunami.
So fast. So deadly.
The new people came.
Irreverent, self-serving people.
They were not one with the land.
To them, land was a commodity.
To them, the spirits were fiction.
To them, only their people mattered.

They claimed Turtle Island was theirs.
"Canada" they called it.
Stealing a word they did not understand
Butchering the sounds that did not belong to them.
"Indians" they called them
Because they didn't understand their own maps.
They decided "Canada" was their land.
Their privilege
Their right.

The new people did not want to share "their" land
With a people whose languages were unfamiliar,
With a people whose customs were different,
Whose skin was a richer color than their own.

The new people never admitted that they were the strange ones.
They were the intruders.

No, to them, they owned the land
The other people were the intruders.
The ones who were there first
Were the intruders,

Assimilation.
That's what the new ones called their mission.
Take the "Indian" out of the child.
What they meant was
Take the culture from the child.
Take the family from the child.
Take the community from the child.
Eradicate the culture.
If they failed at first,
They tried again.
And again.
Each new measure,
Each new policy.
Designed to destroy.
Anything to get rid of them
Like pests,
Like vermin.

But these people were strong.
Powerful.
Resilient.
They would not be destroyed.
They kept coming back,
Stronger.
Louder.
Eventually, the new man,
The white man,
Changed tact.

If the "Indians" would not be destroyed,
They would be hidden.
Trapped.
Caged.
In reservations.
Where white men would not have to see them.
Hear them.
Know them.

But they are still here.
Every minute their voices get louder.
Bolder.
Soon, they will shake the earth with their cries.
They will be heard.
They will not be eradicated. Hidden. Silenced.
They have always been here.
And they always will be
Here,
On Turtle Island.

Contents

Part 4: **The World of Wine**

Annamma Joy

1 Introduction: Critical Perspectives on Art, Fashion and Wine: A Frame Analysis

Erving Goffman's book *Frame Analysis* (1974) provides an appropriate structure for developing critical perspectives in the worlds of art, fashion, and design. A "frame," according to Goffman (1974), provides a window onto a landscape and, as we look through that window, we are guided by what the frame permits us to see: "Frames are constructed in accord with organizing principles that govern both the events themselves and participants' experience of these events" (pp. 10–11). A given frame thus circumscribes shared beliefs, norms, and values, and what things mean in a specific situation (Joy, 1998; Orazi & van Laer, 2023). We must continuously ask what is happening within the frame and how the frame shapes our interpretation—whether that frame is anthropology (Meek, 1988), sociology (Benford & Snow 2000), political science and policy studies (Chong & Druckman, 2007) or some other discipline or perspective. If we expand our frame to include multiple layers, more things become visible to us—although there are limits to this view as well. In our critical examination, we could either continue expanding these frames to include emerging perspectives, or we could limit the framing process, thus limiting the scope of our investigative interpretation.

Jameson (1976, p. 119) notes that Goffman's *Frame Analysis,*

> with its elaborate defense of the proposition that meanings, in everyday life, are the projection of the structure or form of the experiences in which they are embodied, and that they may most adequately be dealt with in terms of the ways in which such experiences are framed, in which they relate to, transpose, or cancel other frames.

The framing process is decisive: it determines what is included or excluded, and in this process it creates a certain order (Joy & Sherry, 2004). It is an ideological signifier of value, edge, border, boundary, and limit. Yet, some of the frames we identify have already materially shaped the world. For instance, a neo-liberal frame is an ideology and governing structure that affects how business operates in advanced capitalism and calls forth remedial action from critical thinkers.

Further, Entman (1993) argues that frames in, for instance, communication can be identified with the communicator, the text, the receiver, and the culture. But even in the context of communication, a frame can structurally emphasize one or more of these elements at the expense of the others. In the context of this book, frames can be seen as both expanding and shifting (Joy, 1999; Joy & Sherry, 2004). When the boundaries are clear, what is circumscribed by the frame provides a perspective on the content related to the frame. A number of chapters in this compendium expand and shift the frame through the critical stance they take. This viewpoint is important in this book because, while a discipline may appear tightly circumscribed, there is constant interrogation of

https://doi.org/10.1515/9783110783933-001

the ontological and epistemological principles guiding the discipline. Thus, for example, while the social sciences may appear to permit more flexibility in the subjects of its study than business schools, reverberations at the periphery will eventually affect the core of the business discipline. In terms of our understanding of art, fashion, and wine, the concept of shifting boundaries allows us to expand what is contained by and what is beyond the frame, thus leading to greater theoretical and methodological reflexivity.

In this introductory chapter, we look from multidisciplinary perspectives at the framing processes in three domains: art, fashion, and wine. The introduction not only encompasses ideas by the authors of the subsequent chapters within specific frames, but it additionally introduces new ideas, thereby expanding the frame. We have multiple frames, each diversifying the content and providing new insights, and we start with a neoliberal frame.

Late Capitalism: A Neoliberal Frame in the Art, Fashion, and Wine Industry

Neoliberalism can be understood as the management of society and individuals through the market. The neoliberal framework supports privatization, liberalization of prices, trade, deregulation, consumerism, and an entrepreneurial self that undermines unions (Bockman, 2007; Ziliberberg & Dholakia, this volume). As the market grows, the neoliberal framework asserts, the long arm of the state will diminish—but in practice, under neoliberalism, it seems that both governments and corporations have expanded their reach to all corners of society. Many consumer researchers have highlighted the dominance of a neoliberal framework in understanding consumption in society (Giesler & Verasiu, 2013; Eräranta et al., 2019; Schmitt, Brakus, & Biraglia, 2022; Zwick, 2018).

Becker, Hartwich and Haslam (2021) note that marketization is the outcome of neoliberal ideas on the importance of a holistically self-sufficient society. In the world of art, marketization has caused major changes in how art is defined, viewed, and supported; art becomes a capitalist enterprise, rather than a creative sector of society. Under neoliberalism, some artists and their works have been made into icons and priced highly, and the museums that hold their works consider them more as commodities to be bought and sold than outcomes that celebrate the creative process. Museums in the twenty-first century, as Eräranta et al. (2019) note, are evaluated in terms of numbers of visitors and other quantifiable measures of success. Eräranta et al. (2019) provide a detailed account of how museums, with their elite visitors and members, have continued to serve the upper classes. Museums like the Guggenheim have hired directors that have an MBA in addition to art expertise. Joy and Sherry (2003) discuss the prevalence of blockbuster shows in museums supported by major corporate sponsors, and how such exhibitions shape our perceptions of art. It is also not surprising that famous museums such as Guggenheim and the Victoria Albert museum have had shows for well-known designers such as Armani and Karl Lagerfeld. Museums and haute-couture seem effectively intertwined (Armitage 2022). Thus, neo-liberal ideas of self-sufficiency—even in domains that are meant to be outside the world of profit-making, such as public art galleries and museums—are reshaping our perception of what does and does not count as an artwork.

Corporations are capitalizing on our shifting understanding of what constitutes art by blurring the line between artworks and consumer products. This process is called artification, and is defined as the process by which non-art becomes art (Kapferer, 2014). Louis Vuitton, Chanel, and Gucci all have elevated their products through their association with art and sacralising the interiors of their flagship stores and other retail spaces through design (Joy, 2022b). Art is in the DNA of luxury brands and is thus central to the strategic choices they make in business (Joy et al., 2014; Kapferer, 2014). Artists have been hired as art or marketing directors of companies such as Louis Vuitton to oversee the process of turning luxury products into art objects. Takashi Murakami, one of the foremost pop artists of our times, is one such artist. Murakami first debuted at the Venice Biennale in 1995 had museum retrospectives shortly thereafter at the Los Angeles MOCA and the MOMA in New York (Thornton, 2009). From 2002 to 2015, Murakami served as an art director at Louis Vuitton Moet and Hennessey (LVMH). Art is in the DNA of luxury brands (Dion & Arnould, 2011; Joy et al., 2014), and when big-name artists collaborate with luxury brands like Louis Vuitton, consumers have additional motivation to buy from them. LVMH is of course not the only luxury company that employs artists; Hermes and Chanel have both included artists in their stable of designers. LVMH, Chanel, Kering, and Hermes have art foundations that support artists and the art world, and these companies also hold art exhibitions within their premises (Joy et al., 2014). Moreover, corporations are collectors of art (Joy, 1998), and art dealers and auction companies such as Sotheby's and Christie's promote artists in their own collections to increase the value of their artworks. Therefore, art is still largely the currency for privilege and wealth under neo liberalism as it did during the time of the Medicis.

The number of biennials and art fairs around the world is also the outcome of the neoliberal framework of viewing art as an enterprise that shapes our world. Art biennials have become reputation-building ventures, and the money-making capacity of such endeavours is well known (Drummond 2006; Rodner et al., 2011). The Venice Biennale is the most successful one, enabling artists to become branded—as was the case with aforementioned artist Takashi Murakami. While in theory, art is sacred and should not be contaminated by commerce, it is at art fairs and art biennales that many artists become famous, and their works sought after (Lee & Lee, 2016). Many biennials have corporate sponsors and other private sources of funding. While Walter Benjamin (2008) talked about the loss of aura of art in an age of mechanical reproduction, the current loss of aura by art is even more pernicious in its impact. Appadurai et al. (2021a) argue that the aura is not associated with a physical product but a service entity that allows financial experts to bet on risk rather than the future value of the commodity, which according to him is essentially lost in the long chain of trade-able risks. As Appadurai & Alexander (2021b, pp. 128–129) suggests,

> Financial capitalism hates the sluggish materiality of the commodity and much prefers its unknown and vaporous future value, whereby any commodity can acquire the aura of uniqueness, distance and immediacy that Walter Benjamin saw as endangered by the growth of the commodity world.

This, he argues, is a tragedy of epic proportions, because it is the exemplar of how things work in late capitalism. Appadurai et al. (2021a) laments the loss of art's aura and suggests that the new auratic [product on the market is not art, but rather a commodity—a financial derivative.

Fashion is the poster child of neoliberalism as well. The way the industry is currently structured under neoliberalism supports the supremacy of fast fashion (Joy et al., 2012). The mantra of the fast fashion industry is: use, trash, and buy new. Feeding the desire of consumers to have the runway look at a fraction of luxury prices, this industry produces cheaply manufactured, poor-quality clothing that is not designed to last. Mirroring the individualistic values of neoliberalism, fast fashion allows consumers to pursue their fashion identity even though landfills cannot hold the resultant clothing and textiles that are trashed (Ertekin & Atik, 2023. Even among companies like Patagonia that collect used clothing from consumers, waste is still a problem, as sometimes these clothes have to be held until they can be disposed of safely (Grohmann, Marengo, & Joy, this volume). According to Hoskins (n.d.), the short turn-around times and low prices of the fast fashion industry mean that resources and labor are exploited in the production process. Money goes where labor is cheap; when individuals do not have a choice but to accept low wages, there is massive exploitation. Fast fashion garments are primarily made in emerging economies such as Bangladesh, Indonesia, and India, where labor costs are low and where rules and regulations are blatantly disregarded. China, according to Hoskins (n.d.), is the biggest producer of fast fashion, with an output twice the combined size of that of countries like India, Vietnam, Bangladesh, Indonesia, and Mexico. While China is no longer a leader in cheap labor, manufacturers believe that the quality of Chinese product is better than any produced in the aforementioned countries. Furthermore, the environmental damage done by the fast fashion industry is enormous; for instance, cotton is a water-intensive crop, and the volume of water used and polluted in the process of its production is significantly high (Henninger et al., 2022). What is more, while some extoll the creativity that fast fashion permits, most of the goods produced are knock-offs and the product quality is abysmally low. The low-quality production is intentional, since every week there are new items to be had in a large swath of stores (Ertekin, 2019). Yet despite the low quality, fashion—fast or luxury, low or high—is a source of substantial wealth. According to Ertekin (2019) and Henninger et al. (2022), the winners of the fashion industry are the big corporations with multiple brands: ASOS has brands such as Topshop and Miss Selfridge, and Condé Nast owns Vogue and Vanity Fair—not producers of fashion, but supporters of fashion discourse (see also Conde Nast, 2022).

The irony here is that while the fashion industry is highly exploitative, consumers have a choice in what they purchase. Thus, many believe that fashion companies are not so much to be blamed for poor labor practices and environmental pollution as the individuals who make purchasing decisions. They have a choice, and, as Hoskins (n.d.) summarizes, "neoliberalism is a system that teaches us that empowerment comes from acting independently (not collectively), that freedom means variety in what we consume, and that we should trust in the system and shop (not fight) our way to a new world" (n.d.). At a time when there is so much concern about climate change and environmental destruction, exercises of such notions of freedom under neo-liberalism require major revision.

Neoliberal frames and the international policies that have accompanied these points of view have likewise affected the wine industry. Since NAFTA came into force in 1994, trade within North American has been liberalized considerably, and Canadian and American federal governments have taken a back seat when it comes to high-value agricultural products such as wine. The United-states-Mexico-Canada agreement (USMCA) that came into effect in 2020 facilitates trade further by helping importers obtain a certification of origin with important elements specified (Gertz, 2018). While such trade agreements have had many benefits for participants land prices became very high, and wineries moved toward producing smaller yields, which increased quality and, with it, prices (Yelvington, Simms, & Murray, 2012). Nowadays, wineries are tourist attractions: visitors come for an authentic experience in a rural setting, enjoying beautiful landscapes as much as quality wines (Joy et al., 2023). However, the same process that generates tourism also leads to the further commodification of wine via large yields and location branding (Poitras & Donald 2009). While the Napa and Sonoma Valleys are not Disneyland, in the summer they are visited by exponentially increasing numbers of global visitors. Moreover, wineries also see the benefit of lending their space for weddings, parties, and conferences, which only further commercializes their vineyards.

According to Yelvington et al. (2012), the term *terroir*—which refers to "taste of place," primarily "nature"—has been replaced with an understanding of *terroir* as a broader natural environment that includes the work of wine-makers (Ulin, 2002). The introduction of the appellation system—a system that identifies where the grapes in a bottle were grown—reduced the push towards total commodification of place because it stipulated certain localities as having specific characteristics (e.g. type of soil) central to the production of quality wine. This system, as in the case of Napa, Burgundy, and Bordeaux, is also significant for the wineries that operate in the Okanagan, a region in British Columbia, Canada. The Okanagan Valley, termed the "Napa Valley of the North," has nine official, protected sub-geographical indications: East Kelowna Slopes, Golden Mile Slopes, Naramata Bench, Okanagan Falls, Lake Country, South Kelowna Slopes, Summerland Bench, Summerland Lakefront, and Summerland Valleys (BC Gov News, 2022). The sub-appellation systems in the Okanagan helps to elevate the location of wineries in the Okanagan and identifies them as producing premium wines.

Thus, place, site, and yield became critical for the premium end of the wine industry, leading to an upscaling of the industry as a whole. Okanagan wines are considered to be premium wines that are available but relatively rare. They are considered to be artisanal in orientation, with narratives built around particular winery terroirs, and thus sold to visitors as a place in a glass. Major conglomerations such as the Constellation Brands—an American producer and marketer of wine, beer, and spirits—started buying small wineries in the early 2000s. While these small wineries operated under the same name, they were still able to put economies of scale into use. As a region develops, however, it becomes harder to argue that its wines are unique and special. Corporate capital, as Yelvington, Simms and Murray (2012) note, was therefore used to grow industry profits, with the state taking a minor role in the gentrification of the rural landscape.

In emerging nations, wine is associated with status and wealth. Unlike beer and most other spirits, wine is considered to be a drink that is knowledge-based, which creates a sense of inadequacy among people who are not in the know (LaTour, Joy, & Noujeim 2021). The tastes of people in emerging states will change as their wealth increases, and we expect that preferences will begin to align with international tastes and styles. In India for instance, Michel Rolland—the world-renowned, Bordeaux-based oenologist—has flown in to advise wineries in the making of wine, as he has done in other wine regions (Joy & Pena 2017). As tastes change, so too are wine-producing regions seeing a gentrification of the countryside, as laborers in vineyards are housed in camps or in lesser-known areas of town (Overton & Murray 2013). In Canada, the number of wineries has grown rapidly, and what was once farmland and orchards has been converted to vineyards, with their associations of rural bourgeoise lifestyles (Overton & Murray 2013). There is a trade-off happening between the return on investment in vineyards and the prestige associated with their products: as wine becomes an elite, luxury good, the people who enable that wine to be produced (commodified labor) face decreasing working and living conditions (Yelvington, Simms, & Murray 2012).

In sum, under neoliberalism and its entrepreneurial emphasis, companies in the art, fashion, and wine industries have commodified labor, place, and the environment. Resultingly, neoliberalism has promoted a hegemonic system that benefits only the few.

Market Socialism in the PRC

While we have mostly focused on capitalist countries with a neoliberal orientation in the West, there are other politically important countries also taking centre stage in the world of art, fashion, and wine. China, with its commitment to market socialism, is the prime example and cannot be ignored in a global consideration of luxury goods.

All societies, whether capitalist or socialist, have a market at their centre, since trade, exchange, and barter are as old as civilization. However, it is the specific role of the market and its coordination that determines whether it has more of a socialist or capitalist tilt. Neoliberalism is strongly associated with free market capitalism, with its emphasis on market orientation and a reduction in the role of the government (Giesler & Fischer 2016). China moved towards the liberalization of its economy through embracing a market orientation and making the market central to the coordination of economy and society. However, there is a key difference between Chinese market socialism and Western neoliberal capitalism. In China, the state still guides the market, preventing the privatization of key industries (Wang & Judge 2012). While entrepreneurship is strongly encouraged and the accumulation of personal wealth is celebrated, the long arm of the State guides this progress (Duckett, 2020). Becoming global, through integration into the global division of labor, is one way China has become more neoliberal in its orientation. But this commodification of labor is still very much in State hands, as the market and private property are still expected to serve the State's agenda of development (Weber, 2020). There seems to be an acceptance of these ways of development within the Chinese population, since even knowledgeable citizens—particularly those working in the outsourcing and back-office service industries—declare themselves proud of their heritage and proud of their country, which is moving to be a world player in terms of economic development (Chong, 2020). Chong (2020) argues that these knowledge workers resist corporate cosmopolitanism, and it seems that their individual views of a cosmopolitan self are more in line with a broader national project of elevating China's development to parallel that of the West (pp. 819–820).

Similar displays of resistance to corporate cosmopolitanism can be seen in the contemporary Chinese art market, which developed when China opened up in the late '70s with the introduction of Deng Xiaoping's socialist market economy (Gao 1999; Joy & Sherry 2004). In the art world, an implicit art-market model is used, yet Deng's call to maintain a "Chinese essence" in artworks produced by Chinese artists remains of great importance (Van Dijk, 1992). There are four important time periods for understanding the current art market in China: the end of the Qing dynasty (1911–1949); the communist regime (1949–1976); from Mao's death until the massacre at Tiananmen Square (1976–1989); and from 1989 to the present (Zhang, 2017). As one time period moved into the next, the communist frame changed, leading to the creation of a frame of market socialism (Van Dijk, 1992). The key term in market socialism is the "market" and, while governmental oversight exists, entrepreneurial-based growth in the art world is encouraged. Hence, the commercial nature of Chinese art is not lost on even the most important of contemporary artists (Dal Lago, 1999; Zhu, 2002).

Joy and Sherry (2004) discussed the new trends in Chinese art since the 1990s and how this demand coincided with the demand for luxury goods in the PRC. Currently China boasts 525 auction houses, 5,354 museums (Daxue Consulting), and a large number of art galleries. The importance of commerce in the art world is evident, for instance, in Shanghai's West Bund Museum, a result of a collaboration between Paris's Pompidou Centre and the Tank Shanghai, a multifunctional art centre. Contemporary art has become very valuable in the PRC.

Consequently, neoliberalism has left an undeniable mark on Chinese art. Harvey (2005) describes the Chinese art market as neoliberal but with Chinese characteristics. As with other business endeavours, entrepreneurial activities in the art world were encouraged by the State, although individuals were ultimately subject to the State. As Zhang (2017) notes, "being afraid of the repercussions of acting boldly as artists and catering to political power has not allowed the art market to flourish" (p. 2036). Nonetheless, China has become the largest contemporary art market in terms of auction and related sales. On Sotheby's 2014 list of rich young artists (based on auction prices), there were 47 Chinese in the top 100 contemporary artists in the world (Zhang, 2017). Those artists who know how to bridge the line between State and non-State policies that govern art are more successful than others in the commercial sales of their works.

Similar to the art world, the fashion industry in China is also an extension of neoliberalism but with Chinese characteristics. Ironically, while the State has control over the market, it wants to project the strengthening of the middle class, a task which is essential to promoting the State's project of economic development and maintaining social stability. Consumption is crucial for the strengthening of the middle class—especially the consumption of luxury goods and well-known Western brands. Globalization within China happens through consumption and is visible in the financial independence of middle-class women. An increase in individual social status is reflected by material symbols of consumption, which bears gendered consequences. The modern ideal female image emphasizes fashion as well as spending power. Consumer goods that are symbols of social status have thus become sources of aspiration and objects of pursuit. In a market like China, economic empowerment and self-reliance brings with them a certain level of empowerment of the gendered female self (Yu, 2018).

A more recent trend has been to revive traditional sartorial style in the PRC (Reinach, 2011). Paraphrasing the words of President of the Central Academy of Fine Arts, Fu (2023) notes that "the 'Chinese dream' is not merely an improvement in material life but also an elevation in tastes and artistic appreciation" (p. 7). Its manifestation in fashion is to reflect a historical tradition with a modern twist—both in terms of national revival and fashion identity construction (Fu, 2023, p. 8). Fashion reflects a country that looks in to its past in order to find solutions to the present and future.

As the Chinese art and fashion markets have changed under a series of state-imposed frames, so too has the Chinese wine market (Andrews & Gao, 1995). Local and international wineries are important to the emergence of the wine industry in China—an industry which has become central to the Chinese economy (Lu & Howson, 2023, in this volume). Kjellgren (2004) argues that the Chinese wine industry has followed a similar trajectory to that of the Chinese art market—a shift that is best understood using a political economy framework. As Kjellgren (2004) notes, "the latest chapter in the history of Chinese wine starts in 1978 with the Third Plenary Session of the Chinese Communist Party, in which Deng Xiaoping's political program was chosen as China's and [the] Communist Party's salvation" (p. 25). At the local level, the shift to Deng's socialist market economy meant the implementation of the market system with private ownership of wineries and overseas investment in vineyards. The three famous Chinese wineries, which were born in the wake of the Third Plenary Session and which still dominate the wine market today, are Dynasty (a Sino-French joint venture established in 1980 with Rem-Cointreau), Great Wall (established in 1983 by China National Cereals and Oils and by the Foodstuffs Import and Export Corporation), and Changyu (a joint venture with the French company Castel) (Auger et al., 2012). LVMH also has vineyards in the Ningxia region and produces wines that equal or exceed quality expectations and are sold at high prices. Drinking wine, especially red wine, has become common amongst China's upper-middle classes, and offering of wine as a gift—in the tradition of offering a gift of the spirit Baijiu—is still very popular. Wine is a product, says Kjellgren (2004), that in China is strongly linked to the project of modernization—yet this modernity adheres to the century-old catch phrase: "make the old serve the present and make the foreign serve the Chinese" (p. 26).

While the Chinese state encourages neoliberalism, it comes with Chinese characteristics: surveillance, and entrepreneurship. In the spheres of art, fashion, and wine, entrepreneurship is encouraged, but it happens under the watchful eye of the State. The contrast and comparisons that we note between China and the West are important in understanding how neoliberalism is at work not only in post-capitalist U.S., but also market-socialist China.

Diverse Frames

The predominance and durability of a neoliberal frame in current contexts, however, does not mean that neoliberalism is the only perspective we can take on art, fashion, and wine. When we expand our frame to include a critical studies perspective, we introduce a new frame and, with it, appropriate concepts essential to the consideration of the content from within this frame. Applying the frame of critical studies allows us to critically revisit the neoliberal frame, because the content within the first frame can be countered, expanded, and explored via the second one, leading to conclusions that are larger in scope than the first frame alone would allow. Moreover, when we expand the frame to consider the decolonization of management theory, the critical studies frame is expanded once again, and now may include a critical understanding of the theory-building process itself. Thus, a dialogical approach between different disciplines can both circumscribe as well as expand our critical understanding of art, fashion, and wine.

Frame 1: Business

Art market researchers are effusive about how art fairs, art biennials, art galleries, museums, and auctions allow a small group of high net-worth individuals—artists, speculators, and retailers—to increase their wealth (Velthuis, 2011). There is no question that, in our neoliberal times, art is viewed through the prism of price, as continuously demonstrated by Sotheby's and Christie's auctions, which reflect a neoliberal view of art and the art world. This view turns art institutions like museums into markets of sorts and individual artists into contestants (Kundu & Kalin 2015). Price determines the value of an artist and their work, much more than the art works themselves. The internet and digital technologies have also changed how art is viewed. Art is not only accessible to larger groups of people than it was in a museum or an art gallery, but the internet also affects the price of the art because of the demand. In the current status quo of digitalization and of price as the stamp of value, the cutting edge of art has been compromised and replaced by the aura associated with the financializaton of capitalism and symbolized in the "derivative" (Appadurai et al., 2021a). The traded derivative, note Appadurai and Alexander (2021), has replaced the traditional speculation associated with art—and with it, the aura associated with art that Benjamin (2008) describes has been replaced as well. What is tragic, Appadurai et al. (2021b) argue, is that under capitalism any commodity can achieve the aura of uniqueness in the same way that Walter Benjamin has described art. Technology, including photography, film, and the internet, has reduced the risks of contingency and duration from the circulation of aesthetic objects.

It is not surprising that, if art can be examined through the business frame, then luxury fashion and fine wines—which because of artification are also not commodities —can be viewed from a business perspective as well. Kapferer and Bastien's (2012) *The Luxury Strategy*, for example, focuses on how to create strategies for marketing products at high levels of profit. Implicit in their text is the assumption that luxury is not for all and that the business model of luxury brands serves only a select few—the very rich. As Armitage and Roberts (2016) note in *Critical Luxury Studies: Art, Design and Media*, luxury brand managers are not concerned with the ethics of inequality on which they build their business strategies. They go on to suggest that managers and scholars of luxury brands are more pragmatic than philosophical. As Berry (2016) has argued, over the centuries, the idea of luxury has changed from being a negative term to being seen in a positive light—what he calls "the gradual demoralization of luxury" (pp. 101–125), a process that emphasizes economic prosperity over political morality. This positive focus on prosperity is precisely the framework used by Kapferer and Bastien (2012). Such a frame does not include the consideration of history or ethics of luxury. Could the approach to such indulgence be changed, however, given the drastic situation the world faces today, asks Berry (2016)? Could climate change provide an important reason for curtailing excesses of luxury consumption?

The book *Luxury Wine Marketing* by Yeung and Thach (2019) likewise exemplifies the frames used by business scholars who have a pragmatic and positive view of luxury wine, without taking into consideration the ethics and inequities embedded in the system. They define luxury wine as "one of the highest quality, coming from a special place on earth [. . . with] an element of scarcity, an elevated price, and [the ability to] provide a sense of privilege and pleasure to the owner" (p. 5). This definition has similarities to how Kapferer and Bastien (2012) define luxury, and it forms the foundation from which they develop their analysis. Yeung and Thach (2019), however, go on to say that luxury wines often incorporate elements of organic and environmentally sustainable practices, even though the wines may not be marketed as such. They also add a note of caution: continuous high quality cannot be maintained if the land used for wine grape production is not viable and fertile, which are statuses that climate change threatens. This cautionary remark is reminiscent of how land has been exploited in the growing of cotton for the fashion industry and how it has wreaked havoc on land use and people around the world (Arthington 1996). Yet, Yeung and Thach (2019) do not go beyond this mere mention of sustainable wine agriculture to consider the ethics of continuing with unsustainable cultivation and production practices.

An example of such reflexivity in the luxury wine business model is only hinted at in the description of sustainability practices by Gaja, a wine company from Piedmont, Italy. According to Yeung and Thach (2019), Gaja has been at the forefront of innovations in the wine market, including being one of the first wineries to introduce green harvesting, using techniques such as small French *barrique* casks and short maceration times. Most recently, they have imported American earthworms to turn cow manure into compost for their vineyards, because this form of composting brings vitality and strength to the vines (see also McInerney, 2016). Without the right soil, the vines will not have the strength to produce quality grapes on an ongoing basis. Selling earthworms to vineyards has now become a viable business. Yet, the motive for this quasi-sustainable practice is to produce high-quality wines, while making profits.

These business frames give us glimpses into sustainable practices within the wine industry, although these ventures are often peripheral to the core purpose of the business: the creation and extraction of profit. The business literature follows a scientific model of knowledge-sharing, most often manifested in published journal articles, book chapters, and books. Such publications generally tack between previous findings and current knowledge with implications for the future. Yet not all studies from a business perspective take this shape. Consumer culture theory has critically questioned this form of theory construction (Arnould & Thompson, 2005). For example, an entire issue of the *Journal of Marketing Management* (Coffin & Hill, 2022) was devoted to non-representational forms of research and writing, to explore a three-dimensional matrix of knowing versus sensation, considerations of subject versus object and closure versus openness of interpretation. One such lens through which we can understand the world—a lens that differs from the conventional without losing its status as "serious scholarship" (Coffin & Hill 2022, p. 1617)—is poetry.

Frame 2: Critical Studies

Like poetry, critical studies seems to raise more questions than it provides answers. While studies that adopt a conventional business frame might focus on principles of managing luxury brands, Armitage and Roberts (2016) argue for expanding the frame by locating a study of luxury within the context of history and politics, and by extension, of ethics—an approach that was missing from the aforementioned consideration of luxury wines by Yeung and Thach (2019). For example, they argue that the field of luxury studies can be viewed as the domain of a network of people, institutions, and luxurious influences. Without such a context, the boundaries between what is luxury and what is not are fuzzy, revealing the artificiality of such boundaries. For instance, Armitage and Roberts (2016) argue that bottles of balsamic vinegar are "removed [. . .] from the ordinary category of human food" because of "their rich producers, their fine taste, their rich consumers and high price" (p. 10). By elevating the creation and maintenance of certain goods, food producers create the category of luxury food and wine not accessible to the common person. As it goes with food, so too can this concept be applied to any number of products, services or experiences.

As Armitage and Roberts (2016) emphasize, the disparities between the wealthy and the poor set the terms for the idea of "luxury-as-dominance" (p. 10). Luxury brands use the cultural and economic capital represented by art to further their own strategies of success (Joy et al., 2014). This is best exemplified by the actions of LVMH. As noted earlier, by hiring the artist Takashi Murakami as their artistic director—as well as a slew of other artists, including Yayoi Kusama, who contributed her artistic vision to LVMH products such as Veuve Clicquot champagne—LVMH acted as an art purveyor as well as a museum, displaying the works of these artists, albeit in the context of luxury (Featherstone, 2016; Joy et al., 2014). The seemingly ubiquitous boundary-spanning activity between these fields is essential to luxury brands' search for revenue. Consider, as a parallel example, Rolex's alignment with the celebrity tennis player Roger Federer—the watchmaker here uses sport and fame to support their image, even though wearing a Rolex to tennis practice seems uncomfortable at best. Luxury brands need cultural capital (Bourdieu, 1984) to make profits, and the appropriation of art and design is a logical choice to make in this process. Using celebrities helps to seal the deal. When brands make their (non-art) products into art—whether through appropriation or commodification—they transform their goods into luxury items—a point that Kapferer (2014) makes, despite not considering the political implications of such a move.

The actions taken by companies such as LVMH are normalized in effect to emphasize artisanal and artistic orientation and to elide references to mass production. In her discussion of the Louis Vuitton website, Rocamora (2016) explores the luxury brand's tactics of hiding and erasure. With the website's elaborate images of handcrafting in ateliers—eliding the mass production processes that happen in LVMH factories around the world—as well as the website's extensive references to the arts and the brand's continuous use of artists to create limited editions, LVMH elevates and differentiates itself from mere commercial production, even though its products are made through such processes. Myth-making is part of this process (Boje et al., 1982; Brown et al., 2013), as the site contains stories of how a young Louis Vuitton got into the business of travel and the creation of trunks for the rich and noble. More importantly, although the site has a global audience, their presentation and sales of their goods focus primarily on North America, Western Europe, and East Asia, leaving out large swaths of the world without the money to access these products. LVMH thereby reinforces the distinction between the core and periphery (Lash and Urry 1994, p. 28).

Another aspect of luxury that is not often discussed is its dark side—notably, the corruption and secrecy of luxury goods and art markets (Backsell & Schwarzkopf, 2023). One exception is Roberts' (chapter in this book) study of free ports—spaces in which goods in transit are exempt from customs duty, and in which there is limited transparency or control over the circulation of goods (Loos, 2017). Roberts (2019) cites a UNESCO document (2016) on free ports that showed that, when high-priced historical and contemporary art is shipped internationally, the spectre of criminal activities is raised. For example, in 1995, looted antiquities linked to the Getty Museum in Los Angeles were discovered in the Geneva Free port, and, as recently as 2014, the Geneva Free port stored a treasure trove of Roman and Etruscan antiquities in crates, labelled with the name of an offshore company (Renauld, 2021). Similarly, in 2022, there was an uproar due to the purchase of art goods by Russian oligarchs (mostly friends of Vladimir Putin) a month prior to the start of the war in Ukraine and then the usage of the Geneva Free port to store art owned by these oligarchs (Harari, 2022). Although many of the stolen goods were eventually returned to their rightful owners, such events reveal that illegal activities take place, and are not infrequent, in free ports. Thus, what ostensibly appears to be a neutral space—a space without a specific government levying fee, as if the land were outside of its territory—may become a space for corruption and criminal activities. Art is mostly implicated, although other luxury goods such as antiques and vintage wines are also transported through and stored in such venues (Renauld, 2021). The juxtaposition of art and luxury goods that are in circulation through dealers, luxury purveyors, museums, auction houses, and collectors—alongside art and luxury goods that are hidden in such secret spaces—allows us to consider the dark side of both art and luxury. Backsell and Schwarzkopf (2023, p. 11) go so far as to show that free ports transforms works of art into financial assets that are generally known as "emotional assets" and "passionate investments." In doing so, these assets maintain the aura associated with a Van Gogh or a Modigliani painting, even though they may be used as mere collateral for financial borrowing. For this to seamlessly happen, Backsell and Schwarzkopf (2023) suggest, requires enablers (usually galleries and auction houses), the clients who have the money, and the art, as well as the critics (journalists and tax accountants) who find the process less than transparent and corrupt.

Kuldova's (2021) interview with Andie Schmeid, the author of *Private Views, Luxury and Corruption* (2021), additionally critiques the dark side of luxury accumulation by high-net-worth individuals and the purveyors of luxury architectural spaces. Schmeid

(2021) focuses on buildings that house apartments of the rich and famous in New York City—the Trump Tower, the Gehry Tower, and West 53, among others—which she visited under cover. Schmeid notes that the Trump Tower used a loophole to develop its building: between the storeys that house apartments, the Trump Tower includes storeys dedicated solely to mechanics, and these floors are not counted in the height of the building. The building thus has empty floors with no apartments—only support columns. By adding multiple mechanical storeys, the developers increased the overall height of the building. This loophole has now been closed, so that permitted cumulative height of mechanical storeys is no more than 30 feet total, although other buildings include one empty floor in every ten floors of construction. Of course, the higher the apartment, the higher a price it can attract. And even in these high-cost apartments, some units sit empty, owned by wealthy people who live elsewhere in the world. In cities like New York, tall, luxury buildings are filled with unoccupied apartments that become little more than storing spaces for paintings, sculptures, and other art items. According to Schmeid (2021), there are tax advantages as well in not occupying or renting these properties, although some governments are beginning to crack down on unoccupied dwellings. In short: critical studies reveal the corrupt, often immoral practices deployed by luxury architecture firms.

Critical cultural studies, as defined by Armitage and Roberts (2016), offers a historical and political context to the study of luxury—a study of art, design and media with a focus on process, as well as a network of relationships. Armitage and Roberts (2016) highlight the struggle that exists over various forms of indulgence between the very rich and others. Yet, as mentioned above, luxury goods such as wine are often connected to knowledge, and the possession of such knowledge relates it to the ownership of cultural capital (Bourdieu 1984). *Habitus*—a concept outlined by Bourdieu (1990)—becomes the process by which individuals are socialized into luxury and make their way through the domains of luxury. Bourdieu (1990) defines habitus as "systems of durable, transposable dispositions, structured structure predisposed to function as structuring structures" (p. 53). For those who are socialized into luxury, knowledge of luxury—of how something is a luxury—is experiential and grows over time. Judgement of taste can only be known if one knows what is appropriate in specific contexts and in the context of one's own class. None of this is cast in stone, however, as changes in context are inevitable. The symbols and meanings associated with the use of a luxury object can be learnt from its promotional material or even watching how it is made, but this knowledge is different from that which is learned through possession and use. While conspicuous consumption might be a mechanism used by the nouveau riche to bypass years of knowledge or experience based on *habitus*, there are nonetheless noticeable differences between the old and new rich. Armitage and Roberts (2016) point to the concept of stealth luxury, whereby gaining acceptance among those with inherited wealth is complex, because people with family money can change the rules of membership (to distance themselves from the new rich) among the upper classes.

Critical luxury studies use a multidisciplinary and critical approach to luxury, drawing on ideas in moral philosophy, Marxism, cultural theories, theories of the object, art, signs, symbols, fashion, and geographies of production and consumption. As Armitage and Roberts (2016) note in their introduction, all the contributors to their book

> seek to situate luxury products and services explicitly in relation to other socio-cultural and historical practices and particularly concerning the politicized structures of luxury capital and labor, democracy, science, the city and other socio-cultural hierarchies such as those advanced by haute couture fashion houses like Chanel, Dior and Versace. (p. 11)

What is also important to note, they argue, is that luxury begins at the point at which humans surpass necessity (Armitage & Roberts 2016). There are two issues to take into consideration: the first is the idea of excess and lavishness embedded in objects that take individuals beyond mere necessities into a desire for more. For instance, a bottle of Dom Perignon—especially when it is purchased for an important celebration—is worth more than the price you pay for an ordinary bottle of wine. For many consumers, high-cost, high-quality champagne can be a justified occasional luxury. The second issue is that our recognition of ourselves as luxury-loving beings, always seeking more, also leads to economic and cultural growth. While being aware of the fine balance between need and indulgence, and aware that the consumption of luxury goods can easily lead to inequities, Armitage and Roberts (2016) also note that productive activities can ensue from luxury—productive activities which satisfy our desires for excess and lead to the creation of ever newer luxuries. Luxury wines are an important example of such goods (Yeung & Thach, 2019); luxury fashion goods are another.

Frame 3: Poetic Lens

Although the use of a poetic frame in business studies may not be mainstream, it stands as an exemplar to demonstrate the vulnerabilities of taken-for-granted concepts in the field (Sherry 1998a; 1999b). In their study "A Role of Poetry in Consumer Research," Sherry and Schouten (2002) provide a poetic frame through which to study consumer behavior. They ask: "if anthropologists use their marginal experiences to understand their own cultures more deeply, might we not use the insight of poets to understand consumer behavior more comprehensively? Especially, when those poets are consumer researchers themselves? Poetry is one effective way of writing intersubjectively" (p. 220). They extol the virtues of poetry to foster "sensuous knowledge and visceral representations" (p. 467), helping us to understand the research context better and to acknowledge the affective nature of consumption (Canniford, 2012, p. 393; Downey, 2016, p. 361). Their work, while peripheral to the conventional business frame, uses an artform to critique studies of the other artforms of interest here —namely of art, fashion, and wine (Sherry 2022).

Similarly, Wijland (2011)—who also applies critical poetics to the study of businesses—notes,

> in its aesthetic presence, marketing expressions are no different from other cultural artifacts in that they are appreciated for their uniqueness [. . .] Given their linguistic, visual and general semiotic components, brands inevitably are the most aesthetic outcome of the marketing process. Poetic textualization may provide a distinctive sceptical reflexivity on the quintessential openness of brands. (pp. 4–5)

Wijland concludes that poetry produces consumer insights that are not managerial in orientation and that allow for an understanding beyond our typical conceptions of marketing and consumer behavior with its links to consumerism (see also Brown & Wijland 2015).

By exploring the concept of poetization, Rojas-Gaviria (2021) takes apart the taken-for-granted concept of consumer identity construction as a wilful and agentic activity articulated through the consumption of products and brands. She summarizes the importance of poetry as a critical framework: "thoughts and ideas in their emerging forms rather than in their finalized version are, for me, what poetry is about" (p. 465). Borrowing from Hirshfield (2000), she argues that "poetizing is not merely an act of will, it is also an act of opening that which lies outside the will, outside the already known" (p. 464). There is a calculative future focus in identity-construction that belies the accidentality of becoming, especially in a vulnerable population with dementia. Her study shows that "heart-breaking times result in consumers being owned by identities rather than being the strategic authors of one" (p. 466). Rojas-Gaviria explores the powerlessness of an individual with Alzheimer's to craft a linear and controllable identity—an exploration that she charts by using categories such as poetic sweats, poetic companions, and poetic projections. Poetic sweats are embodied outcomes that can be managed by some patients through meditation or walks. Poetic companions are ordinary objects that individuals carry with them in order to strengthen themselves such as photos of loved ones. Poetic projections are the use of poetic sweats and poetic and other companions to collectively project into a fragile future; Rojas-Gaviria argues that they are examples of an emergent identity-making and shows that all three concepts are useful in unravelling experiences that are messy, less agentic, and mysterious in our lives. Overall, the insights of poetry with its holistic approach and overall consideration of the human subject are invaluable to marketing and consumer behavior with its emphasis on consumption (Rojas-Gaviria & Canniford, 2022).

Frame 4: Digital Technology

The introduction of art and luxury non-fungible tokens (NFTs) in the early 2020s created ripples in the art world. The auction houses Sotheby's and Christie's were at the forefront, garnering profits made from art NFTs. NFTs are dependent on blockchain technology, which allows, as Abbate et al. (2022) posit, "a radically innovative means of defining and governing transactions among multiple actors (Ying et al, 2023-chapter in this book). [The blockchain] constitutes a peer-to-peer ledger that provides a useful way of information to be recorded, aggregated and shared within a heterogeneous community of participants" (pp. 107–108). Blockchain technology is especially valuable for the worlds of art and luxury, since both spheres have struggled for a long time with fakes and forgeries (Wilcox, Kim, & Sen, 2008.

NFTs also allow for some form of democratization in the art world, enabling unmediated interactions between artists and art collectors, allowing both parties to have trust in each other and the transaction. The relevant package of information accompanying each transaction travels with the product or NFT (Humayun, Belk, & Brouard 2022; Joy et al., 2022a). As Abbate et al. (2022) note, in the art world, while the use of technology is not problematic, there is some resistance to the use of blockchain technology. This resistance is closely linked to the concept of trust—both cognitive and emotional—which, Abbate et al. (2022) argue, should increase if both artists and consumers were to accept transparency, decentralization, and consensus mechanisms on the blockchain. On a cautionary note, they add that key players such as for-profit organizations (e.g. auction houses) might take the lead in this direction. Old-fashioned institutional logics associated with the traditional operations of the art world and art market resist technological logics.

Each time an NFT is created, there are multiple players who are part of this process, and they validate and verify the process. While this concept of validation is a worthy idea, blockchain technologies and NFTs use more electricity than entire countries and, in the process, contribute to pollution and climate change (CCRI, 2022). This excessive energy consumption occurs despite the move towards renewable sources of electricity. In some cases, electricity grids are still reliant on oil and gas, which are the perpetrators of carbon emissions (CCRI, 2022). Ethereum, a blockchain platform that enables NFTs, requires 23 million MWh before its system upgrade in September 2022 (quoted in Zhu et al., in this volume). They argue that while 23 million MWh is sufficient to sustain 1.58 million Canadians for a year, given that in Canada the annual electricity consumption per capita was 14.6 MWh in 2017 (Canada Energy Regulator, 2021). However, according to CCRI (2022) Ethereum has made substantial changes to reduce its use of electricity and has a lower carbon footprint. CCRI notes that the Ethereum network is currently energy efficient and has successfully managed to decrease its electricity consumption by 99.9%. This was possible because they now use low-energy Proof of Stake rather than the high-energy Proof of Work consensus protocol. But they seem to be an exception; numerous other blockchain platforms continue to rely on the energy-intensive mechanism (CCRI, 2022). Because of their substantial carbon footprint, NFTs and the blockchain cannot be the panacea for problems in the art world, art markets, and luxury brands.

In the fashion world, haute couture has begun to make itself felt in the metaverse via skins and avatars. But such digital proxies are a far cry from how haute couture is generally understood in the material world, especially in the value that materials such as fabrics provide clothing, says Armitage (2022). High-fashion designers have specific people in mind when they produce clothes, whereas in the virtual world, creations are made for avatars. According to Armitage (2022, p. 12), "what is being produced, therefore, is not an haute couture collection but a visual representation of an haute couture collection." Armitage goes on to suggest that, while it is possible to make a case for a poetry of avatars and skins, all of this will happen only within the context of video games. He laments "that the composition of a poesis of clothing can never be found in the video games industry" (p. 16).

Digital fashion accessed through virtual reality, augmented reality, and the metaverse has grown by leaps and bounds in the luxury industry (Joy et al., 2022). Kozinets (2023) provides a detailed discussion of the application of the well-established method of netnography (the qualitative study of the internet), and how it can be applied to the study of the metaverse. NFTs in the art world, as mentioned earlier, are one example of how these new forms can be studied. As immersive technologies become more prevalent, the importance of the metaverse cannot be overestimated. Kozinets (2023) cautions us to the problems and prospects of immersive technology, including ethical considerations of using netnography to study the myriad aspects of the metaverse.

Tech company founders generally share the belief that technology can save mankind (Rushkoff, 2022). Problems that humans create, this belief goes, can be resolved with greater advances in technology. As tech companies grow, Rushkoff (2022) argues, so too grows a mindset that he terms "winning" (p. 35); as tech companies become larger, they pivot away from helping others and focus instead on increasing their capital gains. Appadurai and Alexander (2021) provide a more complex take on the topic by exploring regimes of failure. They argue that the interconnections between technology and finance support the view that successes in the market place are the result of technology (and thus of tech producers), while the failures that ensue are caused by investors, users, and consumers. Thus, "failure" becomes normalized and is supported "by the narratives promoted by Wall Street and Silicon Valley" (Appadurai and Alexander 2020, p. 123). Perpetuated in this discourse is the myth of endless progress, which justifies ongoing innovations in technology. Yet when catastrophes relating to climate change and economic collapse occur, the survival of humans and of the planet is at stake. This brings us to the next frame—the ecological frame.

Frame 5: Ecology and Politics

In a paper on the Anthropocene, Banerjee (2021b) asks, "What if we were to make an ecological case for business, instead of the business case for sustainability?" (p. 14). Banerjee's is a fundamental question that brings to the fore typical justifications for a company's existence. He then goes on to identify four shifts that are essential to making ecological matters a central focus of any business's organizational mission. The first is a move towards critical epistemologies, which means a questioning of the consumption model that drives capitalistic concerns of profit-making without a concern for its detrimental outcomes. What should our focus be if we displace economic growth? Banerjee suggests that future research should focus on ecological and social concerns. Will the green solutions being proposed be sufficient to create human–earth ecologies that are available for all people, regardless of wealth and other social inequities? A second shift he proposes is relational thinking. The separation of nature and culture is at the heart of non-relational thinking, which assumes that people possess dominance over everything—a highly anthropocentric view of the world. A relational view would allow us to consider nature as a political subject and therefore engender environmental ethics that encompass both nature and culture.

Banerjee's third shift focuses on interdisciplinarity, which, he argues, should not place the social sciences or humanities as subsidiary to the natural sciences. This conception of interdisciplinarity then leads to the fourth suggestion: engaged scholarship. Banerjee rejects the idea of a neutral, detached or subjective stance to scholarship. Extending this idea, Beacham (2018) suggests an ethics of care to be applied to the more-than-human world. He gives the example of an organic garden, which requires a rejuvenation of the soil—a process that can take seven years to develop. This temporal frame is not a human time frame, but working with the more-than-human world requires that care be given to the necessities of other organisms.

Eco-feminism and its variations have had some success, if only to raise awareness and challenge existing male bias (Maclaran and Chatzidakis, 2022). The environmental movement and its values was combined with the search for equality and justice embodied in the feminist movement. Eco-feminism emphasizes environmental ethics and its links to ethics of care. The dominant theory of moral reasoning, in line with a neoliberal frame, assumes an individual making abstract decisions; ethics of care, on the other hand, assume the interconnectedness of people and the environment (Whyte & Cuomo 2016). Both the environmental movement and feminist movement called for a radical change in human priorities, and advocated for a holistic perspective that critiqued the concept of anthropomorphism.

In the fashion world, the values of saving the planet resonate clearly with designers, as well as some manufacturers and consumers. They all understand the relationship between environmental abuse and the role of women – especially those in emerging economies – who have nowhere else to go. The use of plastics and chemicals have decimated the fertility of their lands and now the oceans. In their study of waste Frantzen and Bjering use the term "hyper abject" to refer to waste that is inert and will not decompose or be absorbed in the ground. The notion of the hyper-abject is a combination of Morton's concept of the hyper-object (Morton 2013) and Kristeva's (1982) concept of the abject. The key difference between the hyper-object and the hyper-abject lies in the importance of political economy to the hyper-abject: the hyper-abject is "not only an extension but inertness and the clogging of economic and ecological circulations produced by this inertness" (p. 89). The term refers to objects in their material reality and to the ways in which these objects have travelled or continue to travel along certain paths without themselves being transformed. For example, when we normally think of waste, we often associate it with transformation and decay. But the hyper-abject is not transformed when it becomes waste; its compelling property is one of inertness. Frantzen and Bjering (2020) give the example of microplastics, which are inundating the earth and the oceans, and are even being ingested by humans. After death, the human body may decay, but the microplastics will still remain. As the hyper-abject, microplastics have no agency; they are rendered thus through human capitalist actions. This form of waste, Frantzen and Bjering (2020) posit, cannot be recirculated through the ecosystem or re-emerge as a resource, so the hyper-abject allows us to look at waste from the point of view of the global infrastructures that create it. If microplastics are an exemplar of the hyper-abject, then the historical situation that creates them—and especially the ravages wrought by the petrochemical industry—needs to be curtailed.

In addition to introducing the concept of the hyper-abject, Frantzen and Bjering (2020) extend the ecological lens to bring into consideration the aesthetic and the political—a critical act they perform via the Danish poet Theis Orntoft, and specifically his 2016 work on the craters in the tundra caused by the loss of permafrost. When living with the Nenets, Indigenous people of the Russian far north, Orntoft was deeply affected by temporal and spatial characteristics of the tundra. He records sensing a unity of everything, encapsulating himself and the landscape. He comes to the conclusion that, from time immemorial, the world and everything in it constituted "messy assemblages," which does not allow for an anthropocentric view (p. 93). Orntoft echoes the ideas of speculative realist philosophers, who argued that the human subject is not ontologically distinct or special when compared to animals, plants, minerals, or other elements of the natural world. The idea of the agentic subject here is itself in question because everything, according to speculative realists, has agency. Entanglement of all human and nonhuman entities is the outcome.

But as Frantzen and Bjering (2020) note, Orntoft's poetry includes a sudden about-face when his poetic outputs moved rapidly from a belief in speculative realism to a more material and political description of the tundra. Orntoft came to call the craters of the tundra "abjects," caused by human activity. They could not be absorbed by or entangled with the "messy assemblages"; humans, by the actions of capitalism, have created the unassimilable. The hyper-abject is thus unusable, neither recyclable nor incorporable into the assemblage of agentic beings—such entities can never be included in any human or biological activity. Such a perspective returns us to the idea of human agency and responsibility. The idea of the hyper-abject requires a politics to either provide ethics of care or to destroy it, which means that late capitalism, as we know it—with its emphasis on production and circulation—will have to be destroyed as well. It is clear from Frantzen's and Bjering's (2020) observations that the neoliberal frame of late capitalism, with its disregard for the world, has contributed to the situation that we find ourselves in currently. Both the fashion and wine industries play a particularly influential role in the destruction of the environment, but perhaps the fashion industry is the main culprit.

Frame 6: Ethics and Social Justice

Art and the exclusion of women artists in its fold led to major movements in the art industry. Ethics and social justice for all, including women of color, is a rallying cry for younger feminists (Verster, 2021).

The exclusion of women in the wine industry is long standing, especially as wine makers, proprietors, and wine experts. They have been underpaid and overworked as in other industries. Ironically, feminine qualities are often associated with wine. Wine is often described as graceful, seductive, fine, delicate, and needing care and attention. As Almila and Inglis (this volume) suggest, gender inequality is as prevalent today as it was a few decades ago, although subtle concessions have been made over time (Matasar, 2010).

In the fashion world, the structure of the industry has had a major impact in celebrating male designers over female designers and the domination of the global North over the global South. Fashion companies—especially fast fashion companies like H&M and Zara—have begun to organize supply chains in parts of the world where the labour is unorganized (non-unionized) and inexpensive. Much of the labour performed within these supply chains is done by women. If sustainable and ethical principles in the fashion world are ever to occur, then we need transparency and good management of supply chains—but such transparency is not yet available in countries like Bangladesh, where H&M and Zara both operate. After the 2013 collapse of the eight-story Rana Plaza factory, in which at least 1,134 people were killed and more than twice that number were injured, two industry-led corporate social responsibility groups came to prominence in Bangladesh: the Bangladesh Accord for Fire and Building Safety (the Accord) and the Alliance for Bangladesh Worker Safety (the Alliance) (Banerjee & Alamgir, 2019). Banerjee and Alamgir's (2019) study of the Accord and Alliance shows that these groups did little to empower Bangladeshi workers or improve their safety in the workplace. Both groups involved workers in their operations only minimally; as brand-led initiatives, they did not specify the mechanisms by which workers could actually participate (Banerjee, 2021), and exploitative working conditions remained unaddressed when the two groups left Bangladesh in 2018. The Accord and Alliance, it seems, were a victory for trade unions outside of Bangladesh, as well as for global brands and retailers—but not for social responsibility or Bangladeshi workers in garment factories. Ironically, while both the Accord and Alliance purported to speak about workers' rights, both appear to have effectively silenced workers' own calls for change. Bangladeshi garment-factory workers—most of whom are women who live in abject poverty—are still in no position to negotiate the low wages they receive (Islam et al., 2023). Moreover, since the Rana Plaza collapse, procurement prices have dropped dramatically, which manifests in continually low wages and poor working conditions. According to Alamgir and Banerjee (2019), development in Bangladesh follows a neoliberal model in which "reconfiguration of state institutions to serve capital is a condition for a neoliberal development state to be embedded into global supply chains" (p. 31). Development under this model in Bangladesh involves the use of state violence to disperse labor protests; as a result, factory owners have become part of the ruling class in the country. In sum: while fast fashion corporations create a seemingly endless chain of organization, little positive change occurs for the lowest level of workers in the industry. As Alamgir and Banerjee (2019) note despite the outcry for social justice, the "creation and appropriation of value from the global supply chain still remains in the hands of providers of capital, global brands and the state" (p. 32). In a neoliberal context, globalization and cheap labor are important attributes of the fashion industry, exemplified in India and Bangladesh, and—to a lesser extent—of the wine industry as well, as wineries in Argentina and Chile exemplify. Not all women can afford to avoid such dangerous employment, as is clear in the case of India and Bangladesh. The conditions of precarity do not allow for redefining the rules that place them in such situations (Joy et al., 2015).

A different spin on social justice through the very rich helping the poor is provided by Bajde and Rojas-Gaviria (2021) in their study of donor behavior in Peru. Ironically, they note, under neoliberalism, even the poor must be transformed into entrepreneurs. These authors connect the concepts of consumer responsibilization and subject formation in their study of micro-lending practices to the entrepreneurial poor. Consumer responsibilization, as discussed by Giesler and Verasiu (2014, pp. 841–842), is a governmental process that constructs consumers "as autonomous, rational and entrepreneurial subjects who bear responsibility for social problems." The myth of shared responsibility is further sanctified in neoliberal frames that naturalizes the "problem-solving" propensity of the individual. While Bajde and Rojas-Gaviria (2021) accept the discourses that contribute to the creation of the subject, they bring affective dynamics in to focus on consumer responsibilization. They advance this understanding into a whole new level by arguing that structures of feeling created by online marketing intermediaries lay the foundation for individual donors to experience aspirational hope and an affinity towards the poor. Through the apparatus of relatability and likeability, these intermediaries act upon their feelings to loan money to the poor. Lenders believe that their actions will change the conditions of the poor in Peru and that, in the process, they would have contributed to changing the inequities between the developed and developing worlds.

Bajde and Rojas-Gaviria highlight the importance of ethics in practice (ethical reflexivity) when they recognize that online marketing intermediaries provide "romanticized depictions of the poor as aspiring entrepreneurs which, in addition to being inaccurate, further marginalizes the poor who are not economically functioning" (pp. 504–505). The authors are also conscious that online marketing intermediaries value some poor subjects over others—those who are more like the lenders (self) than those who cannot bridge this chasm. In the process, the intermediaries reinforce a particular moral order—an order that allows individuals in poor countries to shape themselves in the image of their benefactors as entrepreneurial subjects. If subalterns are given a voice, it is a voice that privileges the market. Perhaps the ultimate pathos is in this seeming unawareness of the constraints on their voice: "while borrowers do receive some compensation for their affective labor (i.e., access to more affordable loans) they remain largely unaware of the complex network of relations they enter—a network in which the lender's capacities to be affected to affect often come first" (p. 509).

Reimagining sustainability in the redistribution of food for those in need in developed countries like Austria is discussed by Gruber and her colleagues (in this volume) in their discussion of hybridization of the food retail sector. They argue that the logics of commercialism in the food sector has begun to be balanced by the ethics of care for the poor.

Frame 7: The Circular Economy

While social justice issues relate to social sustainability, the fashion world in particular is accused of being the worst offender when it comes to environmental sustainability—especially in regards to waste and waste management. A charitable view of how the fashion world can limit waste production, become socially responsible, and reduce its carbon footprint is the use of a circular economy. While the political issues and a critique of neoliberal frames are not prominent in such a view, viewing fashion through the lens of the circular economy enables us to offer possible alterations to some aspects of fashion's business model.

One vision for a circular economy in the fashion industry comes from the Ellen McArthur Foundation, a charity established in 2010 whose mission is to accelerate the global transition to circular economy in order to eliminate pollution and waste (The Ellen McArthur Foundation, 2022): "The circular economy is based on the principles of designing out waste and pollution, keeping products and materials in use, and regenerating natural systems." A circular economy seems the perfect solution to the problem of used garments being burnt or dumped in landfills. In a circular economy, materials for clothing would primarily be ethically sourced and transported to consumers using eco-friendly routes and mechanisms. In addition to being sold to consumers, ready-made garments could be rented or leased. When a product's life cycle comes to completion, its fibres would be recycled to create a new product. The expectation of a circular economy is that nothing would be wasted. Educating consumers to understand this perspective takes time and effort, and incentives should be used to get them on board (Joy & Pena, 2017; Hyass and Pederson (2019). Moreover, when considering a shift to a circular economy, the initial financial costs associated with developing new processes and workflows have to be factored in; for a circular economy to be viable, its value proposition must be incorporated into the business model of fashion companies (Hvass & Pedersen, 2019).

More recently, both luxury and regular fashion brands have been encouraging repair work as a way of saving an item of clothing and reusing it. Indeed, companies like LVMH have images on their websites of people doing repair work as if to show that LVMH is invested in the circular economy. Unlike industrial capitalism and its subsequent variants requiring commoditization—abstracting, dividing, recombining, and exploiting workers and materials for profit-making—repair and caretaking require the collaboration and interdependence of people and things (Corwin & Gidwani, 2021). As Corwin and Gidwani (2021, p. 15) state: "care as involvement in a complex inter-connected world means looking after things, non-humans and ecosystems, as well as people, their living spaces, and the relations that sustain them as social beings." Many brands, however, offer what Maclaran and Chatzidakis (2022) wryly refer to as "care-washing" (p. 100).

Yet even if a circular economy were to come into being, individual consumers would still need to consume less. The circular model gives consumers a false sense of pride that they are contributing to a reduction in carbon emissions because they've bought clothing that has done its circuit in the circular model. Circularity can be seen as making a difference, but the difference is not enough for the fashion industry to say that it has found a way to reduce the pollution it creates. According to the 2021 Circularity Gap Report, our global economy is only 8.6% circular—and that includes all industries, not just fashion (CCRI, 2021). Most fashion companies remain reluctant to use this model, because it generates smaller financial profits than traditional, linear business models. Nonetheless, luxury and fast fashion brands are spouting the importance of the circular model to reduce the ill effects of climate change. This has affected the wine industry as well, as critical factors such as climate, soil, and water require judicious usage (Grohmann, 2023).

Frame 8: Gender, Race and Intersectionality

The social aspects of sustainability do not receive much attention as the environmental and economic considerations, and this lack of attention concerns feminists and the feminist movement. The performative theories of Butler (1993) have been influential to feminist theory and have enabled gender to be seen as an artificial construct (Joy et al., 2015). Butler (1993) argues that repetitive gender performances contribute to gender identities and are not simply based on biological sex or sexed bodies (see also Maclaran & Chatzidiakis, 2022). Her notion of performativity, borrowed from speech-act theory, hinges on the importance of discursive practises that produce what they name. Gender identities can, however, enable power differentials based on discourses that create continuous changes in gender through enactment. Gender is thus fluid and can be refigured through repetitive performance. However, an emphasis on performativity does not do justice to the fact that some women have more power than other women based on their class or race. Historically, Black women have been marginalized by virtue of their race and social standing (Crenshaw, 1991). Currently, it seems that LGBTQ+ people are a much-maligned group, and queer and trans women have less privilege than straight women (Maclaran & Chatzidiakias, 2022, p. 14). These authors suggest that performances by the LGBTQ+ community may be different and even socially tolerated, given the dominant norms of heterosexuality, but that such performances do not contribute as yet to redefinitions of what is central to social formations. They merely become normalized as a deviation from the norm.

Given ongoing power dynamics related to race and class, it is not surprising that, despite their radical questioning of ontological and epistemological understandings of sex and gender, the work of feminists such as Butler (1990) have been critiqued. As a corrective, many cultural scholars have called for the use of an intersectional approach, acknowledging that previous studies have primarily focused on a small group of women—the white, wealthy,and privileged—and in doing so have ignored the experiences of the majority (Crenshaw, 1991; Oksala, 2016). The need to recognize the heterogeneity of women is amplified when we consider how differentially women are treated globally. Context and history are crucial to how we understand gender, and an intersectional approach enables us to consider such differences.

Within an intersectional framework, gender and race are political categories; as such, they often have been accorded legal status (Cooper 2015). This in turn creates interdependent systems of disadvantage. Race and gender can be used to discriminate against people in job markets and even in getting an education, which has an impact on the power and privilege that such individuals might have. Identifying race and gender in this context are political processes that produce the categorisations and characteristics of the powerful and the subordinated Arsel & Crockett 2021).

A question that Crockett (2022) raises in this context is whether brands can remain neutral about a controversial issue especially when the customers and fans want them to take a position. The example Crockett offers is the case of Colin Kaepernick who knelt at the football game in 2016 – a fitting protest against racialized police violence in the U.S. The NFL disavowed the action whereas Nike embraced it. Nike in particular has a long history of courting controversy in its advertising, product innovations and retailing because they see such actions as brand-building opportunities. Yet as Crockett (2022) argues, in the final analysis, the seemingly opposing actions of both brands are largely superficial. Brand avoidance (NFL) or confrontation of stigma (Nike) are just two different expressions of the same brand imperative. In both instances resource allocation done by these brands works around this brand management imperative and confines their efforts to focusing on a narrow set of brand interests. As Crockett (2022: 17) notes, "Many (if not most) organizational missions are tethered to historical and ongoing investments in racial oppression that direct their resource-allocating practices. And in the New Nadir, they do not long tolerate racial projects that would seriously subvert or devalue those investments".

Crockett (2022) and Ger (2018) use intersectionality to understand how inequality and discrimination are generated on the basis of characteristics such as race, gender, class, and disability. By using the framework of intersectionality, the authors explore how inequities of power are embedded in structures of domination (Ger, 2018; Crockett, 2022; see also MacLaran & Chatzidakis, 2022). Ger (2018) suggests that, through intersectionality, we can re-evaluate how we define, for instance, agency, resistance, and subjectivity from a political stance. Because of the overlap of multiple criteria, we are able to critique the validity of the choice-making in consumption processes of specific individuals who exercise their free will. It allows for a deeper understanding of reflexivity that goes beyond the knowledge of the knower and the known (Ger, 2018).

Building on theories of intersectional feminism, scholars go beyond discourse through the use of materialism within their frameworks to discuss inequities in power (Grosz, 2010). Some newer feminist theorists advocate for a post-human feminism which draws on actor-network theory. In this context, agency is allocated to both humans and non-humans who are inextricably entangled with each other (Barad, 2008). The human is not at the centre of decision-making or of importance in the network. At the heart of this concept is that all living systems have a self-organizing vitality at its core that disallows an anthropocentric view of the world (Barad, 2001, 2003, 2008; Braidotti, 2013).

Increasingly, other feminists have begun to also use the concept of materialism to take up the cause of justice and equality. Identity-formation, according to Parkins (2008), is dependent on a subject's interactions with the material world. Both human subject and non-human material object have recognizably mutable, changeable, contingent, and agential qualities.

Applying a feminist frame to the fashion industry can reveal a number of its core paradoxes, notes Parkins (2008). For example, consider the ephemerality of the industry. Fashion changes constantly and is experienced as ephemeral by consumers (Mukendi et al., 2020). The fashion industry is also ephemeral in that planned obsolescence is built into its business model, as silhouettes, colors, and fabrics change with the seasons. Today, fast fashion has a hyper-accelerated concept of time built into the business model, which makes the industry a danger to the environment (Joy et al., 2012). It is in the financial interests of the industry—both the older, established industry and the fast fashion industry—to outdate itself. Yet as it celebrates ephemerality and instability, the fashion industry, says Parkins (2008), also plays a major role in the reification of static images of women's bodies. The idea of changing fashion, however, calls into question the discourses that describe the feminine as static and unchanging, as Parkins (2008) has argued. To focus only on the changeability of the subject, however, is to ignore the role of industry in "the reproduction and instability of identity" (p. 511). The introduction of new fashion products 52 weeks of the year—instead of the historical fashion seasons, three or four times a year—requires a new way of consumer interactions with the material world that is extremely problematic for the future of the planet.

Materiality, fashion, and gender come together in the shape of "popular feminism" (Hopkins 2018, p. 99)—a form of celebrity discourse and attire practiced by the likes of Beyoncé Knowles, Ivanka Trump, and Victoria Beckham. In popular feminism, fashion choices are framed as part of self-expression (Joy et al., 2014; Parkins, 2018), bringing together the ideas of luxury, lifestyles and neoliberal feminism (Hopkins, 2018). What these women have in common are their successful companies: Knowles, Trump and Beckham are entrepreneurs who peddle women's clothing in line with what Hopkins (2018, p. 99) calls "wealth accumulation, monetised motherhood and competitive femininity." Beyoncé, for example, publicly paid tribute to Black culture in her 2016 Superbowl halftime performance, which appeared to reference the Black Panther Party, and in her praise for the Black Lives Matter movement during a June 2020 speech at the Black Entertainment Television (BET) Awards. Ironically, however, her clothing line sells a neoliberal feminism that reinforces white femininity (Vesey, 2015). The gist of the arguments of Knowles, Trump, and Beckman is that the post-feminist woman, if dressed appropriately in luxury fashion, can buy herself advantages in an increasingly male-dominated and uneven competitive world. It is one more example of neoliberal feminism that gets sold as "feminist politics" (Hopkins, 2018, p. 103; see also Parkins, 2018).

Just as the high heel reshapes posture, so too does all fashion—as a power-oriented phenomena—leave traces on the body (Joy et al., 2015). But fashion does not only impact the bodies of those who purchase and wear new articles of clothing. With most new garments sold today being manufactured in emerging economies, the fashion industry leaves traces in these countries as well, as poorly ventilated factories and the toxic dyes make workers ill and pollute local landscapes and waterways. These traces are systemic, and they are the material consequences of industrial production. As fast fashion becomes an increasingly prominent business model with no end in sight, the waste from the developed world is sent back to emerging economies, which contributes to further pollution. These are material realities created by the fashion industry. What is important is that when we talk about the conditions people, especially women working in fashion, face in emerging economies there is race, culture, gender, and class that have to be factored in simultaneously (Crenshaw, 1991. Often our analysis does not capture how some people especially in the global south are subject to all of these conditions. Third-wave feminists suggest that attending to these realities opens up the possibilities of making changes (Parkins, 2008).

As with fashion, an intersectional feminist lens can support novel understandings of the wine industry. Inglis (2019) notes that the language associated with wine is gendered and classed. This association is particularly true of red wine, which is considered a more sophisticated and masculine drink than white or rosé wine (Almila, 2019; 2021)—although, for reasons of profit-making, the red wine market has been extended to include women. According to Almila (2021), "the female wine market has been essentialized as less sophisticated, less knowledgeable and less confident than the male market" (p. 11). Such infantilizing marketing shows how slowly patriarchal ideologies change. Marketing campaigns tend to associate women with wines that are not considered connoisseur drinks, such as rosé—consider, for example, the 2022 film *Rosé All Day*, which features a dominantly female cast, or the similarly titled "Rosé All Day Cosmetics" line of make-up. Such arbitrary yet pervasive gendered associations reflect the standard taken-for-granted cultural assumptions of masculinity and femininity in these contexts (Fitzmaurice, 2017; Velikova et al., 2015). Moreover, this form of marketing also demonstrates the difficulty in displacing the existing definitions of self, subjectivity, and agency in the West.

Regardless of the strides we have made in terms of gender, race, and class, a one-step-forward-two-steps-back situation prevails, particularly in the worlds of fashion and wine. Consider, for example, the number of winery labels that have breasts on them (Styles, 2018). Christina Rasmussen, a wine journalist in the U.K., noted that sexualized labels only serve to objectify women and continue the form of sexism that already exists. The so-called artistic expression that it falls under is clearly not gender neutral (https://www.meiningers-international.com/wine/general/natural-wine-labels-borderline). Non-feminist ideas of gender, art, and wine consumption remain prevalent today, despite many changes mobilized by the feminist movement.

Consumer studies researcher Ger (2018) argues, that we might not even know that the pre-suppositions we bring to research shape our understandings—even as we examine the pre-understandings of the people we study. Intersectional feminist approaches can enable consumer studies researchers to see our work and our subject matter in new ways—including ways that are important for social justice. As researchers including Ger (2018) have argued, in the consumer studies field, we urgently need to consider the role of intersectionality in our choice of topics, our approach to research, our methods of data collection and analysis, and our decisions about where and how we disseminate explanations and discussions.

Some Concluding Remarks

Figure 1.1 summarizes the discussion thus far and, more importantly, provides us with an impetus to push outwards in search of richer understanding that lie outside the frames. In an insightful introduction to a special issue on presentation in marketing, Coffin and Hill (2022) summarize the importance of non-representational thinking and representing in marketing along three lines: knowledge versus sensation, objective distance versus subjective, depth, and interpretive closure versus interpretive openness. Sensation, subjective depth and interpretive openness are closely aligned and allow for a greater and more nuanced understanding of the complexity of consumption and marketing. We have already referred to the potency of poetry in evoking insights that simply cannot be imagined if we use scientific discourse (Sherry & Schouten, 2002; Rojas-Gaviria, 2021). While vision and the scopic regime has dominated marketing research, a multi-sensorial approach and the openness it entails, Coffin and Hill (2022) argue, is long overdue.

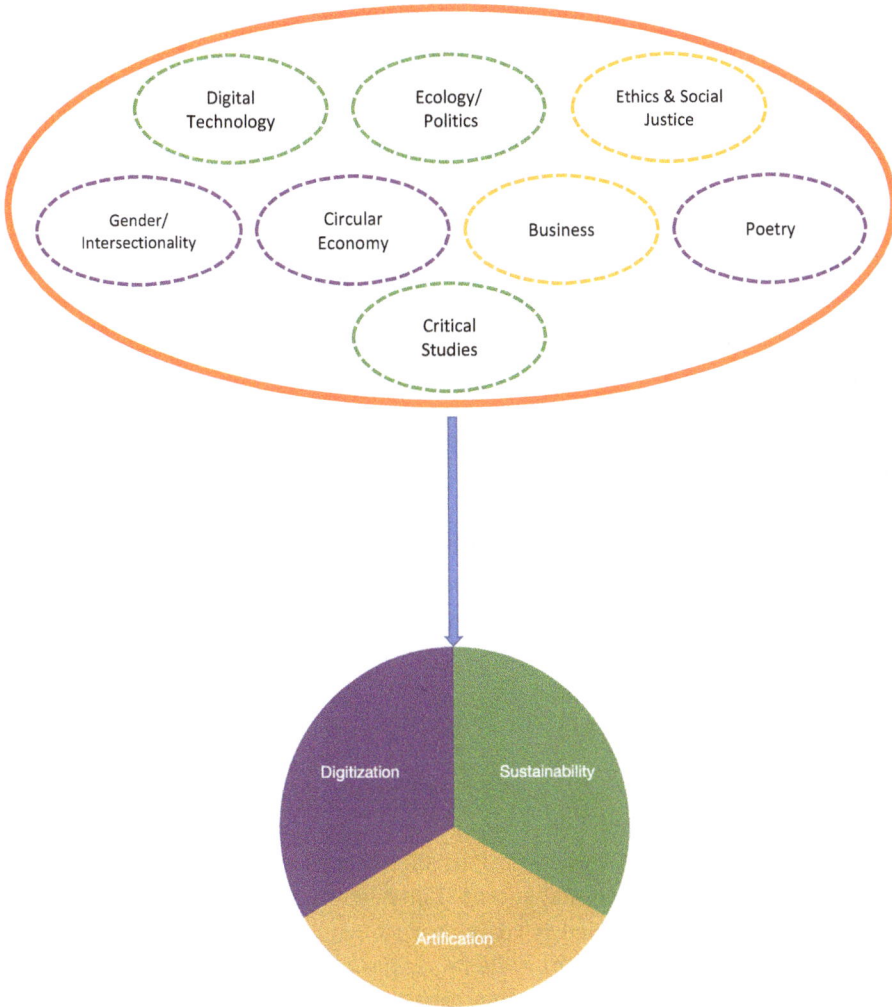

Digital Technology

Ecology/ Politics

Ethics & Social Justice

Gender/ Intersectionality

Circular Economy

Business

Poetry

Critical Studies

Digitization

Sustainability

Artification

Figure 1.1: Critical Perspectives on Art, Fashion & Wine.

I am reminded of Cezanne's observations about color and its connections to how a painting emerges: "the first a systolic moment in which confused sensations condense into definite forms; the second a diastolic moment when there is no longer anything except colors and in them only clarity" (quoted in Bogue, 1996, p. 259). Deleuze (discussed in Bogue 1996, pp. 34–35) likewise, in a comparison of Francis Bacon and Cezanne, notes: "when Bacon speaks of sensation, he says two things which are very similar to Cezanne. Negatively, he says that the form related to the sensation (the Figure) is the opposite of the form related to an object that it is supposed to represent (the figuration) [. . .] sensation is that which is transmitted directly, and avoids the detour and boredom of conveying a story." Coffin and Hill (2022) capture some of this fluidity and ambiguity in their discussion of the differences between knowing and sensing—between representation and non-representation. We need both representational and non-representational techniques to critically understand and shape our world. Having considered the importance of reflexivity needed to do our research, we are ready to look at the contributions made by authors in our compendium.

The Structure and Organization of the Compendium

The first three chapters work together in providing the broad strokes that are central in this compendium. In Chapter 1, I have identified the broad contours of the compendium with a focus on various frames that can be used to study the worlds of art, fashion, and wine. The chapter begins by applying a neoliberal frame to our understandings of these three domains. I then propose eight frames and demonstrate how each frame illuminates and ignores certain issues, with particular attention to sustainability, digitalization, and artification. It also considers what is happening to art, fashion, and wine in the People's Republic of China with its emphasis on market socialism although there are similarities between the outcomes of market socialism and a neo-liberal framework dominant in the West. This chapter not only recognizes the various contributions to knowledge from the scholars in this edited volume, but additionally examines framing as a critical process and highlights new frames that have been ignored in previous discussions of luxury goods.

In Chapter 2, Ziliberberg and Dholakia explore the challenges that arise from the interplay of sustainability and neoliberalism. According to sustainability advocates, the changes driven by neoliberalism are leading to climate catastrophe, while champions of neoliberalism argue that sustainability-driven changes would result in an economy strangled by rules and regulations. Each ideology has also created its own legitimation system in order to prove its value. The authors introduce the 10R framework of the circular economy to illustrate the issues arising from this discussion both generally and in specific reference to the fashion industry.

In Chapter 3, Gruber, Holweg, and Lienbacher provide a reimagination of sustainability in the context of poverty and food redistribution systems. While this chapter has a limited discussion of luxury brand consumption, the authors emphasize the importance of social justice issues within consumption studies. Social supermarkets are purpose-driven retailscapes that have proliferated across Europe to combat food waste and to assist people at risk of poverty with their food expenses. The authors conduct a comparative case analysis of two social supermarkets to explore the tensions that managers experience when navigating between a logic of commerce and a logic of care. They detail how managers ensure that social supermarkets uphold their crucial contributions to the well-being of vulnerable people and the reduction of food waste.

Section on Art

In Chapter 4, Firat investigates the contemporary status and role of art and fashion in the context of the conditions that humanity faces resulting from modern constructions of art and fashion. He reminds us that, as is the case with all concepts, art and fashion do not have a consistent meaning across all historical epochs or cultural contexts, even when they may possess some essences that contain a degree of continuity of popular conception. In each epoch and in every culture, however, art and fashion take on certain particularities imbued in them according to the symbolic dynamics of the time and context.

In Chapter 5, Pilar and colleagues focus on the importance of affective atmospheres in immersive encounters. As they argue in this volume, immersion "is a lived form of intersubjectivity and affectivity; yet the literature on how immersion is mediated in the marketplace remains scarce" (p. 110). Through a study of "Punch Drunk" theatre, they demonstrate that the design of immersive environments is a form of affective governmentality which requires greater attention from researchers. They further suggest alternate methodologies to study non-representational forces and effects that are central to immersive contexts.

In Chapter 6, Roberts examines the transformation of works of art into financial assets through the use of free ports, which store artworks and other valuable collectables while also offering significant tax advantages. While art has aesthetic and emotional value as well as cultural significance, over recent decades, the possession of art for financial gains and as a store of value has increased—and the process of financialization has been supported by growing numbers of free ports. Roberts argues that this trend towards art's financialization may be viewed as indicative of the de-artification of cultural goods.

In Chapter 7, Zhu, Zaitoun, and Joy present an overview of the applications of blockchain technology, cryptocurrency, and non-fungible tokens (NFTs) in the art and luxury fashion industries. The authors identify five brands in these industries—Louis Vuitton, Burberry, Balenciaga, Christie's, and Sotheby's—that represent current trends associated with adopting these innovative technologies and applying them to marketing strategies, branding, and consumer engagement. Although blockchain technology, NFTs, and cryptocurrency have the power to positively transform the art and luxury industries, they also come with costs, such as negative impacts on the environment because of excessive energy consumption. This chapter, in turn, outlines the environmental impacts of such practices, especially according to the concept of metawashing. The authors conclude by suggesting research questions that art and luxury markets should address when adopting these new technologies.

Section on Fashion

Fernandez argues, in Chapter 8, that circular consumption must complement circular production if we are to create a sustainable society. To ensure that resources are not wasted, lost or discarded, consumers must reduce their consumption of new products, extend product usage, and employ disposition methods that minimize resource loss. Re-use plays a role in all three of these pathways. Unfortunately, consumer re-use of fashion is difficult to achieve, and so this chapter discusses how contamination and cultural norms influence fashion re-consumption. Fernandez considers luxury fashion, fast fashion, slow fashion, vintage fashion, retro fashion, and re-commerce, with the goal of encouraging and facilitating the re-use of fashion.

In Chapter 9, Frig, Polsa, and Kerrigan argue that fashion is unsustainable, particularly due to its role in the production of pollution, waste, and social inequality. The chapter explores different methods by which these unsustainable practices could be reduced. The authors present the different motivations behind the sustainable practices of reduce, reuse, repair, recycle, and rent of clothing. They scrutinise the differences between the practices of reuse and recycle, showing what motivates consumers to either reuse or recycle their clothing. Finally, they compare different types of fashion libraries and ask what values consumers get from fashion libraries.

Atik and Ertekin note in Chapter 10 that democratization of fashion has been a topic of interest both in academia and popular media. Research shows that, at the consumer level, persistent problems of sustainability and diffusion of fashion to larger consumer segments do not necessarily indicate that fashion is democratized. In this chapter, the authors explore this topic from the broad institutional level, showing how the practices of the multiple constituents of the fashion supply chain are democratizing for everyone involved in the making of fashion. For such an assessment, the authors investigate the power structures and labor dynamics of the industry and offer suggestions for a more sustainable future in the fashion industry.

In Chapter 11, Henninger et al. provide insights into what colonialism implies, asking how far the phenomenon still exists within the Ethiopian fashion and textile supply chain. Although Ethiopia has only been colonially occupied for a brief part of its history, oppression is nonetheless observed. Whilst oppression may not necessarily be unique to the Ethiopian context, discussions of fashion are stimulated on how to overcome barriers to promote decolonization.

In Chapter 12, Iran et al. discuss interconnections between sustainable fashion consumption, minimalism, and luxury fashion, arguing that minimalism promotes the idea of owning fewer items, which can lead to a rise in the demand for high-quality, durable, and timeless pieces that can be worn for years to come. At the same time, luxury brands are taking notice of sustainability trends and are starting to incorporate such practices into their production processes, while additionally offering timeless and durable pieces that can be passed down through generations. Hence, it seems that luxury and minimal wardrobes could lead to more sustainability in the fashion industry—as long as consumers do not engage themselves in practices that bring rebound effects (e.g., fast replacement of their luxury garments).

Focusing on the case of the Patagonia brand, Chapter 13 authors Grohmann et al. examine the sustainability paradox in the fashion industry. This paradox arises when a brand's sustainability attracts a growing number of consumers, which results in increased production and brand consumption. This, in turn, leads to negative environmental and social consequences, such as increased emissions, waste, or the inclusion of less socially responsible suppliers to meet increasing demand, which ultimately threaten the brand's sustainability. This chapter sheds light on the sustainability paradox and discusses the brand's recent shift from conscious capitalism to philanthropocapitalism to mitigate the negative impacts of their success.

Section on Wine

In Chapter 14, Pena explores three distinct approaches to sustainable wine making: conventional, organic, and natural, focusing on widely adopted practices for each approach. The comparison between these three approaches is done for the full wine-making process, considering ecosystem management, soil and nutrition management, viticultural and pest management, water management, energy management, winemaking, cellaring, and social aspects involving employees, neighbors, and community. The chapter develops a robust understanding of what sustainability means in the wine world.

In Chapter 15, Almila and Inglis argue that, although there have been shifts in wine culture over the recent decades, wine production, distribution, and consumption remain subject to multiple forms of division and inequality along gender lines. This includes processes by which wine phenomena are subjected to artifying strategies for marketing purposes. When winemakers are presented as artists, and oenology is presented as an artistic practice, deeply masculinist notions of artistic genius are commonly invoked. The authors reflect upon gendered phenomena in wine marketing, pointing out the potential gender risks embedded in wine artifying pursuits, as well as instances of resistance and alternative ways of existing and acting in the world of wine.

Finally, in Chapter 16, Ly and Howson discuss the production and consumption of fine wine in China. China has been considered a growing market for imported wine—notably, luxury consumption by the wealthy in order to show off their status. Meanwhile, the reputation of Chinese domestic wine went from low quality and mass produced to earning praise from international critics. In this chapter, Ly and Howson examine how luxury multinationals and local private entrepreneurs have reshaped the image of Chinese wine and earned the respect of local wine enthusiasts who drink for aesthetic pleasure rather than status signaling. However, the authors demonstrate that while fine wine producers continue to develop their brands around sustainability and the art of winemaking, water scarcity could pose a major challenge.

References

Abbate, T., Vecco, M., Vermiglio, C., Zarone, V., & Perano, M. (2022). Blockchain and art market: resistance or adoption? *Consumption Markets & Culture, 25*(2), 105–123. http://doi.org./10.1080/10253866.2021. 2019026

Almila, A. (2019). Wine, women and globalization: the case of female sommeliers. In D. Inglis & A. Almila (Eds.), *The globalization of wine* (pp. 191–212). Bloomsbury. https://doi.org/10.5040/9781474265027. ch-011

Almila, A. (2021). A wine flight of gendered sociology: vignettes of (Apparent) Trivialities. *Journal of Cultural Analysis and Social Change, 6*(2), 1–14. https://doi.org/10.20897/jcasc/11449

Almila, A., & Inglis, D. (2022). Threats of pleasure and chaos: wine and gendered social order. In S. Charters, M. Demossier, J. Dutton, G. Harding, J. Smith Maguire, D. Marks & T. Unwin (Eds.), *The Routledge Handbook of Wine and Culture* (pp. 311–319). Routledge.

Andrews, J., & Gao, M. (1995). The avant-garde challenge to official art. In D. Davis (Ed.) *Urban Spaces, autonomy, and community in contemporary China*. Cambridge University Press.

Appadurai, A., Bockman, J., Heinich, N., Konings, M., La Berge, L.C., Lovink, G., Ignacio M. Sánchez Prado, I.M., & Thayer, W. (2021a). Art under neoliberalism. *ARTMargins, 10*(3), 126–158. doi: https://doi.org/ 10.1162/artm_a_00303

Appadurai, A., & Alexander, A. (2021b). *Failure*. Polity Press: New York.

Armitage, J. (2022). Re-thinking haute couture: Julien Fournié in the virtual worlds of the metaverse. *French Cultural Studies*, 1–18. https://doi.org/10.1177/09571558221109708

Armitage, J., & Roberts, J. (2016). *Critical luxury studies: art, design and media*. Edinburgh University Press.

Armitage, J., & Roberts, J. (2016). Critical luxury studies: defining a field. In J. Armiage & J. Roberts (Eds.), *Critical cultural studies: Art, design and media* (pp. 199–220). Edinburgh University Press.

Arnould, Eric J., & Thompson, C.J. (2005). Consumer culture theory (CCT): twenty years of research. *Journal of Consumer Research, 31* (March), 868–82.

Arsel, Z., Crockett, D., & Scott, M.L. (2022), Diversity, Equity and Inclusion: A Curation and Research Agenda. *Journal of Consumer Research, 48*(5), 920–933.

Arthington, A. (1996). The effects of agricultural land use and cotton production on the tributaries of the Darling River, Australia. *Geo Journal, 40*, 115–125.

Auger, U., Chen, J., Ho, C., & Rowe, A. (2012). Uncorking China's wine market. In *Knowledge at Wharton*. https://knowledge.wharton.upenn.edu/article/uncorking-chinas-wine-market/.

Ayscough, A. (2020, December 16). *Natural wine labels on the borderline*. Meininger's Essential Readings for the Wine and Drinks Industry International. Retrieved December 6, 2021. https://www.wine-business-international.com/wine/general/natural-wine-labels-borderline.

Backsell, J.I., & Schwarzkopf, S. (2023). Hiding in plain sight: organizational magic as a contested process of revelation and concealment. *Organization Studies*. https://doi.org/10.1177/01708406231151494

Bajde, D., & Rojas-Gaviria, P. (2021). Creating responsible subjects: the role of mediated affective encounters. *Journal of consumer research, 48*(3), 492–512.

Alamgir, F. & S. B. Banerjee (2019). Contested compliance regimes in global production networks: insights from the Bangladesh Garment Industry. *Human Relations, 72*(2), 272–292. https://doi.org/10.1080/ 0969160X.2020.1795453

Banerjee, S.B. (2021a). Decolonizing deliberative democracy: perspectives from below. *Journal of Business Ethics*. https://doi.org/10.1007/s10551-021-04971-5

Banerjee, S.B. (2021b). Decolonizing management theory: a critical perspective. *Journal of Management Studies, 59*(4), 1074–1087. https://doi.org/10.1111/joms.12756

Barad, K. (2001). Re(con)figuring space, time, and matter. In DeKoven, M. (Ed.), *Feminist locations: global and local, theory and practice*. Rutgers University Press.

Barad, K. (2003). Post-humanist performativity: toward an understanding of how matter comes to matter. *Signs: Journal of Women in Culture and Society, 28*(3), 801–31.

Barad, K. (2008). Queer causation and the ethics of mattering. In M.J. Hird & N. Giffney (Eds.), *Queering the Non/Human*. Ashgate.

Beacham, J. (2018). Organizing food differently: towards a more-than-human ethics of care for the Anthropocene. *Organization, 25*(4), 533–549.

Becker, J., Hartwich, L., & Haslam, A. (2021). Neoliberalism can reduce well-being by promoting a sense of social disconnection, competition and loneliness. *British Journal of Social Psychology, 60*, 947–965.

Belk, R., Humayun, M., & Brouard, M. (2022). Money, possessions and ownership in the metaverse: NFTs, cryptocurrencies, Web 3 and wild markets. *Journal of Business Research, 153*, 198–205.

Benford, R., & Snow, R. (2000). Framing processes and social movements: an overview and assessment. *Annual Review of Sociology, 26*, 611–639.

Benjamin, W. (2008). *The work of art in the age of mechanical reproduction*. Penguin.

Berry, Ch. (2016). Luxury: A dialectic of desire. In J. Armitage & J. Roberts (Eds.), *Critical cultural studies: art, design and media* (pp. 199–220). Edinburgh University Press.

Bockman, J. (2007). The origins of neoliberalism between Soviet socialism and Western capitalism: "a galaxy without borders." *Theory and Society, 36*(4), 343–371.

Bogue, R. (1996). Gilles Deleuze: The aesthetic of force. In P. Patton (Ed.), *Gille Deleuze: a Critical Reader*, 257–269. London: Blackwell.

Boje, D., Fedor, D.B., & Rowland, K.M. (1982). Myth making: a qualitative step in OD interventions. *The Journal of Applied Behavioral Science, 18*(1), 17–28.

Bourdieu, P. (1984). *Distinction: a social critique of the judgement of taste*. Harvard University Press.

Bourdieu, P. (1990). Structures, habitus, practices. In *The Logic of Practice* (pp. 52–65). Polity.

Braidotti, R. (2013). Posthuman Humanities. *European Educational Research Journal, 12*(1), 1–19. https://doi.org/10.2304/eerj.2013.12.1.1

Brakus, J. Joško, Schmitt, B.H., and Zarantonello, L. (2009). Brand experience: What is it? How is it measured? Does it affect loyalty? *Journal of Marketing, 73*(3), 52–68.

Brown, S., & Wijland, R. (2015). Profit from poetry: bards, brands, and burnished bottom lines. *Business Horizons, 58*(5), 551–61. https://doi.org/10.1016/j.bushor.2015.04.003

Brown S., MacDonagh, P., & Schutz, C. (2013). Titanic: consuming the myths and meaning of an ambiguous brand. *Journal of Consumer Research, 40* (December), 595–614.

Butler, J. (1990). *Gender trouble. Feminism and the subversion of identity*. Routledge.

Butler, J. (1993). *Bodies that matter: on the discursive limits of sex*. Routledge.

Canada Energy Regulator (2021, May 19). What is in a Canadian Residential Electricity Bill? Canada Energy Regulator. Retrieved February 7, 2022, from https://www.cer-rec.gc.ca/en/data-analysis/energy-commodities/electricity/report/canadian-residential-electricity-bill

Canniford, R. (2012). Poetic witness: marketplace research through poetic transcription and poetic translation. *Marketing Theory, 12*(4), 391–409. https://doi.org/10.1177/1470593112457740

Chong, D., & Druckman, J. (2007). Framing theory. *Annual Review of Political Science, 10*, 103–126.

Chong, K. (2020). Cosmopolitanism and the global economy: notes from China's knowledge factories. *Journal of the Royal Anthropological Institute, 26*, 805–823.

CCRI. (2021). *Circularity Gap Report 2021*. https://www.circularity-gap.world/2021

CCRI. (2022). *Circularity Gap Report 2022*. https://www.circularity-gap.world/2022

CCRI. (2022). The Merge: implications on the Electricity consumption and carbon footprint of the Ethereum network. A commissioned report by CCRI for ConsenSys Software Inc.

Coffin, J., & Hill, T. (2022). Introduction to the special issue: presenting marketing differently. *Journal of Marketing Management, 38*(15–16), 1613–1632. DOI: 10.1080/0267257X.2023.2149947

Conde Nast. (2022). https://www.condenast.com/about

Cooper, B. (2015). Intersectionality. In L. Disch & M. Hawkesworth (Eds.), *The Oxford handbook of feminist theory* (pp. 385–406). Oxford University Press. https://doi.org/10.1093/oxfordhb/9780199328581.001.0001

Corwin, J., & Gidwani, V. (2021). Repair work as care: on maintaining the planet in the Capitalocene. *Antipode*. https://doi.org/10.1111/anti.12791

Crenshaw, K.W. (1991). Mapping the margins: intersectionality, identity politics, and violence against women of color. *Stanford Law Review, 43*(6), 1241–99.

Crockett, D. (2017). Paths to respectability: consumption and stigma management in the contemporary black middle class. *Journal of Consumer Research, 44*(3), 554–81.

Dal Lago, F. (1999). Personal Mao: Reshaping an icon in contemporary Chinese art. *Art Journal, 58*(2), 46–59.

Dion, D., & Arnould, E. (2011), Retail luxury strategy: assembling charisma through art and magic. *Journal of Retailing, 87*(4), 502–520.

Downey, H. (2016). Poetic inquiry, consumer vulnerability: realities of quadriplegia. *Journal of Marketing Management, 32*(3), 357–364.

Drummond, K. (2006). The migration of art from museum to market: consuming Caravaggio.*Marketing Theory and Practice, 6*(1), 85–105.

Duckett, J. (2020). Neoliberalism, authoritarian politics and social policy in China. *Development and Change, 51* (2), 523–539.

Ellen Macarthur Foundation. https://ellenmacarthurfoundation.org/

Entman, R. (1993). Framing: toward clarification of a fractured paradigm. *Journal of Communication, 43*, 51–58.

Eräranta, K., Moisander, J., & Penttilä, V. (2019). Reflections on the marketization of art in contemporary neoliberal capitalism. In *Museum Marketization*. Routledge. https://doi.org/10.4324/9780429401510

Ergene, S., Banerjee, S.B., & Hoffman, A. (2021). (Un)Sustainability and organization studies: towards a radical engagement. *Organization Studies, 42*(8), 1319–1335. https://doi.org/10.1177/0170840620937892

Ertekin, Z. (2019). Can luxury fashion provide a roadmap for sustainability? *Markets, Globalization & Development Review, 4*(1), Article 3. https://doi.org/10.23860/MGDR-2019-04-01-03

Ertekin, Z., & Atik, D. (2023), Luxury fashion and Sustainability: Challenges, conflicts and possibilities. In A. Joy (Ed.), *New directions in Art, Fashion and Wine: Sustainability, Digitalization and Artification* (pp. 103–118). Lexington Books: Maryland.

Featherstone, M. (2016). The object and art of luxury consumption. In J. Armitage & J. Roberts (Eds.), *Critical cultural studies: art, design and media* (pp. 108–128). Edinburgh University Press. https://doi.org/10.3366/edinburgh/9781474402613.003.0006

Fitzmaurice, C. (2017). How Rose became high class: categorical divestment and evaluation. *Poetics*, 61, 1–13.

Frantzen, M.K., & Bjering, J. (2020). Ecology, capitalism and waste: from Hyperobject to Hyperabject. *Theory, Culture and Society, 37*(6), 87–109.

Fu, C. (2023). New fashion identity and the state in China: a decolonial interpretation. *Fashion Theory*. https://doi.org/10.1080/1362704X.2023.2166205

Gao, M. (1999). *Inside/out: New Chinese art*. Berkeley: San Francisco Museum of Modern Art and Asia Society Galleries. University of California Press.

Ger, G. (2018). Research curation: Intersectional structuring of consumption. *Journal of Consumer Research, 45*, 1–12.

Gertz, G. (2018). NAFTA on the Brink. *Intereconomics 53*, 291–292. https://doi.org/10.1007/s10272-018-0768-x

Giesler, M., & Veresiu, E. (2014). Creating the responsible consumer: moralistic governance regimes and consumer subjectivity. *Journal of Consumer Research, 41*(3), 840–857. https://doi.org/10.1086/677842

Giesler, M., & Fischer, E. (2016). Market system dynamics. *Marketing Theory, 17*(1), 3–8.

Goffman, E. (1974). *Frame analysis: An essay on the organization of experience.* Harvard University Press.

Grosz, E. (2010). Feminism, materialism, and freedom. In D.H. Coole & S. Frost (Eds.), *New materialisms: Ontology, agency, and politics*, 139–157. Duke University Press.

Harari, A. (2022, April 4). Sanctions on Russian oligarchs put focus on assets and art stowed away in Swiss freeports. *The Art Newspaper.* https://www.theartnewspaper.com/2022/04/04/freeport-secrecy-veils-oligarch-art-assets

Harvey, D. (2020). Neoliberalism 'with Chinese Characteristics'. In *A Brief History of Neoliberalism.* Online edn, Oxford Academic, 12 Nov. 2020.

BC Gov News (2022). https://news.gov.bc.ca/releases/2022AF0045-001014

Henninger, C., Bydges, T., Jones, C., & Normand, A. (2022). That's so trashy-artification of waste in the luxury fashion industry. In A. Joy (Ed.), *The future of luxury brands: sustainability and artification.* [it is Artification and not Ratification] De Gruyter.

Hirshfield J. (2000). Kingfishers catching fire: seeing with poetry's eyes. *The American Poetry Review, 29*(1): 9–12.

Hopkins,S. (2018). Girl power-dressing: fashion, feminism and neoliberalism with Beckham, Beyoncé and Trump. *Celebrity Studies, 9*(1), 99–104. https://doi.org/10.1080/19392397.2017.1346052

Hoskins, T. Neoliberalism and fashion. (n.d.). The OLR. https://oxfordleftreview.com/olr-issue-14/tansy-hoskins-neoliberalism-and-fashion

Hvass, K., & Pederson, E. (2019). Towards circular economy fashion: experiences from brands product take-back initiative. *Journal of Marketing and Management, 23* (3), 345–365.

Inglis, D. (2019). Mutating and contested languages of wine: heard on the grapevine. In S. D.

Brunn & R. Kehrein (Eds.), *Handbook of the changing world language map* (pp. 4033–4058). Springer. https://doi.org/10.1007/978-3-030-02438-3_205

Islam, M., Abbott, P., Haque, S., & Gooch, F. (2023). *Impact of global clothing retailers' unfair practices on Bangladeshi suppliers during Covid 19.* University of Aberdeen. https://www.abdn.ac.uk/news/docu ments/Impact_of_Global_Clothing_Retailers_Unfair_Practices_on_Bangladeshi_Suppliers_During_ COVID-19.pdf

Jameson. F. (1976). On Goffman's frame analysis. *Theory and Society, 3*, 119–133. https://doi.org/10.1007/ BF00158482

Joy, A. (1998). The framing process: The role of galleries in the circulation of art. In J.F. Sherry Jr. (Ed.), *Servicescapes: the concept of place in contemporary markets.* NTC Business Books.

Joy, A., & Sherry, J.F. Jr (2004). Framing considerations in the PRC: Creating value in the contemporary Chinese art market, *Consumption Markets & Culture, 7*(4), 307–348.

Joy, A., Wang, J.J., Chan, T.S., Sherry, J.F. Jr, & Cui, G. (2014). M (Art) worlds: consumer perceptions of how luxury brand stores become art institutions, *Journal of Retailing, 90*(3), 347–364.

Joy, A., Belk, R., & Bhardwaj, R. (2015). Judith Butler on performativity and precarity: Exploratory thoughts on gender and violence in India, *Journal of Marketing Management, 31*(15–16), 1739–1745.

Joy, A. (2022a). *The Future of Luxury Brands: Sustainability and Artification.* Boston: De Gruyter.

Joy, A. (1999). Artists, artworks and the discourse of art. In *Research in Consumer Behavior.* JAI Press.

Joy, A., & Pena, C. (2017). Sustainability and the fashion industry: conceptualizing nature and traceability. In Henninger et al. (Eds.), *Sustainability in fashion, a cradle to upcycle approach*, 31–54. Palgrave Macmillan.

Joy, A. & Sherry, J. F. (2003). Speaking of art as embodied imagination. *Journal of Consumer Research, 30*(2), 259–282. https://doi.org/10.1086/376802

Joy, A., & Sherry, J.F. Jr. (2004). Framing considerations in the PRC: Creating value in the contemporary Chinese art market. *Consumption, Markets and Culture, 7*(4), 307–348.

Joy, A., Sherry, F.J., Venkatesh, A., Wang, J., & Chan, R. (2012). Fast fashion, sustainability and the ethical appeal of luxury brands. *Fashion Theory, 16*(3), 273–296. https://doi.org/10.2752/175174112X13340749707123

Joy, A., & Venkatesh, A. (1994). Post-modernism, feminism and the body: the visible and the invisible in consumer research. *International Journal of Research in Marketing, 11* (4), 333–357.

Joy, A., Wang, J.J., Tsang-Sing, Chan., Sherry, J.F. Jr. & Cui, G. (2014). M(art) worlds: consumer perceptions of how luxury brand stores become art institutions. *Journal of Retailing, 90*(3), 347–364.

Joy, A., Zhu, Y., Pena, C., & Brouard, M. (2022b). Digital Future of luxury brands: Metaverse, digital fashion and non-fungible tokens. *Strategic Change* (31), 337–343.

Joy, A., J. Wang., D. Orazi, S. Yoon, K.Latour and C.Pena (2023), "Co-creating Affective Atmospheres in Retail Experience," Journal of Retailing, Vol 99, issue 2 p.297–317

Kapferer, J.N., & Bastien. V. (2012). *The luxury strategy: Break the rules of Marketing to build luxury brands.* (2nd ed.). Kogan Page.

Kapferer, J.N. (2014). The artification of luxury: From artisans to artists. *Business Horizons, 57*(3), 371–380.

Kjellgren, B. (2004). Drunken modernity: wine in China. *Anthropology of food.* https://doi.org/10.4000/aof.249

Kozinets R. (2023). Immersive netnography: a novel method for service experience, research in virtual reality, augmented reality and metaverse contexts. *Journal of Services Marketing, 34*(1), 100–125.

Kuldova, T.O. (2021). On private views, luxury and corruption. Andie Schmied interviewed by Teresa Kuldova. *Journal of Extreme Anthropology, 5*(2), 124–141. https://doi.org/10.5617/jea.9566

Kundu, R., & Kalin, N.M. (2015). Participating in the neoliberal art museum. *Studies in Art Education: A Journal of Issues and Research, 57*(1), 39–52.

Lash, S., & Urry, J. (1994). *Economies of signs and space.* Sage.

LaTour, K.A., Joy, A., & Noujeim, R. (2021). Developing wine appreciation for new generations of consumers. *Cornell Hospitality Quarterly* special issue on the Wine Business, *62*(3), 337–345. https://journals.sagepub.com/doi/10.1177/1938965520978382

Li, X. (1993). Major developments in the development of contemporary Chinese art. In V.C. Doran (Ed.), *China's New art: Post-1989* (pp. 10–22). Hanart T. Z. Gallery.

Loos, F.A. (2017). *Freeports as ecosystems for the preservation of fine art value and the acceleration of related businesses* [Master's thesis, University of Rotterdam]. https://thesis.eur.nl/pub/39521/Loos-Famke.pdf

Matazar A.B. (2010). *Women of wine: the rise of women in the global wine industry.* University of California Press.

Maclaran, P., & Chatzidakis, A. (2022). Introduction: an overview of gendered marketing. In P. Maclaran & A. Chatzidakis (Eds.), *Gendered marketing.* Edgar Elgar Publishing.

McInerney, J. (2016, October 11). The Gajas are the first family of Italian wine. *Town and Country.* https://www.townandcountrymag.com/leisure/drinks/a8078/gaja-family-italian-wine/

McNay, L. Agency. In L. Disch & M. Hawkesworth (Eds.), *The Oxford Handbook of Feminist Theory* (pp. 39–60). Oxford University Press. https://doi.org/10.1093/oxfordhb/9780199328581.001.0001

Meek, L. (1988). Organizational culture: origins and weaknesses. *Organization Studies, 9*(4),453–473.

Morton, T. (2013). *Hyperobjects: Philosophy and Ecology after the End of the World.* University of Minnesota Press.

Mukendi, A., Davies, I., McDonagh, P., & Glozer, S. (2020). Sustainable fashion: current and future research directions. *European Journal of Marketing.* https://doi.org/10.1108/EJM-02-2019-0132

Oksala, J. (2016). Affective labor and feminist politics. *Signs, 41*(2), 281–303.

Orazi, D., & van Laer, T. (2023). There and back again: bleed from extraordinary Experiences. *Journal of Consumer Research, 49*(5), 904–925. https://doi.org/10.1093/jcr/ucac022

Overton, J., & Murray, W.E. (2013). Class in a glass: capital, neoliberalism and social space in the global wine industry. *Antipode, 45*(3), 702–718. https://doi.org/10.1111/j.1467-8330.2012.01042.x

Parkins, I. (2008). Building a feminist theory of fashion. *Australian Feminist Studies, 23*(58), 501–515.

Poitras, L., & Donald, G. (2006). Sustainable wine tourism: the host community perspective. *Journal of Sustainable Tourism, 14*(5), 425–448. https://doi.org/10.2167/jost587.0

Reinach, S. (2011). The identity of fashion in contemporary China and the new relationships with the west. *Fashion Practice, 4*(1), 57–70.

Renauld, M-M. (2021, May 1). *Geneva Free port: The most secretive art warehouse*. The Collector. https://www.thecollector.com/geneva-free-port-the-worlds-most-secretive-art-warehouse/

Armitage, J., & Roberts, J. (2016). Knowing luxury: From socio-cultural value to market price. In J. Armitage & J. Roberts (Eds.), *Critical cultural studies: art, design and media* (pp. 199–220). Edinburgh University Press.

Roberts, J. (2019). Secret spaces of luxury: Ignorance, free ports and art. In J.Roberts & J. Armitage (Eds.), *The third realm of luxury: connecting real places and imaginary spaces* (pp. 159–176). Bloomsbury Publishing.

Rocamora, A. (2016). Online luxury: Geographies of production and consumption and the Louis Vuitton website. In J. Armitage & J. Roberts, *Critical Cultural Studies: Art, Design and Media* (pp. 199–220). Edinburgh University Press.

Rodner, V., Omar, M., & Thomson, E. (2011). The brand-wagon: emerging art markets and the Venice Biennale. *Marketing Intelligence & Planning, 29* (3), 319–336.

Rojas-Gaviria, P., & Canniford, R. (2022). Poetic meditation: (re)presenting the mystery of the field. *Journal of Marketing Management, 38* (15–16), 1821–1831. https://doi.org/10.1080/0267257X.2022.2112611

Rojas-Gaviria, P. (2021). Poetizing to improve consumer representation. *Marketing Theory, 21*(4), 463–79.

Rojas-Gaviria, P. (2023). Poetic orientation for creating and writing.*Marketing the Arts Breaking Boundaries*, ed. Finola Kerrigan and Chloe Preece. London: Routledge.

Rushkoff, D. (2022). *The survival of the richest*. Norton & Company.

Schmeid, A. (2020). *Private views: A high-rise panorama of Manhattan*. VI Per Gallery.

Sherry, J. F. (2022). Nodding by the fire: Appreciation of the Derry Temple. *Journal of Marketing Management, 38* (15–16), 1633–1650. https://doi.org/10.1080/0267257X.2020.1851746

Sherry, J.F. (1998a). Nothing but net: Consumption, poetry and research pluriculture (in the sixth moment) presidential address presented at the twenty sixth annual conference of the association for consumer research, Montreal.

Sherry, J.F (1998b) Three poems: Hump flute, market music, one tuna caught this day in diamant. In B. Stern (ed.), *Representing consumers: voices, views an visions*, 303–305. New York: Routledge.

Sherry, J.F. Jr., & Schouten, J.W. (2002). A role for poetry in consumer research. *Journal of Consumer Research, 29*(2), 218–34.

Sherry J.F.R., & Kozinets, R. (2022). Being at burning man: fabulations and provocations in the future of luxury brands artification and sustainability, ed. Annamma Joy. De Gruyter: Berlin/Boston.

Sherry J.F. Jr. (2022). Nodding by the fire: appreciation of the Derry Temple. *Journal of Marketing Management, 38*(15–16), 1633–1650.

Styles, O. (2018). Is slapping breasts on wine labels now more "sex and the silly" than seductive? https://www.wine-searcher.com/m/2018/07/lousy-labels-wont-go-away.July 21, 2018.

Thornton, S. (2009). *Seven days in the art world*. W. W. Norton & Company.

Ulin, R. (2002). Work as cultural production: Labour and self-identity among southwest French wine growers. *Journal of the Royal Anthropological Institute, 8*(4), 691–712. http://www.jstor.org/stable/3134939

UNESCO. (July 2016). ICPRCP/16/20.COM/12. Free Ports and risks of illicit trafficking of cultural property (Intergovernmental Committee for Promoting the Return of Cultural Property to its Countries or Origin or its Restitution in Case of Illicit Appropriation). Paris. https://unesdoc.unesco.org/ark:/48223/pf0000372793

Van Dijk, H. (1992). Painting in China after the cultural revolution: Style developments and theoretical debates. *China Information, 6*(3), 1–21.

Velikova, N., Charters, S., Bouzedine-Chameeva, T., Fountain, J., Ritchie, C., & Dodd, T.H. (2015). Seriously pink: a cross-cultural examination of the perceived image of rose wine. *International Journal of Wine Business Research, 27*(4), 281–298. http://doi.org.//D10.1108/IJWBR-10-2014-0050

Velthuis, O. (2011). Art markets. In R. Towse (Ed.), *Handbook of cultural economics* (2nd ed.). Edward Elgar.

Verster, H. (2021). Intersectionality visualized: An analysis of global feminisms. https://ir.lib.uwo.ca/cgi/viewcontent.cgi?article=1002&context=undergradawards_2021.

Vesey, A. (2015). Putting her on the shelf: pop star fragrances and post-feminist entrepreneurialism. *Feminist media studies, 15*(6), 992–1008. https://doi.org/10.1080/14680777.2015.1033639

Visconti L.M., Sherry, J.F. Jr, Borghini, S., & Anderson, L. (2010). Street Art, Sweet Art? Reclaiming the "Public" in Public Place. *Journal of Consumer Research, 37* (October), 511–529.

Wang L., & Judge, W.Q. (2012). Managerial ownership and the role of privatization in transition economies: The case of China. *Asia Pacific Journal of Management, 29*, 479–498.

Weber, I. (2020). Origins of China's contested relation with neoliberalism: economics, the World Bank, and Milton Friedman at the dawn of reform. *Global Perspectives, 1*(1) 12271. https://doi.org/10.1525/gp.2020.12271

Wilcox K., Kim, H.M., & Sen, S. (2008). Why Do Consumers Buy Counterfeit Luxury Brands? In Claudia R. Acevedo, Jose Mauro C. Hernandez, and Tina M. Lowrey (Eds.), *Latin American Advances in Consumer Research Volume 2* (pp. 176–177). Duluth, MN: Association for Consumer Research.

Whyte, K., & Cuomo, Ch. (2016). Ethics of caring in environmental ethics: indigenous and feminist philosophies. In Gardner, S., & Thompson, A. (Eds.), *The Oxford Handbook of Environmental Ethics* (pp. 253–267). Oxford University Press.

Wijland, R. (2011). Anchors, mermaids, shower-curtain seaweeds and fish-shaped fish: the texture of poetic agency. *Marketing Theory, 11*(2), 127–41. https://doi.org/10.1177/1470593111403217

Yelvington, K.A., Simms, J., & Murray, E. (2012). Wine tourism in the Temecula Valley: neoliberal development policies and their contradictions. *Anthropology in Action, 19*(3), 49–65. http://dx.doi.org/10.3167/aia.2012.190305

Yeung, P., & Thach, L. (2019). *Luxury wine marketing: The art and science of luxury wine branding*. Infinite Ideas Limited.

Yu, S-L. (2018). The rise of neoliberal Chinese female subject in Go Lala Go. *Comparative Literature and Culture* (CLC WEB), *20*(6). Article 3. https://doi.org/10.7771/1481-4374.3322

Zhang, J. (2017). Commodifying art, Chinese style: the making of China's Visual art market *Environment and planning, 49*(9), 2025–2045.

Zhu, Y. (2002). Commercialization and Chinese cinemapost wave. *Consumption, Markets and Culture, 5*(3), 187–211.

Zwick, D. (2018). No longer violent enough?: creative destruction, innovation and the ossification of neoliberal capitalism, *Journal of Marketing Management, 34*(11–12), 913–931.

Part 1: **Neo-Liberal Framework and Social Justice**

Nikhilesh Dholakia and Cristian Ziliberberg

2 Change and Legitimation Narratives in the Intertwined Market Discourses of Sustainability and Neoliberalism

Introduction

Sustainability and neoliberalism are major contemporary idea systems that permeate a lot of the discourse in media, corporate board rooms, policy forums, research settings, and classrooms. While sustainability – as a term and concept – is invoked freely in such settings, neoliberalism operates in a somewhat stealth fashion. Only the critics of neoliberalism name and (attempt to) shame it; its advocates prefer to champion neoliberalism via proxy terms such as freedom of choice and rejection of stifling regulation.

In terms of the interplay of sustainability and neoliberalism, the fashion industry is a case in point. Sustainability aspects of fast fashion get high visibility, particularly when activists and investigative reporters get involved. The neoliberal engines driving the growth of fast fashion remain very much in the shadows. While critics of fast fashion raise the specter of massively discarded fast fashion garments – including brand new items – choking up various places on the planet, including vast stretches of the pristine Chilean Atacama high desert (Bernetti & Al Jazeera, 2021), the fact that fast fashion is a global profit engine – and a highly exploitative one, in terms of sweatshop labor, for hundreds of fashion and retail firms – is kept mostly out of sight of media observers (Ozdamar-Ertekin, 2017).

In this chapter, we sketch these two major contemporaneous idea-systems – sustainability and neoliberalism – and then turn to the individual, organizational, and macro-level process that seem to be at play to create the changes that these two ideologies seek to promote and champion. We also offer views on the resulting socio-economic-political-ecological end-states that each of these ideologies desires, as well as on the actual end-states that result from the interactions and clashes of sustainability and neoliberalism ideas. We find that, for each idea-system, there are active legitimation processes to promote the preferred ideal states, as well as processes to delegitimate and dislodge the undesired ideas and states. In the last part of the chapter, we revisit the dilemmas and challenges that the interplay of sustainability and neoliberalism create for markets, marketers, manufacturing, channel organizations, and, finally, for consumers.

https://doi.org/10.1515/9783110783933-002

Sustainability and Neoliberalism: Brief Overviews

The conceptual range of these two idea systems – sustainability and neoliberalism – is vast and cannot be covered in the confines of a chapter. It is important, however, to provide overviews that provide the needed background for later discussions.

Sustainability

In the contemporary global discourses, sustainability is a new idea. Earlier, it was confined to the narrow eco-botanical field of forestry management – forests, especially when used for timber, had to be managed sustainably. With the rising recognition of the climate crisis, however, this term acquired global currency rapidly (Philipsen, 2022). Not just timberland forests but the entire ecosystem of planet Earth needed to be managed sustainably. Thus, the term sustainability has become central to the ecological/environmental discussions happening in government agencies, international organizations and forums, corporate boardrooms, and activist movements. The launch – on the first day of 2016 – of the 17 United Nations Sustainable Development Goals (SDGs), to be achieved by 2030, put an official imprimatur on all these sustainability discourses.

In practical terms, especially relevant to industries such as fashion, sustainability requires economic processes that are based on a resource-conserving "circular" economy rather than in a resource-wasting "linear" economy (Jørgensen & Pedersen, 2018). To make the circular strategies even clearer, a variety of frameworks were developed like 3-R (reduce, reuse, recycle), 5-R (reduce, reuse, remanufacture, recycle, and recover), and an even 10-R framework is available (Campbell-Johnston et al., 2019; J. Cramer, 2017; J. M. Cramer, 2020; Reike et al., 2018). Simply put, the R-elements are all about resource conserving practices at various levels: extraction, manufacturing, distribution, consumption, and disposal. In total, up to 38-R strategies are mentioned in the literature, namely, "re-assembly, recapture, reconditioning, recollect, recover, recreate, rectify, recycle, redesign, redistribute, reduce, re-envision, refit, refurbish, refuse, remarket, remanufacture, renovate, repair, replacement, reprocess, reproduce, repurpose, resale, resell, re-service, restoration, resynthesize, rethink, retrieve, retrofit, retrograde, return, reuse, reutilise, revenue, reverse and revitalize" (Reike et al., 2018, p. 253). In this chapter, we will focus on 10 R-elements that help understand the sustainability and circularity issues in the economy and eco-system of the fashion industry (see Table 2.1 for an initial look).

The circular economy strategies for the fashion industry are not yet universally accepted and widely implemented – they are mostly at the incipient and aspirational level. Thus, their implementation is part of the change narratives and agenda of the sustainability advocates. For this change agenda to succeed, however, first, the idea of sustainability per se must be legitimated, and second, the change agenda to achieve sustainability must be legitimated. This is burdensome because the rival ideology of neoliberalism has its own agenda of change, and this neoliberal agenda often challenges sustainability and its promotion of 10-R practices.

Table 2.1: Circular economy – The 10R Framework.

Element	Definition, Brief Explanation	Fashion Sector: Notes, Examples
Refuse	Do not buy, buy less, buy green	In 2020 Americans bought five times more clothing than in 1980.
Rethink	Reconsider ways of making, marketing, consuming. Before buying, consider if need is real.	VEJA sneakers: cool, minimalist, long-lasting style. Eco-friendly, socially conscious manufacturing methods.
Reduce	Buy less, buy in bulk and unpackaged, borrow and/or share. Reduce resources to maintain products.	Buy clothing made with naturally renewable, organic, or recycled fiber. Use detergents suitable for cold water wash.
Reuse	Rather than discarding or destroying, reuse items	thredUP has an online platform to buy and sell used clothes.
Repair	Fix or mend rather than discard	Fashion retailers Zalando and H&M offer garment repair services.
Refurbish	Inspect, repair, recondition, restore to like-new condition	In North Face Renewed program, items are cleaned, inspected, repairs made (e.g., stitching up tears), quality checked for The North Face standards, then offered online for resale.
Remanufacture	Employing used, waste, excess, trimmed material to make items better in quality than newly made items	California based R Collective uses European luxury design houses' cutting floor scrap to make sustainable, durable, high-style clothing
Repurpose	Creative reuse of existing items or materials into entirely new designs, with minimal application of new materials. Also called upcycling	Used clothing converted to knotted, braided rugs, quilts. Also, personal repurposing: tie/dye, cut-resew into various clothes, accessories
Recycle	Besides direct reuse and repurposing of discarded items, ultimately, disassemble used items as raw material for new items	Resortecs specializes in garment disassembly technology: efficient ways to separate fabrics from buttons, labels, zippers – so textiles can reenter the circular economy
Recover	Rather than waste filling up dumping sites, it serves a useful purpose, replacing other (including new) materials	Recover [company name], in Los Angeles, replaces water and pesticide intensive farmed cotton with premium recycled cotton and cotton blends

Source: Based on authors' research of multiple sources (e.g., Kirchherr et al., 2017; Morseletto, 2020; Muthu, 2019; Reike et al., 2018)

Neoliberalism

Neoliberalism is the late twentieth century reincarnation of older ideas from neoclassical economics, Germanic ordoliberalism, and Austrian School economists (see Dholakia, Ozgun, & Atik, 2021). The ideas emerged from writings of certain economists, but they received a massive policy boost when Prime Minister Margaret Thatcher in the United Kingdom and President Ronald Reagan in the United States started enacting programs and policies – deregulation and privatization, in particular – based on the key ideas of neoliberalism. Since then, governments the world over – regardless of the declared ideological tint of the party in power – have been pursuing neoliberal policy agendas. Interestingly, unlike sustainability, the term neoliberalism is almost never employed by the advocates and champions of this way of politico-economic thinking and policymaking. Indeed, the term is used rarely even by those political players and activist organizations that oppose many neoliberal policies. The term comes into play mainly when blunt and eye-opening critiques of neoliberal policies are launched in the media (e.g., Monbiot, 2016) or in academic writings (e.g., Harvey, 2007).

Neoliberalism also has a change narrative, one of increasing the power of free market and reducing the regulatory power of the state. For that, it also must legitimate itself as an ideology, to be supported by the voters, corporations, and policymakers. And it also must fight and delegitimate the rival ideology of sustainability, which starts from a different set of values and requires extensive regulations such as impelling the adoption of 10-R practices, including in the garment and fashion industry.

Interwoven Change and Legitimation Narratives and Processes

The world – as is – is not acceptable to sustainability advocates. The existing world also usually is not to the liking of the acolytes of neoliberalism. Sustainability advocates envision a harmonious society of responsible people who live in a green, clean, and peaceful world. Because of global warming, imbalanced population geographies, and inequality, such a green, clean, and peaceful world does not exist at this point in time. On the other side of the ideological spectrum, the neoliberalism advocates envision a minimally regulated society of free and rational people who achieve global progress and prosperity through free market competition. Because of regulations, often escalating through political liberals (yes, confusingly, the opposite of neoliberals), the neoliberal "free" state also does not exist.

Where the world may move, if left to inertia, is also not acceptable to the acolytes of the neoliberalism or to the champions of sustainability, because it will not end up even close to their ideal vision of the world. Thus, both sides are apprehensive about what they see ahead.

For sustainability advocates, the inertial movement is towards our planet hurtling into a climate catastrophe. The policy-oriented advocates want to see international and national policies, as well as organizational strategies, that stop the rapid advance toward a climate catastrophe and usher in "green" ways of doing things. They want strong policies in place to conserve, preserve, renew, repair, and restore the ecology of our planet (e.g., the 10-R elements of Table 2.1). The highly activist sustainability champions – such as for example, Greta Thunberg – are often not satisfied by the gradualist pace of policy reforms. They agitate for precipitate action, to create a global mass movement that demands immediate actions to arrest the degradation of ecology and to launch wide-ranging projects for clean, renewable ways of making and consuming. No matter what the approach, if desired changes come about, the resultant state is of a harmonious society of responsible people living in a green, clean, peaceful world.

For champions of neoliberalism, the inertial movement is towards gradual layering-up of rules and regulations, a creep toward the despised system of "socialism." Policy-oriented neoliberals want national policies in place that dismantle most rules and regulations: tax cuts, deregulation of industries as well as nonprofit institutions, privatization of state-controlled economic activities, and even non-economic activities (e.g., schooling, policing, etc.). The strongly activist advocates of neoliberalism often do not want to wait for the legislative machinery to grind on slowly towards deregulation – they want instant action, as was attempted by the short-tenured British Prime Minister Liz Truss. Again, regardless of the approach, the desired end state that neoliberals want is of a minimally regulated society of free and rational people, a society and a system that enables global progress and prosperity.

To implement their vision of the world, the champions of neoliberal policies feel so strongly that they hasten to precipitate actions that endanger the entire economic system of a nation. This is what happened, for example, during the brief tenure and abrupt resignation of the neoliberal British Prime Minister Liz Truss – who pushed for immediate, massive, unfunded tax cuts as well as extensive, unpopular deregulation, throwing the UK economy into a tailspin (Lawless, 2022). Conditions in the British economy deteriorated so fast that she was forced to leave her position in just 49 days. Similarly, some sustainability champions may feel so strongly that they may engage in drastic and disruptive practices that at best keep the situation in place and annoy the neoliberals, instead of bringing the world closer to the sustainable vision.

To achieve global hegemony, and implement their agenda of change, the proponents of both positions – sustainability and neoliberalism – need legitimation from new audiences. Thus, both these positions keep generating narratives revolving around the fundamental notions of change and legitimacy. These narratives are based on, and invoke in their communication and rhetorical strategies, fundamental values that are very reasonable sounding and thus largely impervious to counterarguments. For champions of sustainability, some of these values are "Responsibility, Stewardship, and Security," the last aspect referring to planetary ecology as well as securing the future of successive generations. For advocates of neoliberal policies, the core values are equally solid and attack-proof: "Freedom, Progress, and Rationality." With such solid bedrocks, both the idea systems, and their proponents, come to regard their preferred ideology as an imperative one – designed, if not destined, for global hegemony.

As a condensed portrayal of these competing mega-idea-systems, we introduce Table 2.2 here. The table shows the essential aspects of the change and legitimation of these idea systems.

Table 2.2: Change and legitimation narratives – a framework.

Aspect	Sustainability	Neoliberalism
Motivating Sources	Responsibility (of institutions, governments, people)	Freedom (of choice, of enterprise)
	Stewardship: Mother Earth (our planetary home)	Progress (prosperity)
	Security (over generations)	Rationality (being sensibly logical)
Convincing Narrative Mechanism	For inter-generationally safe, healthy, and habitable earth, we need to act now and responsibly for a sustainable future.	If we care about freedom, progress, and rationality, then we need to let people, with the support of market forces, decide what is good for them.
Target	Sustainability ideology, with its associated practices.	Neoliberalism ideology, with its associated practices
Function	Enforcement and promotion of the sustainability ideology, and defense against rival ideologies. The goal is to become a hegemonic ideology.	Enforcement and promotion of the neoliberal ideology, and defense against competitive ideologies. The goal is to become a hegemonic ideology.
Audiences	International organizations, national governments, academia, the industry	Lawmakers, regulators, academia, large corporations
Vision of the world	A harmonious society of responsible people living in a green, clean, peaceful world.	A minimally regulated society of free and rational people that enables global progress and prosperity.

Source: Based on authors' research.

It is interesting to explore further how sustainability and neoliberalism frame their change and legitimation narratives. The change processes that the advocates of sustainability and neoliberalism engage in are intertwined, interwoven, and frequently (though not always) conflictual.

Circular Economy and Fashion Industry

The interplay of the sustainability and neoliberal change and legitimation narratives is well illustrated when looking at the circular economy as applied to the fashion industry. For most champions of sustainability, the idea of creating a circular economy is quite popular (Jørgensen & Pedersen, 2018). The idea is particularly strongly discussed – in business as well as academic and public policy settings – in the fashion industry (Dissanayake & Weerasinghe, 2022), like for instance in the case of the fashion retailer H&M (Rana & Tajuddin, 2021). A circular economy is one that wastes almost nothing. The waste minimization is not just at the end of a product's life but also in the early stages: when a product is being imagined, designed, its components are being sourced, and ways to make and distribute it are being developed. In an ideal circular economy, there is minimal energy expenditure, minimal impact on natural and ecological systems, and strong reliance on renewable materials and energy resources. Reviews of the circular economy indicate that all actors in the production, marketing, and consumption systems – designers, resource extractors, manufacturers, suppliers, retailers, recyclers, and consumers – must pitch in, fully and cooperatively, to achieve the goal of creating a smoothly functioning circular economy (Kirchherr, Reike, & Hekkert, 2017). What is not understood well is how to do this.

To illustrate the challenges and dilemmas, let us turn again to the popular hands-on 10-R frameworks for a circular economy (revisit Table 2.1). It is interesting to note that the initial framework consisted of just 3 R-elements: Reduce, Reuse, Recycle. Through the interactions of pressures and thrusts from both camps – sustainability advocates and neoliberalism champions – the framework has expanded to 10 R-elements (and sometimes even more R-elements are added). The expansion to 10 R-elements happened because sustainability advocates want specific ways to prevent ecological damage, and also specific ways to cut waste (see, e.g. Joy et al., 2012).

Neoliberalism champions do not particularly favor the controls that sustainability policies introduce, especially when these controls challenge their vision of the world and interfere with the profit-making processes. Thus, for each of the 10-R processes neoliberals propose their own alternative, typically stemming from an ideal of a "free-to-choose" consumerist society.

Table 2.1, introduced earlier, provides a basic overview of the 10-R framework. It also lists some of the action possibilities in the fashion sector for each R – and selects few of the already operating case studies, which can serve as models. Based on the discussion so far, we introduce Table 2.3. This table illustrates the challenges that neoliberalism could (and often does) introduce to the working of a circular economy. If neoliberal ideas dominate, then many of the R-elements are opposed or rejected outright, and others must operate in ways that are geared toward creating competitively profitable opportunities for private firms. Under neoliberal dominance, a circular economy cannot operate in a pure form: at various points, such an economy must compromise and bend to the profit-enabling dictates of neoliberalism.

For instance, for the sustainable 10-R practice of Reusing, neoliberals would promote the idea of replacing one's wardrobe whenever fashion changes. For the practice of Rethinking, they would promote the idea of freedom, as manifested in following one's impulses in buying clothes that are in line with the ideals of beauty that are currently in vogue. For the practice of Reducing, consumerist neoliberals would promote the idea of buying more clothes, of a large diversity. For the practice of reusing the same clothes, they would emphasize the focus on new, the latest trend. Overall, any and all of the 10-R elements – to obtain any degree of neoliberal support – must enhance consumer choice and offer new profitmaking paths.

Table 2.3: Circular economy – neoliberal challenges to The 10R Framework.

Element	Neoliberal Views, Positions, Challenges, Pressures	Notes
Refuse	Buy the latest and greatest version	Many replace their fashion garments after one season. People replace their iPhones every three years. The idea of "Refuse" is anathema to neoliberalism.
Rethink	Follow impulses – be free, unconstrained	Hedonic ads (chocolates, clothes, wine, cruises) invite buyers to act on their impulses. Buy the clothes that they like now.
Reduce	Buy more, buy multiples, buy bigger	Buying more and bigger signals power and strength: more clothes, big car, big mini-mansion style house.
Reuse	Plan obsolescence, refocus on experiences	Make some components fail (appliances) or quickly obsolete (fashion). Discourage reuse. Emphasize new experiences – fashion, art, travel – requiring repeated one-time consumption shots.
Repair	Replace; get rid of the broken and the obsolete	For most clothes, appliances, and electronics, it is easier and cheaper to replace rather than repair. Neoliberalism favors low-skilled-and-waged mass manufacturing labor over skilled repair-shop labor.
Refurbish	Upgrade	Refurbishing could cost more than upgrading. Profits are far greater for upgrading to new models than for refurbishing old ones.
Remanufacture	Reinvent	Neoliberalism may encourage enterprises that create new items from used, recovered materials.

Table 2.3 (continued)

Element	Neoliberal Views, Positions, Challenges, Pressures	Notes
Repurpose	Buy specific items for each purpose; proliferate product and brand variants	Proliferation of specialized products and variants (colors, flavors etc.) is far more profitable than repurposing/reusing existing products.
Recycle	Recycle whenever consumers' free labor can create recycled bottles, plastic granules, paper etc.	In general, neoliberals love settings where consumers provide free labor (Zwick, Bonsu, & Darmody, 2008). They oppose cases where corporate costs go up to develop products that are easily recyclable.
Recover	Abandon, discard	In general, material recovery – in a circular fashion – is expensive with only niche business opportunities. A linear economy offers far more profit opportunities than a circular one.

Source: Based on authors' research of multiple sources.

If some of the 10-R policies and practices are unavoidable (because of intense media outcry about waste and eco-despoliation), then the neoliberal position wants increasing number and greater range of profit-making opportunities, and thus favors expanding the R-elements in ways that generate such opportunities.

Markets, Marketing, Brands, Channels, and Consumers

Sustainability and neoliberal change narratives and legitimation narratives influence and are instantiated in the various business models. This of course is so very evident in the fashion sector. Till the last decades of the last century, fast fashion proliferated – at the consumer and retail levels as well as in the global outsourcing of garment manufacturing base. Neoliberalism ruled for the most parts – companies kept shifting their production bases to lower wage settings to maximize profitability. Not just lower wages but lax or nonexistent safety and environmental standards in the low-wage nations controlled the costs even more, and further boosted profitability. Even the high-fashion labels of France and Italy, while keeping the essential design and making processes "local" – in Paris and Milan – had no choice but to outsource the manufacturing of mass versions of their designs to low-wage locations. Then, from the 1990s, concerns of sustainability as well as critiques of exploitative outsourcing began to surface, first slowly and then more cogently. In the twenty-first century, things are shifting; of course, only gradually at the time of this writing.

The ongoing tussles, and occasional convergences, of sustainability and neoliberalism can be observed in the way companies choose their markets and target segments, position and build their brands, channel their goods and services as well as messages, and formulate and execute their marketing plans generally.

In terms of markets, companies promoting the sustainability agenda signal focus on local markets: such markets support communities and keep the scale of operations at levels that are not ecology-damaging. Companies more in line with the neoliberal agenda focus on global markets, pervasively powerful brands, and massive scale of operations distributed strategically to minimize costs and maximize revenues. Take as an example Whole Foods Market, which tries to position itself under the sustainability agenda. It prides itself in terms of selling cheese, wine, crafts, and other products from local producers. The products that come from non-local markets, however, constitute the majority at Whole Foods. This is not emphasized: the company projects its retail brand image as rooted in local markets. On the other hand, a company like Unilever produces and distributes the same product worldwide. Even if the product is manufactured at a factory nearby, this is not advertised. This shows that companies that signal their sustainability allegiance attempt to show that they manufacture in, and sell to, the local markets. Similarly, the "slow fashion" trend promotes local production, by local artists, for local buyers, which are more sustainable than garment production that entails long global supply chains and labor-intensive manufacturing operations often located in poorer nations with lax environmental and safety standards (Fletcher, 2014).

In terms of consumers, the companies signaling connection with the sustainability ethic would primarily target the morally conscious consumers, such as consumers who want to save the planet, become vegan to decrease cruelty towards animals and prevent deforestation, and seek ethically manufactured and fair-traded goods, or at least are considering these issues. These consumers would wear clothes and shoes that were produced in accordance with fair trade principles, from recycled materials. The other brands (the majority, indeed) – by default, falling in the neoliberal camp – will focus on the general mass of consumers for whom price, practicality, and rapid style shifts are more important than the ethical considerations.

In terms of marketing, companies following sustainability tend to emphasize the responsibility values, while those more aligned with the neoliberal ideology tend to emphasize hedonistic or pragmatic human tendencies – including indulgence, impulse buying, and extravagance in terms of variety sought and variants bought. One of the messages of the sustainability focused firms like Patagonia is to stress that buying their products is a responsible way to go, because they protect the ecology and ensure that the workers receive a fair wage. A more mainstream company like L'Oréal, on the other hand, would emphasize the beauty and the healthiness one achieves by using their products.

Brands with strong sustainability positions will clearly mention the ecological, fair-trade, and other responsible aspects in their marketing communications. They would employ terms like local, recyclable, sustainable, and similar labels that signal the brand's sustainability alignment. For instance, if we look at Patagonia, their marketing screams that they plead for sustainability. It is not so with the brands that are more aligned with the neoliberal ideology. No brands – except perhaps those of gun-makers and similar – tout the unregulated, unfettered aspects of their product positioning. In most cases, neoliberal positions of brands remain latent; some may even create a façade of responsible-ethical positioning even without practicing it.

Channels of distribution and communication – mass as well as interactive social media communication – could also be selected to align with the ideologies. The more neoliberal oriented brands are more likely to use mass media and wide-reaching social media and sell products through physical and e-commerce channels with very wide reach, compared to sustainability-oriented brands. This is for the simple reason that the neoliberal oriented brands appeal primarily to the general mass market, not niche segments that sustainably positioned brands appeal to. The sustainability-oriented brands, because they are more locally oriented and focused on responsible and morally conscious consumer segments, are more likely to avoid general mass media and prefer specialized social as well as selective regular media spaces (such as sponsorship of PBS and NPR, for example, in the U.S.). In terms of distribution, these brands are likely to sell through e-commerce as well as physical retail channels that are selective.

Overall, the two mega-ideologies of the contemporary era influence the business models, marketing strategies, and brands differently (see Table 2.4). With the passage of time, if the sustainability seeking market segments become large enough, and coa-

Table 2.4: Markets, marketing, brands, channels, consumers – clashing perspectives.

Aspect	Sustainability	Neoliberalism
Markets	Focus on local markets	Focus on all markets: local, regional, global
Consumers	Morally conscious consumers	Hedonistic, often impulsive consumers
Marketing and Positioning	Emphasize responsibility: from product design to production, distribution, consumption, and disposition	Emphasize impulses, excitement, variety, incessant newness
Brands	Local brands or sub-brands	Global brands, unless the local one can out-compete the global: Let the best brand win
Channels	Specialized physical, e-commerce, conventional media and social media channels. Selective ways to communicate and distribute, to reach committed segments.	Mass conventional media channels as well as social media channels of communication. Mass distribution and merchandising through wide-reaching physical retail and e-commerce retail channels.

Source: Based on authors' research of multiple sources.

lesce, to constitute mass markets, then we can expect significant shifts in business models and strategies. One potential approach could be the sustainability driven business model creation using the storytelling approach (Boje & Rana, 2021). For researchers and analysts, it is imperative to be alert to such shifts, in the incipient stages as well as, of course, when idea-system-switch gains momentum.

Discussion of the Change/Legitimation Framework

Change narratives and legitimation narratives for sustainability as well as for neoliberalism span large conceptual territories.

Change happens through processes that are natural and inertial, driven by momentum that is often perceived as unstoppable. Change also happens through active, intentional, and determined efforts to create change. The in-between position is one where ongoing historical change processes with strong, inertial momentum but intense activism – often led by a vanguard that inspires mass movements – are able to reshape and reorient the direction and trajectory of change.

In the case of each idea system, strong, inertial negative forces with a lot of momentum exist. In addition, there are ideological opponents who are sometimes able to bring in direct countervailing forces to oppose the goals of sustainability or neoliberalism. For these reasons, the two idea systems being discussed in this chapter – indeed, all idea systems that seek a global hegemony – need legitimation narratives that keep the advocates solidly anchored to the positions of the ideology, narratives that constantly (preferably rapidly) bring in new supportive audiences and adherents, and narratives that delegitimate opposing viewpoints.

To guide the ensuing discussion on the interplay of these idea systems in the context of the fashion industry, the condensed framework of Table 2.2 captures these change and legitimation processes in a telegraphic fashion – with of course full awareness of the required detailed discourses on the complexities and depth of these ideas.

In essence, the condensed framework of Table 2.2 lays out the main sources, mechanisms, targets, and sought-for end-state outcomes of the two mega-idea-systems: sustainability and neoliberalism. In a larger document (see Dholakia & Ziliberberg, 2023), we offer greater probing of the considerable depth and detail that can be added to the change processed and legitimation seeking processes that are shown in a condensed fashion in Table 2.2. Without taking a major detour into change and legitimation practices and theoretics, some of the details would become clearer in the ensuing discussion.

Future of the Interplay of Sustainability and Neoliberalism

The foregoing has shown that sustainability and neoliberalism, the two mega-idea-systems of the contemporary world, frequently come into conflict. The future interaction can result in four scenarios: (1) the continuation of the tussle-struggle; (2) the victory of the sustainability agenda for change over neoliberalism; (3) the victory of the neoliberalism agenda for change over sustainability; and (4) the convergence or inter-mixing of sustainability and neoliberalism which could give rise to new ideology.

For the true, dedicated advocates of sustainability, it has become clear that sustainability and capitalism are simply not compatible (Philipsen, 2022). If – for preservation of our planetary ecology and for the wellbeing of future generations – sustainability is an imperative, then capitalism must change. The prevalent globalized neoliberal capitalism must be replaced by a mix of options that include democratic socialism, various forms of post- or alt-capitalism (Kasmir, 2016), and multiplying formats of localism (Varman & Belk, 2022). Indeed, on the untenability of capitalism if we desire a sustainable world, in a prefatory note to an interview of sustainability advocate and scholar Dirk Philipsen (see Philipsen, 2022), Hertrick (2021) offers this view:

> Capitalism is an unsustainable economic system. That idea may seem radical or extreme, particularly since the vast majority of us have been taught about and regularly experience neoliberal economics, but the truth is our current economic system is designed for consumption and growth, creating unsustainable conditions that are depleting our planet.

The ideas of Dirk Philipsen deserve scrutiny: he was a founding member of the Green Party in Germany – a party that is a member of the ruling coalition of Germany in 2023 – prior to becoming a faculty member and sustainability scholar at Duke University. The ideas about sustainability that the Green Party offers thus exist not just at the theoretical level but have made inroads into policy spheres, especially in Europe.

When stripped to its essence, sustainability rejects capitalism and of course rejects even more strongly neoliberal capitalism. Similarly, in an essentialist form, neoliberalism rejects the sustainability idea as well as the sustainability agenda.

There are, however, points of convergence and cooperation also, especially when sustainability solutions are seen as possible profitmaking opportunities. Such convergences usually require compromises, especially on the part of sustainability advocates. Often, the only way to get some – and almost never adequate – funding for sustainability efforts is by creating profitmaking business models that, while making money for the enterprise, achieve some of the sustainability goals. This of course means sustainability efforts remain fragmented, often at the margins of major industry sectors, unable to make a comprehensive push toward a future characterized by a harmonious society of responsible people living in a green, clean, peaceful world. Similarly, neoliberalism is unable to usher in a minimally regulated, privatized, profit-driven competitive world which – by the miracle of the all-seeing market – would bring progress and prosperity to all. In practical terms, to understand this global ideological interplay, it is useful to keep our attention focused on a sector like the fashion industry. The interactions and interplays are easier to observe and analyze than, say, in a domain such as the energy sector. Researchers as well as policymakers, by focusing on the fashion industry, can gain many specific insights into the ways sustainability and neoliberalism forces interact. With clearer insights, there may emerge practicable pathways to resolve the struggle between neoliberalism and sustainability. It may be possible to craft legitimation and change narratives of these two mega idea-systems in ways that lead to real progress rather than a hopeless stalemate.

Concluding Observations

With neoliberalism pervasively dominant in the world – with only kleptocratic oligarchism as a minor variant in some geopolitical settings – sustainability efforts have an uphill climb. Albeit minor at this point in time, there are illustrative economic efforts happening that are not under the neoliberal or kleptocratic umbrellas. The Mondragon group of cooperatives, headquartered in Spain, offers a strong alternative model to the oligarchic capitalist enterprises (Kasmir, 2016; Romeo, 2022). Started as a small cooperative project in the 1950s, Mondragon evolved into a group with over 250 business enterprises employing over 70,000 workers. In the cooperative parts of Mondragon, the earnings ratio of top-to-bottom salaries is 9:1, compared to 127:1 for Spain overall. The enterprise's brands have a reputation of high reliability and non-exploitative manufacturing. To compete with global neoliberal brands, however, Mondragon has expanded via acquisitions and low-wage outsourcing – to China, for example – just like any neoliberal capitalist firm. The total employee base now comprises of only one third as owning-members, the rest being contract employees in Spain or wage workers abroad (Kasmir, 2016). For sustainability advocates this raises the question as to whether the Mondragon type coop creates a worker-and-ecology protecting system, or a tiered workforce with privileged coop-owner-workers at top and exploited contract and wage workers at the bottom. Major organizational innovations are required if Mondragon is not to become just a utopic socialist subsystem sitting atop a larger, exploitative neoliberal subsystem.

Another avenue, for sustainability supporters, is to promote and encourage entities that promote localism, as antithesis of neoliberal brand behemoths. Varman and Belk (2022) profile a group in India that relies on Gandhian principles of localized simplicity. The group urges its followers to shun not only foreign multinational brands but also brands of Indian mega-corporations, both being variants of global neoliberalism. This group not only promotes locally made products of small local enterprises, but also advances non-market consumer solutions such as use of neem twigs for brushing teeth. Such interest in localism is becoming pervasive globally. Kurland, McCaffrey, and Hill (2012) find four key elements in successful localism-focused con-

sumption movements: independent ownership, local buying, local sourcing, and pragmatic partnering. As the Whole Foods and many other cases show, however, the
coopting of "localism" trends by mega-brands – retailers as well as manufacturers – is
common. Sustainability champions need to do a lot more experimentation and exploration to find ways to make true localism flourish.

Apart from policies and practices, if sustainability efforts are to have rapid and
visible successes, then major cultural shifts are required. Neoliberal ways of doing
things have been infused into the very cultural fabric of our consumption spheres.
Take the case of the fashion industry. Enterprises and nonprofit organizations that
promote sustainable fashion solutions, via one or more of the R-elements of Table 2.1,
are proliferating. Some consumers are willing to shift from ecologically destructive
fast fashion behaviors to pro-sustainability behaviors. For many of these consumers,
however, even with the shift to sustainable fashion products, the "need for speed"
does not get attenuated. In the December 15, 2022 edition of *Vogue Business* it was reported that many who have switched to sustainable repurposed wearables and accessories kept asking for new designs (Cernansky, 2022). Moving away from fast non-
sustainable fashion, these consumers want fast sustainable fashion, partially defeat-
ing some of the R-elements such as Refuse, Rethink, and Reduce. On a broader conceptual plane beyond just the fashion industry, based on a study of digital consumption,
Hoang, Cronin and Skandalis (2023) conclude that in "the absence of any unifying and
politically-centered solidarity projects, mere gestures of resistance are undertaken towards managing personal dissatisfactions with – instead of collectively transforming –
. . . [the prevalent neoliberal] structural conditions" (p. 1).

The neoliberal cultural transformation – sustainability advocates may use a term
such as "corrosion" or "corruption" rather than transformation – of consumer culture
has taken deep roots. In the age of Instagram and Tik Tok, the enduring cultural shift
required by movements such as the "Cittaslow" or "Slow City" model – with Slow
Food and general deceleration of frenetic life (as well as intensification of conviviality
and bonhomie) – has become very challenging. We conclude this chapter on the interactive tension between sustainability and neoliberalism not with an academic but a
practitioner voice, that of the mayor of Izmir, Turkey, Tunç Soyer (Metropolis, 2021),
who emphasizes the overarching importance of culture:

> Being fast and big are the main reasons why we have destroyed our countries, and we know that
> this is not sustainable . . . It's time to apply the Cittaslow criteria to metropolises . . . This is in-
> trinsically linked to culture. There is a struggle between [neoliberal] economics and [sustainable]
> ecology, which is also destroying the future. We have to find a balance between the two, and this
> is a question of culture. Without culture, if you have an economy, you will have inequality and
> autocracy. That's why culture is essential.

References

Bernetti, M. & Al Jazeera. (2021, November 8). Chile's desert dumping ground for fast fashion leftovers. *Al Jazeera*. Retrieved from https://www.aljazeera.com/gallery/2021/11/8/chiles-desert-dumping-ground-for-fast-fashion-leftovers

Boje, D. M., & Rana, M. B. (2021). Defining a sustainability-driven business modeling strategy with a storytelling science approach. In *Handbook of Sustainability-Driven Business Strategies in Practice* (pp. 59–77). Edward Elgar Publishing.

Campbell-Johnston, K., Cate, J. ten, Elfering-Petrovic, M., & Gupta, J. (2019). City level circular transitions: Barriers and limits in Amsterdam, Utrecht and The Hague. *Journal of Cleaner Production, 235*, 1232–1239.

Cernansky, R. (2022, December 15). Sustainable fashion is stuck in 'pilot phase.' *Vogue Business*. Retrieved from https://www.voguebusiness.com/sustainability/sustainable-fashion-is-stuck-in-pilot-phase

Cramer, J. (2017). The Raw Materials Transition in the Amsterdam Metropolitan Area: Added Value for the Economy, Well-Being, and the Environment. *Environment: Science and Policy for Sustainable Development, 59*, 14–21.

Cramer, J. M. (2020). Implementing the circular economy in the Amsterdam Metropolitan Area: The interplay between market actors mediated by transition brokers. *Business Strategy and the Environment, 29*, 2857–2870.

Dholakia, N., Ozgun, A., & Atik, D. (2021). The unwitting corruption of broadening of marketing into neoliberalism: A beast unleashed? *European Journal of Marketing, 55*, 868–893.

Dholakia, N., & Ziliberberg, C. (2023). *Sustainability and Neoliberalism: Impossible Coexistence, Improbable Adaptation, or Imperative Transformation*.

Dissanayake, K., & Weerasinghe, D. (2022). Towards Circular Economy in Fashion: Review of Strategies, Barriers and Enablers. *Circular Economy and Sustainability, 2*. https://doi.org/10.1007/s43615-021-00090-5

Fletcher, K. (2014). *Sustainable Fashion and Textiles: Design Journeys*. New York, N.Y: Routledge.

Harvey, D. (2007). Neoliberalism as Creative Destruction. *The Annals of the American Academy of Political and Social Science, 610*, 22–44.

Hertrick, S. J. (2021, September). The elephant in the room: Capitalism is not sustainable. Retrieved April 19, 2023, from Circular Triangle website: https://www.circulartriangle.org/blog/the-elephant-in-the-room-capitalism-is-not-sustainable

Hoang, Q., Cronin, J., & Skandalis, A. (2023). Futureless vicissitudes: Gestural anti-consumption and the reflexively impotent (anti-)consumer. *Marketing Theory*, 14705931231153192.

Jørgensen, S., & Pedersen, L. J. T. (2018). The Circular Rather than the Linear Economy. In S. Jørgensen & L. J. T. Pedersen (Eds.), *RESTART Sustainable Business Model Innovation* (pp. 103–120). Cham: Springer International Publishing.

Joy, A., Sherry, J. F., Venkatesh, A., Wang, J., & Chan, R. (2012). Fast Fashion, Sustainability, and the Ethical Appeal of Luxury Brands. *Fashion Theory, 16*, 273–295.

Kasmir, S. (2016, February 13). The Mondragon Cooperatives: Successes and Challenges. *Global Dialogue*. Retrieved from https://globaldialogue.isa-sociology.org//articles/the-mondragon-cooperatives-successes-and-challenges

Kirchherr, J., Reike, D., & Hekkert, M. (2017). Conceptualizing the circular economy: An analysis of 114 definitions. *Resources, Conservation and Recycling, 127*, 221–232.

Kurland, N. B., McCaffrey, S. J., & Hill, D. H. (2012). The Localism Movement: Shared and Emergent Values. *Journal of Environmental Sustainability, 2*, 1–14.

Lawless, J. (2022, October 20). Truss quits, but UK's political and economic turmoil persist. *AP NEWS*. Retrieved from https://apnews.com/article/liz-truss-europe-economy-business-e18e6e6007c28f6e11cc1a201c545b71

Metropolis. (2021, September 27). The spirit of Cittaslow has sidled into the metropolis. *Metropolis*. Retrieved from https://www.metropolis.org/news/spirit-cittaslow-has-sidled-metropolis

Monbiot, G. (2016, April 15). Neoliberalism – the ideology at the root of all our problems. *The Guardian*. Retrieved from https://www.theguardian.com/books/2016/apr/15/neoliberalism-ideology-problem-george-monbiot

Morseletto, P. (2020). Targets for a circular economy. *Resources, Conservation and Recycling, 153*, 104553.

Muthu, S. S. (Ed.). (2019). *Circular economy in textiles and apparel: Processing, manufacturing, and design*. Duxford, United Kingdom ; Cambridge, MA: Woodhead Publishing, an imprint of Elsevier.

Ozdamar-Ertekin, Z. (2017). The True Cost: The Bitter Truth behind Fast Fashion. *Markets, Globalization & Development Review, 2*. https://doi.org/10.23860/MGDR-2017-02-03-07

Philipsen, D. (2022). What Counts – Why Growth Economics is Failing Us. *Journal of Consumer Culture*, 146954052211362.

Rana, M., & Tajuddin, S. (2021). Circular Economy and Sustainability Capability: The Case of H&M. In *New Perspectives on the Modern Corporation Series*. *Upgrading the Global Garment Industry: Internationalization, Capabilities and Sustainability*. Cheltemham, UK: Edward Elgar Publishing.

Reike, D., Vermeulen, W. J. V., & Witjes, S. (2018). The circular economy: New or Refurbished as CE 3.0? – Exploring Controversies in the Conceptualization of the Circular Economy through a Focus on History and Resource Value Retention Options. *Resources, Conservation and Recycling, 135*, 246–264.

Romeo, N. (2022, August 27). How Mondragon Became the World's Largest Co-Op. *The New Yorker*. Retrieved from https://www.newyorker.com/business/currency/how-mondragon-became-the-worlds-largest-co-op

Varman, R., & Belk, R. (2022). Privileging Localism and Visualizing Nationhood in Anti-Consumption. *Markets, Globalization & Development Review, 7*. https://doi.org/10.23860/MGDR-2022-07-04-02

Zwick, D., Bonsu, S. K., & Darmody, A. (2008). Putting Consumers to Work: 'Co-creation' and new marketing govern-mentality. *Journal of Consumer Culture, 8*, 163–196.

Verena Gruber, Christina Holweg, and Eva Lienbacher

3 Juggling Janus: Managing Retailscapes at the Frontier of Logics of Commerce and Care

Organizations operate in institutional fields that are guided by logics which inform the objectives, assumptions, values, and practices of these organizations (Thornton & Ocasio, 1999). The food distribution sector is a large and complex industry, and home to many different types of organizations that are informed by two main logics. On one side, there is a logic of commerce that prioritizes efficiency and rationality. This logic guides the operations of traditional retail stores such as supermarkets or discount stores, manufacturers, and the service sector, with restaurants and delivery services. It builds on the notion of food distribution as a quest of process optimization with the aim to increase profitability, often to the detriment of the people involved (Gruber, Holweg, & Teller, 2016). Food is not seen as an important pillar of well-being (Block et al., 2011) but as inventory that needs to be managed in a manner to minimize shrinkage (Avery, McKay, & Hunter, 2012). The logic of commerce is one of rationalization and "McDonaldization" (Ritzer, 1983). On the other side, there are food distributors such as food banks, which are informed by a logic of care that prioritizes the supply of food to those in need, as well as human and environmental well-being. The logic of care is informed by an understanding of food as more than its instrumental value but instead as an important aspect of cultures and traditions, as well as a source of comfort, pleasure, and community (Block et al., 2011; Rozin, 2005). It questions narrow conceptions of food waste and focuses on its potential for human, animal, and planetary well-being (Gruber, Holweg, & Teller, 2016). Social supermarkets (SSMs) represent an alternative retail format that operates at the frontier of these two logics. SSMs are purpose-driven retailscapes that aim to provide access to affordable food for at-risk-of-poverty consumers. They do so by selling surplus products provided for free by manufacturers, such as products with suboptimal packaging, or products close to expiration, which would otherwise be declared food waste by traditional retail stores or manufacturers (Gruber, Holweg, & Teller, 2016; Holweg & Lienbacher, 2011).

This chapter focuses on SSMs as they are found in an interesting space between the dominant institutional logics of commerce and care that characterize the food distribution sector. More specifically, we are interested in the unique perspective of individuals managing these retailscapes. Just like the Roman god Janus, they must look in two different directions when organizing day-to-day operations. These managers are susceptible to isomorphic pressures of market efficiency, yet at the same time are guided by their volition to uphold humanity in their retailscapes, and to act in line with environmental objectives and a logic of care (DiMaggio & Powell, 1983; Thornton, Ocasio, & Lounsbury, 2012). Scholars have noted that organizations might blend insti-

https://doi.org/10.1515/9783110783933-003

tutional logics (Ertimur and Coskuner-Balli, 2015), but there is little insight on the experiences of managers who find themselves at the frontier of these logics. A notewor-
thy exception is the recent work of Welté, Cayla, and Fischer (2022), who study
management practices at the intersection of different institutional logics in the field
of luxury retail. The authors uncover a set of hybridization practices that retailers employ to strategically leverage the distinct institutional logics. Our objective in this
chapter is to offer a complementary perspective by investigating the tensions that
SSM managers face in their daily operations. The long-term engagement with two
SSMs allows us to provide thick descriptions of managers' reality (Geertz, 1973). Our
research uncovers four sources of tensions that emerge due to SSMs' unique position
on the fault line of two logics: the composition of the product assortment; the unique
customer profiles; the idiosyncrasies of employees; and the engagement with and relative dependency of other stakeholders. These tensions speak to the complexity for
social organizations, such as SSMs, to pursue their missions within a neoliberal environment that coerces practices into rigid structures and prioritizes competitiveness
and profitability over service to the collective (D'Enbeau & Buzzanell, 2011). The managers in our case study resort to different strategies to navigate these tensions. These
strategies add to the extant knowledge on managers' and organizations' practices that
help balance the demands of distinct institutional logics (Thornton & Ocasio, 1999).
Our findings also add to the literature on both ecological and social sustainability (Ly
& Cope, 2023): describing their efforts to stay economically viable, to minimize food
waste, and to uphold humanity while assuring food security, the accounts of the managers we followed tell a new story about sustainability in the food sector.

Theoretical Background

Two streams of literature are relevant for the present context and guide our investigation of SSMs and the individuals who manage them. One the one hand, work on institutional logics informs our understanding of the underlying prescriptions, as well as
the values, objectives, and practices prevalent in the sector of food distribution. On
the other hand, the literature on hybrid organizations provides insights into the particularities of managing different organizational objectives.

Institutional Logics

Companies operate against the backdrop of institutional logics that shape and inform
the values, objectives, and practices of a field. Formally defined, institutional logics
represent "the socially constructed, historical pattern of material practices, assumptions, values, beliefs, and rules by which individuals produce and reproduce their ma-

terial subsistence, organize time and space, and provide meaning to their social real-ity" (Micelotta, Lounsbury, & Greenwood, 2017; Thornton & Ocasio, 1999, p. 804). In other words, an institutional logic consists of a set of "organizing principles that shape the behavior of field participants" (Reay & Hinings, 2009, p. 631). Institutional logics are not bound to the broad organizing principles of a society, for they can de-velop at various levels, including organizations, industries, or organizational fields (Ramus, Vaccaro, & Brusoni, 2017; Thornton & Ocasio, 2008). They are decoded and elaborated at the field and the organizational level by the individuals whose behavior is structured or oriented by them (Gawer & Phillips, 2013; Nigam & Ocasio, 2010).

The concept of institutional logics is important for understanding different types of dynamics prevalent in organizational fields. There are often multiple institutional logics that exert an influence on an organizational field (Thornton, 2004): there are organizational fields that maintain pluralistic institutional logics despite the emer-gence of a dominant one (Van Gestel & Hillebrand, 2011); there are relatively stable fields which either contain two simultaneously active institutional logics (Reay & Hin-ings, 2005; 2009) or have seen sudden shifts in logics followed by settled periods (Greenwood & Hinings, 2006). Whenever a field is characterized by simultaneously present logics, organizations must address this duality, often navigating between dif-ferent demands while addressing the challenges and tensions that arise from them (Gigliotti & Runfola, 2022; Smith, Gonin, & Besharov, 2013). There may also be logics that co-exist in a field and that prescribe contradicting understandings and actions, thus requiring institutional actors to show a certain ambidexterity when operating in the field (Ertimur & Coskuner-Balli, 2015).

Parmentier and Fischer (2021) illustrate how designers who manage their own professional brands while also being employed by a fashion house find themselves negotiating, in their work, between the logic of commerce and the logic of art that dominate the field of fashion (Scaraboto & Fischer, 2013). The authors show the ten-sions regarding resources and identity that designers experience, as well as the strate-gies they employ to overcome these tensions. In a similar vein, Welté, Cayla, and Fischer (2022) discuss the various logics that influence the field of luxury retailing. A logic that has traditionally been very important in that field is the logic of distinction, which has guided luxury brands in the usage of social class in their service operations (Dion & Borraz, 2017). At the same time, new logics have increasingly gained a foot-hold in the luxury retail sector and have reoriented organizations towards a focus on experiences (Joy et al., 2014) and sustainability (Keinan et al., 2020). To navigate these conflicting logics in the luxury servicescape, managers deploy technological, spatial, and interactional hybridization practices that allow them to capitalize on the syner-gies between the logics (Welté, Cayla, & Fischer, 2022). The research of Welté, Cayla, and Fischer (2022) illustrates the importance of addressing the specifics of different retail environments to understand the unique challenges that managers face when operating at the interface of distinct institutional logics. The institutional logics in food retailing are arguably different from those in luxury retailing, and SSMs differ from luxury brands as they have a social and environmental mission at the core of their business model. We turn to the literature on hybrid organizations to highlight the particularities of organizations with dual missions.

Hybrid Organizations

Social enterprises (SEs) or social hybrid organizations are characterized by a pursuit of environmental and social goals while catering to a business logic (Jolink & Niesten, 2012; Maier, Meyer, & Steinbereithner, 2016; Rama Murthy, Roll, & Colin-Jones, 2021). This means that these organizations concurrently pursue both profit and social, or environmental, objectives (Mair, Mayer, & Lutz, 2015; Pache & Santos, 2013). At times, these objectives are in conflict and this discord gives rise to tensions and trade-offs that need to be managed (Doherty, Haugh, & Lyon, 2014). Smith, Gonin, and Besharov (2013) provide a systematic review of the tensions that arise and how they manifest. In doing so, they draw on Smith and Lewis' (2011) categorization of tensions as performing, organizing, belonging, and learning. Performing tensions arise because the organization is concurrently pursuing two different objectives, which are associated with different metrics and stakeholder demands (Smith, Gonin, & Besharov, 2013). Organizing tensions capture the different structures, practices, and processes, such as how to hire, integrate, and train employees. Belonging tensions relate to the organizational identity that is difficult to articulate and that is instrumental in the way the organization positions itself vis à vis its different stakeholders. Learning tensions arise as the distinct objectives go along with different time horizons (Smith, Gonin, & Besharov, 2013). In their review, Smith, Gonin, and Besharov (2013) interpret these four tensions based on different theoretical streams, among them institutional theory. Scholars in this tradition, as discussed above, think of such organizations as being informed by different logics, that is a social welfare logic and a commercial logic. Smith, Gonin, and Besharov (2013) acknowledge that the intersection of logics is a place of great potential for innovation but also challenges.

The literature that focuses more specifically on SEs argues that it is the development of certain capabilities that helps with facing these challenges and pursuing distinct objectives (Bhardwaj & Srivastava, 2021). Dynamic capabilities are defined as "the ability of a firm to build, integrate and reconfigure internal competencies as well as external competencies to address a changing business environment" (Bhardwaj & Srivastava, 2021: p. 3). In their systematic review, the authors find the following key capabilities: (1) bricolage, which is the acquisition and combination of (scant) resources; (2) alliance building, which is collaboration with other organizations to jointly address social problems; (3) legal and formal support, such as from governments, to address new opportunities; (4) learning capability, which is experimentation and the development of innovative solutions; (5) effectuation, which is the strategic use of ecosystems to shape opportunities; (6) improvisation, which includes deviation from regular strategic plans to address new opportunities; (7) knowledge management, which is crucial for encountering constantly changing environmental dynamics; (8) innovation capability, which is an organization's ability to seize opportunities and carry out innovative activities; (9) marketing capability, which is the ability to understand customer needs and to achieve product differentiation and superior brand value; and lastly (10) co-specialization, which is "the ability of a firm to recognize, develop, and use co-specialized resources" (Bhardwaj & Srivastava, 2021: p. 19). In concluding their systematic review, the authors reflect on the importance of resources when developing dynamic capabilities, and thus in the management of dual objectives in SEs.

To better understand the possibilities for SSMs in acquiring resources and developing capabilities, we turn to the field of food distribution. We first briefly address the importance of food to individual well-being and the role it plays for vulnerable consumers in particular. We then dissect the food retail landscape and discuss the influence of different institutional logics and the distinct distribution formats present in the food sector. Afterwards, we introduce SSMs as the context for the subsequent empirical investigation.

Food Industry Transformation

The Importance of Food

Food is central to individual and societal well-being (Block et al., 2011) and constitutes one of the most important categories of household expenditure. For financially vulnerable individuals, housing and food even represent the most important pillar of household expenditure (49% compared to 20% for high-income households (Statistics Austria, 2022)). Thus, these consumers often use food as a lever in times of financial constraint because food expenses can be adjusted more easily than, for example, housing or medical care expenses. As a consequence, vulnerable consumers are disproportionately affected by, and more concerned about, rising food prices. Statistics Canada reports that one in five Canadians expect to use food banks or community organizations to obtain meals free of charge (Statistics Canada, 2022), while the UK-based Institute for Grocery Distribution (IGD) warns that they "are already seeing households skip meals – a clear indicator of food stress" (IGD, 2022). This problem does not just affect a small minority. In 2020, more than 37 million people in the United States were living in poverty (US Census, 2022); in the European Union about a fifth of the population lives at risk of poverty, a threshold set at 60% of the national median income (Eurostat, 2021). The situation has only been exacerbated as sanitary and geopolitical crises have put a lot of pressure on supply chains, which in turn has led to rising prices for many day-to-day expenditures. In combination with steadily increasing consumer inflation, households see themselves confronted with growing financial concerns. There are not only differences in terms of the financial means to afford food but also large disparities in individuals' physical access to food (Rose et al., 2010). Once again, it is often the most disadvantaged socioeconomic areas that have the worst access to healthy and nutritious food (Ball, Timperio, & Crawford, 2009). Due to the importance of securing access to food, a variety of distribution formats have emerged in the food sector.

The Food Distribution Landscape

The retail and distribution landscape is an intricate system that is home to many different types of organizational formats, yet often dominated by a few major players. In 2020, among the 250 leading retailers around the world monitored by Deloitte (2022), the top ten retailers accounted for 34.6% of retail revenue. For most of the leading retailers, such as Walmart, The Schwarz Group, or Target, food is the key revenue source. In parallel to market concentration, the retailing sector has undergone a major restructuring since the 1960s. The rise of information technology, increased automatization, the optimization of merchandising systems, and the introduction of bar codes have allowed for more efficient processes in retail environments (Grewal et al., 2021). Consequently, merchandise flows in grocery supply chains have accelerated and led to lower inventory costs, more efficient assortments, faster product replenishments, and new product introductions, among other things (Kotzab, 1999).

The food sector is a very dynamic sector that continuously sees the emergence of new retail and distribution formats that often have other objectives than the pursuit of profits that is prevalent among more traditional retail forms. In addition, there are alternative distribution formats surfacing around the globe that move away from linear systems and instead try to integrate principles of circularity in their operations. In Italy, Solidarity Purchase Groups (Gruppi di Acquisto Solidale or GAS) emerged as grassroot networks to enable the collective provision of food and other household items (Grasseni, 2013). In several US states and in Canada, farm-to-school or farm-to-cafeteria networks were established to support sustainable and regional food deliveries to schools and universities (see, for example, F2CC, 2022; Sanger & Zenz, 2004). Ho and Shirahada (2021) explain that, in Japan, the quickly aging population is facing increasing difficulties accessing food retailers, which have withdrawn from areas that can be reached by public transport. Mobile supermarkets have emerged in response to this challenge. Other examples include Food Coops, Farmers' Markets, vending machines that directly offer produce to the final consumer, app-based formats such as Too Good To Go, and social start-ups such as the Sirplus markets in Germany that tackle food waste by reintegrating surplus products in their online shops. In addition to these alternative retail formats, there are also non-profit organizations active in the food distribution sector, such as parroquias or food banks. These food distribution formats pursue very specific objectives, such as helping the most vulnerable members of society. Food banks collect food products from retailers, restaurants, or other premises, and redistribute them for free to organizations that help people in need, such as homeless shelters. First founded in the US in 1967, food banks operate in more than 200 countries globally (Global Foodbanking Network, 2015). Parroquias are similar to food banks but also offer a soup kitchen. They are linked to the church in Spain and are well-established across that country (Corporación Aragonesa de Radio y Televisión, 2023).

In summary, there are various types of organizations operating in the food distribution sector, from global giants like Walmart to local Spanish parroquias, that all aim to create value for consumers. Arguably, these organizations are embedded in different institutional logics. Classic retail organizations operate in a logic of commerce that prioritizes process efficiency in supply chains, the optimization of inventories and food assortments, and the maximization of profits. Automatization and the ubiquity of information technology have led to a further acceleration and rationalization of food distribution (Kotzab, 1999; Ritzer, 1983). Efficiency, competitiveness, and ultimately profitability are guiding values in this logic and inform the daily practices of companies. This is in stark contrast to organizations such as food solidarity purchase groups, which are embedded in a logic of care that prioritizes people and the planet, and acknowledges the preciousness of produce and the importance of humanity in the distribution of food. As in the case of institutional logics in other fields (Parmentier & Fischer, 2021; Welté, Cayla, & Fischer, 2022), these two logics are not mutually exclusive; organizations driven by care need to ensure viability to sustainably serve their purpose, and organizations guided by a logic of commerce have increasingly sought to integrate empathy and humanity into their daily operations. A recent example includes the Dutch supermarket chain Jumbo, which introduced a slow checkout lane to combat loneliness: instead of focusing on speed and efficiency, these checkouts deliberately counter the prescriptions of a logic of commerce and focus on customers who feel lonely and would like to chat with their cashiers (Raj, 2023).

Figure 3.1 provides a categorization of selected types of organizations and illustrates them in line with the dominant, institutional logic they operate in (logic of commerce or logic of care). In addition, we highlight the extent to which these organizations cater to vulnerable consumers. In this figure, we also include SSMs, which are mostly embedded in a logic of care but often need to adhere to the rules and beliefs prescribed by a logic of commerce.

Social Supermarkets and their Stakeholder Network

SSMs are purpose-driven retailscapes that aim to provide affordable access to food for consumers at risk of poverty, while simultaneously reducing food waste in the supply chain by selling surplus products, suboptimal products, or products close to expiration (Gruber, Holweg, & Teller, 2016; Holweg & Lienbacher, 2011). SSMs are a

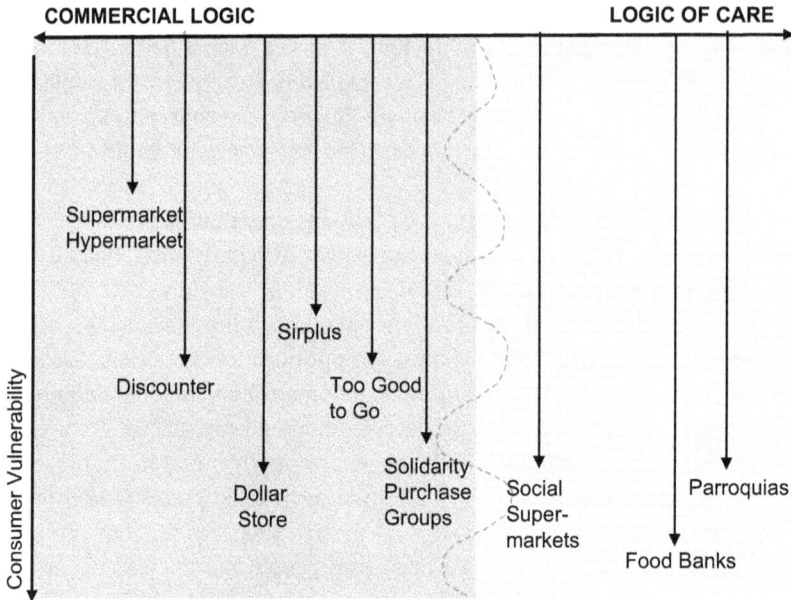

Figure 3.1: Selected organizations in the food distribution landscape.

specific type of retail environment that emerged in France in the 1980s and have since surfaced in many European countries, including some of the most economically prosperous and wealthy cities, such as Vienna (Austria) and Zurich (Switzerland) (Caritas Markt, 2023; Holweg & Lienbacher, 2016; SOMA, 2023). They operate in 13 European countries, with slightly different concepts, such as, for example, "épicerie sociale" and "épicerie solidaire" in France (about 820 stores), "Caritas Markt" in Switzerland (about 20 stores), and the "Sozialmarkt" in Austria (about 100 stores) (Holweg & Lienbacher, 2021). The concept of SSMs has extended to the US, with the first stores established there as early as 2012 in the Boston area (Daily Table, 2023).

SSMs are designed as retail spaces that mirror classic retail stores, especially those operating in the discount segment. Prices are "symbolic" and set to around one third of the prices in traditional retail stores. The assortment mainly consists of food products, and some stores also offer a small non-food assortment, with hygiene and cleaning products, for example, as well as body and baby care (Holweg & Lienbacher, 2016). In comparison to charities, SSMs deliberately charge a price (as mentioned, about a third of those of conventional stores) to encourage shoppers to perceive themselves as consumers rather than as welfare recipients, as might be the case with food banks. Furthermore, SSMs need the revenue to cover some parts of their operational costs, such as rent or electricity (Holweg & Lienbacher, 2011).

Another key characteristic of SSMs is their limited assortment, which only comprises surplus products, supplied for free by retailing and manufacturing companies

(Holweg & Lienbacher, 2011). These products are still fit for human consumption and adhere to food security standards but can no longer be sold in conventional retail stores for reasons related to industry standards or store policies, with regards to packaging or expiration dates. Volunteers or employees of SSMs collect the products in trucks, thus helping the sponsoring organizations to reduce food waste and to save on the costs of municipal waste removal. As SSMs only offer what is provided by retailers or manufacturers, their assortment is limited. These products are not considered to be donations, because SSMs are considered to be providing certain services in return, for example collecting, sorting, and presenting the products in their stores. Moreover, as mentioned, the SSMs enable retailers and manufacturers to save on some municipal waste collection costs, as the products would often have been disposed of otherwise. A last differentiating characteristic of SSMs is that they regulate store access and are only open to individuals who are at risk of poverty, defined as having an income below 60% of the national median income. Access to SSMs is organized and controlled via identification cards that are issued by the stores upon presentation of an income statement and proof of residence. The reduced product assortment mentioned above is to a certain extent also a deliberate choice, to ensure that customers will also frequent more traditional stores. In terms of their legal constitution, most SSMs are non-profit organizations and operate with the support of volunteers as well as long-term unemployed persons, who work in the SSMs for some months as part of workforce reintegration programs.

SSMs represent an interesting case for studying management at the frontier of institutional logics. On the one hand, they are embedded in a logic of care for both the planet and its people, in that their mission requires them to focus on integrating the long-term unemployed as employees, and help reduce food waste in the supply chain by redistributing items rejected by mainstream retailers, thus supporting vulnerable consumers. On the other hand, the store managers are informed by a logic of commerce in that they have to generate profits for self-sustenance and therefore need to focus on key indicators such as efficiency of operations or sales. Managers face the difficult task of decoding on a daily basis the demands stemming from the different logics in which they operate. In this project we aim to uncover the areas in which the conflicting demands can lead to tensions, and to investigate the strategies managers use to address these tensions. To do so, we will adopt a qualitative methodological approach.

Methodological Approach

Our investigation follows Zilber's (2016, p. 149) "call to follow the work of institutional logics in interactions among actors within organizations, in situ and in vivo; and to appreciate not only how people within organizations engage with, interpret and use institutional logics – but also how, by doing so, they actually constitute them." To achieve this, we build on an in-depth analysis of two SSMs in Vienna that differ with respect to their formal set-up, their institutional background, and their internal rules and proce-dures. Our approach is informed by comparative case analysis and our selection of cases guided by theoretical considerations (Bartlett & Vavrus, 2017; Eisenhardt, 1989; Yin, 2009). Table 3.1 provides short descriptions of the two stores and their managers.

Table 3.1: Description of cases.

	SSM 1	SSM 2
Brief description	This SSM is located in a central location in Vienna and has a comparatively large store surface of ca. 400 m² and a storage area of ca. 200 m².	This SSM is located in a suburban area of Vienna and operates with a relatively small store surface of ca. 120 m² and a storage area of ca. 60 m².
	It has 5,500 registered customers and is managed by six full-time employees and three part-time employees, as well as two volunteers. A total of 44 long-term unemployed people have worked there as part of their workplace reintegration program.	It has 800 registered customers and is managed by one full-time employee, three part-time employees, and 22 volunteers. One person is working there as part of their workplace reintegration program.
	The main assortment is food; a small non-food assortment includes children's toys, second-hand computers, and stationery products, for example. The SSM further offers a small café and a meeting area where customers can receive support from social welfare workers. Occasionally, the SSM provides training on proper food handling, for its workers, and on applying for jobs, for both workers and customers.	The main assortment is food; a small non-food assortment includes second-hand clothes and some stationery products. Once a year, the store runs a workshop on dental care, supported by the national dentist association. This SSM belongs to a national charity organization which runs two SSMs in total.
	Key stakeholder relations that this SSM entertains are with an affiliated local non-governmental organization specializing in community support and the national employment service (AMS).	
Managers	Sandra and Colin	Gary and Andrea

Given that prolonged engagement in and observation of store reality and culture are essential to understanding the experiences of managers (Hill & Stamey, 1990), we joined the two SSMs as observers and volunteers before the start of our research project. Two authors have been active volunteers supporting the board for more than seven years. Continuous participation in the store operations thus enabled us to gain deeper insights into the processes and challenges of the store managers. In total, we spent close to four weeks in various functions at the SSMs, from back-office support to frontline work at the fresh food counter or check-out. This time allowed us to get first-hand insights on the tensions arising in SSMs on a daily basis, and to witness how managers anticipate, face, and address these tensions. Moreover, we conducted in-depth interviews with four senior store managers who have an average experience of six years managing their respective SSMs. Their long involvement allowed them to share rich accounts of the difficulties they experience in the management of these retailscapes. The interviews lasted, on average, one hour, and were audio-recorded and later transcribed. All interviews were supported by at least two observational rounds, covering the store, the warehouse area, and the managers' offices. Additionally, we drew upon our field notes and several additional data sources in the form of brochures, online materials, and leaflets about the SSMs.

Our analysis started with the reading of all transcripts, field notes, and additional documents, and we made sure to identify and contextualize both the similarities and the differences in terms of the tensions experienced and strategies employed. Our coding was both grounded and theoretically informed.

Findings

The inductive analysis of the interview and ethnographic data gave rise to four distinct yet interrelated sources of tensions in the daily operations of SSMs: (1) assortment composition; (2) customer profiles; (3) employee idiosyncrasies; and (4) stakeholder engagement.

Tensions Related to the Composition of the Product Assortment in Social Supermarkets

The assortment of SSMs mainly consists of products received from manufacturers, retail stores, and some private donations. It is impossible to plan ahead regarding when products will be available, and the deliveries often include only a very restricted range of products. The assortment in SSMs is in general much smaller than in traditional retail stores, and managers have virtually no influence on the kind of products they get: "At the moment, we have four different types of chips. One type would probably be enough. And we'd rather have other things, but we just can't choose" (Gary). The restricted assortment requires attention from SSM managers and often forces them to manage customer flows to ensure a fair distribution of available quantities to their clients. Sandra recounts that "customers often wait in front of the store by 8:30 a.m., even though we only open at 10 a.m. They think that if they come in first, they get more of the cake, so to say." To manage the inflow of customers, managers resort to proactive communication, for example when trying to adjust clients' expectations. Colin explains how he handles this at the SSM he manages:

> We explain to them [customers] that they can also come at 11. The products that we don't have at 10 o'clock, we won't have them at 11 either. You can't get that [fear of missing out] out of a person, but nevertheless, we are trying everything . . . we try to explain that they can come at different times, but eventually we can't stop them from lining up. And of course, there is a queue, because we only let customers in block wise. We can't let all the people in at once. That would only lead to complications. It's also about the safety of the people.

Communication skills are also needed when managers must question the decisions of some of their customers, for example when they take a markedly large amount of a product. Sandra acknowledges that this is a delicate matter but often necessary to ensure distributive justice. To this end, SSMs often restrict the number of products that clients can purchase. Gary recounts situations in which clients expressed incomprehension and asked, "why don't you just order some more [of the product] at Billa [a local supermarket]'? And then I need to explain to them that this is not how the system works." Often, managers not only have to set rules to ensure justice but also pursue certain clients if they take more than is allowed:

> Sometimes, people haven't seen that there is a limit to how much they can take, and they fill up the whole shopping cart, then of course I don't have any more of it [the product]. Then the next customer says, 'well yeah but he has 20 pieces!!!' Then I have to intervene, tell him, 'No, that is not ok' and I explain to the other customer that he can't take twenty, but only two, so that we can distribute the remainder again to other customers. (Colin)

Communication is also needed to guide customers' movements in the store, such as when Sandra reminds her clients "to please continue to the checkout because there won't be more [products] coming in, and it is a pity [if] they wait for nothing."

Another strategy that managers employ to manage customer streams is to strategically use the material structure and store equipment available in the supermarket. The SSM managed by Gary is very small and thus he cannot allow customers to linger for a prolonged period in the store. He has established a one-way system to facilitate the flow of customers through the store. This means that customers cannot turn back, even if a previous section has been replenished with donations while they are still in the store. Another piece of store equipment that Gary uses is the shopping cart:

> We can only let in as many people as we have carts. We have 25 carts. So now there are sometimes 40 people standing outside. That means that, in the first three quarters of an hour, someone is always standing by the door to prevent more people from coming in than we have carts.

Tensions Related to the Unique Customer Profiles

Another tension that SSM managers need to navigate stems from the unique profiles of the customers they serve. Individuals who shop in SSMs are financially vulnerable but also often face additional vulnerabilities, such as health issues, or they may live in generally precarious situations. This means that SSM managers cannot always adhere to the normal "rules of the game" and have to apply leniency and allow for flexibility. Sandra shares that she might give a free loaf of bread to someone without an entry pass, and Colin recounts a similar situation:

> From time to time we get this customer who says, 'Please, I need some food now, because I'm hungry and I have no money whatsoever' and you worry that if he doesn't get something to eat now, he'll collapse. So you simply have to react. You have to differentiate between situations.

Bending the rules is not only restricted to giving products away for free, something barely imaginable in classic distribution organizations that work with strict inventories and indicators, but even extends to illegal behaviors:

> It often happens that we catch customers stealing . . . unfortunately . . . but we don't call the police or anything. Normally, you even feel bad yourself because you've caught the person. And you wish you had another choice than taking the pass [to access the SSM] away from the person. You know that the person is needy, but then we may have no other option because theft does cost us money as well. The pass is confiscated, and they have a shopping ban, a house ban, so to say . . . Because theft is normally reported to the police, but we don't do this. I think the shame of losing the pass is punishment enough. (Sandra)

Individuals who visit SSMs often do so because, without the drastically cheaper prices of the products there, they would not be able to make ends meet. Not every customer is at peace with this situation and many of them would prefer to be invisible when visiting the store. They miss the anonymity that they have in "normal" supermarkets because, in SSMs, anonymity does not exist. Customers need to register for an access card; thus, the store necessarily has a lot of personal information on them, and the staff generally know their identity. Gary recounts often having to manage customers' emotions and navigate around the ambivalence and shame they experience.

Another main difference compared to classic retail environments is that SSM managers might experience positive feelings when they "lose" customers. Gary, who is also actively involved in the admission procedures and creation of access passes, shares that each year about a third of those passes will not be renewed. He considers this "a positive sign because it means someone earns more than he is allowed to for accessing the market, which is good, which means they gained a foothold."

Tensions Related to Employee Idiosyncrasies

Employees at SSMs are a mix of the formally employed, volunteers, and long-term unemployed persons. The composition of the workforce is related to the social mission of the organization and has implications for the organizational intelligence. Colin explains that they "neither have the personal resources, nor the skills, to do something with the customer information we collect." This idiosyncrasy creates situations in which clients might also come in to help as volunteers, and where they might hope to have preferential access to products. Managers are also confronted with the challenge of organizing and managing a diverse set of employees.

Volunteers are not engaged in a binding manner, but managers still need them to show professionalism when collecting donations and dealing with customers. How should one tell a volunteer, who has sacrificed their leisure time to help, that they are not doing a good job? Gary recounts that the opening hours of the store will depend on the person working that day:

> It always depends on who is at the checkout. For example, if there are smokers at the cash register, it's more difficult because they naturally want to have a smoke before they open. Then, we rarely manage to open the doors earlier. If there are non-smokers, then we just open the doors. These are things that just . . . . you can't change that. Because I mean, I can't say to a volunteer 'Just smoke earlier!'

The long-term unemployed and some of the volunteers may not have been in a working environment for quite some time. They will often lack basic skills on how to present themselves to customers (for example with regards to proper attire) or how to communicate with customers. Employees also have to follow basic hygiene standards when handling food. Thus, managers have to invest a lot in training and in actively communicating the respective standards. They do so by "writing detailed job descriptions and putting reminders on the wall to wash hands or to wear gloves when touching bread . . . this helps a lot in creating a common understanding" (Sandra).

Andrea shared a similar experience with us, with regards to volunteers:

> The volunteers . . . you know . . . with them it's a bit of a balancing act. To give you an example, we had someone who was responsible for cleaning the machine, and then two weeks or three weeks ago, a service technician had to come because the machine was completely clogged up. The volunteer said to me 'well what is the big deal? It does not really matter' and I told him that it was his responsibility to keep it clean and that the machine costs three and a half thousand euros. I told him that 'If it is your store, and your machine, then you can say "it does not matter" but you work for us and we care.' He simply lacked this sense of responsibility that normally comes when you get paid for your labor.

SSM managers often struggle with the attitudes of volunteers and long-term unemployed and also find the compulsory training the latter receive as part of their labour market preparation to be inapt for the work they do at the SSM. Rather than focusing on technical skills, they say, training should help the long-term unemployed acquire "social skills" that they will need when interacting with the unique customers in an SSM: "The long-term unemployed are paid by the unemployment service, not by us. These individuals only stay with us for about half a year. I have the impression that the way this program is set up is to benefit the unemployment service, not us" (Gary).

A strategy that managers employ to manage the idiosyncrasies of the workforce is to organize frequent meetings and debriefings. This helps ensure that everyone in the team is on the same page, that employees share their experiences, and that a community spirit is fostered. Sandra explains that they talk a lot in their team: "We talk about situations when something odd happens, about problems with customers . . . we have a familiar atmosphere and talk very openly about it. That gives us support and strength. And when we have talked about it in the team, I can go home calmly."

Tensions Related to the Engagement with Different Stakeholders

A fourth tension in the daily operations of managers emerges from the fact that SSMs are closely intertwined with, and often dependent on, other organizations. Dealing with these stakeholders is not as straightforward as relations between partners in a linear supply chain. First, managers might experience a shortage of product supply due to competition between SSMs. Sandra says that

> because more people are in need, there are more social supermarkets, but at the same time companies produce less, which means that we do not get as much merchandise. But we depend on our sponsors. I have realized that our assortment was larger and more diverse seven years ago.

It is important to stress that, while there is competition for products, in the sense that all SSMs need them, the stores themselves do not view each other as competitors. They often belong to the same umbrella association and pursue the same mission of catering to people in need and reducing food waste. Andrea explains the logic:

> We certainly don't take anything away from each other. On the contrary, if Alfred, who called me just before, says: 'There is so much of this product, do you want to get some of it?' And if I have a lot of chips, for example, then I would also give them to him and we exchange with each other, and that's how it should be. Because it's not just about everyone making sure that they have as many sales as possible, which is of course also important. But it's also simply about complementing each other, so that you don't have to throw anything away. That's the most important thing.

Sometimes, partners stop donating products without much prior notice. Colin explains that "if a company tells me 'I won't do this [provide products to the SSM] anymore,' then there is not much I can do about it. We had a large partner, and then within two months they stopped all kinds of donations or deliveries because they said they'd rather find their own way to sell the products." Colin believes that companies do this in an effort to become more self-sufficient and to make sure that everything counts towards the bottom line.

As managers struggle to fill their shelves, they often become proactive and send out emails to potential partners such as retail companies or manufacturers. Andrea explains that "it is essential to stay in the minds of partners." Sometimes, it is even necessary to appeal to a wider audience for donations. However, this might result in additional work for the managers, for example when private citizens try to provide donations. Colin explains that, while they appreciate people's goodwill, they cannot just take donations from anyone:

> We've recently launched an appeal, advertising that we need food. There are always private people who would like to donate something, and I always think that's great, but unfortunately, we can only accept donations from organizations, especially for refrigerated goods. Private donations are nice, but as we would want to sell or give away these goods, we have to guarantee food safety. And therefore, we cannot accept such donations.

Discussion

Our findings illustrate four distinct origins to the tensions that managers of SSMs face on a daily basis. Table 3.2 summarizes these sources and highlights the respective strategies employed by managers.

Table 3.2: Overview of tensions and strategies in the management of social supermarkets.

Origin of tension:	Limited product assortment	Unique customer profiles	Employee idiosyncrasies	Stakeholder relations
Strategies employed:	Proactive communication with customers	Individual customer communication	Individual and group training	Expansion of co-operation with partnering companies
	Use of material structure and store equipment	Practicing leniency and flexibility	Establishing meetings and debriefings	Proactive communication with new stakeholders and donors

Our research adds to extant work addressing the particularities of organizations and managers that operate at the interface of conflicting logics (Ertimur & Coskuner-Balli, 2015; Parmentier & Fischer, 2021; Welté, Cayla, & Fischer, 2022). We illustrate that, in the sector of food distribution, organizations likely subscribe to either a predominant logic of commerce or a predominant logic of care. The space occupied by SSMs is somewhat unique in that it is at the very fault line of these two logics, which gives rise to several "trouble spots."

The strategies that managers employ are reminiscent of the strategies reported by Welté, Cayla, and Fischer (2022) in the context of luxury retailers. Luxury brands employ strategies of hybridization to leverage the synergies between different institutional logics that inform their operations. The spatial hybridization strategy, for example, is not unlike the space-related practices SSM managers use to navigate tensions due to their limited assortment. Whereas a jewellery store might create a specific material structure, such as a "bridal bar," to guide customers' experiences (Welté, Cayla, & Fischer, 2022), SSM managers resort to the use of shopping carts and one-way systems in the store to ensure a structured flow of customers. In a similar vein, the relational hybridization strategy that addresses interactions with customers and employees is somewhat reminiscent of the active communication with customers and staff, in the form of meetings and debriefings, in which SSM managers engage to address tensions related to assortment size and employee idiosyncrasies.

Our discussion of the sources of tensions in the management of SSMs also provides insights for organizations that are guided by a predominant logic of commerce but are interested in selectively integrating practices that are informed by a logic of care. The slow checkouts in the Dutch supermarket chain Jumbo, mentioned earlier, are a good example of a traditional retail outlet acknowledging the diversity of their customers' profiles and needs, and institutionalizing practices informed by a logic of care. Moreover, we believe that our discussion of the causes of tensions will be interesting for future work in (food) retailing looking at more circular business models. Classic retail traditionally follows a very linear path from production to consumption. This path is well-oiled, and every value chain member can efficiently execute their well-defined tasks. Our analysis of the tensions arising in the management of alternative food organizations identifies the departure from this linear path as a potential hotbed of tensions. We contend that retail organizations' difficulties in embracing a transformation towards a circular economy might stem from a similar reason.

Conclusion and Recommendations

This research illustrates the complexity that SSM managers face as they concurrently cater to a logic of commerce and a logic of care. The case of SSMs also highlights the trailblazing work of organizations that are guided by a logic of care. SSMs offer services for people such as vulnerable consumers and the long-term unemployed, and address problems such as food waste, for which there are as yet no functioning systemic solutions. Against this background, these organizations address sustainability issues for which societies are yet to establish corresponding structures.

To ensure that managers can rise to the challenge of operating at the intersection of the logics of commerce and care, we recommend that the following aspects are integrated into introduction and initiation processes for new SSM managers: (1) create an environment that supports flexible mindsets; (2) foster capabilities that facilitate interactions with idiosyncratic customers and employees; and (3) endorse the development of emotional resilience, potentially with the assistance of outside providers such as mediators, to ensure that managers can deal with the additional mental and emotional demands of concurrently looking in two different directions.

Our findings contribute to the debate on the importance of reimagining sustainability in sectors such as food distribution. We argue that sustainability in food retail cannot be solely achieved through a focus on optimizing supply chains to reduce food waste (Gruber, Holweg, & Teller, 2016), or through donations of produce as part of a company's Corporate Social Responsibility (CSR) agenda. Instead, organizations need to be receptive to the values and prescriptions of a logic of care that requires managers to be empathetic, to occasionally bend the rules of the game (such as when SSM managers do not report theft to the police), and to courageously incorporate practices that contradict rules of efficiency and optimization (as in the case of the slow checkout lanes at Jumbo).

References

Avery, D. R., McKay, P. F., & Hunter E. M. (2012). Demography and disappearing merchandise: how older workforces influence retail shrinkage. *Journal of Organizational Behavior*, *33*(1), 105–20.

Ball, K., Timperio, A., & Crawford, D. (2009). Neighborhood socioeconomic inequalities in food access and affordability. *Health & Place*, *15*(2), 578–585.

Bartlett, L., & Vavrus, F. (2017). Comparative case studies: an innovative approach. *Nordic Journal of Comparative and International Education (NJCIE)*, *1*(1), 5–17.

Bhardwaj, R., & Srivastava, S. (2021). Dynamic capabilities of social enterprises: a qualitative meta-synthesis and future agenda. *Journal of Social Entrepreneurship*, 1–29.

Block, L.G., Grier, S.A., Childers, T.L., Davis, B., Ebert, J.E., Kumanyika, S., Laczinak, R.N., Machin, J.E., Motley, C.M., Peracchio, L., Pettigrew, S., Scott, M., & van Ginkel Bieshaar, M.N.G (2011). From nutrients to nurturance: a conceptual introduction to food well-being. *Journal of Public Policy & Marketing*, *30*(1), 5–13.

Caritas Markt. (2023). CARITAS Markt. https://www.caritasmarkt.ch/de. Accessed February 15, 2023.

Corporación Aragonesa de Radio y Televisión. (2023). Las 'colas del hambre'. Accessed February 20, 2023. https://www.cartv.es/aragonnoticias/noticias/colas-del-hambre-mucho-mas-que-comida-2557

Daily Table (2023). About. Accessed April 24, 2023. https://dailytable.org/about/#banner

Deloitte (2022). Global Powers of Retailing 2022. Accessed November 6, 2022. https://www2.deloitte.com/content/dam/Deloitte/global/Documents/Consumer-Business/gx-global-powers-of-retailing-2022.pdf

D'Enbeau, S., & Buzzanell, P.M. (2011). Selling (out) feminism: sustainability of ideology-viability tensions in a competitive marketplace. *Communication Monographs*, *78*(1), 27–52.

Dion, D., & Borraz, S. (2017). Managing status: how luxury brands shape class subjectivities in the service encounter. *Journal of Marketing*, *81*(5), 67–85.

DiMaggio, P.J., & Powell, W.W. (1983). The iron cage revisited: institutional isomorphism and collective rationality in organizational fields. *American Sociological Review*, *48*(2), 147–160.

Doherty, B., Haugh, H., & Lyon, F. (2014). Social enterprises as hybrid organizations: a review and research agenda. *International Journal of Management Reviews*, *16*(4), 417–436.

Eisenhardt, K.M. (1989). Building theories from case study research. *Academy of Management Review*, *14*(4), 532–550.

Ertimur, B., & Coskuner-Balli, G. (2015). Navigating the institutional logics of markets: implications for strategic brand management. *Journal of Marketing, 79*(2), 40–61.

Eurostat. (2021). One in five people in the EU at risk of poverty or social exclusion. Accessed July 18, 2022. https://ec.europa.eu/eurostat/web/products-eurostat-news/-/edn-20211015-1

Farm to Cafeteria Canada (F2CC). What is farm to cafeteria Canada? Accessed September 11, 2022. https://www.farmtocafeteriacanada.ca/about-us/our-vision-values/

Gawer, A., & Phillips, N. (2013). Institutional work as logics shift: the case of Intel's transformation to platform leader. *Organization Studies, 34*(8), 1035–1071.

Geertz, C. (1973). *The interpretation of cultures* (Vol. 5043). Basic books.

Gigliotti, M., & Runfola, A. (2022). A stakeholder perspective on managing tensions in hybrid organizations: analyzing fair trade for a sustainable development. *Business Strategy and the Environment, 31*(7), 2767–3688.

Global Foodbanking Network. (2015). What is food banking? Accessed April 24, 2023. http://www.foodbanking.org/about/foodbanking.html

Grasseni, C. (2013). *Beyond alternative food networks: Italy's solidarity purchase groups*. Bloomsbury Publishing.

Greenwood, R., & Hinings C.R. (2006). Radical organizational change. In S.R. Clegg, C. Hardy, C. Lawrence & W.R. Nord (Eds.), *The SAGE Handbook of Organization*, 814–842. Sage publications, 2nd Edition.

Grewal, D., Gauri, D.K., Roggeveen, A.L., & Sethuraman, R. (2021). Strategizing retailing in the new technology era. *Journal of Retailing, 97*(1), 6–12.

Gruber, V., Holweg, C., & Teller, C. (2016). What a waste! Exploring the human reality of food waste from the store manager's perspective. *Journal of Public Policy & Marketing, 35*(1), 3–25.

Hill, R.P., & Stamey, M. (1990). The homeless in America: an examination of possessions and consumption behaviors. *Journal of Consumer Research, 17*(3), 303–321.

Ho, B. Q., & Shirahada, K. (2021). Actor transformation in service: a process model for vulnerable consumers. *Journal of Service Theory and Practice, 31*(4), 534–562.

Holweg, C., & Lienbacher, E. (2011). Social marketing innovation: new thinking in retailing. *Journal of Nonprofit & Public Sector Marketing, 23*(4), 307–326.

Holweg, C., & Lienbacher, E. (2016). *Social supermarkets in Europe – investigations from a retailing perspective in selected European countries*. Vienna: Institute for Retailing and Marketing. ISBN: 978-3-200-04756-3.

Holweg, C., & Lienbacher, E. (2021). The ecosystem of social supermarkets – an industry specific CSR initiative. *Colloquium on European Research in Retailing* (CERR conference), Sophia Antipolis (France), online. July 15–16, 2021.

Institute for Grocery Distribution (IGD). (2022). Food inflation likely to reach 15% this summer hitting most vulnerable households hardest. Accessed July 18, 2022. https://www.igd.com/articles/article-viewer/t/food-inflation-likely-to-reach-15-this-summer-hitting-most-vulnerable-households-hardest/i/29803

Jolink, A., & Niesten, E. (2012). Recent qualitative advances on hybrid organizations: Taking stock, looking ahead. *Scandinavian Journal of Management, 28*(2), 149–161.

Joy, A., Wang, J.J., Chan, T.S., Sherry, J.F., & Cui, G. (2014). M(Art)worlds: Consumer perceptions of how luxury brand stores become art institutions. *Journal of Retailing, 90*(3), 347–364.

Keinan, A., Crener, S., & Goor, D. (2020). Luxury and environmental responsibility. In F. Morhart, K. Wilcox, & S. Czellar (Eds.), *Research handbook on luxury branding*, 300–323. Edward Elgar Publishing.

Kotzab, H. (1999). Improving supply chain performance by efficient consumer response? A critical comparison of existing ECR approaches. *Journal of Business & Industrial Marketing, 14*(5/6), 364–377.

Ly, A.M., & Cope, M.R. (2023). New conceptual model of social sustainability: review from past concepts and ideas. *International Journal of Environmental Research and Public Health, 20*(7), 5350.

Maier, F., Meyer, M., & Steinbereithner, M. (2016). Nonprofit organizations becoming business-like: a systematic review. *Nonprofit and Voluntary Sector Quarterly, 45*(1), 64–86.

Mair, J., Mayer, J., & Lutz, E. (2015). Navigating institutional plurality: organizational governance in hybrid organizations. *Organization Studies*, *36*(6), 713–739.

Micelotta, E., Lounsbury, M., & Greenwood, R. (2017). Pathways of institutional change: an integrative review and research agenda. *Journal of Management*, *43*(6), 1885–1910.

Nigam, A., & Ocasio, W. (2010). Event attention, environmental sensemaking, and change institutional logics: an inductive analysis of the effects of public attention to Clinton's health care reform initiative. *Organization Science*, *21*(4), 823–841.

Pache, A.C., & Santos, F. (2013). Inside the hybrid organization: selective coupling as a response to competing institutional logics. *Academy of Management Journal*, *56*(4), 972–1001.

Parmentier, M.-A., & Fischer, E. (2021). Working it: managing professional brands in prestigious posts. *Journal of Marketing*, *85*(2), 110–128.

Raj, R. (2023). In brands we trust: what a Dutch supermarket chain can teach us about building community and earning loyalty. *Fast Company*. Accessed April 24, 2023. https://www.fastcompany.com/90856855/in-brands-we-trust-what-a-dutch-supermarket-chain-can-teach-us-about-building-community-and-earning-loyalty

Rama Murthy, S., Roll, K., & Colin-Jones, A. (2021). Ending business-non-profit partnerships: the spinout of social enterprises. *Scandinavian Journal of Management*, *37*(1), 101136.

Ramus, T., Vaccaro, A., & Brusoni, S. (2017). Institutional complexity in turbulent times: formalization, collaboration, and the emergence of blended logics. *Academy of Management Journal*, *60*(4), 1253–1284.

Reay, T., & Hinings, C.R. (2005). The recomposition of an organizational field: health care in Alberta. *Organization Studies*, *26*(3), 351–384.

Reay, T., & Hinings, R.C. (2009). Managing the rivalry of competing institutional logics. *Organization Studies*, *30*(6), 629–652.

Ritzer, G. (1983). The 'McDonaldization' of society. *Journal of American Culture*, *6*(1), 100–107

Rose, D., Bodor, J.N., Hutchinson, P.L., & Swalm, C.M. (2010). The importance of a multi-dimensional approach for studying the links between food access and consumption. *The Journal of Nutrition*, *140*(6), 1170–1174.

Rozin, P. (2005). The meaning of food in our lives: a cross-cultural perspective on eating and well-being. *Journal of nutrition education and behavior*, *37*, S107–S112.

Sanger, K., & Zenz, L. (2004). Farm-to-cafeteria connections: marketing opportunities for small farms in Washington state. (2nd ed.). Washington State Department of Agriculture Small Farm and Direct Marketing Program. Accessed March 24, 2008. http://agr/wa/gov/Marketing/SmallFarm/102-FarmToCafeteriaConnections-Web.pdf

Scaraboto, D., & Fischer, E. (2013). Frustrated fatshionistas: an institutional theory perspective on consumer quests for greater choice in mainstream markets. *Journal of Consumer Research*, *39*(6), 1234–1257.

Smith, W. K., Gonin, M., & Besharov, M.L. (2013). Managing social-business tensions: a review and research agenda for social enterprise. *Business Ethics Quarterly*, *23*(3), 407–442.

Smith, W.K., & Lewis, M.W. (2011). Toward a theory of paradox: a dynamic equilibrium model of organizing. *Academy of Management Review*, *36*(2), 381–403.

SOMA. (2023). SOMA Österreich und Partner. Accessed February 15, 2023. https://somaoesterreichundpartner.at/

Statistics Austria. (2022). Verbrauchsausgaben 2019–20 (Consumer expenditures 2019–20). Accessed March 24, 2023. https://www.statistik.at/fileadmin/publications/Verbrauchsausgaben2019–20_Sozial statistische_Ergbnisse.pdf

Statistics Canada. (2022). Rising prices are affecting the ability to meet day-to-day expenditures for most Canadians. Accessed July 18, 2022. https://www150.statcan.gc.ca/n1/daily-quotidien/220609/dq220609a-eng.htm

Thornton, P.H. (2004). *Markets from culture: institutional logics and organizational decisions in higher education publishing*. Stanford University Press.

Thornton, P.H., & Ocasio, W. (1999). Institutional logics and the historical contingency of power in organizations: executive succession in the higher education publishing industry, 1958–1990. *American Journal of Sociology*, *105*(3), 801–843.

Thornton, P., & Ocasio, W. (2008). Institutional logics. In R. Greenwood, C. Oliver, K. Sahlin, & R. Suddaby (Eds.), *Handbook of organizational institutionalism*, 99–129. London: Sage Publications.

Thornton, P.H., Ocasio, W., & Lounsbury, M. (2012). *The institutional logics perspective: a new approach to culture, structure, and process*. Oxford University Press on Demand.

United States (US) Census. (2022). National poverty in America awareness month: January 2022. Accessed April 24, 2023. https://www.census.gov/newsroom/stories/poverty-awareness-month.html

Van Gestel, N., & Hillebrand, B. (2011). Explaining stability and change: the rise and fall of logics in pluralistic fields. *Organization Studies*, *32*(2), 231–252.

Welté, J.-B., Cayla, J., & Fischer, E. (2022). Navigating contradictory logics in the field of luxury retailing. *Journal of Retailing*, *98*(3), 510–526.

Yin, R. K. (2009). *Case study research: design and methods*. Sage.

Zilber, T. B. (2016). How institutional logics matter: a bottom-up exploration. In J. Gehman, M. Lounsbury, & R. Greenwood (Eds.), *How institutions matter!* (Research in the Sociology of Organizations, Volume 48A), 137–155. Emerald Group Publishing Limited.

Part 2: **The Art World**

Fuat Firat

4 Art, Fashion, and the Human Condition

In this chapter, I wish to investigate the contemporary status and role of art and fash-ion together with the conditions that humanity faces resulting from modern construc-tions of art and fashion. I begin with the understanding that, as is the case with all concepts, art and fashion do not have a meaning that endures across all historical epochs or cultural contexts, even when they may possess some essences that make it possible to have a degree of continuity of popular conception across time and context. In each epoch and in every culture, however, they take on certain particularities im-bued in them according to the symbolic dynamics of the time and context.

Modern Separations of Domains

To understand the contemporary meanings and roles of art and fashion, we need to contextualize their existence in modernity. Here, by modernity I mean the epoch that started, scholars generally agree, with Enlightenment in the mid-seventeenth century. I would argue that the seeds of modernity were planted with the Renaissance, about three centuries earlier. It was originally the artists of the Renaissance that insisted that the human being could be in the center of attention, the subject, as opposed to earlier art that centered around heavenly entities, such as deities, angels, and de-mons. This was a time when the traditional cultural mythologies that focused on forces above and beyond the human, on faith and fate, were challenged by new artis-tic sensibilities, by a focus on the nature of the Earth and the universe, and on the human being as part of this nature and as the worthwhile subject matter.

Thus, the Renaissance gave impetus to the idea that created the Enlightenment, the turn from abandoning human destiny to heavenly forces to the idea that human beings could determine their own destinies by discovering and understanding the na-ture of the universe through scientific technologies (Angus, 1989). This would indeed make the human being the subject, one who could and did act upon nature (including the human being's own nature), the totality of objects surrounding the subject, to de-termine destiny and build a grand future society that would provide the foundation for all individuals to realize their utmost potential, through culture, all that is created by humans. This was the modern project, but to realize it a new set of norms and principles of human existence had to be institutionalized. The traditional orders had to be dismantled and a new, modern order had to be constructed.

Modernity rejected the traditional orders but did not abandon the idea of the ne-cessity of an order. After all, the modern project, or any project, could not be accom-plished in a state of chaos or fluidity (Bauman, 2000), a new order of human existence

https://doi.org/10.1515/9783110783933-004

had to be institutionalized. This was the task that occupied early modern thinkers and politicians. A new set of norms were eventually organized around separated discursive and practical domains of modern culture. Informed by Weber, Habermas has articulated that the architects of modernity conceptualized three foundational domains around which the norms were organized (Foster, 1983). These were the domains of science, morality, and art. Interestingly, early constructors of modern norms thought that these three domains needed to remain separated from each other, because they thought that the principles of each, if they blended, could contaminate the principles of other domains and derail each domain's purpose. Thus, they thought, each domain needed to follow its own principles, pure and uncontaminated, if each domain was to accomplish its necessary goals for modernity to fulfill its project.

The principles of the domain of morality were fairness and justice. These were necessary for each individual of modern society to have equal access to the right of life and to resources needed to fulfill each one's true and independent potential. The principle of the domain of art was aesthetics, the quality that either attracts—beauty—or repels—ugliness—(Feagin and Maynard, 1997). This was considered necessary for human beings to have a sense of life, and appreciation of each other and things around them. The principles of the domain of science were objectivity and reason. These were principles absolutely required in order to be able to know the universe and how the forces of nature that operate in it act. As knowing subjects, then, human beings could weather these forces as well as use them to their own ends. Such scientific knowledge was deemed central and key to humanity's taking control of its own destiny and, thus, science was considered to be the central foundational domain for realizing the modern project.

It was, therefore, especially important that the principles of fairness or of aesthetics ought not to contaminate the domain of science, because the influence of considerations of what is or would be beautiful or fair could subvert the purely objective knowledge of the universe, leading to biases and to failures in being able to deal with the forces of nature and accomplishing control over them to determine humanity's fate.

Thus started the advent of separations that seem to be endemic in the modern ordering of life. Practical domains of modern culture, most significantly the economic, the social, and the political, were also separated, each with its own principle—respectively, economic value optimization through efficient allocation of economic resources, civility, and democracy. Each domain had its key institution(s)—respectively, the market, the nuclear family and public education, and the nation-state—as well as its scientific discipline—respectively, economics, sociology, and political science—to enable the exercise of the principle of each domain toward realization of the modern project. Most other norms to give order to and guide humanity toward the completion of the modern project were also based in separations into bipolar oppositions, with one pole representing the proper and the positive and the other the improper and the negative orientation (see Table 4.1).

Table 4.1: Oppositional separations in modern culture
(Adapted from Fırat, 1994).

Feminine	Masculine
private	public
home	workplace
consumption	production
Woman (female)	Man (male)
consumer	producer
passive	active
incapable	capable
Body	Mind
emotional	rational
sensation	reason
submissive	assertive
powerless	powerful
Moon	Sun
nature	culture
Profane	Sacred
worthless	valuable
Property	Owner
product (object)	person (subject)

Art, Fashion, and Modernity

As modernity advanced, the economic concerns increasingly took a growing central role in ordering all other domains and the market increasingly became the sole organizing institution in what has come to be known as market society (Slater and Tonkiss, 2001). This development further established consumer culture as the dominant culture of modernity. I wish to illustrate that these occurrences along with the original construction of modern institutionalizations briefly touched upon above have produced two events, significant among others, that have greatly contributed to the disenchantment of modern life and to the degradation of the environment. One of these events is the eventual separation of art from everyday life. The second is the fashioning of all relations that people have with things (Fırat, Atik, and Ertekin, 2023).

Separation of Art from Everyday Life

As briefly discussed above, the original separation of art from other foundational domains of culture, specifically scientific enquiry, was an early part of the discursive ordering of modernity. Also, possibly with the influence of the Renaissance in modernity, art occupied a special space as a specialized domain of artists. Later, with the advent of marketization of modern culture, artistic products were also coopted into the market as commodities to be planned and produced for the market. Yet, as the market for artworks matured, distinctions that began to appear between craft and art and fine art provided the ground for a further separation of the market into a commodified art market and a market for art that was deemed not as a commodity but as cultural artifact, seemingly non-commodity artwork. Such fine artwork, now occupying a special market, a speculative market available only to museums and a few exclusive speculators and art aficionados, commanded extreme prices and did not follow the typical demand and supply rules of the regular market. A small number of artists who earned the status of creators of such artwork by the community of art critics and art dealers became the focus of the modern cultural understanding of the meaning of art in all categories of art, including painting, sculpture, music, photography, and architecture, among others. Art was an endeavor by especially talented "great artists." It was not for everyone to be engaged in; everyone else was an audience to the creations by the true creators.

The speculative art market, distinct from the regular market, is, nevertheless, an extension of the logic of the market that has the impulse to coopt all relationships into the market exchange domain and maximize exchange value in all ways possible in order to optimize accumulation of economic value—to be converted into capital in capitalism. A distinction between the regular and speculative art market does exactly that. Exchange values of artworks that can be brought into the speculative art market are maximized. Of course, there is the discourse that such great artworks are thus made available to the public who otherwise would have no chance of enjoying and experiencing them through, for example, museums and galleries. The catch in modernity is that this availability to the public happens and has to occur through the exchanges that take place in the market.

In this occurrence, there is the process that can be metaphorically called the staging of the theater of life. As Fırat and Dholakia (2006, p. 133) explain,

> Modern theater is a 'staging' of representational, artistic expressions of the human condition. It is a means of reflecting or representing the evocative aspects of humanity to 'spectators' for purposes of entertainment, education, reflection, or discussion. Modern theater is a detachment, a wrenching from pre-modern moments, of everyday life in which everyone participated. In modern theater, professionals came to re-present and reflect stylized moments of everyday contexts. The masses became an 'audience' rather than participants in the act. From the common ground that previously included everyone, an elevated 'stage' arose. The stage was accessible only to the professional actors and directed from the 'backstage', based on screenplays that became enduring through documentation. At its core, the institution of the modern market has a process that parallels the emergence of the modern theater.

Staging the theater of life is a common process in modern culture; it is a necessity for the market to function to its full potential. When production turned socially organized, not to fulfill the producers' desires but to fulfill the expected desires of others who constituted "the market," the offerings exchanged in the market became commodities. For others to have a desire for commodities, they had to be perceived to be of value that those who exchanged for it could not otherwise produce. That is, they had to be produced by those who had expertise or skills beyond what the purchasers had, similar to the actors on stage who had the superior skill to act to be on the stage. They were professionals, acquiring skills through training on top of special talents they may have had. Thus, they could evoke the perception that what they could do others in the audience, the market, could not. To have the experience, those in the audience had to access the products of the skilled, since they could not create the same quality of experience themselves. Thus, as the market increasingly became the almost sole means through which people could have access to commodities, "artful" skills were increasingly divorced from their everyday lives. To have music they had to get access to skilled, professional musicians, to enjoy a play they had to get access to the staged theater, to have good food they had to access the skilled chefs, and so on. In the modern market society people's belief in their own abilities to accomplish different things in order to have access to the art of producing many of the sought experiences had to be diminished for the market to thrive. Eventually, commodities came to be perceived to possess the qualities that were desired and belief in one's own personal capabilities became minimized.

With the staging of the theater in all walks of life in modernity, professionalization of different skills and specializing into professions became the norm. Finance was best left to the financiers, music was best left to musicians, communication was best left to those who were experts in producing communications technologies, and so on. This compartmentalization of what one could do was reflected in all areas, even in science, which, as mentioned earlier, was specialized into disciplines.

Fashioning of Relations with Things

Modern market society transformed fashion from being a cycle of new styles trending from superordinate classes to subordinate classes, activated by the processes of differentiation and emulation (Simmel, 1957), into a key principle of market dynamics (Atik and Fırat, 2013). Growth in the population is not sufficient for the market to continuously grow to keep accumulating economic value. Consumer units, whether individuals, households, or organizations, have to periodically renew the commodities they have acquired in the market for continuous market growth. Fashioning of relations consumers have with things, specifically commodities, helps to accomplish this market requirement. Called planned obsolescence in marketing literature, continuously introducing new fashions in all categories of consumption, through new technology, new styles, new features, as well as recycling fashion from earlier periods using nostalgia, images of authenticity, and the like, keeps the cycle alive.

Always looking for novelty in the commodities we surround ourselves with and in our relationships with others has indeed become a way of life in modern consumer culture. This is partly inscribed in our acculturation into the modern, project culture.

While traditional cultures turned to past traditions to organize present life, modern culture turned its gaze onto the future, to, as mentioned earlier, create a grand future society in which all individuals could realize their utmost potentials. This was a culture of a project to be realized. As there was the project for humanity to realize, the grand society of the future, so was there a project for each individual to realize, the ideal self. With consumer culture, the ideal self increasingly came to be defined in terms of ownership of commodities, new and improved. A better and larger home, a finer set of things to wear, a better equipped automobile, more travel experiences, etc.

Modern marketing, the institutionalized practices of the market, has adopted fashion as its principle to keep this project alive and never ending, because with ever changing fashion there is always more and better to reach. As has been argued (Freedman, 2002), the project of modernity is always in progress but never completed, as is the individual project each consumer follows. Each improvement towards accomplishing the project brings with it new improvements to realize. Thus, fashioning of relationships with things contributes to the ever-continuing cycle of more consumption based on exchanges in the market.

Contributions of Fordism and Post-Fordism

The implications of separation of art from everyday life and the fashioning of people's relations to things have been exacerbated by the advents of Fordism and later by post-Fordism. Taylorism (Taylor, 1911/1998), in what was considered to be a scientific approach at the time, specialized each worker's role on the production line to maximize productivity that by that time was defined in solely economic terms. Fordism's feat was to organize workers' lives beyond the factory to make sure that they could devote all their productive energies to the production line to help maximize productivity (Link, 2020). This meant that workers' lives outside of the factory were organized to be solely devoted to replenishing their energies through consumption of food, entertainment, and recreation. They were to become true consumers in their private lives, their public lives socially organized in production. Of course, this meant that their private lives were just as much socially organized, producing them as consumers internalizing their consumer subjectivity along with their identity as productive workers.

Post-Fordism is partially a result of this internalization as it is also a result of the new social organization of work (Murray, Gilbert, and Goffey, 2015; Vallas, 1999). With post-Fordism, people bring their work into their homes, their private lives, where their devotion to being productive begins to organize even their relationships with their family members. Work is often carried into the private home interfering with social relationships with family members and friends. Sometimes family members are drawn into helping the worker to accomplish productive work, without, of course, compensation (Amin, 1994). Workers' lives and relationships outside of work are sacrificed to reinforce socially organized production for the market. In effect, work for economic production dominates life.

Implications of the Modern History of Art and Fashion

There are serious implications of the above discussed history of modern market society and the roles of art and fashion in it for the future of humanity. For one, art, which should be a part of everyone's life in a way that integrates the aesthetic experience for a complete sense of being in the world, enchanting everyday lives, is on the one hand commodified and on the other hand distanced from most of the people who can access it only as an audience, as spectators or buyers, who are left without the confidence of being participants in art. This is a key element in the discontent and disenchantment that many feel (Marsh, Caputo, and Westphal, 1992; Ritzer, 2010) in their modern lives. For another, becoming consumers of fashion absorbs people's energy into constantly following and catching up with new fashions, depleting their interest for endeavors other than consuming.

In advanced modern market society, all is organized and institutionalized to realize the organizing principle well represented in the dominant ideology of the time, neoliberalism. This organizing principle is (optimization of economic) value. Value, now specifically thought of as economic value, was not always the sole organizing principle in modern society. Democracy and civility were also organizing principles in original conceptualization of modern society. Yet, as the economic domain gradually took center stage and its principle eventually became the sole organizing principle, with the neoliberal ideology gaining ground with global marketization, the idea that if given a free reign the market would work to realize all modern principles (Harvey, 2005), including democracy and civility, became quite hegemonic. Currently, we are living the legacy of this development, which culminated in the USA and UK during the overlapping tenures of Reagan and Thatcher. Both Reagan and Thatcher were ardent promoters of neoliberalism. Although all indicators illustrate that this ideology has not worked well in even accomplishing a healthy market (see, for example, Piketty, 2017), its influence is very dominant in global marketization (Chaudhuri and Belk, 2020), including the so-called Second World and Third World (Fırat, 2020).

Original modernist thinkers did not intend the kind of unidimensionalization of the organizing principle and, as a result, the organization of life. They were, on the contrary, conceptualizing a system of different domains with different principles that would both balance each other but also guide each other toward an organization of life that would enhance the varied dimensions of being human as well as assure their relatively independent but necessary existence. The principle of democracy of the political domain would promote each individual's participation in humanity's affairs without impositions by others upon each one's free will. The principle of civility of the social domain would ascertain respect and understanding of each other providing the environment for progress toward a common vision democratically established. The principle of value of the economic domain would help humans to accomplish the significant tasks toward the grand future without lacking the necessities for a nourished and healthy human existence. These key domains and principles were all needed, among other supportive ones, for an ordered and balanced progress toward the completion of the modern project.

Eventually, this desired balance has been lost with the economic domain gaining primacy as discussed. Implications of this loss of balance in the ordering of modern society have been significant for humanity. Unfortunately, most of these implications are negative.

We are all aware of the consequences of human beings turning to consumption as the means of finding meaning in their lives. Consumer culture—a consequence of the late modern (Jameson, 1991) hegemonic influence of the market, as the institution of the economic domain, which requires constant growth—as a culture of people's internalization of the idea that success and accomplishment in life, even the sense of being someone worthwhile, is measured by how much and how well one is able to consume, has created a non-sustainable exploitation of Earth's resources. Constant insistence by supporters of incessant market growth that technological developments will resolve the issue of non-sustainability misses the fact that it is the selection of technologies to be developed in a culture of economic value production that exacerbates the problem of non-sustainable consumption in the first place. In effect, throwing more technology on to the fire is unlikely to resolve the problems facing the coming generations.

In addition to these negative consequences of a unidimensional focus on the production of economic value, for the future of humanity as a whole, there are also immediate negative consequences that the great majority of individuals living currently on Earth experience due to the developments discussed. One consequence has already been mentioned, the loss of enchantment in life due largely to people's engagement with art, except as audiences, being divorced from everyday life moments.

Without experiencing and/or relating to the art in what one does or practices, without the feeling that one is engaged in artful activity, tasks people perform become chores, taking the enjoyment out of the process, thus disenchanting moments of life. Further, specialization in the work most people perform restricts the number of activities and deprives people of well-rounded, multidimensional lives, adding to this disenchantment. Professionalization distances people from each other due to specialized tasks they are engaged in and compartmentalizes activities peopledo, often with specialized vocabularies, making it less likely for social relationships and mutual understanding to develop. Relations even among neighbors and family members become less organic and often superficial. Together with the calls for individualism in modern culture and echoed in neoliberalism, people turn into themselves, focus on individual identity projects—closely connected to the modern ideal-self project—largely supported by and acted through engagement with fashion.

Consumer subjectivity that became dominant in late modernity (Fırat and Dholakia, 2017) leads to representation of self and identity largely through what one consumes. Rather than what one thinks, intends, or endeavors for, people judge themselves and others by what they can observe in terms of how people look and what people wear, drive, live in, in general, what they consume. In the custom of neoliberal market competition, representing identity also becomes a competitive practice/play, which in a market of fashion requires constant renewal, each individual always having to up the ante as the one with the more fashionable identity.

In late modern market society, fast fashion has enabled much larger proportions of the world's population to join this cycle of "fashioned" consumption (Ertekin and Atik, 2014). Deemed as a democratization by some, this diffusion of fashion consciousness and inclusion in fashion cycles of larger proportions of consumers is, indeed, far from democratization (Atik et al., 2022) and it exacerbates non-sustainable exploitation of resources. Fast fashion in the clothing industry encourages "buy→wear a few times→discard to buy the new fashion" cycle. This continual renewal of what one consumes for a constant renewal of oneself is indeed not sustainable given the destruction it causes in people's psyche as much as in the environment that can no longer catch up with the speed of disposal to diffuse the harmful effects left behind by non-biodegradable, toxicity producing materials discarded.

With specialization and professionalization constraining people into restricted agency by allowing them few activities to be engaged in and depleting their confidence in having multidimensional capabilities and existence, and fashioning of people's relations with things, which absorbs their energy in catching up with fashion as consumers, not leaving much energy for well-rounded public engagement and governance of human affairs, construction of individuals as consumers in late modernity seems complete. As consumers, people expect to be offered alternatives that they can choose from rather than be engaged in the determination of alternatives that will be offered. Having choice becomes the substitute in conceptualizing freedom in place of democracy where people are expected to be participants in the public arena determining the choices that will become available. Political agency is thus ceded to corporations that tend to make fashion choices that will expand the market and optimize accumulation of economic value.

This phenomenon is not observed in only capitalist market economies. We see the same progression of affairs in other countries of the world as well, where private corporations yielding power are substituted by corporatized states run by politicians just as interested in accumulation of economic value, which they and their cronies appropriate the large part of. Control over economic value, put to use for employing labor to accumulate more economic value, or capital, has become the key arbiter of power in modernity, which consequently has enslaved people to economic interests (Chomsky, 1999). The health of the economy has taken precedence over the health of the people as political actions and their consequences in death have shown during the COVID-19 pandemic. In such a market culture, people are left to fend for themselves and their loved ones on their own, without very little, if any, social support, and consequently without any energy, or indeed any interest, for the welfare of others. The truth that unless everyone is safe on this Earth no one can be truly safe gets lost in such a culture.

Are There Remedies?

The way that the role of art and fashion, in addition to implications of modern institutionalized systemic order and ideology, has been presented so far may have given the reader an impression that fashion and art are problematic dimensions of human life. I wish to argue that it can be, and ought to be, the opposite. The problem is with the way that, in modern organization of life, art and fashion have been conceptualized and institutionalized, especially once the economic domain of human culture took center stage, with its organizing principle, the optimization of (economic) value, becoming fundamentally the sole arbiter of how people came to think of the meaning (fulness) in life.

There is a general agreement among philosophers that meaning indeed constitutes what is central to humanity's search (Cooney, 2000), even in the most horrific times (Frankl, 1959). Across history, what people find to have meaning has changed. In traditional cultures, meaning was often found in the spiritual, the connections people imagined among the many elements of the universe, humans included. With modernity, meaning was originally found in liberty, the independent agency of the human being liberated from all impositions from each other and from the forces of nature. Later, as mentioned, having access to economic value came to be thought to be the highway to having meaning in life. The great majority of the world's population had lost control over any resource but their labor, and their labor was controlled by corporate interests—whether private corporate or corporate state. Thus, the only illusion left was that they could have control over their consumption choices—without, as discussed, control over what the choice alternatives would or could be.

Both art and fashion could be great sources of re-enchantment. This would, however, require a new conceptualization and institutionalization of art and fashion, different from their modern conceptualizations. Fashion can indeed be a means of self-expression as well as other expression. Yet, this is not possible when fashion remains to be a market principle. Unique and truly creative expression is not possible when fashion is based on choice among limited, no matter how many, alternatives, which results in multiple others wearing, using, driving, saying, etc., the same choice. Fashion based on the market suppresses creativity beyond the ability to select, as others can do also, from among those alternatives that are made available by organizations working with the principle of maximizing their economic value returns.

Creativity in fashion has also been suppressed by the separation of art from everyday life as discussed. People lose confidence that they can engage in artful living, because art is something artists with special talents do; because art is professionalized, they adopt the consumer mentality and think that they can only make choices among artistic products produced by artists, feeling they cannot create as good artistic experiences. Clearly, there is nothing wrong with the condition that some people are better at certain artful endeavors than others. There is also nothing wrong with people wanting to experience the art of fine artists of all genres. The problem is in the professionalization of art in such a way that those who are not professionals can access the art solely through the market and that they feel they cannot engage in art themselves.

One doesn't have to be a musician to enjoy the aesthetics of doing music themselves, as one also enjoys the professional musician's music. One need not be the great chef to enjoy the art of cooking. One shouldn't feel s/he cannot and should not paint to experience the art of it because s/he isn't an accomplished painter. Art, that is, ought not be "staged," but a domain that everyone can participate in during their everyday activities. One need not have to be producing art for the market to be able to participate in its creation.

How can we, then, experience and enjoy artful moments in our everyday lives to reenchant our existence in the universe? Given our experience with the history of modernity, the answer begins with the recognition that the rigid separation of domains of culture and the unidimensionalization of the organizing principle around which all relations are institutionalized did not work. Further, fashion as a principle of expanding the market does not serve the human purpose but creates a cycle of constant replacing and discarding of commodities before they have outlived their usefulness.

The above insights from history indicate that separating culture into different domains, while may be useful in recognizing and organizing its complexity, has not been meaningful for humanity when each domain has been compartmentalized, specialized, and professionalized. A clear recognition should be that culture is an integrated and complex whole. Experience with modern culture has illustrated that when human projects are focused on the principle(s) of a single domain, or when solutions to problems are sought thinking that any one domain independent from all others among culture's domains can provide an answer, disillusion is inevitable. There is not a solely economic or solely social or solely political solution possible to problems or to completion of human projects. Culture must be accepted and engaged with in its full complexity, its dimensions or domains not forced to be independent from each other, but each requiring its relationships with other dimensions; a holistic organization of life is needed.

Art and Fashion of the Future?

Similarly, art and fashion need to be institutionalized as integral to people's everyday life moments, as part of the culture they inhabit at every moment. This will give greater meaning to life. Integration of art, as the unison of concept, technique, and the aesthetic (Fırat, 2023), can provide a sense of purpose in proposing a concept, a sense of capability in mastering a technique, and a sense of emotional release in offering the aesthetic experience, as opposed to being simply the follower of preset actions in socially organized production or the consumer of predetermined commodities produced for the market. As, on the one hand, modern culture revered and intended to liberate the individual, on the other hand it rendered her/him simply a member of the market, the audience in the highly staged organization of production of commodities for expanding economic value as the organizing principle.

Similar to art, fashion, which in its general sense could be defined as creative styling of things, actions, and experiences, needs to be integrated in people's everyday lives as part of their performances, not trends that they have to follow in the market. In effect, the market's hegemony over all other dimensions of human life needs to be overcome. The market can be reconstructed as one of the many institutions and on an equal footing. Fashion, then, instead of a market principle, can become a creative activity that all people can engage in, enchanting lives.

Postmodernism, as a critique of modern organization of life, detected the problems with the hegemony of singular narratives (Lyotard, 1974), as well as with establishment of modern norms based on separations and polar oppositions causing disenchantment (Marsh, Caputo and Westphal, 1992). By recognizing multiplicity and the necessity of tolerance for different narratives, postmodern critiques offered some hope for re-enchantment of the lives of consumers by suggesting the possibility of a different subjectivity (Fırat and Dholakia, 2017). Yet the iconographic character of postmodern culture has largely limited people's agency to the fullest. Iconographic culture favors omnipresent commercial references that are influential. These references penetrate deep into everyday social, political, and economic discourses, and they refer to what resembles familiar and pleasant experiences constantly evoking consumptive behaviors and desires. The Internet and social media, for example, have disappointed many who initially were excited that potential democratic and independent voices would now find free means of expression. Instead, we see people using these media in a very large majority, repeating and replicating the commercial, consumptive, and already dominant ideological elements.

Yet, there is still the possibility of conceptualizing and institutionalizing art and fashion in a manner that gives agency to the multitudes. The symbolic nature of human existence on Earth seems to inevitably force a trend toward a fully symbolic culture to flourish. As the symbolic is culturally constructed and thus free from reference to what already exists, a wider distribution of human agency seems possible, if, of course, humanity is able to resolve current existential problems of global warming and the buildup of military mass destruction weapons, thus not extinguishing itself first.

References

Amin, Ash, ed. (1994), *Post-Fordism: A Reader*, Maiden, MA: Blackwell Publishers Inc.

Angus, Ian (1989), "Circumscribing Postmodern Culture," in *Cultural Politics in Contemporary America*, I. Angus and S. Jhally (eds.), New York: Routledge, 96–107.

Atik, Deniz, Lena Cavusoglu, Zeynep O. Ertekin, and A. Fuat Fırat (2022), "Fashion, Consumer Markets and Democratization," *Journal of Consumer Behaviour* 21, 5, 1135–1148.

Atik, Deniz, and A. Fuat Fırat (2013), "Fashion Creation and Diffusion: The Institution of Marketing," *Journal of Marketing Management*, 29, 7–8, 836–860.

Bauman, Zygmunt (2000), *Liquid Modernity*, Cambridge, UK: Polity Press.

Chaudhuri, Himadri R., and Russell W. Belk, eds. (2020), *Marketization: Theory and Evidence from Emerging Economies*, Singapore: Springer.

Chomsky, Noam (1999), *Profit Over People: Neoliberalism and Global Order*, New York: Seven Stories Press.

Cooney, William (2000), *The Quest for Meaning: A Journey Through Philosophy, the Arts, and Creative Genius*, New York, NY: University Press of America, Inc.

Ertekin, Zeynep O., and Deniz Atik (2014), "Sustainable Markets: Motivating Factors, Barriers, and Remedies for Mobilization of Slow Fashion," *Journal of Macromarketing*, 35, 1, 53–69.

Feagin, Susan, and Patrick Maynard, eds. (1997), *Aesthetics*, Oxford, UK: Oxford University Press.

Fırat, A. Fuat (2023), "Contemporary Implications of Aestheticization," in *New Directions in Art, Fashion and Wine: Sustainability, Digitalization and Artification*, A. Joy (ed.), Lanham, MD: Lexington Books, 29–42.

Fırat, A. Fuat, Deniz Atik, and Zeynep O. Ertekin (2023), "Fashioning Marketing and its Consequences," in *Marketing Fashion: Critical Perspectives on the Power of Fashion in Contemporary Culture*, K. Ekström (ed.), London, UK: Routledge, 41–55.

Fırat, A. Fuat (2020), "The Nature of Modern Marketization," in *Marketization: Theory and Evidence from Emerging Economies*, H.R. Chaudhuri and R.W. Belk (eds.), Singapore: Springer, 21–29.

Fırat, A. Fuat, and Nikhilesh Dholakia (2017), "From Consumer to Construer: Travels in Human Subjectivity," *Journal of Consumer Culture*, 17, 3, 504–522.

Fırat, A. Fuat, and Nikhilesh Dholakia (2006), "Theoretical and philosophical implications of postmodern debates: Some challenges to modern marketing," *Marketing Theory*, 6, 2, 123–162.

Fırat, A. Fuat (1994), "Gender and Consumption: Transcending the Feminine?" in *Gender Issues and Consumer Behavior*, J.A. Costa (ed.), Thousand Oaks, CA: Sage Publications, Inc., 205–228.

Foster, Hal (1983), "Introduction," in *The Anti-Aesthetic: Essays on Postmodern Culture*, H. Foster (ed.), Townsend, WA: Bay Press, ix–xvi.

Frankl, Victor E. (1959), *Man's Search for Meaning*, Boston, MA: Beacon Press.

Freedman, Carl (2002), *The Incomplete Projects: Marxism, Modernity, and the Politics of Culture*, Middletown, CT: Wesleyan University Press.

Harvey, David (2005), *A Brief History of Neoliberalism*, Oxford, UK: Oxford University Press.

Jameson, Fredric (1991), *Postmodernism, or, The Cultural Logic of Late Capitalism*, Durham, NC: Duke University Press.

Link, Stefan J. (2020), *Forging Global Fordism: Nazi Germany, Soviet Russia, and the Contest Over the Industrial Order*, Princeton, NJ: Princeton University Press.

Lyotard, Jean-François (1984), *The Postmodern Condition*, Minneapolis: The University of Minnesota Press.

Marsh, James L., John D. Caputo, and Merold Westphal, eds. (1992), *Modernity and its Discontents*, New York: Fordham University Press.

Murray, Robin, Jeremy Gilbert, and Andrew Goffey (2015), "Post-Post-Fordism in the Era of Platforms: Robin Murray talks to Jeremy Gilbert and Andrew Goffey," *New Formations*, 84/85, 9, 184–208.

Piketty, Thomas (2017), *Capital: in the Twenty-First Century*, Cambridge, MA: Harvard University Press.

Ritzer, George (2010), *Enchanting a Disenchanted World: Continuity and Change in the Cathedrals of Consumption*, Thousand Oaks, CA: Pine Forge Press.

Simmel, Georg (1957), "Fashion," *American Journal of Sociology*, 62, 6, 541–558.

Slater, Don, and Fran Tonkiss (2001), *Market Society: Markets and Modern Social Theory*, Cambridge, UK: Polity.

Taylor, Frederick W. (1911/1998), *The Principles of Scientific Management*, Mineola, NY: Dover Publications, Inc.

Vallas, Steven P. (1999), "Rethinking Post-Fordism: The Meaning of Workplace Flexibility," *Sociological Theory*, 17, 1, 68–101.

Chloe Preece and Pilar Rojas-Gaviria

5 The Affective Atmospheres of Immersion

Immersive Experiences

The term "immersion" has become a buzzword within the context of the experience economy, used in various contexts including: new technologies such as augmented reality and virtual reality which are thought to facilitate immersion; in tourism and retail, where extraordinary experience promise to enchant the consumer, for example dark restaurants, escape room games, transgressive nightclubs, and secret cinemas (Sherry, 1998); and within the arts and creative industries where the immersive experience is defined as a "state of intense engagement" with "high levels of concentration, an emotional, visceral response. It is the sensation of heightened experience in a piece of work, the phenomenon of 'losing yourself' in it, of losing track of time" (Biggin, 2020, p. 75).

More specifically, theatre and the performing arts have been at the heart of the surge of interest in immersion and immersive techniques. Immersive theatre is "an exhilarating live experience based on the palpable interactions with a performance environment and its inhabitants" (Eglinton, 2010, p. 55). As such, it includes a variety of styles, forms, and approaches, ranging from one-on-one pop-up encounters to mass interventions. However, as Bucknall (2023) argues, the term immersive in theatre is itself the product of marketing and promotion and in "the past decade, 'immersive' has become one of the most overused terms to describe theatre productions that aim to involve audiences in unconventional ways" (Lopes et al., 2020, p. 4).

What immersive theatre can do though, given the right expertise, context, funding, and skills, is build encounters which activate the senses of audiences/participants. Adam Alston (2013, p. 3) posits that "immersive theatre might be distinguished by the sensory acts which it demands of audiences, such as touching and being touched, tasting, smelling, and moving – this latter often (but not always) being characterized by freedom to move within an aesthetic space." For immersion to occur, the theatrical must be lived through in some embodied sense, something which distinguishes immersive theatre from more traditional forms of theatre. This allows for the opening of ludic and liminal space which engages the audience in collaboration to co-create fictive worlds and thus "holds the possibility of potential forms, structures, conjectures and desires" (Broadhurst 1999, p. 12). The material and affective relations between actors, audiences, and spaces are central to immersive performances: "participation is the activation of the audience through performative acts; acts that *affect* the very fabric of the performance itself" (Bucknall, 2023, pp. 144–5). In order to be lived through, the audience must seek out, activate, and inhabit the space(s) through corporeal, synaesthetic engagement. Yet, much of the appeal of immersive theatre is within the realm of secrecy and elusivity, as Bucknall (2023) theorises. Each participant is prom-

https://doi.org/10.1515/9783110783933-005

ised a unique, bespoke, and personal experience within a mysterious landscape through productive participation and co-creation which involves uncovering, discovering, and exploring.

Immersion is therefore a process as well as a specific quality; it is not instantaneous and as such must engage with the agency of individual audience members (Whittaker, 2023). As Slaby and von Scheve (2019, p. 1) note, immersion "emerges through dynamics of affecting and being affected, and is characterized by a dense involvement of the subject in an interactive and inter-affective context that entangles thinking, feeling and acting." Sense (in terms of feeling both sensation and emotion) is fused with sense ("meaning making"), so meaning-making is highly embodied (Wetherell, 2012, p. 4). The sensory shifts that an immersive experience can create have the potential of affecting participant's internal states and, in turn, these internal states are externalized and will also affect the collective atmosphere of the experience (Preece, Rodner, & Rojas-Gaviria, 2022). Audiences therefore must "become attendant" through a "reciprocal sensual relationship [which is] established between self, space and other bodies in the space" (Machon, 2013, p. 83). This affective orientation or disposition to be immersed is therefore highly individual; the individual has a certain potential to be immersed, however, the specific framing of an inter-affective and relational context can unleash and harness that potential in specific ways. When effectively immersed, the possibility of distancing is temporarily blocked; they are at the mercy of the inter-affective context but also contribute to and participate within the context. This results in both a sense of vulnerability and uneasiness but also of glamor and mystery. It is within these intensities, emerging from the interaction between bodies and objects, that the atmospheres of immersion can enchant. Through the "manipulation of surfaces" (Thrift, 2008, p. 1) and the balance of intimacy and distance, the mundane and ordinary can be transformed into visions of the sublime and extraordinary, endowing those audience members disposed to suspending their disbelief the illusion of being part of a plot they may influence. The craft involved in creating these theatrical atmospheres is thus as much about what is hidden and withheld as the spectacle on show.

Affective Atmospheres

As noted, immersion unfolds as a result of finding oneself embedded in some sort of affective arrangement (Slaby & von Scheve, 2019). There has been a recent surge in interest in the study of affect and specifically affective atmospheres in the marketing and consumer research literature (Hill, Canniford, & Eckhardt, 2021; Preece et al., 2022; Steadman et al., 2020) as part of a wider turn towards the non-representational and more embodied perspectives (Biehl-Missal & Saren, 2012; Canniford, Riach, & Hill, 2018; Hill, Canniford, & Mol, 2014; Patterson & Larsen, 2019; Scott & Uncles, 2018; Stevens, Maclaran, & Brown, 2019), in order to account for new ways of consumer sense-making by taking into consideration both the affective and the sensual in various forces and human and non-human entities. Atmospheres, as a particularly intense affect (Anderson, 2009) largely composed of un-representational and immaterial forces, present a particular problem for consumer researchers. They have long been noted to have significant impact and their curation has been shown to move consumers in certain ways, resulting in higher sales, for example, as the retail and services literature has shown (Bitner, 1990; Kotler, 1973; Yakhlef, 2015). Yet, how exactly the various aspects that make up an atmosphere come together in order to move people and the nuanced ways in which consumers are moved as they "land" in these atmospheres is still cloaked in mystery (Hill et al., 2022; Preece,et al., 2022). What this literature does evidence is that consumers' responses to affective atmospheres are highly mediated; personal biographies and socio-political contexts create complex entanglements. While what is felt and experienced may, on the one hand, be orchestrated by service providers and result in collective feelings of entrainment (Hill et al. 2022), it may also, on the other hand, be registered by bodies unprepared for the intensities of these affective atmospheres (Preece et al., 2022). What is of note is that, in fact, the majority of the most intense consumer experiences (Scott & Uncles, 2018; Stevens, Maclaran, & Brown, 2019) are often characterized by mixed feelings on the part of consumers: pain and pleasure, disgust and desire, form part and parcel of the "extraordinariness" of the experience.

Extraordinary experiences have received significant attention in the consumer research literature, highlighting the multi-sensory and emotive dimensions of consumption behavior (Holbrook & Hirschman, 1982; Kozinets et al., 2004; Schmitt, 1999). This literature has focused on various contexts including natural environments (Arnould & Price, 1993; Belk & Costa, 1998; Canniford & Shankar, 2013), ludic retail environments (Diamond et al., 2009; Kozinets et al., 2004; Sherry, 1998), athletic/physical encounters (Celsi, Rose, & Leigh, 1993; Tumbat & Belk, 2011; Scott, Cayla & Cova, 2017), and religious experiences (Higgins & Hamilton, 2019; Husemann & Eckhardt, 2019), attempting to unpick the dynamics which allow for a transcendent escape from marketplace logics through imaginative play from which consumers return restored and transformed. Key to this transformation, however, is a sense of immersion. In their recent paper on live action role play, Orazi & Van Laer (2023) start to unpack the distance consumers can feel in transitioning into – and out of – extraordinary experiences. They conceptualize the tension between the ordinary and extraordinary (principally) negatively as "bleed." While they focus on the frames and roles that govern the actions of consumers within extraordinary experiences, by focusing on affective atmospheres, we, instead, try to unpick this distance through a focus on the reciprocal sensorial and embodied shifts that result in the heightened intensities of extraordinary experiences. In doing so, we paint a more nuanced and complex picture of these shifts to account for both disruption, delight, and distress.

While some of the consumer research literature has highlighted the significance of the arts in resulting in heightened embodied extraordinary experiences, whether (at least partly) through music (Goulding, Shankar, & Elliot, 2002) or aesthetics (Kozinets, 2002), this literature is sporadic at best. Despite the significance of the arts in eliciting emotional reverberations, there have been few considerations of the quality of this engagement and what it requires from consumers. Joy & Sherry's (2003) multisensory and embodied approach to the aesthetic experience is the one notable exception. In their study, they consider how the body informs the logic of thinking about and interpreting artwork to demonstrate how perception and understanding are the product of not only the act of seeing but are impressed upon the body through various sensations. In exploring the link between the body, vision, and the mind, they show the need for marketers to attend to the body for memorable consumer experiences. Our exploratory work in this chapter aims at continuing these efforts through a visit to an immersive theatre production, via Punchdrunk's *Burnt City*, a theatrical experience illustrating how enchantment and frustration intertwine in affective atmospheres of immersion. This emotional intertwinement operates as a creative, dialectic tension.

Context: Punchdrunk's *The Burnt City*

The work of Punchdrunk offers a striking case study to elaborate our theoretical conception of affective atmospheres of immersion. Founded in 2000, Punchdrunk is largely acknowledged to have pioneered immersive theatre in rejecting the passive obedience of traditional theatregoing (Higgin, 2017). Part theatre, part dance, part giant immersive art installation, space is at the heart of a Punchdrunk piece and brought to life through intricate set dressing, epic visual scenes, low atmospheric lighting, filmic soundtracks, and distinctive scents, creating a highly intimate yet sprawling environment. Indeed, the name of the company itself is meant to elicit a feeling of "being bombarded with storytelling through every sense, an overload of stimuli that has a deep emotional and physical impact on the audience" (Higgin, 2017). Text and spoken word are used sparingly; the narrative is primarily communicated through choreography and the company is made up of mostly contemporary dancers. In particular, the work devised is distinguished by the fact that no audience member has the same experience. Due to the multiple threads offered simultaneously, whereby the action of the play is deconstructed and played all at once in different parts of the building, the audience is free to choose what to watch and where to go, resulting in many different possible experiences. Audience members are encouraged to explore and often stumble across scenes, often in mid-flow, they can follow specific characters, or roam free through the fictional world alone, opening drawers, reading letters they may find there, etc. As a result, the work tends to attract devoted fans who return many times to witness the production from different perspectives and try and piece together the narrative and soak up the space. Masks are the other signature element of Punchdrunk's work; every audience member is masked resulting in both a sense of anonymity and freedom in exploring the surroundings. As such, Punchdrunk are masters in creating affective atmospheres, immersing their audiences in storyworlds which resonate long after the performance, processed through layers of memory and sensory associations. Machon (2009, p. 4) argues that this requires "(syn)aesthetic work" on the part of audiences "which shifts between the sensual and the intellectual, the somatic, ('affecting the body' or 'absorbed through the body') and the semantic (the 'mental reading' of signs)."

We focus specifically on Punchdrunk's 2022–23 London show *The Burnt City* (TBC hereafter) where the action of the play is deconstructed with multiple scenes playing across two former ammunition factories combining 100,000 square feet. As appropriate for this space, the subject at play is war, the waging of it and its devastating effects. The source texts (very loosely interpreted) are Aeschylus' *Agamemnon* and Euripides' *Hecuba*, Greek tragedy inflected by more contemporary (comparatively to Ancient Greece, at least) references, particularly Fritz Lang's *Metropolis*, Weimar decadence, and costumes seemingly inspired by Alexander McQueen. These vast industrial buildings conjure both infinite space through a maze of rooms, corridors, and floors but also intimate spaces due to the attention to detail. As is typical of Punchdrunk work, rather than relying on words, the production employs mainly mime, movement, and dance to create distilled moments which capture a sense of timelessness.

For this chapter, we draw on netnographic research (Kozinets, 2019) and participant observation. In particular, we draw on the closed Facebook group of "The Burnt City Discussion Group" as a site for rich, relevant, active, interactive, substantial, and heterogenous data. As the most active site of fan discussion, there are currently over 3,100 members in the group who must answer two Punchdrunk-related questions in order to join. Discussions speculate, theorize, and discuss TBC, yet are careful not to reveal any secrets in order not to reveal anything that could spoil other fans' visits. In systematically following these online fan interactions, we observed, read, and archived posts from March 2022 when previews for TBC opened. As we did so, given the quantity of material available, we homed in on the sensual or affective manipulations of the immersive context of TBC. As this focus emerged, we noted two significant yet seemingly contrasting sentiments which lie at the heart of immersion: a fear of the unknown and an illusionary power in perceptually re-negotiating one's positioning in the immersive context which are experienced collectively as a tension or hesitation between being lost and taking control.

The Dialectic of Immersive Atmospheres: Navigating the Fear-of-Missing-Out (FOMO)

Slaby and von Scheve (2019, p. 4) note the that the "phantasmic topos" of total immersion "combines both the desire for immersing oneself in a pleasurable mode of manipulation and the fear of being immersed without recognizing it." It is clear when looking at the fans' comments on their experiences in TBC that what makes a Punchdrunk immersion more complete than other immersive theatre companies is the success of its "in-its-own world quality" (Machon, 2013, p. 93). This is both enticing and frightening. The world of Punchdrunk is a felt totality but it can only be experienced by audience members as fragments which they must puzzle together. This is described by a fan's first visit:

> When I entered the show, I was able to just be there, with no idea what was going on, and really enjoyed that sense of being in a world which appeared coherent and detailed, but only really being able to grasp a fragment of what was happening, without feeling I was missing something, because it was all interesting and absorbing. I don't think I even followed a character, because they seemed to be surrounded by people and moving really quickly. I saw some intimate moments and some big set pieces, but my overarching sense was this was a world that I wanted to know more about, and which had the depth to reward me for that . . .

We see here a sense of oceanic distance: the beauty of the experience, the perception of being in a universe of representation so detailed and so vast that the participant can't conquer it in its wholeness. This beauty also involves a sense of foreboding or disorientation. Another first-time audience member discusses how she loved "the scale, the detail and beauty of the set, the ambition of the undertaking, the sense of adventure and discovery and magic, and of course the sense of being immersed in another world." Yet she found that her "first Punchdrunk experience did however leave me feeling frustrated and confused. (. . .) This was especially true as I was not treated as a participant. Although I inhabited the same world as the characters, as they did not acknowledge me in any way, I felt I was haunting or intruding."

In response, another fan suggests that rather than a negative feeling that you are haunting or intruding, this "is the whole point for me, I love it! But totally understand it's not for everyone; the inevitable FOMO is frustrating but also, I think, what keeps some of us coming back for more." There is another side to the coin then, a need to understand. Indeed, Prudhon (2018) suggests that cultivating the frustration of the audience and the mystery of the narrative is a way of "trapping" audiences and encouraging them to return. The show is designed so that the different storylines – one for each character – follow their own directions, overlapping at certain moments and unfolding both horizontally (character's pathways) and vertically (the superimposition and crossing of these pathways). Even if audience members decide to follow the same character throughout their entire loop, they will still miss a major part of the show and the journey itself may be interrupted or lost, as one fan described: "losing sight of characters while they go down long corridors; missing which direction they went and losing them altogether was very frustrating on my third visit" and results in being "pulled out of the immersion experience." Furthermore, it is physically impossible for an audience member to follow each one of the 20 or so characters in one night, rendering the experience necessarily partial and personal. Therefore, many of the fans feel they can only achieve true closure once they have explored the entirety of this world, some going back dozens of times.

A sense of vastness is therefore at the heart of TBC, with the set designed as a maze of small rooms so that the audience member has the impression that it is never-ending and they cannot reach its edges. Therefore, rather than passively waiting for the narrative to unravel, it is necessary to actively map the fictional world and try and find its edges. It is the desire to reach their frontiers and the drive to see what happens elsewhere at the same moment that impels the audiences to move around. There are numerous references to FOMO, fear-of-missing-out, in the data: "I've noticed that the rhythm of a Punchdrunk show is this: great periods of stillness punctuated with more frenetic scenes. And FOMO (. . .) makes it hard to settle into that rhythm." As well as escaping physical boundaries, due to the action looping and the performance starting before the audience gets in, the impression is of a world existing on its own and escaping temporal considerations. Scenes are performed whether there are people to witness them or not, with this world seeming to exist independently of audiences being there. Temporality therefore plays a strong role in FOMO. Sara Ahmed (2004, p. 65) notes that "fear projects us from the present into a future. But the feeling of fear presses us into that future as an intense bodily experience in the present." Through FOMO we see the psychic projection of the self into another time and place, magnifying and making urgent the experience of time passing through this dislocation so that it is not fear of the future, but rather fear of the now, "or all the nows that the subject is not part of" (Nolan, 2021, p. 237). FOMO as Nolan (2021) discusses, despite being used as a casual cyber-slang term (usually associated with digital participatory cultures on social media in the context of apparent entertainment and pleasure), is a powerful form of social anxiety which references an effect of fear. The anxiety that exciting events may currently be happening elsewhere leads to an underlying uneasiness, a state of watching and being watched, where fears and desires are heightened, producing bodily sensations due to enmeshed affective relationships to others. Nolan discusses how FOMO is mobilized by marketers to promote excessive consumption through herd behaviors. As such, it is structurally and systematically produced, instrumentalized within Western consumer capitalism. In our case, the liveness of the performance dissolves the binary of observer/observed.

The masks, while creating a boundary between the audience and performers, also allow the audience to dissolve into generic, ghostly presences allowing them to be more voyeuristic than they might normally be and to lose some of their inhibitions. One fan discusses how: "I was the only spectator in that room witnessing the event (. . .). It was incredible. I felt as if I shouldn't be there, spying on two people in the throws of passion and when the female approached me and almost treated me like a mirror it was very uncomfortable but very intense at the same time."

Liveness, affect, and human connection are central to the performance, with FOMO therefore not a discrete affect but symptomatic and emblematic of the embodied nature of TBC and the sensory qualities of the materials and objects which create its "haptic visibility." This impression of endlessness is overwhelming yet the proliferation of minute details which relate things together also serves to provide a sense of intimacy and emotional engagement:

> I watched the actors intently, sometimes from a distance, and sometimes incredible proximity' [sic] each of them engaged with me in some small way during their journey. I sobbed; I cried; I was swept up in their tragedy. In the midst of the experience, I was conscious of the power of this immersive format to give me such intense insight – I could see all the small changes of expression on their faces and tension held in their bodies; I would not have been so swept up watching the same performances on a stage while I sat in my seat.

It is in the shifts from grandeur to intimacy, from distance to close-ups, that the tension builds. Indeed, most of the characters have a one-on-one at some stage in their loop and these are extremely coveted amongst fans who often discuss techniques to try and "score" one:

> I get that managing FOMO can be hard. (. . .) I can think of one genuinely useful tip: keep an eye out for characters that seem quieter (. . .). Then stick with them and see what happens. The 1:1s I have had have almost universally come when I've been the only follower or one of two or three who have stuck it out, rather than getting lucky in the throng. Even if the character you light on doesn't do 1:1s, the thrill of being alone for a scene or one of a few is very special, and you are more likely to be rewarded with some form of interaction.

These one-on-ones, by their nature, expose audience members' vulnerability, somehow being performed as both personal and private and staged and public: "without going into detail, it struck a personal chord, so much so that I teared up a little but in a good way. I felt comforted. I guess it all demonstrated the power of talented, intuitive immersive performance to soothe and calm."

FOMO must therefore be put aside for enjoyment: "focus on what the actors are doing in front of you and enjoy it rather than worry about what you are missing elsewhere." Yet as a form of affective labor it keeps audience members persistently engaged, seeking an unattainable satiation. The frustration inherent in FOMO seems to be central to the pleasure; it heightens the emotional experience and operates as a motivational factor. The members of the audience are confronted with the limitations of the immersive experience, not being able to overcome the power imbalances between producers and consumers. As Biggin develops:

> Environmental theatre works to diminish the literal distance between audience and performers; the question therefore becomes one of whether a fictional distance is maintained. Anonymous masked audience members are in many ways distant from the performers they may be physi-

cally close to, separated from the environment they temporarily inhabit: the rules of the mask (no touching, no talking) and the performance style of the performers (ignoring the audience members except during one-on-one scenes) may emphasise this distance within physical proximity. (Biggin, 2017, p. 186)

Through frustrations like these ones, TBC presents a challenge which needs to be overcome. Indeed, Nylund and Landfors (2015) discuss how carefully constrained frustrations can be a powerful tool in gaming, leading to addictiveness. The complexity and fragmented nature of the Punchdrunk production ensures that audience members do not get bored, with its anxious pacing by nature a scarcity model which is self-consciously imposed. Audience members therefore extend Punchdrunk's world through their sharing of their different individual experiences in an attempt to try and reconstruct the narrative puzzle through their embodied memories. These discussions extend to the virtual sphere where they build a collective inventory of the different scenes and maps of the performance space. This is an intent purely developed by the audience to navigate the power distances between consumers and producers. As one fan notes: "this group plays a big part in my enjoyment and understanding of the show." However, fans are extremely conscious of spoilers and warn that: "I think in a way, finding online discussion about Punchdrunk too early isn't a positive because it gives you that FOMO feeling like you're not getting something that everyone is. Most people do not come away with a truly deep understanding of the show's many layers, especially after one visit – it's more something to be experienced and accepted." Therefore, some posit that: "I'm actually in favour of not trying to make sense of it. It's going to feel a bit like a fever dream when you're new to it, and I think that it's worth leaning into that until it starts to make sense to you more organically."

The enticement of the mystery lingers on as: "the fun is in what I don't see – what my imagination has to fill in or what I have to try and work out. I don't think we as white masks are meant to be doing anything – the mask is the fourth wall, allowing [the] audience to view a story from inside it, intimately, and no one person's view is right or valid or whole, which for me is the beauty of it – I'm not being told what I have to take from it and that feels freeing to me." Immersion is therefore fragile, hard to achieve, and easy to destroy but it is this very fragility and an illusory feeling of nearly "having got it" that makes the experience tantalizing so that "the more you see, the stronger the addiction grows."

Immersive Atmospheres as Casting a Magical Spell through Glamor

The power of the aesthetic of Punchdrunk productions has already been noted. The history of immersion is intimately linked to the history of illusionist art (Slaby & von Scheve, 2019), and the individual audience member's strategies to distance themselves from or draw themselves into this immersion has to be continually renegotiated as we have seen. The audience's orientation towards ongoing perceptual, sensual, and affective manipulations of TBC requires further analysis. Another concept which appears repeatedly in fan discussions online is that of glamor: "Glamor, in the original sense of the world is a magic trick. A whole heap of sensory detail – the set, sound, the smells, the quality of the light – all the stuff we take for granted which builds the world. We don't need to work so hard to suspend our disbelief because we're up to our elbows as soon as we step over the threshold."

Stevens, Cappellini and Smith (2018, p. 581) theorize glamor as an experiential site of consumer desire which "can dazzle or enchant our eyes as senses" through a visual language of seduction. As such, it is remote, beyond our reach, mysterious, and is associated with the "manipulation of surfaces" (Thrift, 2008, p. 1). Indeed, this manipulation is noted by the fans as enchanting: "somewhere there's a fabulous and mysterious mixologist, mixing up otherworldly Punchdrunk scents . . . the nose knows." Glamor is artfully concealed. However, when it doesn't quite work, glamor can be brutally disrupted: "Troy feels more like its own place – sleazy, detailed, a little dangerous. The effect of the light there is incredible. I've experienced magic there even in an empty room, which is about as Punchdrunk as you can get. For me Mycenae still feels like a set, and it breaks the spell a bit."

The glamorous otherworldliness of TBC heightens the immersion. Indeed, the dreamlike state which the experience induces is its appeal, resulting in an "open ended, personal dream-like experience." Imagination is once again significant here: "what I love about Punchdrunk is making up my own ideas about what's happening around me, feeling immersed in a world, and experiencing everything like in a dream without putting two and two together." As Postrel (2013) highlights, glamor requires distance to remain alluring, which is what inspires imaginative longings. This distance is achieved through, as one fan puts it, "a constant tension around what is and isn't real, with unreliable narrators aplenty and an escalatingly vertiginous sense of derealization (and depersonalization)." It is through such tensions that fans become "emotionally invested" as "the stakes feel higher." We see these intensities play out in this fan's account of the highlight of one show:

> We stuck with Kronos and ended up sitting in the small square while he was hidden away in a locked room until eventually the woman gave up and went off to explore other things. I stayed and watched the action in the square until Kronos eventually came out. Then he did some actions with a torch looking at parts of the set in detail and in particular following a cable back to his room . . . and being there at that time resulted in me getting a one-to-one with him! No details here but the "reveal" set my heart racing and it took me several minutes to get back to a normal pulse. When I got back into the main area, I had to go to the bar for a drink of water to calm down again.

We see here the effort and affective labor required by the audience member as well as the performer. Glamor emerges from the interaction between performer and audience as well as the objects and materials of the set. High and low, distant and intimate, indifferent and affective, unattainable yet all-encompassing, the shifts in scale and intensity charm and enchant: "I find TBC incredibly glamorous. The costuming on this show is my favourite yet. I love how fresh it feels (. . .). The mix of Grecian austerity and luxury and Trojan pseudo-sleaze is *chef's kiss*." Glamor thus depends on what is withheld, allowing fans to dream of what they could be. Significantly, glamor can make the ordinary sublime through enchantment. This promise of enchantment is what makes the immersive theatre experience magical:

> just a quick note to say that – for me – TBC continues to improve and inspire. Last night's show (. . .) both broke my heart and brought me overwhelming joy. If the performers read this, I'd just like to thank them for making us feel so special and such a part of their art: a hand on the shoulder, a look in the eye, a smile – it's all transformative.

> words about scale, scope, artistry, is like writing about the Pyramids of Giza or the Northern lights: reading about it won't ever suffice, you have to see it in person, once in your lifetime.

The immersive experience, through a glamorous spell consisting of scenography, intertwined plots, and a multisensorial experience on the move, promises the audience, and often achieves, a magical, liberatory experience:

> What I loved about my very first visit (. . .) was that I didn't *have* to do anything in particular; I paid the ticket price and then could do whatever I liked – it took me about an hour to latch on to this, but then I didn't follow anyone for the next 2 hours, I wandered around the set and read letters in drawers and watched as actors appeared, danced and then moved on – and was just left speechless at the scale and detail of the world, like I was in the kind of video game you can just wander around in.

This "apparent" freedom of the experience on the move is, however, illusory and temporary. Seemingly free, liberated from traditional seated theatre, the audience members are oriented in certain directions, as made more evident in the finale where the entire audience is guided to the space where the closing scene is performed. The finale marks the end of the show and highlights how the individual adventure turns into a collective celebration, at the bar, where the more transactional and commercial elements such as paying for drinks remind the audience that the fiction is about to end (Biggin, 2017). While seemingly at odds with the rest of the experience, it does provide an illusory feeling of closure and underlines the artificiality and manipulation of the audience. As Stevens et al. (2018 p. 589) note, glamor is "a form of communication and persuasion," in this case providing audiences a sense that they "got" at least part of "it."

Conclusion

Our focus on the affective atmospheres of immersion reveal a number of tensions due to the reciprocal dynamics of affecting and being affected, of activity and passivity, movement and sensation. Immersion, in contrast to what much of the literature suggests (Suh & Prophet, 2018), does not solely overwhelm or overpower the immersed subject, rendering them passive. Rather, through an entanglement of active and passive involvement, immersion is neither a property of a certain subject alone or of a certain situated arrangement, but emerges through the interplay of both. Constellations in which this relational dynamic operates cast a spell on the audience member being immersed, capturing them completely in a specific local frame which functions as a "social, affective, discursive, symbolic and institutional force field" (Slaby & von Scheve, 2019, p. 7). The individual's affective, cognitive, and bodily potential is harnessed to become a part of the larger ensemble at play and depending on the intensity of the emotional involvement, different possibilities, feelings, and actions are available. The specific context and mode of involvement modulates the level of immersion possible. We see in our context that audiences are in turn bewildered, exasperated, frustrated but also enchanted and left in wonder. The bleed (Orazi & Van Laer, 2023) experienced by consumers as they are immersed is therefore not necessarily bad; it is in this tension as subjects shift from intimacy (which can be frustrated) to distance (which is both glamorous and illusory) that new perspectives emerge, maintaining the tension and magic spells of immersive atmospheres.

We find the focus on immersion and immersive techniques in marketing and consumer spheres to be somewhat limited to date. Immersion is either considered solely as a characteristic of the technology or the focus is entirely on the context of immersion; there has been limited attention to the reciprocity between the context and the consumers/audiences. Yet, any analysis of immersion, as shown in this chapter, must start with the individual consumer and their subject positionings or orientations. Rather than closing the door to uneasiness we argue we must investigate it, and this requires moving beyond the binary modes of thinking exhibited in this chapter; it is not simply active versus passive, absorption versus reflection, proximity versus distance or manipulation versus agency, but rather it is in the transitional between them that intensities are felt and feelings are heightened. What Punchdrunk does so well is shift the audience's status within the work, where they are seemingly at the center of the action yet, of course, there is still a neoliberal ethos at work here in the form of "entrepreneurial participation" where rewards come to those who make their own opportunities (Alston, 2013). Immersion is a lived form of intersubjectivity and affectivity yet the literature on how immersion is mediated in the marketplace remains scarce. What this chapter demonstrates, from a more critical perspective, is how the design of immersive environments is a modern technique of affective governmentality requiring closer examination. The ways in which immersion can prevent moments of distancing and critique and normalize escapism through managing our attention and co-opting our engagement deserve further attention given the hype around immersive techniques (scenography and scent design in retail for example) and technologies (augmented and virtual reality) in marketing (Slaby & von Scheve, 2019). Furthermore, the ways in which these environments spatially and temporally embed individuals in environments and how is highly unequal; for example, Bucknall (2023) shows the inaccessibility inherent in how immersive theatre favors the able bodied, neurotypical participant. Another critical aspect requiring examination is how immersive techniques create an affective background for specific relations that can be labeled as consumers' attachments (Borghini et al., 2021). Anderson (2022, p. 15) defines attachments as holding a promising value: "a distinct kind of relation orientates inquiry to how some objects within a way of life accrue a promissory value and come to be differentiated from others. Attachments are selective." It is necessary to better understand the processes of attachment that unfold in immersive atmospheres because such processes of affective governmentality (Bajde & Rojas-Gaviria, 2021) may support addictive behaviors in immersive experiences such as video gaming, bringing to light wider consumer and societal wellbeing concerns.

Finally, in order to study these affective atmospheres, we highlight the need for alternative methodologies to understand these non-representational forces and affects. As we show, audiences' emotional responses to TBC are produced by the process of engaging with the work rather than the individual elements found within the work alone. This process is non-verbal and expresses something beyond what can be said with language, manifesting a different form of knowledge which cannot be fully captured through standard interviews. Poetic methodologies (Canniford, 2012; Preece et al. 2022; Rojas-Gaviria, 2021; Sherry, 2008; Sherry & Schouten, 2002) have been noted as a useful tool to capture lived, embodied experiences that could otherwise go unnoticed and cannot be articulated, particularly in heightened emotive and affective moments, sometimes even providing participants and researchers with therapeutic and cathartic relief. Yet, these methods are still predicated on the written word. In examining a form of theatre that rejects the passive obedience of traditional theatre-going, namely immersive theatre, we ask what alternative arts-based methodologies could help capture the emotional reverberations and liveness of this context. Reason's (2010) creative-reflective research methodologies using drawing, for example, could be useful as a way for participants to account for the non-linguistic experience of bodies moving in spaces, allowing for greater scope for sensorial responses to emerge and become articulated. More embodied methods, guided by dancers or performers, could also hold great potential. Further research is needed to better account for the affects of immersion.

References

Ahmed, S. (2004). *The cultural politics of emotion*. London: Routledge.

Alston, Adam. (2013). Audience participation and neoliberal value: RISK, agency and responsibility in immersive theatre. *Performance Research*, *18*(2), 128–138.

Anderson, B. (2009). Affective Atmospheres. *Emotion, Space and Society*, 2(2),77–81.

Anderson, B. (2022). Forms and scenes of attachment: a cultural geography of promises. Dialogues in Human Geography.

Arnould, E., & Price, L. (1993). River magic: extraordinary experience and the extended service encounter. *Journal of Consumer Research*, *20*(1), 24–45.

Bajde, D., & Rojas-Gaviria, P. (2021). Creating responsible subjects: the role of mediated affective encounters. *Journal of Consumer Research*, *48*(3), 492–512.

Biggin, R. (2017). *Immersive Theatre and Audience Experience: Space, Game and Story in the Work of Punchdrunk*. Springer International Publishing.

Borghini, S., Sherry, J.F., Joy, A., et al. (2021). Attachment to and detachment from favourite stores: An affordance theory perspective. *Journal of Consumer Research*, *47*(6): 890–913.

Belk, R., & Costa, J. (1998). The mountain man myth: a contemporary consuming fantasy. *Journal of Consumer Research*, *25*(3), 218–240.

Biehl-Missal, B., & Saren, M. (2012). Atmospheres of seduction: A critique of aesthetic marketing practices. *Journal of Macromarketing*, *32*(2), 168–180.

Bitner, M.J. (1990). Evaluating service encounters: the effects of physical surroundings and employee responses. *Journal of Marketing*, *54*(2), 69–82.

Broadhurst, S. (1999). *Liminal acts: a critical overview of contemporary performance and theory*. London, Cassell.

Bucknall, J. (2023). Selling secrets: the role of "elusivity" in the liminoid invitations of immersive theatre. In F. Kerrigan & C. Preece (Eds.), *Marketing the arts: breaking boundaries* (2nd Ed.) (pp. 139–154). Routledge: London.

Canniford, R. (2012). Poetic witness: marketplace research through poetic transcription and poetic translation. *Marketing Theory*, *12*(4): 391–409.

Canniford, R., Riach, K., & Hill, T. (2018). Nosenography: how smell constitutes meaning, identity and temporal experience in spatial assemblage. *Marketing Theory*, *18*(2), 234–248.

Canniford, R., & Shankar, A. (2013). Purifying practices: How consumers assemble romantic experiences of nature. *Journal of Consumer Research*, *39*(5), 1051–1069.

Celsi, R., Rose, R., & Leigh, T. (1993). An exploration of high-risk leisure consumption through skydiving. *Journal of Consumer Research*, *20*(1), 1–23.

Diamond, N., Sherry, J., Muñiz Jr, A., McGrath, M., Kozinets, R., & Borghini, S. (2009). American girl and the brand gestalt: closing the loop on sociocultural branding research. *Journal of Marketing*, *73*(3), 118–134.

Eglinton, A. (2010). Reflections on a decade Punchdrunk of theatre. *Theatre Forum*, *37*, 46–55.

Goulding, C., Shankar, A., & Elliott, R. (2002). Working weeks, rave weekends: identity fragmentation and the emergence of new communities. *Consumption, Markets and Culture*, *5*(4), 261–284.

Goulding, C., & Saren, M. (2009). Performing identity: an analysis of gender expressions at the Whitby goth festival. *Consumption Markets & Culture*, *12*, 27–46.

Higgin, P. (2017, September 7). A Punchdrunk approach to making theatre. British Library, available at: https://www.bl.uk/20th-century-literature/articles/a-punchdrunk-approach-to-making-theatre

Higgins, L., & Hamilton, K. (2019). Therapeutic servicescapes and market-mediated performances of emotional suffering. *Journal of Consumer Research*, *45*(6), 1230–1253.

Hill, T., Canniford, R., & Eckhardt, G.M. (2022). The roar of the crowd: how interaction ritual chains create social atmospheres. *Journal of Marketing*, *86*(3), 121–139.

Hill T., Canniford R., & Mol, J. (2014). Non-representational marketing theory. *Marketing Theory*, *14*(4), 377–394.

Holbrook, M., & Hirschman, E. (1982). The experiential aspects of consumption: Consumer fantasies, feelings, and fun. *Journal of Consumer Research*, *9*(2), 132–140.

Husemann, K.C., & Eckhardt, G.M. (2019). Consumer deceleration. *Journal of Consumer Research*, *45*(6), 1142–1163.

Joy, A. & Sherry, J.F. Jr. (2003). Speaking of Art as Embodied Imagination: A Multisensory Approach to Understanding Aesthetic Experience. *Journal of Consumer Research*, *30*(2),259–282.

Kotler P. (1973). Atmospherics as a marketing tool. *Journal of retailing, 49*(4), 48–64.

Kozinets, R. (2002). Can consumers escape the market? Emancipatory illuminations from burning man. *Journal of Consumer Research, 29*(1), 20–38.

Kozinets, R. (2019). *Netnography: The Essential Guide to Qualitative Social Media Research*. London: SAGE Publications.

Kozinets, R., Sherry, J., Storm, D., Duhachek, A., Nuttavuthisit, K., & DeBerry-Spence, B. (2004). Ludic agency and retail spectacle. *Journal of Consumer Research, 31*(3): 658–672.

Lopes Ramos, J., Dunne-Howrie, J., Maravala, P.J., & Simon, B. (2020). The post-immersive manifesto. *International Journal of Performance Arts and Digital Media, 16*(2), 196–212.

Machon, J. (2013). *Immersive theatres: intimacy and immediacy in contemporary performance*. Houndmills, Basingstoke, Hampshire: Palgrave Macmillan.

Machon, J. (2009). *(Syn)aesthetics: redefining visceral performance*. Springer.

Nolan, K. (2021). Fear of missing out: performance art through the lens of participatory culture. *International Journal of Performance Arts and Digital Media, 17*(2), 234–252.

Nylund, A., & Landfors, O. (2015). Frustration and its effect on immersion in games: A developer viewpoint on the good and bad aspects of frustration. Available at: https://www.diva-portal.org/smash/get/diva2:821653/FULLTEXT01.pdf.

Patterson, M., & Larsen, G. (2019). Listening to consumption: towards a sonic turn in consumer research. *Marketing Theory, 19*(2), 105–127.

Orazi, D. & van Laer, T. (2023). There and Back Again: Bleed from Extraordinary Experiences. *Journal of Consumer Research, 49*(5),904–925.

Postrel, V. (2013). *The power of glamour: Longing and the art of visual persuasion*. New York, NY: Simon & Schuster.

Preece, C., Rodner, V., & Rojas-Gaviria, P. (2022). Landing in affective atmospheres. *Marketing Theory, 22*(3), 359–380.

Prudhon, D. (2018). Punchdrunk's immersive theatre: from the end to the edge. *Sillages critiques* (24).

Reason, M. (2010, October). Watching dance, drawing the experience and visual knowledge. In *Forum for Modern Language Studies* (Vol. 46, no. 4, pp. 391–414). Oxford University Press.

Rojas Gaviria, P. (2021). Poetizing to improve consumer representation. *Marketing Theory, 21*(4): 463–479.

Scott, R., Cayla, J., & Cova, B. (2017). Selling pain to the saturated self. *Journal of Consumer Research, 44*(1), 22–43.

Schmitt, B. (1999). Experiential marketing. *Journal of Marketing Management, 15*(1–3), 53–67.

Scott, R., & Uncles, M.D. (2018). Bringing sensory anthropology to consumer research. *European Journal of Marketing, 52*(1/2), 302–327.

Sherry, J.F. Jr. (1998). The soul of the company store: Nike town Chicago and the emplaced brandscape. In *Servicescapes: the concept of place in contemporary markets* (pp. 109–46). NTC Business Books.

Sherry J.F. (2008). Three poems on markets and consumption. *Consumption, Markets and Culture, 11*(3): 203–206.

Sherry J.F., & Schouten J.W. (2002). A role for poetry in consumer research. *Journal of Consumer Research, 29*(2): 218–34.

Slaby, J., & Von Scheve, C. (2019). Introduction: affective societies–key concepts. In *Affective Societies* (pp. 1–24). Routledge.

Steadman, C., Roberts, G., Medway, D., Millington, S., & Platt, L. (2020). (Re)thinking place atmospheres in marketing theory. *Marketing Theory, 21*(1): 135–154.

Stevens, L., Cappellini, B., & Smith, G. (2018). Nigellissima: A study of glamour, performativity and embodiment. In Celebrity, Convergence and Transformation (pp. 125–146) in *Celebrity, Convergence and Transformation*. London: Routledge.

Stevens, L., Maclaran, P., & Brown, S. (2019). An embodied approach to consumer experiences: the Hollister brandscape. *European Journal of Marketing, 53*(4), 806–828.

Suh, A., & Prophet, J. (2018). The state of immersive technology research: A literature analysis. *Computers in Human Behavior, 86*, 77–90.

Thrift, N. (2008). The material practices of glamour. *Journal of cultural economy, 1*(1), 9–23.

Tumbat, G., & Belk, R. (2011). Marketplace tensions in extraordinary experiences. *Journal of Consumer Research, 38*(1), 42–61.

Yakhlef, A. (2015). Customer experience within retail environments: An embodied, spatial approach. *Marketing Theory, 15*(4), 545–564.

Wetherell, M. (2012). *Affect and emotion: a new social science understanding*. London: SAGE.

Whittaker, L. (2023). Onboarding and offboarding in virtual reality: a user-centered framework for audience experience across genres and spaces. *Convergence*. 13548565231187329.

Joanne Roberts
6 Art, Financialization and Free Ports

Introduction

The transformation of works of art into financial assets through the use of free ports is the focus of this chapter. Of course, works of art do have a financial value and as long as they are desired by individuals or public organizations they always will. However, the purpose of art is more than financial; importantly, it has aesthetic and emotional value together with cultural significance. Yet, over recent decades, the financialization of art has accelerated the desire to possess art for financial gain and to hold it as a store of value. This process of financialization has been supported by the expansion of free ports, which store artworks and other valuable collectables while also offering significant tax advantages. On the one hand, free ports have expanded to meet the need for appropriate storage space for art and luxury collectables and, on the other hand, the spread of free ports offering specialist services for the storage of fine art and luxury collectables has encouraged the further financialization of art. The trend towards the financialization of art may be viewed as indicative of the de-artification of cultural goods including art. The term de-artification is used here to capture the process by which the artistic element of a piece of art, or other cultural object, is diminished or even nullified. In the case of an artwork, financial motives result in its de-artification through the appropriation of its economic value at the expense of its aesthetic, emotional, and cultural value.

By exploring the role of free ports in the financialization of art, this chapter seeks to identify not only the immediate impact of free ports but also other related forces, some of which are enabled by free ports. Such forces include changes in the financial nature of art, the evolving nature of collectors of art, the rise of digital art and Non-Fungible Tokens (NFTs), and new ownership models. This chapter addresses the following questions: what impact does the financialization of fine art stored in free ports have on the aesthetical value of art? Is art reduced to just one more asset for the financial markets to appropriate or does its aesthetic, emotional and cultural value remain?

The chapter begins by exploring the relationship between art and finance. The nature of free ports is then examined before the relationship of fine art and its financialization is investigated in the context of the free port. The chapter concludes with reflections on the role of free ports and related developments in promoting the de-artification of art through its financialization.

https://doi.org/10.1515/9783110783933-006

Art and Finance

The history of art can be traced back many thousands of years. Early examples of art that have survived the passage of time include the cave paintings at Lascaux in France that date from 15,000 to 10,000 BC (Gombrich, 1950). Art exists in all societies across the globe. Sometimes it has functional attributes, as in architecture, and, at other times, art exists purely for its aesthetic value. This chapter is concerned with fine art and its current relationship to finance. Therefore, it is important to appreciate what fine art is in the contemporary era. Fine art (henceforth art and fine art are used interchangeably) refers to the expression or application of human creative skill and imagination, typically in a visual form such as painting or sculpture, producing works to be appreciated primarily for their aesthetic or emotional power. In this sense, for art to fulfil its purpose, it must be experienced and generate meaning through being exposed to human perception (Klamer, 1996a). As Arjo Klamer (1996b: 21) notes, "Art exists not in the physical form of a painting or a performance but in the moment of wonderment, of the question mark that the physical form evokes in our minds." So, from this perspective, art has value that defies measurement and therefore it cannot be equated with a monetary sum. Nevertheless, a price is allocated to a piece of art when it is exchanged, whether through an auction house, gallery, or private transaction. Consequently, works of art have economic value and can be regarded as economic capital or financial assets.

Yet, the value of art can be experienced by many, without diminishing the potential for such art to offer value to others. For example, works of art held in museums can offer valuable experiences to the many visitors. Indeed, the more a piece of art is viewed the more its monetary and experience value can rise. In some senses, art is like knowledge, in that sharing knowledge does not diminish the amount available to others. Nevertheless, there is an underlying value to the tangible form of a work of art and through private ownership that value can be captured in economic terms. Additionally, through private ownership the audience for an artwork can be controlled and individuals can be excluded from the benefits of experiencing it. In the same way that intellectual property rights can exclude people from access to knowledge, private ownership may restrict access to artworks. Consequently, the aesthetic and emotional value that art is capable of generating can be limited by restricting its audience.

Although a work of art can be exchanged as economic capital it also has a role as cultural capital. For Pierre Bourdieu (1986), the consumption of art as an objectified form of cultural capital requires not only legal ownership but also embodied cultural capital in the form of, for instance, long-lasting dispositions of the mind and body. Additionally, art as objectified cultural capital requires the support of cultural capital in its institutionalized state because the cultural value of art must be validated by way of, for example, an appropriately qualified individual or group, that constitute and are supported by institutional structures including recognized educational qualifications. According to Bourdieu (1993: 7), art can also be viewed as symbolic capital for it offers a "degree of accumulated prestige, celebrity or honour and is founded on a dialectic of knowledge (connaissance) and recognition (reconnaissance)." In his book *Distinction*, Bourdieu (1984: 279) examines art as symbolic capital, arguing that:

> Of all the conversion techniques designed to create and accumulate symbolic capital, the purchase of works of art, objectified evidence of "personal taste", is the one which is closest to the most irreproachable and inimitable form of accumulation, that is, the internalization of distinctive signs and symbols of power in the form of natural "distinction", personal "authority" or "culture".

Consequently, art can act as a form of economic capital held for investment purposes, as cultural or symbolic capital, as an object of conspicuous consumption, which provides a means of signaling one's wealth to others (Veblen 1899), as decoration, as a source of pleasure offering emotional value, or as a combination of these. Deloitte and ArtTactic's (2021) survey of 115 collectors' motivations in buying art shows that the emotional value is the top motivation, with 93% of those surveyed noting this motivation compared to 36% noting investment returns. However, 47% noted social value as a motivation for buying art and other motivations identified included: a safe haven (32%); a luxury good (40%); a form of portfolio diversification (40%); and a means to hedge against inflation (27%) (Deloitte and ArtTactic 2021: 102). The motivation concerning social value and luxury goods identified by Deloitte and ArtTactic (2021) bears out the role of art as a form of conspicuous consumption. Indeed, fine art is among the nine categories of luxury goods that Bain and Company (2020) regularly include in its assessment of the luxury market. Although a small segment of the overall market, which was valued at 1.14 trillion Euros in 2021 (Bain and Company, 2021: 7), fine art is nevertheless an important element of the luxury market, accounting for an estimated 34 billion Euros in 2021, having rallied with growth of 18–20% after the decline of 35–40% due to the COVID-19 crisis during the previous year (Bain and Company, 2020: 8; 2021: 7).

Collecting fine art is a pastime of many of the super-rich or High Net Worth Individuals (HNWIs) who use art to adorn the entrance halls and walls of their multiple residences, to signal status, and to diversify their holdings of wealth. According to Credit Suisse (2021), the total wealth of High Net Worth (HNW) adults has grown from USD 41.5 trillion in 2000 to USD 191.6 trillion in 2020, and their share of global wealth has risen from 35% to 46% over the same period (Credit Suisse 2021: 18). Importantly, High Net Worth Individuals (HNWIs) are not a homogenous group. Capgemini (2021: 10) identifies three tiers within global HNWIs: firstly, the wealthiest are the 0.20 million Ultra-HNWIs (UHNWIs) with wealth of more than US$30 million, accounting for 34% of the total wealth of HNWIs in 2020; secondly, there are the 1.89 million mid-tier HNWIs with wealth of US$5–30 million, accounting for 22.7% of the total wealth of HNWIs in 2020; and, lastly, there are the 18.74 million millionaires next door tier HNWIs with US$ 1–5 million, accounting for 43.3% of the total wealth of HNWIs in 2020. The number and wealth of these categories of HNWI is growing. For instance, between 2019 and 2020, the number of UHNWIs grew by 9.6% while their wealth increased by 9.1%, the number of mid-tier HNWIs expanded by 7.8%, with their wealth increasing by 7.9%, and the number of millionaires next door grew by 6.1%, with their wealth expanding by 6.3% (Capgemini 2021: 10). Clearly, those with the highest wealth were able to benefit most from the investment growth opportunities, and this was particularly evident during the COVID-19 pandemic (Jones and Romei, 2020).

As the number and wealth of HNWIs has grown, so too has the demand for art and art management related services. Indeed, art is of great interest to the world's billionaires. For instance, Wealth-X (2021a) notes that art is among the top five interests and passions of ultra-wealthy individuals whose fortunes stem solely from inheritance and seventh among those with a combination of inherited and self-made wealth. This is reflected in the size of the global market for art and antiques, which peaked at $68.2 billion in 2014. Yet, growth in the art market has not been consistent; rather, the market has experienced volatility over the last decade or so. In particular, the Great Financial Crisis resulted in a fall in sales value to a low of $39.5 billion in 2009 (a total decline of 40% from a peak in 2007) (McAndrew, 2021: 31). After a strong recovery, the market peaked in 2014, but by 2019 the market was worth $64.350 billion. However, the COVID-19 pandemic created the biggest recession in the art market since 2009, such that by 2020 it was estimated to be worth $50.1 billion, a 22% decline on the 2019 market size (McAndrew, 2021: 30). Nevertheless, by 2021 the art market had rebounded and was worth $65.1 billion (McAndrew, 2022a: 25).

When considering art from an economic perspective it is vital to note that, unlike the market for many other financial investments, the art market does not operate in a predictable manner. For example, Baumol (1986: 10–11) identifies the following characteristics that set the art market apart from the stock market: (1) widely known paintings and sculptures are unique, and even two works on the same theme by a given artist are imperfect substitutes; (2) the owner of a Caravaggio holds a monopoly on that work of art; (3) the resale of a given art object may not even occur once in a century; (4) the price at which art work is acquired is frequently known only to the parties immediately involved; (5) it is questionable whether the true equilibrium price of a work of art can be known. Furthermore, art is subject to fashion and changes in taste: "Only those critics who have succeeded as instruments for the redirection of general tastes seem really to have been in a position to profit from their judgement" (Baumol, 1986, p. 14).

Nevertheless, the acquisition and retention of art remains a significant means by which the wealthy invest in both cultural, symbolic, and economic capital. The value of wealth associated with art and collectables was estimated to be $US 1,481 billion in 2020 (Deloitte and ArtTactic, 2020: 11). HNWIs are keen to secure their wealth, and this requires privacy and secrecy in relation to banking, investments, tax issues, inheritance planning, and, of course, their personal possessions and their own physical security. Holding a diversified portfolio of assets is one way of protecting and securing wealth. In recent years, art has become an asset held by the wealthy as a purposeful means of diversifying their investment portfolios (Thompson, 2008). Moreover, given the historically low levels of interest since 2008 together with higher levels of economic uncertainty, holding wealth in forms other than familiar financial instruments has become increasingly popular (*The Economist*, 2013). There is, then, a growth in the use of luxury cars, fine wines, and fine art as investment assets. Indeed, Deloitte and ArtTactic (2021) notes that the financial dimension of art collecting has become increasingly important over the last 10 years, with art increasingly positioned as a capital asset that requires stewardship by wealth managers.[1]

Art and collectables make up a notable portion of HNWIs' wealth. Drawing on a survey of 2,709 High Net Worth (HNW) collectors from across the globe, McAndrew (2022b: 62) states that 66% of HNW collectors reported an allocation of over 10% to art in their overall wealth portfolios. The importance for HNWIs of holding wealth in the form of art is also evidenced by the growth of wealth managers seeking to support the management and achievement of maximum return on such assets through the provision of consulting, legal, and tax advisory services (Deloitte and ArtTactic, 2021). Certainly, wealth managers collaborate with art professionals to support the management of their HNW clients' art collections, and they increasingly provide related services, including art valuations to provide a consolidated view of wealth, estate planning in relation to art collections, and the management of art related philanthropy.

Furthermore, younger art collectors are increasingly viewing art as a financial investment and this group gives more weight to the social value of art (Deloitte and ArtTactic, 2021). According to Wealth-X (2021b), $18.3 trillion worth of wealth will be transferred by 2030 with 90% of the donors being men, and their ages ranging from 70 and 80 years. The beneficiaries of this wealth transfer will predominantly be Millennials and Generation Z.[2] Given the older generation's interest in the development of art collections, there will be the transfer of a significant amount of art, which will need to be managed by wealth management consultants with art expertise to ensure tax liability efficiency. Given the different motivations for holding art between the older and younger generations, as the young come into their inheritance there is likely to be an impact on how HNWIs hold art collections.

Investment in art is encouraged by the returns that such assets generate. According to the Sotheby's Mei Moses World All Art Index, a leading barometer of art returns, as an investment, fine art provided a return between 1950 and 2021 of a compounded annual growth rate of 8.5%.[3] Moreover, Artnet's indices suggest that art

---

1 Deloitte is a leading provider of audit and assurance, consulting, financial advisory, risk advisory, tax, and related services (https://www2.deloitte.com/uk/en/legal/about-deloitte.html accessed December 19, 2022). Its Deloitte Private division, which focuses on the specialized needs of the ultra-affluent, is well positioned to offer the services required to manage art as a capital asset.
2 Millennials are generally defined as those born between 1980 and 1994 and Generation Z are usually defined as those born between 1995 and 2009.
3 Sotheby's https://www.sothebys.com/smm (accessed December 19, 2022).

offers strong returns in the short term and more moderate returns in the long term (Deloitte and ArtTactic, 2021: 226). Such indices provide an indication of the overall market made up of a multitude of individual transactions, some of which give rise to high returns while others are less successful. Also, it is notable that such indices do not capture the prices gained in the private sale of artworks because such information is not publicly available. Hence, such factors must be borne in mind when using these indices to assess the investment returns on works of art.

Although art is an investment asset (McAndrews, 2010; Deloitte and ArtTactic, 2021), whether it is a sound one when compared to other assets is debatable (Baumol 1986; Gerlis 2014). However, there are tax advantages to be gained from holding art rather than cash or other assets, including inheritance planning benefits. Furthermore, art can be a safe haven in periods of economic uncertainty and a means of storing wealth. As a store of value art displays a strong positive correlation with other asset classes used as a store of wealth such as gold (Deloitte and ArtTactic, 2021: 222). The role of art as a safe haven is borne out by the experience of the art market during periods of economic disruption. So, for instance, although art sales declined sharply in the aftermath of the 2008 Global Financial Crisis, the art market recovered quicker than the economy as a whole (McAndrew, 2017). Still, the art market is tied to the wider economic context, particularly in relation to those factors affecting the growth and distribution of private wealth. Nonetheless, with the increasing numbers of wealthy people across the globe, supported by growth in the emerging markets, the demand for art is likely to increase in the longer term. However, there are other issues to consider when investing in art, including verifying authenticity, fraud, the use of art for money laundering, and the lack of sector specific regulation. These factors encourage the purchasers of art to use trusted intermediaries.

In addition, when considering art as an investment, the cost of keeping it securely and preserving it in pristine condition as well as insuring it against damage or loss must be considered (Baumol, 1986). Hence, it is hardly surprising that the growth in the market transactions of works of art has led to a rise in the use of free ports as locations to store art while in transit and increasingly for longer periods of time, especially when art is purchased specifically as an investment asset. Holding wealth in the form of works of art presents significant security issues. This is because family homes and additional residences, which can be protected via an array of security measures (Wingfield, 2010; Arlidge, 2015; Cox, 2016), are limited in their capacity to hold tangible goods. Moreover, just as securing wealth requires the diversification of assets, the protection of one's tangible assets can be enhanced by using multiple locations for storage to take account of potential dangers arising from natural disasters, including floods, fires, and earthquakes, and the risks resulting from terrorism and political upheavals. Hence, the diversification of wealth portfolios to include luxury goods like classic cars, fine wine, jewels, and works of fine art accounts for the increasing demand for secure and private storage spaces. Furthermore, items purchased purely as investments rather than for display require safe and tax efficient storage. This demand has contributed to a growth in the number of free ports with specialist storage facilities to accommodate fine art and other collectable luxuries. Consequently, attention now turns to the nature of free ports.

Free Ports

The first free port was founded in Geneva in 1854. Originally, free ports were solely facilities for the storage of goods in transit. According to UNESCO (2016: 2):

> Free ports are tax-free warehouses that were initially created to store raw materials and, later, to hold manufactured goods for a short period of time before their transportation, transit and reshipment.

The "free" aspect of free ports refers to the suspension of customs duties and taxes. Today, goods may be kept in free ports for an unlimited period of time and at minimal expense. While goods are stored at free ports, owners pay no import taxes or duties until the goods reach their destination. If a work of art goes straight from the gallery or auction house to the free port, no sales tax is paid – this only becomes due when the work reaches its final destination. If the good is sold at the free port, the owner pays no transaction tax either. Therefore, free ports are more than storage facilities because they offer advantages arising from their legal status. Free ports allow collectors to store unlimited quantities of cultural objects without paying customs duties, Value Added Tax (VAT) or other sales taxes.[4] Furthermore, art can be sold within the free port for substantially higher amounts than the purchase price without incurring capital gains tax. Additionally, in many nations, the storing of goods or artifacts in a free port only requires a declaration of the nature of the asset and the name of the depositor, but not the name of the owner of the object (UNESCO, 2016: 2). This provides anonymity and privacy for the ultimate beneficiary. However, in recent years, there have been moves to change this, for instance through the 5th Anti-Money Laundering (AML) Directive in the EU, to deter the use of free ports for illegal activities, including money laundering and the storage and sale of contraband (European Parliament, European Parliamentary Research Service, & Ex-Post Evaluation Unit, 2018).

The privacy that free ports afford to clients can be further enhanced when works of art are owned through offshore shell companies. Moreover, owners benefit by establishing a shell company in the most favorable tax location, namely tax havens like the British Virgin Islands. For some, this enhances privacy, while for others it is a way to legally avoid tax or to structure inheritance planning; and for yet others, it is a means to distance themselves from illegal activity, including tax evasion, money laundering, and fraud. Legal advisers providing services to establish such offshore shell

---

4 Value Added Tax is a sales tax raised in the European Union.

companies include the now notorious Mossack Fonseca & Co., a Panamanian law firm and corporate service provider founded in 1977, which was once the world's fourth biggest provider of offshore services. This company was largely unknown until the widespread reporting of the leaked Panama Papers in 2016 (Obermayer and Obermaier, 2016), which exposed its role in tax evasion schemes and other dubious activities. In March 2018, Mossack Fonseca & Co. announced that it was shutting down, because of the economic and reputational damage caused by the disclosure of its role in global tax evasion (Slawson, 2018).

Free port storage facilities take the form of anonymous buildings. They are generally located close to airports for the convenient receipt of goods and visitors wishing to view their own stored items or to peruse items on sale. Such buildings are inaccessible to the public at large, who are often unaware of their role as locations for the storage of high value goods. Free ports offer high levels of security and privacy. The short-term use of free ports may result from situations when items are in transit or waiting for their final destination to be prepared. For example, museums may use free ports to hold works of art safely and securely that are in transit between exhibition locations or as additional storage space. The long-term use of free ports may be associated with the storage of items held as investments.

Due to the tax and legal advantages that free ports offer, they are increasingly being used by the world's super-rich to store their investments in luxury goods ranging from works of art and fine wine to jewelry and classic cars (*The Economist*, 2013). Moreover, free port providers have upgraded their facilities to offer places to store precious items safely and securely, and, crucially, with the appropriate level of care, including restoration services .

The free port facilities in Geneva have expanded over the years to accommodate the storage of luxury collectables, such that they now include high security storage with sophisticated surveillance and climate control systems together with private showrooms. Driven by the growth in wealth and the resultant increase in demand for facilities to store high value goods, since 2010 there has been a significant expansion in the number and geographical spread of free ports specializing in the storage of fine art and other luxury collectibles (see Table 6.1).This expansion also reflects the growth and globalization of the luxury market, including the art market, which has been bolstered by the rise in demand from emerging countries, especially China (McAndrew, 2017). Furthermore, with the tightening of tax regulation and requirements for greater transparency in relation to tax havens the incentives to exploit the tax advantages offered by free ports have grown (Helgadóttir, 2020).

The increase in the number of these specialist free port facilities in China (Bejing and Shanghai) reflect the expansion of wealth and number of HNWIs in the Asia Pacific region during the last decade (Capgemini, 2021: 11), as well as the role of Asia Pacific region HNWIs in boosting the global art market in the aftermath of the Great Financial Crisis.

Table 6.1: Free ports specializing in the storage of fine art and other luxury collectibles.

Location	Date of Establishment
Geneva, Switzerland	1854
Singapore, Singapore	2010
Monaco, Monaco	2013
Luxembourg, Luxembourg	2014
Beijing, China	2014
Delaware, USA	2015
Shanghai, China	2017
New York, USA	2018 (closed 2020)

Source: compiled from Ditzig, Lynch, and Ding (2016: 184); Geneva Free port and Warehouses Ltd (http://geneva-freeports.ch/en/ (accessed May 6, 2018); SMT Fine Art (https://www.smt.mc/en/smt-fine-art/monaco-freeport/ (accessed May 6, 2018); and ARCIS (http://www.arcisartstorage.com/news/ accessed May 6, 2018); Kinsella (2020).

In the UK, the current Prime Minster and former Chancellor of the Exchequer, Rishi Sunak, announced during the 2021 budget that eight new free ports would be created in England (East Midlands Airport, Felixstowe & Harwich, Humber, Liverpool City Region, Plymouth & South Devon, Solent, Teesside, and Thames). The Teesside and the Thames free ports opened towards the end of 2021 (Webb and Jozepa, 2022). While there is no mention of these free ports having facilities for the storage of art and high value collectables, given London's position in the art market, a free port specializing in the storage of fine art and other luxury collectibles in England may be a future addition to those listed in Table 6.1.

The companies that manage the space within free ports and deliver specialized logistics and storage services are known for their discretion. Once works of art are placed in the secure storage facilities of the free port, owners can be sure of their safety. Of course, there are costs involved; for instance, Maertens (2013) reports that prices range from 250 to 700 euros per square meter per annum. In addition, holding tangible assets incurs insurance costs. Nevertheless, in 2013, the Geneva free port was estimated to have held around 1.2 million artifacts, and approximately three million bottles of vintage wine and several tons of gold bars (Maertens, 2013). In 2019, Deloitte and ArtTactic (2019, p. 237) estimated that the assets in the Geneva Free port were worth between $80–100 billion. Given the number of free ports globally, the value of works of art held in these facilities is undoubtedly significant.

One of the most notable companies offering free port services is Fine Art Logistics Natural Le Coultre, which was established over 150 years ago.[5] This company provides

---

[5] Much of the information presented on Fine Art Logistics Natural Le Coultre derives from pages of the company's website: https://www.falnlc.lu/luxembourg/ and https://www.falnlc.lu/network/ (accessed July 27, 2018). The former CEO of this company was Yves Bouvier who since 2017 has been involved in an ongoing legal case in which he is accused of fraud in his role of art dealer. In 2017 Bouvier sold Natural Le Coultre

expert advice and solutions in the area of fine art logistics to a select global group of museums, galleries, and collectors through its headquarters in Geneva and its sister companies in Singapore and Luxembourg. In total, Natural Le Coultre manages over 30,000 square meters of fine art storage worldwide, and thereby claims that it contributes to the protection and maintenance of the cultural heritage of humanity. Its warehouse located at LE FREEPORT Luxembourg, which is the highest rated maximum-security vault in Europe, was launched in September 2014. This facility has over 13,000 square meters of fully climate- and humidity-controlled storage space for fine art, four fine wine cellars, and dedicated storage rooms for classic cars and precious metals. Additionally, the company's clients have access to a scientific laboratory and a restoration workshop as well as eight showrooms and an imposing reception area for events, private exhibitions, and the purchase and sale of fine art.

Consequently, free port facilities go beyond the provision of mere storage space. Free ports have become one-stop shops for the management and secure storage of collections of art and other high value possessions, providing all the services required to keep such goods in pristine condition. Furthermore, galleries and art advisers have offices in free ports where clients can view, buy, and sell art. What, then, is the relationship between art, financialization and free ports?

Art, Financialization and Free Ports

As noted above, investors view art as a store of value as well as having potential for financial returns. As assets, works of art are not liquid but they can be used as security to borrow funds. Deloitte and ArtTactic (2021: 23) estimate the size of outstanding loans secured against art to be between US$24 billion and US$ 28.2 billion in 2021 and expect this figure to increase to US$31.3 billion in 2022. Growth in such loans has been driven by the need for liquidity for private business operations during the COVID-19 pandemic; as an alternative to selling art works during the pandemic; to release capital for other investments; to pay estate taxes or fund a trust without having to sell works of art; and to provide the funds to extend art collections (Deloitte and ArtTactic, 2021: 199). However, lenders face several challenges related to art secured loans such as lack of liquidity, an unregulated market, deficiency of knowledge (internal expertise); valuation risk; and the need for due diligence (Deloitte and ArtTactic, 2021). Nevertheless, as the market for art secured loans matures and expands in size these challenges are being addressed through the development of in-house skills and collaboration with art market specialists.

Geneva free port to the French logistics company André Chenue, which specializes in the packing, storage, transportation, and installation of works of art (Bowley, 2017). In 2022, the Natural Le Coultre Singapore free port was sold to Chinese crypto billionaire Jihan Wu (*ARTFORUM*, 2022).

Free ports support the financialization of art because storing works of art in free ports makes it easier to use them as collateral for loans (Deloitte and ArtTactic, 2014: 88). As art becomes a financial instrument, like bonds, stocks, and shares, for its owner the tangibility and cultural and symbolic value of art becomes secondary to its economic value. Art can be stored away in free ports like money in the bank and rarely withdrawn. Indeed, art can be owned by art funds that have multiple investors. In this way, a wider range of individuals can benefit through fractional ownership from art as an investment and store of value. Additionally, such forms of ownership allow a wider range of individuals to gain from the tax advantages of storing art in a free port.

Furthermore, the free ports in Luxembourg and Singapore are permitted, under national regulations, to allow the owners of works of art to remove them temporarily for local exhibition without incurring the tax costs that would normally arise when moving assets from free ports. The aim of this arrangement is to support local cultural industries through the exhibitions that result from the presence of the free port. At the same time, owners can get the pleasure and benefits of exhibiting their art, while also maintaining the free port tax advantages. Making use of such opportunities to show art may be more than a philanthropic act as the inclusion of works in exhibitions can contribute to a strategy designed to increase the value of an art portfolio (Thompson, 2008).

Despite the impact of the EU's recent 5th AML Directive on the sector (Gerlis, 2019), the art market remains relatively unregulated, which presents benefits and risks. Zarobell (2020) argues that the unregulated nature of the art market intersects with the offshore domain nature of free ports, which provide tax-free storage facilities across the globe. While financial speculation in art has grown and has promoted the expansion of free port facilities globally, this trend is also encouraged by the desire of the owners of art works to exploit the tax avoidance opportunities offered by free ports. Hence, increasing amounts of art are being taken out of circulation and deposited in free ports where they are beyond the view of regulatory authorities. This is further encouraged by the tightening up of offshore finance through multilateral efforts to crack down on tax evasion and banking secrecy (Helgadóttir, 2020). For instance, the Foreign Account Tax Compliance Act (FATCA) in the USA (2010) and OECD's 2014 Common Reporting Standards (CRS) make it difficult for individuals to avoid taxation on the proceeds of funds held in bank accounts (European Parliament, European Parliamentary Research Service, & Ex-Post Evaluation Unit, 2018: 13).

Despite the deregulation that has occurred since the widespread adoption of neoliberal policies in the 1980s, the exploitation of regulatory loopholes associated with tax havens has attracted much attention from international organizations such as Transparency International and Tax for Justice and national and international policymakers. For example, Transparency International revealed that almost 40% of multinational companies' profits are transferred to tax havens resulting in lower tax revenues for the countries which host their production and sales facilities (Pearson,

2020). The tax losses from corporate tax avoidance are significant and consequently they draw the attention of politicians and policymakers to tax havens, which are used by corporations and wealthy individuals. While there is an ongoing tightening of regulation related to tax havens, free ports have avoided much of the impact of the legal developments directed at tax avoidance and evasion and banking secrecy. Hence, Weeks (2020) asks if artworks linked to free ports have become the contemporary version of the numbered Swiss bank account or the suitcase full of cash. However, the question arises: why have free ports been spared tighter regulation? Perhaps this is because those who exploit the tax and legal advantages of free ports are the super-rich who champion globalization and neo-liberalism and who, according to Wilkin (2015), wield political influence through their lobbying and political donations.

Nevertheless, critics, such as Gilmour (2022), have raised concerns that free ports could be used to hide illegally acquired assets, to launder money, or evade tax, and they call for greater regulation to prevent such activities. The use of free ports to store illegally acquired and trafficked goods is evidenced by the case of the Swiss authorities seizing artifacts looted from Syria's ancient Semitic city of Palmyra after they were discovered in the Geneva free port (Agerholm, 2016). Moreover, given the relatively unregulated nature of the art market, it has in the past been possible to buy a work of art for half a million US dollars without the need for one's identification to be verified. However, current EU AML regulations require art market participants to undertake greater due diligence on transactions of over 10,000 Euros (Gerlis, 2019). Nonetheless, most art is highly portable and easily shipped abroad and, since its value can be difficult for a non-expert to assess, it provides a vehicle for moving funds across borders and for money laundering. The former Brazilian banker Edemar Cid Ferreira, who was convicted of money laundering and bank fraud, stored millions of dollars in art works, including the $8 million painting titled Hannibal by Jean-Michel Basquiat, which was smuggled into the United States with a customs form saying it was worth $100 (O'Murchu, 2015). Such examples undermine the protests of art market intermediates and the operators of free ports who reject the view that such dubious activities provide a case for more robust regulation of art markets. Indeed, the argument for greater regulation is countered by the fact that customs officers in the various jurisdictions have access to inventory data of what is stored in the free ports. However, for most free ports, information on beneficial ownership is not captured (FT.Com, 2017). As a result, the client anonymity and privacy facilitated by free ports is open to abuse by criminals and may encourage illegal activities with negative consequences for victims of the theft of high value goods whether these are members of the super-rich, private, or state museums and institutions, or countries whose national treasures have been plundered in times of conflict.

The management of art is a growing area of business for wealth managers and facilitating the use of free ports is an important means to minimize tax liabilities and facilitate inheritance planning. Unsurprisingly, wealth managers that offer art management services are keen to encourage regulatory developments that would distance the use of free ports from the criminal activities that can arise due to the lack of transparency concerning, for instance, the obscuring of beneficial ownership and details of items deposited (Deloitte and ArtTactic, 2021). The EU's adoption of the 5th AML Directive in July 2018, with implementation by member states by January 2020, has increased the transparency of ownership in EU free ports. Yet, although information on beneficial ownership is gathered, this information is not necessarily publicly available. Furthermore, unlike the market for financial assets, such as equities, the art market is not subject to direct regulation (Thompson, 2008). For instance, there are no qualifications required by law for an individual to begin trading as an art advisor or dealer. As such, the art market is vulnerable to abuse, including fraud, money laundering, tax evasion, trading on inside information, and price manipulation (Gapper and Aspden, 2015).

Nonetheless, free ports and the logistical, legal, and financial services that support their activities are promoting the financialization of art. Moreover, they facilitate the trend towards art investment funds and fractional ownership models, which extend art investment to a wider population beyond the HNWIs. Given the openness of younger art investors to such ownership modes, these types of investments are likely to increase. Investment in physical art remains dominant, but alternative forms of ownership are emerging, including Non-Fungible Tokens (NFTs) (Deloitte and ArtTactic, 2021). Capgemini (2021) notes that NFTs provide a new class of assets that can be traded on a blockchain platform, which is a digital ledger technology behind Bitcoin (Iansiti and Lakhani, 2017). NFTs are so-called because while "one bitcoin is directly interchangeable with another, meaning they are fungible, NFTs are the opposite because the underlying assets are unique in some way and can't be exchanged like for like" (Bowden and Jones, 2021). While some sales of art through NFTs are merely a new way of selling tangible art held by investment funds that use cryptocurrencies and blockchain (Barrett, 2021), other sales involve digital art works. The attraction of NFTs in the art market is evidenced by Sotheby's sale of "The Fungible Collection," a collection of digital art produced by the anonymous creator Pak, an artist at the forefront of digital art and crypto media, for US$17 million in 2021.[6] Young investors are favorably disposed to such investments, firstly because it allows investment in art at accessible prices and secondly because young investors are far more comfortable with digital forms of ownership compared to older generations. However, while investments in tangible art may make use of free port storage facilities, investments in digital art have no need for such physical storage and can be held in the digital realm – although it would be wrong to think that this realm does not have a tangible manifestation.[7] Additionally, the regulation and financial infrastructure associated

---

6 Sotheby's: https://www.sothebys.com/en/digital-catalogues/the-fungible-collection-by-pak (accessed December 15, 2022).
7 While no physical object exists the storage of the data that makes up the digital art is stored in a physical location in terms of a computer drive or a server farm.

with the developments concerning NFTs is emerging (Deloitte and ArtTactic, 2021). Interestingly, in 2022 the Singapore free port was sold to the Chinese crypto billionaire Jihan Wu (ARTFORUM, 2022), perhaps pointing to some commercial convergence between the tangible free port and the digital realm of art in the contemporary era.

Essentially, when art is stored as an investment asset, its nature and relation to its owner changes. Art transforms from being a tangible object that has some perceptual impact on the owner's existence, and all who have access to the work, into an abstraction: an abstraction that is disconnected from the everyday life of the owner through its incorporation into a set of financial assets. Art's tangibility is neutralized in the strong rooms and vaults of the free port. It moves from the real places of owners' lives to the imagined spaces of the abstract world of financial assets (Roberts, 2020). Hidden out of sight, works of art cease to produce emotional reactions and moments of wonderment in a viewer. Accordingly, the value of such art becomes purely financial. Individual works of art lose their uniqueness and become homogenized as a set of financial assets. Taking on the characteristics of a financial instrument, art's only solidity becomes its value listed on a balance sheet. There is a de-artification process in which art assets become financial assets. Consequently, just as the ownership of stocks and shares can be transferred in the abstract world of electronic financial markets, the ownership of art may change easily from individuals to companies and arts-based investment funds, without the need for the work to be physically moved from its free port location. Although free ports do have showrooms to allow owners the opportunity to reconnect with, and maintain distanciated possession of, their art collections, such facilities are just as likely to be used for inspections, valuations, and sales of the items in storage.

The tax avoidance and evasion that free ports facilitate reduces the tax revenue available for the public realm and services, with negative implications for the quality of life of those individuals reliant on state support. Moreover, the secrecy afforded by free ports ensures that not only the tax authorities but also the public at large remains ignorant of the true wealth of the super-rich. Such ignorance supports the growing income and wealth inequality that has characterized the global economy, and particularly the UK and US economies, since the 1980s (Dorling, 2014; Piketty, 2014). Ultimately, the continued growth of inequality has consequences for the governance and stability of democracies (Piketty, 2014). It also raises moral questions concerning the consumption of luxuries including art by the super-rich (Roberts, 2019; 2022).

Crucially, by promoting the holding of art as a financial asset, free ports deprive growing proportions of humanity of access to cultural artifacts. As increasing quantities of cultural artifacts are hidden away in free ports, society becomes culturally impoverished. Opportunities for creativity resulting from exposure to, and engagement with, such items in exhibitions, museums, and public and private collections are lost, with consequences for the future development of knowledge. The study of works of art and cultural artifacts is limited by what is available and known. In addition, the ownership of such items is difficult to trace and works of national significance may potentially be moved offshore and disappear into a free port storage facility without adequate notice being given to cultural institutions or national authorities. Essentially, artifacts that could enrich culture remain out of view.

Conclusion

This chapter has identified a number of trends promoting the financialization of art. These include the greater availability of free ports with art management resources through which owners are assured that their artworks will not only be secure but also protected through specialist services. New models of ownership, including through art funds and shared ownership, require spaces for the safe keeping of art, thereby contributing to the demand for free port space. Likewise, the growing market for lending against art facilitates a demand for free port space where the lender can be sure of the safety of a piece, given that the title to the work of art will usually be transferred to the lender for the duration of the loan. The changes in the nature of art collectors are also influencing the use of free ports. Older collectors are likely to have a stronger emotional bond with their works of art, whereas younger collectors are more concerned about the social and investment value of artworks. Moreover, younger generations are more comfortable in the digital world of intangible goods, hence the popularity of NFTs among this group. Similarly, art works deposited in free ports, whether owned in full or through shared ownership, are works that become intangible on spread sheets. Of course, the use of free ports for tax advantages is also an important driver of the financialization of art. This trend is promoted by the growing global requirements for greater transparency in relation to tax havens, which drive tax avoidance and evasion into the still opaque location of the free port. Hence, the nature of free ports together with a number of accompanying trends promotes the drive towards the financialization of art. In the process of financialization de-artification occurs through which a major purpose of art transforms from the aesthetic and emotional to the economic.

Fundamentally, when art is hidden from view and held in free ports as an investment asset, it loses its real and fundamental purpose for the individual and for society. To fulfill its purpose, art must be experienced and exposed to human perception. The storage of art in free ports not only diminishes the quantity and quality of art available to the public though exhibitions in public or private museums and galleries but also the essential cultural role of art is challenged. Art becomes merely economic capital and loses its role as cultural capital. Hidden away in a free port, a work of art cannot have both financial and cultural value. Cultural value, in terms of aesthetic and emotional value, can only be accessed through engagement with art. As the cultural value of art declines, so too does the embodied cultural knowledge required to appreciate it. No longer prized for its aesthetic or emotional power, but for its financial value alone, art's fundamental value is nullified, and it loses its true purpose in part or in total. Through free ports, cultural capital, together with the knowledge associated with it, is thereby diminished together with the creativity it inspires. In this way, the privacy and tax advantages that free ports provide for a select few diminishes society at large.

References

Agerholm, H. (2016), 'Stolen Artifacts from Palmyra and Yemen seized in Geneva: Relics Date Back to Third and Fourth Centuries,' *The Independent*, December 4. Available at: http://www.independent.co.uk/news/world/europe/stolen-artifacts-palmyra-yemen-geneva-enesco-switzerland-a7454001.html (accessed May 7, 2018).

Arlidge, J. (2015), 'The Paranoid World of London's Super-rich: DNA-Laced Security Mist and Superyacht Getaway Submarines,' *Evening Standard*, October 22. Available at: http://www.standard.co.uk/lifestyle/esmagazine/the-paranoid-world-of-londons-superrich-dnalaced-security-mist-and-nuclearproof-panic-rooms-a3096491.html (accessed May 7, 2018).

ARTFORUM (2022), 'Crypto Pioneer Buys Yves Bouvier's Singapore Freeport for $28.4 Million, September 20th. Available at: https://www.artforum.com/news/singapore-s-le-freeport-sold-to-crypto-billionaire-89272 (accessed December 15, 2022).

Bain and Company (2020), *The Future of Luxury: Bouncing Back From Covid-19*. Available at: https://www.bain.com/globalassets/noindex/2021/bain_digest_the_future_of_luxury_bouncing_back_from-covid-19.pdf (accessed March 17, 2022).

Bain and Company (2021), *From Surging Recovery to Elegant Advance: The Evolving Future of Luxury*. Available at: https://www.bain.com/insights/from-surging-recovery-to-elegant-advance-the-evolving-future-of-luxury/?utm_medium=email&utm_source=mkto&utm_campaign=AT-retail-2022-01-03&utm_term=from-surging-recovery-to-elegant-advance-the-evolving-future-of-luxury (accessed December 13, 2022).

Barrett, Helen (2021), 'NFTs transform the art market for young novice buyers', FT.COM, September 2. Available at: https://www.ft.com/content/39c5ef2b-c69c-4611-88f5-f5a7f611d8c8 (accessed April 1, 2022).

Baumol, W.J. (1986), 'Unnatural Value: Or Art Investment as Floating Crap Game,' *The American Economic Review*, 76 (2), Papers and Proceedings of the Ninety-Eighth Annual Meeting of the American Economic Association (May), 10–14.

Boucher, B. (2016), 'See What Experts Have to Say About Sotheby's Acquisition of the Mei Moses Art Indices,' *Artnet News*, October 29. Available at: https://news.artnet.com/market/sothebys-acquisition-mei-moses-art-indices-725648 (accessed May 6, 2018).

Bourdieu, P. (1993), *The Fields of Cultural Production: Essays on Art and Literature*, edited and introduced by Randal Johnson, Cambridge: Polity Press.

Bourdieu, P. (1986), 'The forms of capital'. In J. Richardson (Ed.), *Handbook of Theory and Research for the Sociology of Education* (New York, Greenwood), 241–258.

Bourdieu, P. (2010[1984]), *Distinction: A Social Critique of the Judgement of Taste*, Abington: Taylor & Francis Group.

Bowden, J., and Jones, E.T. (2021), 'NFTs are much bigger than an art fad – here's how they could change the world', *The Conversation*, April 26, 2021, 11.24am BST. Available at: https://theconversation.com/nfts-are-much-bigger-than-an-art-fad-heres-how-they-could-change-the-world-159563 (accessed March 6, 2022).

Bowley, Graham (2017), 'Yves Bouvier Sells His Geneva-based Art Storage Company', *The New York Times*, October 27, 2017, https://www.nytimes.com/2017/10/27/arts/yves-bouvier-sells-his-geneva-based-art-storage-company.html (accessed December 15, 2022.).

Capgemini (2021), *World Wealth Report 2021*, Capgemini Research Institute. Available at: https://worldwealthreport.com/wp-content/uploads/sites/7/2021/07/World-Wealth-Report-2021.pdf

Credit Suisse (2021), *Global wealth report 2021*, June, Credit Suisse Research Institute. Available at: https://www.credit-suisse.com/about-us/en/reports-research/global-wealth-report.html (accessed March 6, 2022).

Cox, H. (2016), 'Safe as Houses: How the Super-Rich Make Their Homes Super-Secure,' September 7, *Financial Times* (FT.com). Available at: https://www.ft.com/content/069be746-6f92-11e6-a0c9 -1365ce54b926 (accessed May 29, 2017).

Deloitte and ArtTactic (2021), *Art & Finance Report 2021*, Deloitte Luxembourg and ArtTactic. Available at: https://www2.deloitte.com/lu/en/pages/art-finance/articles/art-finance-report.html (accessed April 1, 2022).

Deloitte and ArtTactic (2019), *Art & Finance Report 2019*, Deloitte Luxembourg and ArtTactic. Available at: https://arttactic.com/product/art-finance-report-2019/ (December 19, 2022).

Deloitte and ArtTactic (2016), *Art & Finance Report 2016*, 4th edition, Deloitte Luxembourg and ArtTactic. Available at: https://www2.deloitte.com/content/dam/Deloitte/lu/Documents/financial-services/ar tandfinance/lu-en-artandfinancereport-21042016.pdf (accessed April 16, 2017).

Deloitte and ArtTactic (2014), *Art & Finance Report 2014*, Deloitte Luxembourg and ArtTactic. Available at: https://www2.deloitte.com/content/dam/Deloitte/es/Documents/acerca-de-deloitte/Deloitte-ES-Opera_Europa_Deloitte_Art_Finance_Report2014.pdf (accessed April 17, 2017).

Ditzig, K., Lynch, R., and Ding, D. (2016), 'Dynamic Global Infrastructure: The Freeport as Value Chain,' *Finance and Society*, 2 (2): 180–88. Available at: http://financeandsociety.ed.ac.uk/issue/view/139 (accessed April 17, 2017).

Dorling, D. (2014), *Inequality and the 1%*, London and New York: Verso.

The Economist, (2013), 'Freeports: Über-warehouses for the Ultra-rich,' *The Economist*, November 23. Available at: http://www.economist.com/node/21590353/print (accessed July 30, 2018).

European Parliament, European Parliamentary Research Service, & Ex-Post Evaluation Unit (2018), *Money laundering and tax evasion risks in free ports: Study at the request of the special committee on financial crimes, tax evasion and tax avoidance* (TAX3). Available at: https://op.europa.eu/en/publication-detail /-/publication/362d2465-e3d4-11e8-b690-01aa75ed71a1/language-en (accessed December 19, 2022).

FT.COM (2017), Lexicon: Freeport, *Financial Times*. Available at: http://lexicon.ft.com/Term?term=Freeport (accessed April 16, 2017).

Gapper, J. and Aspden, P. (2015), 'Davos 2015: Nouriel Roubini Says Art Market Needs Regulation,' *FT.COM*, January 22. Available at: https://www.ft.com/content/992dcf86-a250–11e4-aba2–00144feab7de (accessed April 16, 2017).

Gerlis, Melanie (2019), 'UK art galleries prepare for Brexit', *FT.COM*, February 15, https://www.ft.com/con tent/20184526-2f83-11e9-80d2-7b637a9e1ba1 (accessed December 15, 2022).

Gerlis, M. (2014), *Art as an Investment? A Survey of Comparative Assets*, Farnham, Surrey: Lund Humphries.

Gilmour, P.M. (2022), 'Freeports: Innovative trading hubs or centres for money laundering and tax evasion?', *Journal of Money Laundering Control*, 25 (1), 63–71.

Gombrich, E.H. (1950), *The Story of Art*, New York: Phaidon Press.

Helgadóttir, Oddný (2020), 'The new luxury freeports: Offshore storage, tax avoidance, and 'invisible' art', Environment and Planning A. Available at Online First https://doi.org/10.1177/0308518X20972712 (accessed December 19, 2022).

Iansiti, Marco and Lakhani, Karim R. (2017), 'The Truth About Blockchain: It will take years to transform business, but the journey begins now'. *Harvard Business Review*, January–February. Available at: https://hbr.org/2017/01/the-truth-about-blockchain (accessed March 7, 2022).

Jones, Sam, and Romei, Valentina. (2020), 'Pandemic makes world's billionaires', *FT.COM* – and their advisers – richer', *FT.COM*, October 23. Available at: https://www.ft.com/content/ab30d301-351b-4387-b212-12fed904324b (accessed March 7, 2022).

Kinsella, Eileen (2020), 'New York's Ultra-High-Tech Art Warehouse and Freeport ARCIS Is Abruptly Closing After Just Two Years', *Artnet News*, September 2. Available at: https://news.artnet.com/art-world/arcis-warehouse-shutting-down-1905756 (accessed December 14, 2022).

Klamer, A. (1996a), 'Introduction,' in A. Klamer, *The Value of Culture: On the Relationship Between Economics and Arts*, 7–12, Amsterdam: Amsterdam University Press.

Klamer, A. (1996b), 'The Value of Culture,' in A. Klamer, *The Value of Culture: On the Relationship Between Economics and Arts*, 13–28, Amsterdam: Amsterdam University Press.

Maertens, M. (2013), 'Dans le secret des Ports Francs,' *Connaissances des Arts*, January 16. Available at https://www.connaissancedesarts.com/marche-art/dans-le-secret-des-ports-francs-11136/ (accessed December 19, 2020).

McAndrew, C. (2017), *The Art Market 2017*, An Art Basel and UBS Report, Basel, Switzerland. Available at: https://d33ipftjqrd91.cloudfront.net/asset/cms/Art_Basel_and_UBS_The_Art_Market_2017.pdf (accessed May 7, 2018).

McAndrew, C. (2022a), *The Art Market 2021, An Art Basel and UBS Report*, Basel, Switzerland. Available at: https://d2u3kfwd92fzu7.cloudfront.net/Art%20Market%202022.pdf (accessed December 14, 2022).

McAndrew, C. (2022b), *A Survey of Global Collecting in 2022*, An Art Basel and UBS Report, Basel, Switzerland. Available at: https://d2u3kfwd92fzu7.cloudfront.net/A_Survey_of_Global_Collecting_in_2022_.pdf(accessed December 14, 2022).

McAndrew, C. (2021), *The Art Market 2021, An Art Basel and UBS Report*, Basel, Switzerland. Available at: https://d2u3kfwd92fzu7.cloudfront.net/The-Art-Market_2021.pdf (accessed March 4, 2022).

McAndrew, C. (ed.) (2010), *Fine Art and High Finance*, New York: Bloomberg Press.

Obermayer, B., and Obermaier, F. (2016), *The Panama Papers: Breaking the Story of How the Rich & Powerful Hide Their Money*, London: One World.

O'Murchu, C. (2015), 'Art: A Market Laid Bare,' *Financial Times*, Ft.com, April 7. Available at: https://www.ft.com/content/a91a1608-d887-11e4-8a23-00144feab7de (accessed May 7, 2018).

Pearson, L. (2020), 'Money lost to corporate tax havens could be funding our health services through the crisis,' March: http://transparency.eu/corporate-tax-covid19/ (accessed January 10, 2023).

Piketty, T. (2014), *Capital in the Twenty-First Century*, Cambridge, MA: Harvard University Press.

Roberts, J. (2022), 'Luxury and Economic Inequality: A Critical Luxury Studies Approach.' In *The Oxford Handbook of Luxury Business* edited by Pierre-Yves Donzé, Véronique Pouillard, and Joanne Roberts (New York: Oxford University Press), 503–524.

Roberts, J. (2020), 'Secret Spaces of Luxury: Ignorance, Free Ports and Art,' in Roberts, J. and Armitage, J. (eds), *The Third Realm of Luxury: Connecting Real Places and Imaginary Spaces* (Bloomsbury Visual Arts, Bloomsbury Publishing), 159–176.

Roberts, J. (2019), 'Is Contemporary Luxury Morally Acceptable? A Question for the Super-rich,' *Cultural Politics*, 15 (1): 48–63.

Roberts, J. (2018), 'Luxury and Ignorance: From 'Savoir Faire' to the Unknown,' *Luxury: History, Culture, Consumption*, 5 (1): 21–41.

Slawson, N. (2018), 'Mossack Fonseca Law Firm to Shut Down after Panama Papers Tax Scandal,' *The Guardian*, March 14. Available at: https://www.theguardian.com/world/2018/mar/14/mossack-fonseca-shut-down-panama-papers (accessed May 7, 2018).

Thompson, D. (2008), *The $12 Million Stuffed Shark: The Curious Economics of Contemporary Art*, London: Aurum Press.

UNESCO (2016), *Intergovernmental Committee for Promoting the Return of Cultural Property to Its Countries of Origin or Its Restitution on Case of Illicit Appropriation*, Twentieth Session UNESCO Headquarters, Room II, September 29–30, 2016, ICPRCP /16/20.COM/12, Paris, July 2016. Available at: http://www.unesco.

org/new/fileadmin/MULTIMEDIA/HQ/CLT/pdf/2_FC_free_port_working_document_Final_EN_revclean.
pdf (accessed July 30, 2018).

Veblen, T. (1899), *The Theory of the Leisure Class: An Economic Study in the Evolution of Institutions*, New York, London: Macmillan.

Wealth-X (2016), *Billionaire Census Highlights*, Wealth-X. Available at: http://www.mediapool.bg/files/252/Billionaire_Census_2015–2016_HIGHLIGHTS.pdf (accessed April 16, 2017).

Weath-X (2021a), *World Ultra Wealth Report 2021*, Wealth-X.com. Available at: https://go.wealthx.com/world-ultra-wealth-report-2021 (accessed December 19, 2022).

Wealth-X (2021b), *Preservation and Succession: Family Wealth Transfer 2021*, Wealth-X.com. Available at: https://eur03.safelinks.protection.outlook.com/?url=https%3A%2F%2Fgo.wealthx.com%2Fe%2F311771%2Family-wealth-transfer-2021-pdf%2Fnxrz4%2F467915764%3Fh%3DvNn4WDERn0DI2uCzWeRsAQYNzW8OZDliAMG39K_BkKY&data=04%7C01%7Cj.roberts%40soton.ac.uk%7Cd44595c97e4f45e964c208d9fd0f9b48%7C4a5378f929f44d3ebe89669d03ada9d8%7C0%7C0%7C637819065733147433%7CUnknown%7CTWFpbGZsb3d8eyJWIjoiMC4wLjAwMDAiLCJQIjoiV2luMzIiLCJBTiI6Ik1haWwiLCJXVCI6Mn0%3D%7C3000&sdata=uMvyZ5aR%2FCdCctHu8YCpt2bwby26%2B790IRngmIaUSmQ%3D&reserved=0 (accessed December 19, 2022).

Webb, Dominic and Jozepa, Ilze. (2022), *Government Policy on Freeports*, House of Commons Library, February 14. Available at: https://researchbriefings.files.parliament.uk/documents/CBP-8823/CBP-8823.pdf (accessed March 4, 2022).

Weeks, S. (2020), 'A Freeport Comes to Luxembourg, or, Why Those Wishing to Hide Assets Purchase Fine Art,' *Arts*, 9, no. 3: 87. https://doi.org/10.3390/arts9030087 (accessed July 23, 2023).

Wilkin, S. (2015), *Wealth Secrets of the 1%: The Truth about Money, Markets and Multi-Millionaires*, London: Sceptre.

Wingfield, B. (2010), 'Security Concerns of the Super-Rich,' *Forbes*, October 20. Available at: https://www.forbes.com/sites/brianwingfield/2010/10/20/security-concerns-of-the-super-rich/#4a0a258a4a70 (accessed May 7, 2018).

Zarobell, J. (2020), 'Freeports and the Hidden Value of Art,' *Arts*, 9, no. 4: 117. https://doi.org/10.3390/arts9040117 (accessed July 23, 2023).

Ying Zhu, Raneem Zaitoun, and Annamma Joy

7 Application of Blockchain Technology, NFTs, and Cryptocurrency in the Art and Luxury Industries

Introduction

In the past few years, both the art and luxury industries have embraced blockchain technology—and its implications, such as non-fungible tokens (NFTs) and cryptocurrency—as new ways to innovate marketing practices and attract consumers. In March 2021, Christie's auction house sold a collection of digital art by the artist Mike Winkelmann (aka Beeple) in the form of NFTs for US$69.3 million, the highest price ever paid for a digital artwork in history (Christie's, 2021a). As one of the first high-profile art sales, it received widespread attention from the general public and the media (e.g., reported by publications such as *The New York Times*, *Forbes*, and *Washington Post*). Weeks later, on April 4, 2021, the first digital timepiece was released for auction by Jacob & Co. as a three-dimensional, animated NFT; the SF24 Tourbillon NFT started at US$1,000 and sold for US$100,000 (Shirley, 2021). By April 2022, Jacob & Co., in collaboration with UNXD, an NFT marketplace for luxury products, had launched the Jacob & Co. Metaverse, hosting NFT collections and physical watches. The NFTs serve as exclusive membership passes to unlock future benefits and privileges (Jacob & Co., 2022). These events suggest a new era as blockchain-backed NFTs enter the realms of art and luxury.

Before exploring these business practices in more detail, we briefly introduce the concepts of blockchain technology, NFTs, and cryptocurrency. First, blockchain refers to digital records organized in blocks chained together by cryptography and stored on a network of computers (Narayanan et al., 2016). Blockchain technology is an innovative technology for record-keeping; it embraces a distributed, decentralized, and immutable digital ledger system that allows consumers to track assets and record transactions in a collaborative peer-to-peer network of computers without a central authority (Ahram et al., 2017; Niranjanamurthy et al., 2019). Second, NFTs are digital assets that are not interchangeable (i.e., non-fungible) and reside on the blockchain (Narayanan et al., 2016). Third, cryptocurrency is a digital currency that commonly uses blockchain technology to record and secure transactions (Härdle et al., 2020).

Blockchain technology is an ideal candidate for combating counterfeiting because it can prevent record tampering and provide provenance for artworks and luxury products (Joy et al., 2022). Because data recorded on the blockchain cannot be altered or deleted, the art and luxury industries are turning to this technology as a reliable and secure way to conduct transactions. For example, if an artist sells either digital art in the form of an NFT or physical art accompanied by an NFT to an art collector, a unique

https://doi.org/10.1515/9783110783933-007

digital identifier within the NFT allows the buyer to verify both the authenticity of the art/product and its ownership. If the art/product is sold, the transaction record (payment, quantity, and time) is stored in a decentralized digital ledger on the blockchain. Because both the NFT and the transaction record are stored on every computer across the blockchain network, the blockchain provides a transparent and secure way for sellers and buyers to track and verify NFTs and their associated business transactions, thereby reducing risks of fraud and counterfeiting. Thus, blockchain technology will likely be indispensable and reshape future businesses, especially in the art and luxury spaces.

The rest of the chapter is organized in the following ways. We begin by exploring the impact of blockchain technology and its implications, in the form of NFTs and cryptocurrency, on the structure of the art and luxury industries. By analyzing industry structures from a technology perspective, we can summarize foundational changes introduced by these technologies. We then outline five case studies in the art and luxury industries that delineate marketing practices related to blockchain technology, NFTs, and cryptocurrency. Although each of these technologies has merits, they can be misused by businesses and result in negative consequences. We address, in particular, the potential negative impact of these technologies on the environment, then conclude with directions for future studies, including both academic and practical questions and some challenges the art and luxury markets need to address regarding evolving technologies.

Disruptions of the Art Market by Blockchain, NFTs, and Cryptocurrency

In this section, we first describe the structure of the art market, followed by delineating the disruptions of the art market by blockchain, NFTs, and cryptocurrency. In the traditional art market, the key players are artists as creators; collectors, investors, and museums as buyers; and dealers, galleries, auction houses, curators, and art critics as intermediaries (Velthuis, 2011). Successful artists possess a combination of original ideas, marketing, and networking skills (Allen et al., 2022). To sell their work in the traditional art market, they must leverage network skills and work with dealers and gallerists, who act as their agents, build their reputations, provide opportunities to expose their artwork to more audiences, and exhibit their work to collectors (Velthuis, 2011).

Acting as liaisons between artists and buyers, dealers are the primary sellers of artists' work. It is not uncommon for dealers to share less than 50% of their profit with artists (Velthuis, 2011). Buyers purchase works at values set by the dealers; however, the worth of a piece can change depending on the opinion of influential critics in the market. Most artists are not paid until the gallery sells their work. Some artworks are sold at high prices to exclusive groups of art collectors, who tend to be wealthy, and their purchase decisions are likely influenced by seasoned art consultants who provide advice on the artistic and economic value of the work (Woodham, 2017). Because the goal of many collectors is to use art as a financial investment, they resell it to make a profit. Such practices tend to reduce owner transparency and traceability of the art.

However, the development of blockchain technology has shifted the structural paradigm surrounding key players such as artists, art critics, dealers, auction houses, and gallerists. Specifically, the advent of NFTs and cryptocurrency is changing the structure of the art world by reducing the need for traditional intermediaries (e.g., galleries). It also grants artists more freedom, greater transparency, and increased traceability of their work and alters the profit-sharing structure among players. We discuss some of these disruptions in detail.

First, blockchain technology enables artists' liberation and freedom of creation by reducing the roles of conventional intermediaries. Traditionally, artists might create portraits and sculptures to please the art market by tailoring them to the taste of influential art critics, gallerists, and auctioneers. Moreover, public discourse is shaped by critics' comments on particular works of art, thereby influencing public perceptions of what constitutes "good" art and determining how certain artists and their works are regarded (Arora & Vermeylen, 2013). Their commentary comes in several forms, including reviews, feature writing, and summaries. Critics, artists, dealers, and buyers all interact in this delicate ecosystem of exchange.

Due to the emergence of NFTs, the reduced needs of galleries, gallerists, and art critics from the industry also pushed traditional auction houses to establish digital art divisions and work collaboratively with new intermediaries such as OpenSea and Nifty Gateway to sell digital art. Renowned auction houses such as Christie's and Sotheby's have exhibited the NFT collections of emerging digital artists; Sotheby's developed its own metaverse for the exhibition and sale of digital art (Mattei, 2021). Christie's teamed up with OpenSea (Christie's, 2021b), and Sotheby's partnered with Nifty Gateway to sell their NFT collections (Akhtar, 2021). Following record sales in both auction houses, a significant investment in blockchain technology has accelerated the development of digital art. In this newly evolved industry, gallerists face a situation where they are no longer needed. Art critics are also urged to understand this new art form; however, unlike in traditional art realms, influential personnel have not yet emerged to shape this new generation's perceptions of digital art in the form of NFTs.

Second, NFT artists, compared to traditional artists, have more freedom to create self-expressive artwork and receive strong support from decentralized art communities. Access to NFT art is no longer limited to a private group of wealthy individuals on an exclusive collector list because NFTs are available for any consumer to purchase on the Internet's open market. In particular, the introduction of NFTs in the art market could reshape the traditional path to becoming a successful artist. Instead of heavily depending on a gallerist's connections for exposure, an artist's NFT network sets the discourse around a piece of artwork. Through community referrals, the artist can gain recognition and engagement. Rather than leaning intensively on reviews by traditional art critics, consumers can practice due diligence in discovering an artist through their networks, media publications, and features. Digital art communities weaken the need for gallerists, agents, and critics to authenticate artists and their work prior to purchasing (Belk et al., 2022). Artists rely less on the approval of art critics for industry recognition in the digital world. Reducing once-integral roles (e.g., the art critic, gallerist, and auction house) could potentially enhance artistic freedom and expand the market's consumer base.

Third, the emergence of NFTs has altered the art market's consumer base, changing the structure of the profit-sharing model among artists, dealers, gallerists, critics, and curators. Traditionally, when setting the value of art pieces, critics are sometimes regarded as more important than the artists themselves (Allen et al., 2022). It is not uncommon that dealers reap up to 50% of the profit on any piece of work, and gallerists determine an artist's collector list, art valuation, and the promotion strategy of the art (Velthuis, 2011). Because of the structural change due to NFTs, critics, dealers, and gallerists exert less influence on pricing and receive less profit. The advent of blockchain technology promotes new market structures that provide artists with greater autonomy and flexibility. Artists can market their own NFTs, determine their clientele, and receive all the profits from the sale of their creations (van Haaften-Schick & Whitaker, 2022). They no longer rely substantially on dealers and gallerists to pay them a fraction of the sales price of their artwork.

Disruptions in profit distribution among gallerists and dealers have affected not only primary markets but also secondary markets. In addition to maximizing profits from the sale of their work at the primary market, artists can now receive royalty fees from the resale of their NFTs. In particular, NFT artists can utilize smart contracts, a critical component of blockchain technology, to generate income from the secondary market when the artwork sells again. Smart contracts are transaction protocols created to execute, govern, and document legally substantial activities and events based on the terms and conditions specified in a contract or an agreement without the need for human intervention (Khan et al., 2021). Artists can write the royalties into the smart contract that provides self-contained enforcement of royalties through private agreement (cf. legislation). Smart contracts are straightforward to execute since they do not rely on trust in transaction participants, intermediaries, or governmental entities (van Haaften-Schick & Whitaker, 2022). On the OpenSea platform, creators of NFTs can establish resale royalties up to 10%, with the platform taking 2.5% of each transaction in 2021 (Ashmore, 2022). Recent platforms such as Nifty Gateway and SuperRare have adopted similar resale royalty rates for creators (van Haaften-Schick & Whitaker, 2022).

Although blockchains have afforded digital artists increased autonomy due to their decentralized nature and the separation of "voice" from centralized control, it is important to recognize the possibility of control from newly established entities (e.g.,

NFT marketplace). For example, OpenSea, as one of the largest NFT marketplaces, in February 2023, decided to temporarily suspend its fees and replace its full support on loyalties (e.g., typically 5%–10%) with optional creator earnings with a minimum of 0.5% (Hayward, 2023). This indicates a new market structure involving artists, intermediaries, and buyers.

Fourth, although NFTs are rich with meaning, they do not follow the same technique as traditional art forms, especially for tangible art pieces (e.g., paintings and sculptures) that require certain physical materials. Specifically, since NFTs are digital based, even a 3D NFT piece does not involve physical materials. As digital artists do not need to purchase physical art materials such as brushes, canvas, and paint, or develop relationships with art suppliers, the supply chain dynamics for digital artists would diverge significantly from those of traditional artists. Consequently, NFT art also cannot be analyzed and evaluated by art critics in the same way as traditional art. The conventional approach to evaluating artists' proficiency by analyzing their use of materials and their command of artistic techniques, including brushwork and blending, may not be applicable to digital artists. However, to date, there are very few notable art critics who review NFTs and crypto collectibles, and there is no established criterion in the art industry for evaluating NFT art. Consequently, consumers are beginning to formulate their own interpretations and significance in relation to NFTs.

Disruptions of the Luxury Market by Blockchain, NFTs, and Cryptocurrency

The luxury market, especially luxury fashion, is renowned for its innovation, brand heritage, and expensive garments. Luxury brands always have been in the business of fabricating elaborate designs for affluent collectors and consumers. In the traditional luxury market, designers are at the forefront of luxury fashion operations. They are the artists behind each piece of work. Designers associate with luxury brand labels, for which they create innovative works of fashion. Prominent designers have the power to lead discourse, push fashion trends into the market, and exhibit their work through various productions.

A designer's work comes to life in the hands of manufacturers or producers. Most luxury brands manufacture their products in locations in which they have access to high-quality fabrics, expert craftsmanship, and reputable production facilities. From manufacturer to retailer, luxury brands operate in major shopping outlets worldwide (Fionda & Moore, 2009). Buyers of luxury brands have expanded to include upper middle-class clientele who are looking for exhibit pieces by reputable brands. Despite representing a small portion of the population, this group of buyers will pay exorbitant amounts of capital for products, thus attributing to the industry's global revenue of €353 billion in 2022 (Statista, 2023).

However, with the advent of blockchain technology, a shift occurred in the structure and operations of the luxury market. First, the imposition of blockchain technology is breaking down barriers to success for emerging designers in the traditional fashion sector. Designers no longer rely mainly on fashion critics or fashion houses for recognition. Now blockchain technology is acting as a medium for creative freedom. For instance, platforms such as OpenSea create spaces for designers to showcase their NFT designs to interested collectors. Fashion brands no longer feel the need to use their in-house designers to create NFTs; rather, they search for popular metaverse or NFT fashion designers to collaborate with because these designers may appeal to consumers beyond the traditional luxury fashion sector.

Second, evaluations of brand reputation have shifted from being based primarily on the quality of tangible goods or the longevity of organizations to including innovation within the product line. Accordingly, high-quality fabrics, expert craftsmanship, and reputable manufacturing will not appeal to NFT consumers as much as they did to traditional fashion consumers. Because digital assets do not require the purchase and production of high-quality materials, blockchain and NFTs have commenced a new age of revolutionary virtual designs that appeal to social media norms. Consumers buy NFT-based digital products for hedonic reasons and to convey their social status and prestige to others, particularly when they aspire to be early adopters of such advanced technological products within their social circles (Sestino et al., 2022). Designers take the place of luxury fashion brands in their ability to display consumer trendiness and social ranking.

Third, the transition to the luxury NFT market implies that shifts in consumer tastes may result in a larger market share for emerging digital designers among younger consumers in the luxury industry than previously anticipated. According to a study by Centra Research, Gen Z consumers represent the majority of the digital fashion market (Stern, 2022). These young consumers differ from conventional retail customers because they care more about showing off their products on social media than owning physical products (Brun, Kishan, & Umer, 2021). As a result, they are more inclined to purchase digital pieces from innovative NFT designers than traditional fashion houses.

As a generation born into the digital age, innovative digital fashion brands such as Republique, along with traditional fashion houses, are recognizing such trends by curating NFT pieces that can be bought solely for sharing them on social media platforms. Specifically, consumers can purchase the NFTs, add them to their posts, and publish them online without ever owning any tangible items. Traditionally, digital assets have been valued less than physical objects as they fail to produce a strong feeling of psychological ownership (Atasoy & Morewedge, 2018) and cannot provide sensory feedback. However, NFT consumers, such as Gen Z, value the unique ownership of the NFT that can be verified on the blockchain (Hofstetter et al., 2022). As Gen

Z moves toward NFT fashion, luxury brands implement new marketing strategies, such as promoting the use of NFTs as their social media profile photo or the purchase of NFT wearables for their avatars in the metaverse.

Fourth, digital luxury fashion NFTs are created distinctively, produced exclusively by an artist, and scarce in supply. This creates a scarcity appeal for consumers as they are the sole owners of a particular NFT. Fashion houses such as Louis Vuitton are leveraging the current generation's fascination with blockchain technology by collaborating with NFT designers and gaming entities to introduce fresh aesthetics for their brands. Louis Vuitton's NFT product line features limited-edition models that make use of Gen Z's desire for uniqueness and scarcity (Cho et al., 2021). Balenciaga and Burberry also have launched their own NFT collections outside their product lines.

Moreover, runways and showrooms embedded into the metaverse platform make it easy for consumers to purchase pieces using augmented reality. In December 2020, Balenciaga created a virtual reality (VR) video game called "Afterworld: The Age of Tomorrow," which featured a virtual fashion showroom where players could browse and purchase items (Mower, 2020). In May 2021, Gucci launched a virtual fashion show called "Gucci Garden" on Roblox, an online game platform; the show featured virtual versions of the brand's history, real-life designs, and viewers could interact with the environment in real time and purchase the digital products (McDowell, 2021).

In addition to introducing NFTs, luxury fashion brands accept payment in nontraditional currencies such as cryptocurrencies ranging from Bitcoin (BTC) to Ether (ETH), Litecoin, Dogecoin, Shiba Inu, and ApeCoin. Gucci is leading the trend by accepting cryptocurrencies such as BTC and ETH in locations including but not limited to Los Angeles, New York, Las Vegas, Atlanta, and Miami, starting in May 2022 (Sottile, 2022). Following Gucci's footsteps, Balenciaga also announced the acceptance of Bitcoin as payment in May 2022 (Amick, 2022). Farfetch Ltd., an online luxury marketplace, followed suit with this trend by accepting cryptocurrencies such as Bitcoin, Ether, and Binance Coin in June 2022. In August 2022, Gucci became the first luxury brand to accept payment in ApeCoin, the Bored Ape Yacht Club-affiliated cryptocurrency. Luxury brands are also exploring cryptocurrency as a potential strategy to engage a new generation of wealthy buyers (Moss, 2022).

Case Studies

Louis Vuitton

Louis Vuitton is a luxury fashion brand founded in 1854, specializing in handbags, shoes, watches, accessories, and clothing (Vuitton, 2022). It began its journey by manufacturing luggage for Paris' elite. The brand remains renowned for its light canvas material, flat-topped trunks, and unique designs, including the distinctive tumbler lock and monogram canvas (Vuitton, 2022). Over time, Louis Vuitton gained world-wide respect for its collaborations with emerging artists and state-of-the-art fragrance collections, designer clothing, and accessories and has been recognized as one of the world's most valuable luxury brands (Davis, 2020).

Despite being a traditional luxury fashion brand, Louis Vuitton has launched several digital initiatives to integrate innovative technologies. One of its first business applications of blockchain technology was to enhance the authenticity of its products. In April 2021, along with Cartier and Prada, the company collaborated with Aura Blockchain Consortium to develop solutions to fight counterfeiting by allowing consumers to authenticate their purchased products using digital certificates (Danziger, 2021; Paton, 2021). According to the Managing Director of Louis Vuitton's parent company LVMH (Rascouet, 2021), by providing consumers with encrypted certificates of guarantee, the company can verify the authenticity of products and ensure they are not counterfeit. Digital certificates show products' journeys from beginning to end, providing information about the raw materials used, places of manufacture, and the locations in which the products were purchased (Sekhose, 2021).

The second digital initiative was to launch NFTs. In 2021, a Louis Vuitton digital initiative featured 30 NFTs in a video game known as "Louis" to celebrate founder Louis Vuitton's two hundredth birthday; the game uses NFT arts to help portray the journey of the company's young founder (Block 2021). The video game follows a mascot named Vivienne as it collects candles set against a unique terrain resembling the monogram of the brand (Lee, 2021). Once unlocked, each candle depicts the historical event of the brand in the young founder's journey of building the company. Among the 30 NFTs, ten were designed by the well-known NFT artist Beeple to be collectibles (Ledger Insights, 2021). The Louis Vuitton monogram appears throughout the game, and players may alter the color schemes and patterns of their characters. The game also informs players about the fashion house's history through historical postcards and memorabilia (Block, 2021).

The third initiative includes enhancing consumer experience through the metaverse and utilizing Web3 technology. Specifically, Louis Vuitton is moving beyond physical fashion pieces toward digital assets in the metaverse; its transition to Web3 technology is a new way to target younger consumers. Web3 is the third iteration of the World Wide Web built upon blockchain technology and creates a new version of the Internet that is decentralized, democratic, and peer-to-peer (Stackpole, 2022). Web3 allows hard-to-impress, innovative Gen Z customers to be engaged in a challenging game and take part in the brand's culture without the need for purchase (Sestino et al., 2022). This initiative is taking Louis Vuitton's exclusive, traditional brand to new heights by introducing it to a new and growing customer base.

Louis Vuitton's utilization of NFT and gamification strategies highlights the potential social benefits that NFTs and games present to conventional luxury companies. By incorporating gamification into its collection, the fashion brand displayed its readiness to explore innovative digital avenues, aiming to appeal to tech-savvy, younger consumers, thus drawing in a fresh cohort of luxury fashion enthusiasts. Selling NFTs or their matching clothing was not the sole goal of the NFT collecting game. Louis Vuitton aims to teach younger users about the legacy of their brand, thus building the latest generation of the luxury fashion community (Vuitton, 2022).

Burberry

Burberry is a British luxury garment company renowned for its winter wear. The founder, Thomas Burberry, launched Burberry to manufacture clothing suited to British weather in 1856. Burberry designs and sells a range of fashionable items ready to be worn, such as leather accessories, shoes, and the brand's iconic trench coats (Burberry, n.d.). Burberry was among the pioneering luxury fashion brands that recognized the importance of incorporating digital technologies into its marketing strategies (Marr, 2017). As early as 2006, Burberry underwent a transformation from an underperforming luxury brand to a successful one by consolidating multiple websites into a singular platform that serves as the centerpiece of its branding and marketing; such strategic change proved successful, as evidenced by a doubling of its revenues within five years, reaching $3 billion by 2012 (Ahrendts, 2013). Burberry also became the first luxury fashion brand to make significant investments in social media and the first to utilize cutting-edge 3D broadcasting technology to concurrently broadcast its fashion show live from London to five cities around the world in 2010 (Phan, Thomas, & Heine, 2011).

As a pioneer in digital transformation for luxury fashion brands, Burberry continuously embraces advanced technologies such as blockchain, NFTs, and the metaverse to enhance the authenticity and traceability of its products and improve customer engagement. To offer consumers more transparency of its apparel, Burberry exploits blockchain technology by partnering with an IBM internship to develop a prototype tracking system named Voyage using blockchain and cloud technologies; this system gives customers more insight into the manufacturing process and life cycle of a particular clothing item by allowing consumers to identify garments by either scanning a near field communication (NFC) tag or manually typing in product information (Lee, 2020). Voyage not only helps verify the authenticity of Burberry products but also enables customers to gain additional information about products, such as materials used to manufacture the clothes (Dawson, 2020).

Burberry again engages its consumers by creating NFT games and building communities. In particular, Burberry partnered with Mythical Games to initiate a multiplayer game under its flagship title, "Blankos Block Party," featuring a Burberry NFT collection and digital characters known as Blankos that exist on a blockchain (Burberry, 2021). In the game, consumers can acquire, trade, and resell Blankos as unique digital assets, and upgrade characters while competing with family and friends through various mini-games. One of the most famous characters from the Blankos Block Party game is Sharky B, and all 750-piece limited-edition Shark B characters in NFT were sold in its first 30 seconds of release, with each priced at US$299.99 (McDowell, 2022). Burberry also sells additional accessories in the form of NFTs for each character, including armbands and bracelets that can be applied and resold. Burberry's effective engagement of consumers through non-fungible tokens (NFTs) was further demonstrated in Tmall's Single's Day Metaverse Art Exhibition, one of the largest e-commerce platforms in China, where Burberry provided a limited collection of NFTs featuring an animated deer adorned with Burberry scarves that was utilized to promote their physical products (Tan, 2021).

To further enhance the consumer experience, Burberry became an early adopter of the metaverse. In November 2022, it partnered with Minecraft to introduce a physical and digital collection named Burberry: Freedom To Go Beyond (Tan, 2022). The purpose of utilizing metaverse games is well summarized by Burberry, such that by merging the virtual and physical worlds, Burberry and Minecraft foster self-expression within communities and provide gamers with customizable outfits and tools for them to design avatars (Finney, 2022). Burberry's digital strategies were acknowledged through the bestowal of the Fashion Award for Metaverse World and Gaming Experience by a global panel of industry specialists in December 2022 (Chitrakorn, 2022).

Balenciaga

Balenciaga, a prominent luxury fashion house, was founded by Cristobal Balenciaga, a Spanish designer, in 1919 (Balenciaga, 2011). Cristóbal Balenciaga, a venerated figure and pioneer in the realm of fashion during the 1950s, was renowned for his innovative approach to dress forms in women's haute couture and was coined "The Master" of haute couture (Victoria and Albert Museum, n.d.). The brand, recognized for its iconic bubble skirt designs, offers an assortment of ready-to-wear clothing, footwear, handbags, and fragrances and has been praised for its innovative practices by the traditional luxury industry (Walker, 2006).

Balenciaga has ventured into the realm of blockchain technology with a novel approach. It has collaborated with the video game Fortnite to enter the NFT and digital gaming space, producing in-game items and an exclusive collection of physical garments in the form of NFTs (Siegfried, 2022). Its first collaboration with the brand came in Fortnite's original game, "Afterworld: The Age of Tomorrow" (Anyanwu, 2021). Players could customize their game characters' skin or purchase real garments; gamers who purchase the full physical garment receive matching compatible skins for their characters. Each digital skin costs US$102 (Siegfried, 2022). These purchases can be made through the Fortnite store or the Balenciaga store.

In addition to custom outfits, players receive special Balenciaga dances to apply to their characters and to show off to other players (Yotka, 2021). Gamers also can customize their looks in the Balenciaga store for the chance to be featured in Fortnite Times Square. In-game designs are based on existing 3D Balenciaga looks (Nast, 2021). This initiative opened a new door for Balenciaga to interact with younger consumers, especially Gen Z. By using NFTs to create a new type of gaming experience, the company was able to engage with its customers more immersively and interactively.

Balenciaga also revealed its adoption of cryptocurrency, including Bitcoin and Ethereum, as a mode of payment, initially implemented at its prime retail stores situated on Rodeo Drive in Beverly Hills and Madison Avenue in New York, with plans for subsequent rollout via online channels in 2022 (Amick, 2022). By enabling the acceptance of cryptocurrencies as a payment option, Balenciaga may successfully appeal to customers interested in such currencies, including those who possess cryptocurrency investments (Bringé, 2022).

Balenciaga made the strategic decision to join the thriving luxury resale market trend. According to an industry report, in 2021, the global luxury resale market was estimated to be worth US$32.61 billion and is anticipated to expand to US$51.77 billion in 2026 (Research and Markets, 2022). In September 2022, Balenciaga joined forces with Reflaunt to introduce a resale initiative for its previously owned clothing and accessories (Benissan, 2022). Balenciaga's partnership with Reflaunt leverages blockchain technology to facilitate the resale of second-hand garments and has the potential to make a significant contribution to the circular economy, an economic system based on reuse, recycling, repair, and regeneration of materials or products (Geissdoerfer et al., 2017; Pearce & Turner, 1989). The Reflaunt platform enables consumers to buy and sell preowned Balenciaga items securely and transparently, reducing the environmental impact of fast fashion and waste disposal. Additionally, the use of blockchain technology ensures the authenticity of each item and enables traceability, which can help eliminate the circulation of counterfeit products (de Boissieu et al., 2021).

Furthermore, according to Balenciaga, its collaboration with Reflaunt is also a step towards fulfilling its mission of being a sustainable enterprise and promoting environmentally friendly practices such as reuse, recycling, and waste reduction (Benissan, 2022). By embracing circular economy principles through this innovative platform, Balenciaga can promote sustainability and environmental responsibility in the fashion industry while satisfying consumer demand for luxury fashion at a reduced cost.

The recent strategic move of the luxury fashion brands such as Louis Vuitton, Burberry, and Balenciaga signify their adept understanding of the potency of NFT and gaming platforms and their ability to leverage the metaverse to elevate the perceived value of fashion products. The luxury fashion industry can potentially capitalize on this emerging market to enhance its marketing efforts and increase the value of its merchandise. Therefore, the actions of luxury fashion brands demonstrate the potential for fashion and gaming to synergistically enhance each other's value propositions.

Christie's Auction House

As one of the leading auction houses, Christie's showcases and sells artwork by renowned artists and collectors through its auctions. Established in 1766, Christie's has hosted historic sales, such as the auction of the "Salvator Mundi" by Leonardo Da Vinci (McLeod, 2008). Christie's history, sale of historic art, and prestige have made it prominent in the traditional art world (McLeod, 2008).

Recently, the auction house has incorporated new digital strategies built on blockchain technology and expanded its exhibitions to include digital artwork. Since blockchain technology could provide the auction house with a decentralized and transparent system for recording transactions, it is an ideal solution for the art world, where transparency and provenance are crucial. Thus, in 2018, Christie's teamed up with Artory, a blockchain digital registry, for the art industry, to register artwork sales on the blockchain, creating a tamper-proof ledger of transactions and ensuring that all information about art pieces is accurate and reliable (Registry, 2018).

By partnering with Artory, Christie's aimed to leverage the immutability feature of blockchain to ensure a secure, encrypted certification of the art transaction. Artory's platform promoting transparency in the art world through its digital registry of precise information regarding artworks and collectibles helped facilitate the smooth implementation of this forward-thinking initiative by Christie's. This collaboration demonstrates Christie's early involvement with blockchain technology as a means of enhancing the security and integrity of its operations.

Christie's also has been proactive in exploring the potential of NFTs in the art market by creating new opportunities for artists, collectors, and investors. Christie's generated nearly $150 million in sales from over 100 NFTs in 2021 and achieved its highest sales in the past five years (Christie's, 2021c). As previously noted, a noteworthy NFT collection auctioned at Christie's was curated and published by Beeple, an unorthodox digital artist who sells artwork that touches on socio-political commentary; the collection includes a collage of Beeple's first 5,000 days of work, which sold for over US$69.3 million in March 2021 (Calma, 2021).

The auction house's expansion into the NFT art format attracted an unconventional collector base and Web3 artist list. According to Neda Whitney, Christie's Head of Marketing for the Americas, incorporating NFTs into the art market has enabled the auction house to attract a substantial number of new buyers, with 74% of its customers being new to Christie's and 72% of those who participated in bidding and purchasing NFTs also new to Christie's in 2021 (Bruell, 2021). By using blockchain technology to establish ownership and provenance, NFTs increase transparency and reduce fraud in art transactions (Valeonti et al., 2021). NFTs also provide artists with a new revenue stream by allowing them to retain a portion of the profits from subsequent resales of their works (Malik et al., 2023) and provide consumers with more payment options by accepting cryptocurrencies (Tarmy, 2021).

In addition to digital art exhibitions, Christie's has launched a Web3 investment fund known as "Christie's Ventures." The fund enables digital artists and companies to increase the "seamless technological consumption of art" (Christie's, 2022). It concentrates on funding goods or services that address business issues, enhance client relationships, and increase development prospects for the art market as a whole and for interactions within it (Christie's, 2022).

Through implementing digital strategies built on blockchain technology, Christie's demonstrates how advanced technology can enhance and transform traditional markets while creating new value for stakeholders in the art world. Furthermore, Christie's integration of technology into traditional markets appeals to a younger, more tech-savvy audience. This trend highlights the potential for digital innovation to create new opportunities and interest in established art industries, expanding the consumer base and driving the market growth.

Sotheby's Auction House

Established in 1744, Sotheby's is recognized as one of the most ancient global auction houses specializing in fine art. The firm generated US$7.3 billion in sales through its 80-office global network in 2021 (Sotheby's, 2021a). This auction house is known for its impact on traditional and modern art, such as through its sales of masterpieces throughout the nineteenth and twentieth centuries, including Pablo Picasso's "Garçon à la pipe" (i.e., Boy With a Pipe) which sold in a New York auction house for US$104.2 million in 2004, and the artwork entitled "Silver Car Crash (Double Disaster)" by Warhol which was sold for a staggering US$108.4 million in 2013 (Sotheby's, n.d.a).

With the advent of blockchain technology, the traditional art market structure has shifted to encompass digital art assets, including NFTs and crypto collectibles. Over the past years, as Sotheby's sought to capitalize on the surge in interest in blockchain-based art assets, it has teamed up with crypto artists, curators, and collectors. Specifically, the longest-standing traditional art house effectively adapts to the rapidly shifting art space by auctioning a series of NFT collections by well-known digital artists (Mattei, 2021).

One of the most significant ways Sotheby's has adopted NFTs is through its partnership with digital artists. In April 2021, its debut NFT sale featured Pak, a crypto designer and digital artist, and Pak's "The Fungible" collection attracted over 3,000 new buyers to Sotheby's and generated more than US$16.8 million in sales (Chandra & Belk, 2022). A few months later, in September, Sotheby's conducted an online auction of 107 cartoon apes from the Bored Ape Yacht Club NFTs collection, which sold for $24.4 million (Howcroft, 2021). These cases are a testament to the high demand for digital arts and highlight Sotheby's successful collaboration with digital artists and experts in selling NFTs.

In addition to its partnerships with artists and NFT marketplaces, Sotheby's has begun to create its own metaverse and launched it as a platform exclusively for its NFT sale in October 2021 (Sotheby's, n.d.b). Utilizing its strengths in innovation, Sotheby's incorporates more marketing features in its metaverse than the common features (e.g., transaction history of the NFT) in other metaverse platforms such as OpenSea;

these new features include providing the artist's biography and a description of each NFT's significance, and, most creatively, offering registered metaverse users a unique profile picture designed by a well-known NFT artist, Pak (Registry, 2018).

Sotheby's metaverse is a significant milestone for the NFT market, as it demonstrated the established auction house's willingness to embrace new digital technologies to expand its offerings and reach new audiences outside the traditional art market. Specifically, the platform serves as an additional avenue for artists to exhibit their work and provides a gateway for younger consumers to the art world, which they might not have experienced in the conventional art space. With its innovative ethos, Sotheby's further leveraged its metaverse platform to organize an NFT charity auction to support front-line health workers during the COVID pandemic through a nonprofit organization, Sostento, in November 2021 (Dickens, 2021).

Sotheby's adoption of blockchain technology also has enabled it to expand its payment method for physical arts. Sotheby's has embraced cryptocurrency through its partnership with Coinbase, an online platform for buying, selling, and trading cryptocurrencies. In May 2021, the company announced it would accept payment for an upcoming auction of a physical painting from street artist Banksy in Bitcoin and Ether (Stankiewicz, 2021). For instance, in May 2021, "Love is in The Air" by Banksy was sold for $12.9 million and became the first physical art that accepted cryptocurrency as a payment (Sotheby's, 2021b). By accepting cryptocurrency, Sotheby's was able to appeal to a new generation of tech-savvy clients who prefer to use digital currencies. This move was a significant cornerstone in integrating blockchain technology into the art industry by being one of the first major auction houses to accept cryptocurrency as payment for artwork (Dolan, 2021). These practices demonstrated Sotheby's commitment to staying ahead of the curve with regard to new technologies.

Art and luxury industries recognize the growing importance of blockchain technology, NFTs, and cryptocurrencies; they have quickly incorporated them into their operations. By embracing new technologies, these industries are meeting the changing needs of their clients and expanding their reach to new audiences. Their adoption of these advanced technologies clearly indicates that the technologies are becoming an increasingly important part of the art and luxury markets and have the potential to transform how art and luxury brands are bought, sold, and owned.

Additional Marketing Implications of Adopting Advanced Technologies

Community is integral to the livelihoods of artists and designers who use blockchain technology. Unlike the traditional luxury fashion or art sector, where designers and artists heavily depend on an exclusive list of wealthy consumers to purchase their products at exorbitant rates, in the digital realm, designers' and artists' communities could determine the value of their work and influence the types of art they create

(Colicev, 2023). Namely, the democratization of art and luxury fashion allows members of artist or designer communities to locate, review, and criticize pieces of work publicly (Wang, 2021). As a result, it has become easier than ever for artists and designers to track consumer behaviour and receive feedback on their digital products (Colicev, 2023). Such feedback and the needs of the community can drive the types of collections the artists and designers release.

Successful NFT artists or designers are those who can serve their communities (Gaur and Gaiha, 2020). Unlike the marketplaces of conventional artists and designers, NFT marketplaces and metaverse communities allow artists/designers to provide exclusive benefits and services to their collectors (Colicev, 2023). Adopting the notion of a "drop" from the fashion world, artists and designers have invented a new terminology, the "NFT drop." By utilizing NFT drops, they create excitement within NFT communities. Like Nike's drops of new shoe designs, an NFT drop implies the release of a collection of NFTs at a specific date and time for purchase. Typically, in successful NFT drops, purchasers receive invitations to member-only gatherings, discussion forums, or even gaming platforms, reinforcing the NFTs' sense of community (Kirjavainen, 2022). This sense contrasts with traditional, physical item purchase scenarios which end at checkout. Added benefits and services make digital assets more desirable and, in turn, increase their worth (Kirjavainen, 2022). They also foster longer-term customer connections (Colicev, 2023). Renowned fashion or auction houses that were once alien to the public can now form more diverse communities that go beyond the inner circles of collectors.

NFT games present new opportunities to conventional luxury and art companies from a social and community building perspective. The gamification of a traditional luxury company's collection demonstrates the willingness of the fashion house to forge new digital paths in an effort to appeal to young, tech-savvy consumers and attract a newer generation of luxury fashion enthusiasts. However, selling NFTs or their matching clothing is not the sole goal of the NFT collecting game; Louis Vuitton aims to teach younger users about the legacy of the brand and build a new generation of the luxury fashion community (Vuitton, 2022).

The advent of blockchain technology also allows traditional luxury brands and auction houses to engage with much younger consumers (Sestino et al., 2022). As mentioned earlier, Balenciaga has collaborated with a children's video game to design NFT fashion items for characters in Fortnite, one of the most popular video games. Balenciaga has integrated its designs into the character skins for a minimal price. Players can purchase skins and receive physical clothing to match their characters. Other traditional fashion houses, such as Burberry and Louis Vuitton, have launched similar initiatives. Their collaboration with popular NFT designers or video games caters to younger communities of consumers looking to purchase their designs.

Environmental Impact

Luxury fashion brands have been criticized for being engaged in "fast fashion," the mass manufacturing and distribution of inexpensive clothing, to supply their outlets with the latest trends. Fast fashion accounts for 20% of global wastewater and half a million tons of microplastic waste, and approximately 92 million tons of waste generated annually are associated with clothing (Mulhern, 2022). Concerns about its environmental impact thus are prominent.

Luxury brands have started to adopt blockchain technology to innovate and expect to divert consumers' attention from the negative environmental impact of fast fashion. However, notably, art and luxury fashion organizations could increase their carbon footprints by operating in energy-intensive blockchain and capitalizing on NFTs, metaverse, and cryptocurrencies while continuing the fast-fashion practices that increase environmental waste. By expanding into NFT projects, luxury fashion brands might consume more energy than their traditional operations. In 2020, a single NFT on Ethereum could consume 340 kWh of energy and generate 211 kg of carbon dioxide (CO_2) (Akten 2020).

Consumers may not be aware of the harmful environmental consequences of blockchain technology, as its endeavors are marketed under the facade of being environmentally sustainable. This process, known as "metawashing," implicates luxury brands tend to market their blockchain initiatives as a globally conscious solution to wasteful fashion practices. They claim that the reduction of material in manufacturing and decrease in fuel for distribution makes NFT shopping an environmentally conscious practice. But such claims downplay the energy-intensive system used to power their digital assets; Ethereum, a blockchain platform that enables NFTs, required 23 million MWh before its system upgrade in September 2022 (Crypto Carbon Ratings Institute [CCRI], 2022). To provide context, 23 million MWh is sufficient to sustain 1.58 million Canadians for a year, given that in Canada the annual electricity consumption per capita was 14.6 MWh in 2017 (Canada Energy Regulator 2021). Although Ethereum has successfully managed to decrease its electricity consumption by 99.9% by shifting from the high-energy Proof of Work consensus protocol to the low-energy Proof of Stake, numerous other blockchain platforms continue to rely on the energy-intensive mechanism (CCRI, 2022).

When consumers purchase luxury brand NFTs, their cryptocurrency payments create alarming carbon footprints. The integration of runways or showrooms onto the metaverse also imposes pollution on the environment through high energy consumption. The metaverse currently creates over 626,000 pounds of carbon dioxide annually, five times greater than the total amount of greenhouse gases emitted by a vehicle throughout its lifespan (Rosenberg, 2022). Over a decade, luxury brands and auction houses' operations in the metaverse will contribute to millions of pounds of carbon dioxide emissions. The luxury fashion industry is not the only sector to face this issue.

Artists and auction houses release substantial amounts of carbon dioxide emissions through their sales of NFT art pieces on marketplaces such as OpenSea. Although artists are replacing their material paintings or sculptures with digital art, they are not reducing their carbon footprints. The majority of their NFT work is powered using Ethereum (White, Mahanti, & Passi 2022). The multiple collections of NFTs that artists release can be even more energy-intensive than traditional art pieces in payment transactions. Auction houses that use metaverse platforms are also increasing their carbon footprints by displaying digital art collections. For example, Christie's investment fund backs blockchain technology startups that enable digital art—a feat that increases the pollution produced by the auction house.

Conclusions

Blockchain technology is revolutionizing the operation and production of art and luxury fashion industries. We investigate the adoption of blockchain technology, NFTs, and cryptocurrencies in these industries through a practical lens. By analyzing five cases, Louis Vuitton, Burberry, Balenciaga, Christie's, and Sotheby's, we delineate the marketing practices and environmental impacts associated with the applications of these new technologies. Our case studies show that the art and luxury fashion industries gradually integrate blockchain, NFTs, and cryptocurrency into their portfolios and operations. In particular, renowned art houses and luxury fashion brands are employing NFTs to attract new consumer bases, enhance customer engagement, and increase product innovation. The emergence of blockchain technology in these industries pushes the boundaries of innovation and poses structural implications and environmental hurdles.

Our research combines existing knowledge of the structure of the art and luxury fashion sectors, prospective views on the NFT market, and environmental analyses of blockchain technology to reveal the implications of advanced technologies in the art and luxury fashion domains, thereby contributing to the current knowledge on the subject. We also summarize the latest marketing techniques and strategies related to these implications and how art and luxury fashion industries use them to attract a younger demographic and sustain relevancy in a fast-paced digitized environment.

Our study reveals the transformation of art and luxury industries as a result of the emergence of blockchain technology, NFTs, the metaverse, and Web3 implications. However, it is important to highlight that the digital art and luxury fashion markets are relatively nascent, and the technologies utilized are constantly evolving. Therefore, continuous research is imperative in the domains of digital fashion and art NFTs to stay current on the latest marketing implications, benefits of innovative technologies, and impending legal developments.

Limitations and Future Research

Our study has several limitations. First, because the blockchain technology sector, along with the luxury fashion and art industry, are continuously advancing, our results should be assessed according to current timing. We analyze only a series of art and luxury fashion initiatives within the digital space, and our sample size is small. Larger-scale empirical studies could help validate our findings. Since our case study relies on content analyses and is exploratory, we urge scholars to conduct interviews and focus groups with leaders in the art and luxury industries to reveal the reasons behind the adoption of blockchain technology, NFTs, cryptocurrency, the metaverse, and Web3.

Second, because we solely review initiatives of blockchain, NFTs, and cryptocurrency that intersect with the luxury and art industries and are available to the public, our findings could possess bias in terms of generalizability. Research should continue to investigate new digital initiatives and compare them with existing initiatives as well as examine initiatives outside of the art and luxury domains. The short- and long-term effects of luxury fashion and art NFT initiatives and adoption of blockchain technology on sales, brand image, and company reputation, as well as on the environment and society, are inconclusive and also need further investigation.

The final barrier to this research is the complexity of the industries themselves. The luxury fashion industry, traditional art industry, and blockchain technology sector feature various conditions with unique implications for this study. Our study delves into how luxury fashion brands and auction houses have integrated advanced technologies; we encourage future research to examine the external factors that influence consumers to purchase NFTs directly from artists and designers. An empirical study of the behaviors of NFT consumer groups is needed to clarify how blockchain technology can revolutionize the luxury fashion and art industry, whether it can be marketed to other consumer groups, and why it interests a niche group of consumers.

As blockchain technology gains attraction, consumers have shown excitement about NFTs, cryptocurrency, and the metaverse. Although brands have begun their transition to Web3, there is only limited data on the number of luxury fashion brands and art houses that are utilizing NFTs, trading cryptocurrency, and expanding their brands into the metaverse. Such topics are worth studying. As blockchain technology advances technically and socially, future studies should focus on the evolving environmental and social concerns surrounding the innovations that reside in the blockchain.

References

Ahrendts, A. (2013, August 1). *Burberry's CEO on turning an aging British icon into a global luxury brand*. Harvard Business Review. Retrieved March 26, 2022, from https://hbr.org/2013/01/burberrys-ceo-on-turning-an-aging-british-icon-into-a-global-luxury-brand

Ahram, T., Sargolzaei, A., Sargolzaei, S., Daniels, J., & Amaba, B. (2017). Blockchain Technology Innovations, in *2017 IEEE Technology & Engineering Management Conference (TEMSCON)*, 137–41.

Akhtar, T. (2021, April 16). Sotheby's NFT auction with artist Pak and Nifty Gateway brings in $16.8m. Yahoo! Finance. Retrieved October 8, 2022, from https://ca.finance.yahoo.com/news/sotheby-nft-auction-artist-pak-153836331.html

Akten, M. (2020, December 14). *The unreasonable ecological cost of #CryptoArt*. Medium. Retrieved March 31 2023, from https://memoakten.medium.com/the-unreasonable-ecological-cost-of-cryptoart-2221d3eb2053

Allen, S., Juels, A., Khaire, M., Kell, T., & Shrivastava, S. (2022). NFTs for Art and Collectables: Primer and Outlook. https://doi.org/10.31235/osf.io/gwzd7

Amick, S. (2022, May 23). *Balenciaga to accept Bitcoin, crypto as payment*. Nasdaq. Retrieved Jan 12, 2023, from https://www.nasdaq.com/articles/balenciaga-to-accept-bitcoin-crypto-as-payment

Anyanwu, O. (2021, September 20). *Balenciaga and Fortnite debut physical, Digital Collections and world*. WWD. Retrieved March 1, 2022, from https://wwd.com/feature/balenciaga-and-fortnite-debut-physical-digital-collections-and-hub-1234930335/

Arora, P., & Vermeylen, F. (2013). The end of the art connoisseur? Experts and knowledge production in the visual arts in the digital age. *Information, Communication & Society, 16*(2), 194–214.

Ashmore, D. (2022, December 6). OpenSea NFT Marketplace Review. Retrieved February 15, 2023, from https://www.nasdaq.com/articles/opensea-nft-marketplace-review

Atasoy, O., & Morewedge, C.K. (2018). Digital Goods Are Valued Less Than Physical Goods. *Journal of Consumer Research, 44*(6), 1343–1357.

Balenciaga. (2011). *Brand history: Balenciaga*. Kering.com. Available at: https://www.kering.com/en/houses/couture-and-leather-goods/balenciaga/history/

Belk, R., Humayun, M., & Brouard, M. (2022). Money, possessions, and ownership in the Metaverse: NFTs, cryptocurrencies, Web3 and Wild Markets. *Journal of Business Research, 153*, 198–205.

Benissan, E. (2022, September 26). *Balenciaga presses go on resale following successful pilot*. Vogue Business. Retrieved February 15, 2023, from https://www.voguebusiness.com/fashion/balenciaga-presses-go-on-resale-following-successful-pilot

Block, F. (2021, August 4). Louis Vuitton launches a video game to target young consumers. Barron's. Retrieved January 7, 2023, from https://www.barrons.com/articles/louis-vuitton-launches-a-video-game-to-target-young-consumers-01628109921

Bringé, A. (2022, July 1). *Council post: How fashion brands can enter the metaverse*. Forbes. Retrieved January 10, 2023, from https://www.forbes.com/sites/forbescommunicationscouncil/2022/07/01/how-fashion-brands-can-enter-the-metaverse/?sh=7415d9724667

Bruell, A. (2021, November 23). *How Christie's is pitching its expansion from Picassos to NFTs*. The Wall Street Journal. Retrieved March 20, 2022, from https://www.wsj.com/articles/how-christies-is-pitching-its-expansion-from-picassos-to-nfts-11637700438

Brun, A., Kishan, V., & Umer, S.M. (2021). *Applications of Non-fungible tokens (NFTs) and the Intersection with fashion luxury industry*. Available at: https://www.politesi.polimi.it/bitstream/10589/182823/1/2021_12_Umer_Kishan.pdf.

Burberry. (2021). Burberry Drops NFT Collection In Mythical Games' Blankos Block Party. *Burberry Official*. https://www.burberryplc.com/en/news/brand/2021/Blankos.html

Burberry. (n.d.). Discover The Story of Burberry. *Burberry*. https://ca.burberry.com/c/our-history/

Calma, J. (2021). *The Climate Controversy Swirling around NFTs*. The Verge. Available at: https://www.theverge.com/2021/3/15/22328203/nft-cryptoart-ethereum-blockchain-climate-change.

Canada Energy Regulator. (2021, May 19). What is in a Canadian Residential Electricity Bill? Canada Energy Regulator. Retrieved February 7, 2022, from https://www.cer-rec.gc.ca/en/data-analysis/energy-commodities/electricity/report/canadian-residential-electricity-bill

Crypto Carbon Ratings Institute (CCRI). (2022). The Merge – Implications on the Electricity Consumption and Carbon Footprint of the Ethereum Network Report. https://carbon-ratings.com/eth-report-2022.

Chandra, Y., & Belk, R. (2022). *Is that Jpeg Worth 70 Million Dollars? Value Construction and Perceptions of Non-Fungible Tokens.* papers.ssrn.com. Available at: https://papers.ssrn.com/sol3/papers.cfm?abstract_id=4235739.

Chitrakorn, K. (2022, December 5). Pierpaolo Piccioli and Wales Bonner among Honourees at 2022 fashion awards. Vogue Business. Retrieved January 25, 2023, from https://www.voguebusiness.com/fashion/pierpaolo-piccioli-and-wales-bonner-among-honourees-at-2022-fashion-awards

Cho, E., Kim-Vick, J., & Yu, U. J. (2021). Unveiling motivation for luxury fashion purchase among Gen Z consumers: need for uniqueness versus bandwagon effect. *International Journal of Fashion Design, Technology and Education, 15*(1), 24–34.

Christie's. (2021a, March 11). Beeple's masterwork: the first purely digital artwork offered at Christie's. https://www.christies.com/features/Monumental-collage-by-Beeple-is-first-purely-digital-artwork-NFT-to-come-to-auction-11510-7.aspx

Christie's. (2021b, December 21). Christie's x OpenSea, Christie's. https://www.christies.com/auctions/christies-x-opensea

Christie's. (2021c, December 20). *Strong results for Christie's in 2021.* Christie's. Retrieved February 1, 2023, from https://www.christies.com/presscenter/pdf/10337/Christie's%20EOY%202021%20Press%20Release_10337_1.pdf

Christie's. (2022). *Christie's Ventures.* Christie's Auction House. Retrieved March 1, 2023, from https://www.christies.com/about-us/christies-ventures.

Colicev, A. (2023). How can non-fungible tokens bring value to brands. *International journal of research in marketing, 40*(1), 30–37.

Danziger, P.N. (2021, April 23). *LVMH, Cartier and Prada partner to fight counterfeits, invite other luxury brands to join.* Forbes. Retrieved August 16, 2022, from https://www.forbes.com/sites/pamdanziger/2021/04/22/lvmh-cartier-and-prada-partner-to-fight-counterfeits-and-invite-other-luxury-brands-to-join/?sh=6ed5a48f3072

Davis, D.M. (2020, January 28). *The 9 most Valuable Luxury Brands in the world.* Business Insider. Retrieved March 18, 2022, from https://www.businessinsider.com/most-valuable-luxury-brands-in-the-world

Dawson, E. (2020, October 8). Burberry supports IBM interns to develop prototype system for product traceability. IBM UK. https://www.ibm.com/blogs/think/uk-en/burberry-supports-ibm-interns-to-develop-prototype-system-for-product-traceability/

de Boissieu, E., Kondrateva, G., Baudier, P., & Ammi, C. (2021). The use of blockchain in the luxury industry: supply chains and the traceability of goods. *Journal of Enterprise Information Management, 34*(5), 1318–1338. https://doi.org/10.1108/JEIM-11-2020-0471

Dickens, S. (2021, November 22). *Sotheby's unveils NFT charity auction to support Front Line Healthcare Workers.* Yahoo! Finance. Retrieved January 10, 2023, from https://ca.finance.yahoo.com/news/sotheby-unveils-nft-charity-auction-174910372.html?guccounter=1

Dolan, L. (2021, May 4). *Sotheby's introduces cryptocurrency sales with a famous banksy work.* CNN. Retrieved March 31 2023, from https://www.cnn.com/style/article/sothebys-cryptocurrency-banksy/index.html

Finney, A. (2022, November 8). *Burberry releases Digital Clothing Collection "for the modern explorer" in video game minecraft.* Dezeen. Retrieved March 31 2023, from https://www.dezeen.com/2022/11/08/burberry-minecraft-freedom-beyond-digital-fashion

Fionda, A.M., & Moore, C.M. (2009). The anatomy of the luxury fashion brand. *Journal of Brand Management, 16*(5–6), 347–363. https://doi.org/10.1057/bm.2008.45.

Gaur, V., & Gaiha, A. (2020). *Building a Transparent Supply Chain*. Harvard Business Review. Available at: https://hbr.org/2020/05/building-a-transparent-supply-chain.

Geissdoerfer, M., Savaget, P., Bocken, N. M. P., & Hultink, E. J. (2017). The Circular Economy – A new sustainability paradigm? *Journal of Cleaner Production, 143*, 757–768. https://doi.org/10.1016/j.jclepro.2016.12.048

Hayward, A. (2023, February 17). OpenSea drops fees, cuts creator royalty protections as rival Blur Rises. Decrypt. Retrieved March 12, 2023, from https://decrypt.co/121638/opensea-drops-fees-royalty-protections-blur-rises

Härdle, Wolfgang Karl, Campbell R. Harvey, & Raphael C.G. Reule (2020). Understanding Cryptocurrencies. *Journal of Financial Econometrics, 18*(2), 181–208.

Hofstetter, R., de Bellis, E., Brandes, L., Clegg, M., Lamberton, C., Reibstein, D., Rohlfsen, F., Schmitt, B., & Zhang, J.Z. (2022). Crypto-marketing: how non-fungible tokens (NFTs) challenge traditional marketing. *Marketing Letters, 33*(4), 705–711. https://doi.org/10.1007/s11002-022-09639-2

Howcroft, E. (2021, September 9). Set of "bored ape" NFTs sells for $24.4 million in Sotheby's online auction. Reuters. Retrieved October 1, 2022, from https://www.reuters.com/article/us-fintech-nft-sothebys-ape-idCAKBN2G51HW

Jacob & Co. (2022). *NFT – Astronomia Metaverso*. Jacob & Co. Retrieved March 31, 2023, from https://jacobandco.com/nft

Joy, A., Zhu, Y., Peña, C., & Brouard, M. (2022). Digital future of luxury brands: Metaverse, digital fashion, and non-fungible tokens. *Strategic Change, 31*(3), 337–343. https://doi.org/10.1002/jsc.2502

Khan, S. N., Loukil, F., Ghedira-Guegan, C., Benkhelifa, E., & Bani-Hani, A. (2021). Blockchain smart contracts: Applications, challenges, and future trends. *Peer Peer Netw Appl, 14*(5), 2901–2925. https://doi.org/10.1007/s12083-021-01127-0

Kirjavainen, E. (2022). The future of luxury fashion brands through NFTs. Available at: https://aaltodoc.aalto.fi/handle/123456789/114089.

Lee, A. (2020, October 7). *Burberry, IBM interns collab on product-tracing system*. Yahoo! Finance. Retrieved March 13, 2023, from https://ca.finance.yahoo.com/news/burberry-ibm-interns-collab-product-230125513.html

Lee, R. (2021). Louis 200: How Louis Vuitton celebrates its founder's bicentennial birthday. Yahoo! News. Retrieved February 22, 2023, from https://ca.news.yahoo.com/louis-200-vuitton-celebrates-bicentennial-birthday-nft-bts-055043993.html

Ledger Insights. (2021, August 3). *Louis Vuitton to launch NFT game with Beeple Art*. Ledger Insights. Retrieved February 15, 2022, from https://www.ledgerinsights.com/louis-vuitton-nft-game-with-beeple-art/

Malik, N., Wei, Y.M., Appel, G., & Luo, L. (2023). Blockchain technology for creative industries: Current state and research opportunities. *International journal of research in marketing, 40*(1), 38–48.

Marr, B. (2017, September 25). *The amazing ways Burberry is using artificial intelligence and big data to drive success*. Forbes. Retrieved March 26, 2023, from https://www.forbes.com/sites/bernardmarr/2017/09/25/the-amazing-ways-burberry-is-using-artificial-intelligence-and-big-data-to-drive-success/?sh=4e5dd5ad4f63

Mattei, S.E.D. (2021, October 19). *Sotheby's launches an NFT-only marketplace*. ARTnews. Retrieved February 10, 2023, from https://www.artnews.com/art-news/market/sotheby-metaverse-nft-only-marketplace-1234607430/

McDowell, M. (2021, May 17). *Inside Gucci and Roblox's new Virtual world*. Vogue Business. Retrieved March 12, 2023, from https://www.voguebusiness.com/technology/inside-gucci-and-robloxs-new-virtual-world

McDowell, M. (2022, June 20). *Burberry brings back the Blankos Block Party NFT-based game*. Vogue Business. Retrieved March 16, 2023, from https://www.voguebusiness.com/technology/burberry-brings-back-the-blankos-block-party-nft-based-game

McLeod, L. (2008). James Christie and his auction house. *Art Libraries Journal*, *33*(1), 28–34. https://doi.org/10.1017/s0307472200015194.

Moss, T. (2022, June 10). *Luxury brands start to take cryptocurrency payments*. The Wall Street Journal. Retrieved March 10, 2023, from https://www.wsj.com/articles/luxury-brands-start-to-take-cryptocurrency-payments-11654860403

Mower, S. (2020, December 6). *Balenciaga fall 2021 ready-to-wear collection*. Vogue. Retrieved March 12, 2023, from https://www.vogue.com/fashion-shows/fall-2021-ready-to-wear/balenciaga

Mulhern, O. (2022, July 24). *The 10 Essential Fast Fashion Statistics*. Earth.org.https://earth.org/fast-fashion-statistics/

Narayanan, Arvind, Bonneau, J., Felten, E., Miller, A., & Goldfeder, S. (2016). *Bitcoin and Cryptocurrency Technologies: A Comprehensive Introduction*. Princeton University Press.

Nast, C. (2021). Balenciaga launches on Fortnite: What it means for luxury. Vogue Business. Available at: https://www.voguebusiness.com/technology/balenciaga-launches-on-fortnite-what-it-means-for-luxury.

Niranjanamurthy, M., Nithya, B.N., & Jagannatha, S. (2019). Analysis of Blockchain technology: pros, cons and SWOT. *Cluster Comput 22*(Suppl 6), 14743–14757. https://doi.org/10.1007/s10586-018-2387-5

Paton, E. (2021, April 20). *LVMH, Richemont and Prada unite behind a Blockchain Consortium*. The New York Times. Retrieved March 13 2023, from https://www.nytimes.com/2021/04/20/business/lvmh-richemont-prada-blockchain.html

Pearce, D.W., & Turner, R.K. (1989). *Economics of natural resources and the environment*. Johns Hopkins University Press.

Phan, M., Thomas, R., & Heine, K. (2011). Social Media and Luxury Brand Management: The Case of Burberry. *Journal of Global Fashion Marketing*, *2*(4), 213–222. https://doi.org/10.1080/20932685.2011.10593099

Rascouet, A. (2021, April 20). *Louis Vuitton, Cartier, prada push blockchain tool to lure shoppers*. Bloomberg.com. Retrieved March 13 2023, from https://www.bloomberg.com/news/articles/2021-04-20/lvmh-cartier-prada-push-blockchain-tool-to-lure-shoppers#xj4y7vzkg

Registry, A. (2018, November 15). *Artory launches the world's first publicly available art and Collectibles Registry on the Blockchain*. Business Wire. Retrieved March 31 2023, from https://www.businesswire.com/news/home/20181115005195/en/Artory-Launches-the-World%E2%80%99s-First-Publicly-Available-Art-and-Collectibles-Registry-on-the-Blockchain

Research and Markets. (2022, May). *Global Luxury Resale Market: Analysis by product, by distribution channel, by gender, by region size and trends with impact of covid-19 and forecast up to 2026*. Research and Markets. Retrieved November 21, 2022, from https://www.researchandmarkets.com/reports/5591754/global-luxury-resale-market-analysis-by

Rosenberg, L. (2022, February 16). *Even though it's virtual, the metaverse does actually impact the environment*. World Economic Forum. Retrieved September 12, 2022, from https://www.weforum.org/agenda/2022/02/how-metaverse-actually-impacts-the-environment/

Sekhose, M. (2021, July 30). *The world's most valuable luxury brand is launching a video game with NFTs*. Business Insider. Retrieved April 13 2022, from https://www.businessinsider.in/cryptocurrency/news/luxury-brand-louis-vuitton-is-launching-nft-video-game-on-android-and-ios-device/articleshow/84883379.cms

Sestino, A., Guido, G., & Peluso, A.M. (2022). The interplay of consumer innovativeness and status consumption orientation when buying NFT-based fashion products. In *Non-Fungible Tokens (NFTs) Examining the Impact on Consumers and Marketing Strategies* (pp. 63–75). Cham: Springer International Publishing. https://doi.org/10.1007/978-3-031-07203-1_6.

Shirley, K. (2021, March 25). *Jacob & Co. to auction first luxury watch NFT in April*. Forbes. Retrieved March 31 2023, from https://www.forbes.com/sites/kristenshirley/2021/03/25/jacob–co-to-auction-first-luxury-watch-nft-in-april/?sh=28e09e2f400d

Siegfried, P. (2022). *The Metaverse: Exploring consumer's expectations, their attitudes, and its meaning to the fashion industry.* papers.ssrn.com.https://papers.ssrn.com/sol3/papers.cfm?abstract_id=4191523.

Sotheby's (n.d.a) The History of Sotheby's Auction House. Retrieved April 10, 2023 https://www.sothebys.com/en/about/our-history

Sotheby's. (n.d.b). *NFT Art Auction Department – sothebys.com.* Sotheby's. Retrieved April 1, 2023, from https://www.sothebys.com/en/departments/nft

Sotheby's. (2021a, December 16). Historic Year in Review. Retrieved October 17, 2022, from https://www.sothebys.com/en/press/2021-historic-year-in-review

Sotheby's. (2021b, May 6). *Cryptocurrency accepted via COINBASE for banksy's 'Love is in the air'.* Sotheby's. Retrieved October 1, 2022, from https://www.sothebys.com/en/articles/cryptocurrency-accepted-via-coinbase-for-banksys-love-is-in-the-air

Sottile, Z. (2022, May 12). *You will soon be able to use Bitcoin to buy Gucci. CNN Business.* CNN. Retrieved March 12, 2023, from https://www.cnn.com/2022/05/08/business/gucci-bitcoin-cryptocurrency-payments-trnd/index.html

Stackpole, T. (2022, May 10). *What is web3?* Harvard Business Review. Retrieved April 1 2023, from https://hbr.org/2022/05/what-is-web3

Stankiewicz, K. (2021, May 4). *Sotheby's to accept bitcoin and ether for an upcoming auction of a banksy painting.* CNBC. Retrieved January 20, 2023, from https://www.cnbc.com/2021/05/04/sothebys-to-accept-bitcoin-and-ether-for-an-upcoming-auction-of-a-banksy-painting.html

Statista. (2023). Value of the personal luxury goods market worldwide from 1996 to 2022. Available at: https://www.statista.com/statistics/266503/value-of-the-personal-luxury-goods-market-worldwide/

Stern, M. (2022, December 27). *Will digital assets stay fashionable with Millennials and Gen-Zers? – RetailWire.* Retail Wire. https://retailwire.com/discussion/will-digital-assets-stay-fashionable-with-millennials-and-gen-zers/

Tan, A. (2022, November 8). *The latest from the fashion metaverse: Rimowa launches NFTs, Burberry's capsule collection on Minecraft and more.* Vogue. Retrieved February 18, 2023, from https://vogue.sg/updates-from-fashion-metaverse/

Tan, H. (2021). Luxury brands like Burberry and Coach are cashing in on Singles' Day shopping in China by creating limited edition NFTs for the event. *Insider.* Retrieved from https://www.businessinsider.com/singles-day-limited-edition-nft-china-luxury-brands-2021-11

Tarmy, J. (2021, February 18). *Christie's auction house will now accept cryptocurrency – BNN Bloomberg.* BNN Bloomberg. https://www.bnnbloomberg.ca/christie-s-auction-house-will-now-accept-cryptocurrency-1.1565195

Valeonti, F., Bikakis, A., Terras, M., Speed, C., Hudson-Smith, A., & Chalkias, K. (2021). Crypto Collectibles, Museum Funding and OpenGLAM: Challenges, Opportunities and the Potential of Non-Fungible Tokens (NFTs). *Applied Sciences, 11*(21), 9931.

van Haaften-Schick, L., & Whitaker, A. (2022). From the Artist's Contract to the blockchain ledger: new forms of artists' funding using equity and resale royalties. *Journal of Cultural Economics, 46*(2), 287–315. https://doi.org/10.1007/s10824-022-09445-8

Velthuis, Olav. (2011). Art Markets. In *A Handbook of Cultural Economics, Second Edition*: Edward Elgar Publishing.

Victoria and Albert Museum. (n.d.). *Introducing Cristóbal Balenciaga.* Victoria and Albert Museum. Retrieved February 1, 2023, from https://www.sothebys.com/en/departments/nft

Vuitton, L. (2022). *A Legendary History | LOUIS VUITTON.* eu.louisvuitton.com. Available at: https://eu.louisvuitton.com/eng-e1/magazine/articles/a-legendary-history#.

Walker, M. (2006). *Balenciaga and his legacy: haute couture from the Texas Fashion Collection.* Yale University Press.

Wang, Y. (2021). A Conceptual Framework of Contemporary Luxury Consumption. *International Journal of Research in Marketing, 39*(3), 788–803. https://doi.org/10.1016/j.ijresmar.2021.10.010.

White, B., Mahanti, A., & Passi, K. (2022, April). Characterizing the OpenSea NFT marketplace. In *Companion Proceedings of the Web Conference 2022* (pp. 488–496). https://doi.org/10.1145/3487553.3524629.

Woodham, D. (2017). *Art Collecting Today: Market Insights for Everyone Passionate about Art*. Simon and Schuster.

Yotka, S. (2021, September 20). *Balenciaga and Fortnite team up for a digital-to-physical partnership*. Vogue. Retrieved January 21, 2023, from https://www.vogue.com/article/balenciaga-fortnite-partnership

Part 3: **The World of Fashion**

Karen V. Fernandez

8 Fashioning Circular Consumption

Fashioning Circular Consumption

To collaboratively shape a more sustainable, equitable and connected society, circular production must be complemented by circular consumption – a closed loop consumption system which has no net loss of resources (Fernandez 2022). However, circular consumption requires that, wherever possible, resources are re-used by oneself or others, instead of being discarded. Despite the increased exhortations to reduce, reuse, and recycle, we are far from achieving circular consumption – and we are not just talking about our usage of plastic or combustion engines. Of all the textiles manufactured each year, approximately 85% ends up in landfill or are incinerated, with just 12% put back into the system through donating or recycling, and less than 1% regenerated into new fiber for new clothes (Ellen McArthur Foundation 2022). This is because re-use is a particularly difficult goal with respect to fashion (branded clothing, footwear, and accessories). The fashion industry has been accused of having a "take-make-waste" business model (Brydges 2021) that negatively impacts the environment during production, consumption, and disposition. Improving the take-make-waste business model to improve circular production is important, but not sufficient. Fashion consumers also have critical roles to play, if we are to successfully combat this global problem. This is because the life of fashion items can be extended by consumers responsibly considering what is acquired, how it is used, and the manner of its disposition.

Acquisition decisions can facilitate circular consumption if they result in acquiring fewer new fashion items, prioritising fashion items that have been made with sustainable and/or re-used materials, or acquiring/borrowing/renting fashion items which have already been used. Consumption decisions can contribute to circular consumption by extending the degree and length of usage of currently owned items, or using borrowed/rented ones. Disposition choices can aid circular consumption if they facilitate the use of the disposed items by others. Consequently, besides repairing, altering or upcycling fashion apparel, consumers need to be encouraged to reacquire (acquire items used by others) or dispose of items more conscientiously to facilitate their re-use. Besides consumer disposal events like car boot and garage sales, and second-hand retail outlets, consumers must be encouraged to participate in clothing exchange events, renting, and borrowing, both as providers and re-acquirers of used fashion. However, these modes of disposition will only contribute to sustainability if the items (or their components) can be reacquired and reused by others. Unfortunately, this is easier said than done with respect to fashion items, because many people resist wearing clothing that has been worn by others (O'Reilly et al. 1984) because of perceived contamination (the

https://doi.org/10.1515/9783110783933-008

perception that the qualities of one entity have been transferred to another through actual or perceived contact).

Consequently, this chapter will pay particular attention to how the nature, extent, and valence of contamination can influence re-use of fashion, and how those perceptions could be addressed. To do so, I draw on two decades of researching the re-acquisition of others' used and/or discarded objects, how people cope with perceived contamination, prior literature on fashion consumption, and ten in-depth interviews that are part of a larger current ethnographic study of vintage-inspired consumption. The rest of this chapter will introduce the theoretical construct of contamination, before describing the context of the fashion industry. Then, I will discuss how contamination sheds light on the appeal of new and used fashion. The chapter will conclude by discussing how the inter-relationships between fashion types, contamination, and culture can be harnessed to fashion a more circular consumption cycle for this industry.

Contamination

Contamination, whether through actual or perceived contact (Argo, Dahl, and Morales 2006; Belk, Wallendorf, and Sherry 1989; Nemeroff and Rozin 1994), potentially transforms the recipients in ways that are positive (Fernandez and Lastovicka 2011) and/or negative (Rozin, Millman and Nemeroff 1986). The essence that is transferred, and hence contamination itself, can be viewed on multiple levels simultaneously, including unseen but inferred biological contamination (e.g. germs: Nemeroff and Rozin 1994), observable physical contamination (e.g. blood: Nemeroff and Rozin 2018), and inferred spiritual contamination (e.g. receiving a blessing from a revered figure or a deity: Fernandez 2015). Another form of contamination that is seldom discussed is that of symbolic contamination, whereby the visual similarity between two objects might be interpreted as one having acquired some of the cachet of the other—as when a less expensive knock-off of an haute couture fashion item is admired online (McFarlane, Hamilton, and Hewer 2022) because of its iconic (visual in this case) similarity to the original luxury branded item.

Contamination can be dependent on contextual expectations. Something in the right context or place may be appropriate and even valued, but once it is out of place it can be viewed as polluted and/or polluting (Douglas 1966). For example, a branded fashion item might seem "dirty" if seen in a pile of items put on the sidewalk, but would not be seen so negatively if offered for sale in a resale boutique (even if there is no claim that it had been cleaned). However, contamination is not always viewed negatively. It could be viewed negatively or positively, depending on the perceiver's knowledge and perceptions of the source of the contamination. For example, if the prior user of a garment is unknown and the item does not display visible indexical (evidentiary) cues of prior usage such as sweat stains, the acquirer might be able to ignore the fact that someone else has used that garment—a phenomenon that Samuel Taylor Coleridge termed the "suspension of disbelief" in 1817. However, if the source of contamination is known, then the valence with which that source is perceived becomes a critical determinant of how that contamination is evaluated. For example, an attractive past user of a garment increases the product's value and intent to purchase it (Argo, Dahl, and Morales 2008).

The Fashion Industry

The terms clothing, apparel, and fashion are often used inter-changeably. While the term "clothing" generally refers to garments that are worn and excludes footwear, and the term "apparel" generally extends to anything that is worn, including footwear, and other accessories, the term "fashion" is generally used to refer to branded clothing, footwear, and accessories. In my view, the distinguishing aspect of fashion, compared to clothing or apparel, is that fashion items tend to have expressive value that is greater and more important to purchasers than their functional values, compared to more utilitarian clothing or apparel. The fashion industry, comprising designers, models, photographers, manufacturers, distributors, retailers and relevant media that are all involved in providing fashion items for end-users, is the fourth biggest industry globally. Its value of USD 3 trillion (USD 3000 billion) is estimated to contribute 2% to gross national product worldwide (Fashion United 2016).

Unfortunately, a variety of factors have contributed to the more than USD 500 billion of value lost annually (Mohr, Fuxman, and Mahmoud 2022). Some technical factors, such as the non-recyclability of fibers which have been blended to improve textile properties (Manshoven et al. 2019), have contributed to the less than one percent of clothing material being recycled into new clothing. Issues like these are relevant to increasing the sustainability of new clothing before it is purchased or otherwise acquired. The sustainability of new clothing is an issue for circular production (reducing resource usage and loss during production), and thus largely outside the scope of the current discussion of circular consumption. The sustainability of clothing once it is purchased, in terms of its usage and disposition is of critical importance to the current discussion of circular consumption. Thus, factors, like the socio-cultural trend of the reduced number of items a single item is worn before being discarded (Ellen MacArthur 2000) are germane to circular consumption, and must be considered. It must be noted however, that circular production choices can, and do limit what is possible, in achieving circular consumption. For example, if textiles made of blended fibers cannot be recycled, then that eliminates one possible disposition choice for the owner of an unwanted item.

Next, three somewhat inter-related types of fashion markets that are relevant to this paper– luxury fashion, fast fashion, and slow fashion–will be briefly discussed in terms of their relevance to circular consumption.

Luxury Fashion

The markets for luxury branded products, including luxury fashion brands like Chanel and Dior, are sizeable and quickly growing worldwide (Karatzas, Kapoulas, and Priporas 2019). Luxury branded products strongly influence the apparel market and have been exhorted to take the lead in mitigating those negative effects (Joy et al. 2012). The full potential of luxury brands to be sustainable has yet to be realized. Although some luxury branded products use materials efficiently, employ assembly techniques that are lower in environmental impact, and offer post-purchase repairs (Joy et al. 2012), technical issues like the non-recyclability of blended fibers (Manshoven et al. 2019) mentioned earlier greatly reduce the circularity of luxury fashion. Yet, luxury fashion is greatly desired because it is perceived as being well-made, with high quality construction and materials, and confers status and distinction to its wearers.

Vintage and Retro Fashion

Besides luxury fashion, "vintage" fashion items are often purchased from specialty re-sellers. The term "vintage" as applied to a fashion item generally refers to authentic, relatively uncommon items that represents the style of a particular past era. Consequently, vintage fashion is virtually always offered for sale as a used item. Some specialty stores also offer "reworked vintage" – vintage style clothing that has been remade from actual vintage textiles (repurposed from clothing of that era) while others offer "upcycled vintage" where actual vintage fashion items have been carefully repaired to emulate the quality of newly bought items. The boundaries between vintage fashion and luxury fashion are increasingly blurry because luxury fashion brands have vintage fashion alongside their new collections (Cervellon, Carey, and Harms 2012), and because the most treasured vintage "finds" are often from luxury fashion brands.

Vintage fashion must be distinguished from retro-fashions, which are new fashion items made of new materials, in the style of older or vintage items (Brown, Kozinets, and Sherry 2003). While vintage fashion is authentically from the period it represents, retro-fashion is created to resemble the period it reflects. Luxury brands have reproduced vintage designs, offered vintage-inspired new designs, and re-used vintage fabrics for new designs (Cervellon et al. 2012), while also blurring the boundaries between luxury and retro-fashions. This is problematic, as I will explain, because vintage, like luxury, tends to remain in use longer, while retro-fashions, like fast fashion, may be disposed of rather more quickly.

Fast Fashion

The term fast fashion refers to the low-cost clothing collections that are inspired by high-cost luxury fashion trends (Joy et al. 2012). The term "fast fashion" was first coined by the New York Times in 1989 (Gazzola et al. 2020). In the two decades since then, the pace of fast fashion has accelerated, with clothes becoming ever cheaper, and fashion cycles relentlessly speeding up. This has resulted in over half of fast fashion items being disposed of in less than twelve months (McKinsey 2016), due to insufficient wardrobe space (Cairns et al. 2021) and because they were not made to last in the first place. Not surprisingly, fast fashion has been characterized as "disposable" fashion (Cairns, Ritch, and Bereziat, 2021, 1270). Ironically, the desire of so many ordinary consumers to gain distinction by emulating higher status luxury fashion consumers by purchasing and wearing fast fashion, results in their similarity to each other, rather than individuality (Cassidy and Bennett 2015).

High street retailers, who are usually associated with fast fashion also have offered new vintage-inspired styles. However, this has blurred the line between vintage and fast fashion for only for the uninitiated, because those "in the know" recognize that the fast fashion/retro fashion is "lacking in authenticity" (Cassidy and Bennett 2015, 255).

Slow Fashion

Over the past decade, the slow fashion movement, an approach that carefully considers what processes and resources are required to make an item of clothing, has been gaining traction. Proponents of slow fashion advocate the purchase of better-quality fashion items that will last longer, asking that consumers reduce fashion consumption, as well as reuse and recycle their purchases (Lee, Seifert, and Cherrier 2017). New Zealand footwear brand Allbirds™ (www.allbirds.com) successfully appeals to the slow-fashion consumer by stressing their sustainable production processes and by using sustainable materials made from merino wool, eucalyptus trees and sugarcane to craft their shoes which feature shoelaces made out of recycled plastic bottles. Together with other like-minded companies such as New Zealand merino clothing brand Icebreaker (www.icebreaker.com), Allbirds has embraced a collaborative sustainable initiative which certifies that the wool used is grown on farms that use regenerative practices (Taunton 2021). Fashion brands utilizing natural materials are particularly well-placed to be perceived highly, because "natural" connotes items that are uncontaminated by humans or additives, and thus "pure" (Nemeroff and Rozin 2018). Such products straddle the middle ground between luxury fashion and fast fashion in terms of cost, offering high quality and longevity because they offer classic styles.

Fashion Market Circularity

The appeal of the three fashion markets of luxury fashion, fast fashion, and slow fashion are inter-related. Luxury fashion is desired for its expressive value and its ability to confer status, but is unaffordable to the masses. The unsatiated desire for luxury fashion, fueled by traditional and social media, has led to the rise of fast fashion, which also offers retro-fashion. The increasingly rapid cycles of take-make-waste fast fashion has led to a minority reconsidering their fashion choices more mindfully, which has been termed slow fashion. The rejection of fast fashion in favor of slow fashion partly explains the growing demand for vintage fashion.

The intersections between the three fashion markets offer new opportunities to extend the product life of fashion items via reacquisition. For example, a key source of value for luxury products derives from their uniqueness (Mochaelidou, Chritodoulides, and Presi 2022). However, uniqueness is a quality that could be marketed to reacquirers of used fashion items as well. For example, a graphic design student I interviewed explained that she shopped in charity shops because "when I shop for stuff it's to be *not*-mainstream" (Tiara, multi-ethnic female, aged 21). Similarly, Janet (WF 45), an event manager who chooses to dress in vintage fashions at work and in her personal life, explained the importance of her vintage fashion in making her unique when she explained that

> people want to look different so they don't want to always look like the chain store. So if you can find a piece that someone else has, that's from a different era, then you know you're going to look different and be, just have, portray a little bit of your personality. There's a confidence that comes with wearing something that's . . . different to what other people are wearing . . . So, you're actually making a bit of a statement about yourself but also you're sort of confident that you know that you're not going to be, don't need to be outshone by anybody else but you're not going to be standing next to someone and have exactly the same outfit on, yeah.

Consequently, used vintage fashion and even used ordinary second-hand fashion can function like new luxury fashion to confer uniqueness on its wearer.

Moreover, vintage fashion is clearly seen by its wearers as an antidote to the cheaper quality, throwaway slow fashion. As Janet explained "over the last 30 years . . . there's a lot more chain stores providing great looks and some pretty dubious fabrics which are going to wear out. So, you're not paying an awful lot for them, which is great. So, you can wear them for a season and if they fall to bits at the end of the season they [the chain stores] don't owe you anything because you've only spent 20 or 30, 40 dollars on it. They're fun items but they won't, and they're not, made to last, you know."

Janet's acceptance of the disposability of fast fashion, even if she did not purchase it personally, contrasted sharply with Iris' (WF35) strongly negative view of fast fashion. Iris, who manages a vintage retail store, described how, when "I moved to England and I worked in the fashion industry over there. And it's such a big consumer culture over there, and everyone's obsessed with just having the latest thing, wearing it once, throwing it away. Incredibly wasteful, like there was these big kind of department stores called Primark, and you could buy dresses for four pounds, you know, and shirts for two pounds. And it was just, it really made me sick actually in the end, just the rampant consumerism, and the churn in fashion is so quick over there. It's a lot slower here [in Australasia]. But you know, like say there's these big High Street brands like Zara and Banana Republic, and they'd change their whole shop floor every two weeks. So a whole new range of clothes ever two weeks. So can you imagine how many clothes have been made to satisfy that demand? It was really disgusting." Consequently, an increase in consumers like Iris rejecting fast fashion has led to the slow growth of the slow fashion movement.

Even collectors of new retro-styled sneakers (limited editions that resemble sneakers worn by basketball legends like Michael Jordon) distinguished between older limited editions that they felt were better quality, and newer releases. For example, when Tim (Chinese male, 34) was asked why he had expressed preferring the less recent sneaker releases to the newer ones, he explained, "the older ones . . . they [Nike] do a lot better job on the older ones than what they're doing now days. Because I've been to a couple of factories before, I've seen the [manufacturing] process and all that stuff. But the ones that older, I think they take more care when they're making it. So like you, for the newer ones you find a lot of them having ink coming out and some places discolouring and some places where it's supposed to be one colour but the colour kind of fades out a little bit. Just the craftsmanship is not so good anymore." Not surprisingly, some consumers have been rejecting fast fashion for its perceived lower quality.

Recommerce and Beyond

The resale of formerly used fashion items is not new—consumers have been purchasing used clothing from thrift stores, charity retail outlets, and, more recently, resale stores and online platforms. These items range from luxury fashion to ordinary, everyday fashion. Even if consumers do not ordinarily associate (Beckham and Voyer 2014) or evaluate (Karatzas et al. 2019) potential luxury purchases on the basis of the brand's sustainability, their desire to be contaminated by the cachet of luxury fashion, and even the previous owners of a luxury fashion item, have contributed to the sustainability of luxury fashion items via reacquisition of others' unwanted luxury fashion items via the growing market for used luxury fashion. Although consignment and second hand fashion stores are not new, second-order marketer TheRealReal (www.therealreal.com) has revolutionised the resale of luxury fashion. TheRealReal sells authenticated, pre-owned luxury fashion items via their online site and 18 retail locations (Danziger 2022a). Despite operating in a niche market, the RealReal was estimated to sell nearly $48 billion worth of used luxury fashion items in 2021 (D'Arpizio et al. 2021) to their more than 24 million members. Another major second-order outlet, ThredUp (www.thredup.com), operates only online, and attribute their success to a new generation of "fashion thrifters" (Danziger 2022b) who are proud to share their "finds," popularizing what Thredup terms "recommerce" (Thredup 2022).

Reacquisition Options Beyond Recommerce

Other possible ways to extend product life include clothing swap events, repair/alteration of existing fashion items, donation to charitable organisations, and renting instead of purchasing items. Swap events can be private offline ones, as when a group of co-workers organize a clothing swap event for charity among themselves, public online ones (e.g.), retail swap-shops (Henninger, Bürklin, and Niinimäki 2019), and sometimes can even be sponsored by luxury fashion brands (Lang and Armstrong 2018). However, these swap events, particularly the privately organised ones, seem to be sporadic and short-lived, with many specific offline and online sites mentioned by earlier researchers no longer appearing to exist.

Henninger et al. (2019, 335) report that although participants are not embarrassed to be participating in a swap event, they reject any items that appear to be of poor quality or appear "soiled" (i.e. bearing obvious signs of physical contamination). Fears of physical contamination explains why successful recommercialization of used fashion tends to be limited to items that have not been worn close to the skin. For example, a very early study of reacquisition of used clothing found that consumers were more reluctant to purchase used underwear than used outerwear such as coats (O'Reilly et al. 1984), speculating that perceptions of contamination due to bodily contact with previous wearers could be a significant deterrent to acceptance of used fashion. This is echoed in Iris' (WF35) explanation that she decided she was "only going to buy vintage or second-hand clothes . . . apart from underwear and maybe running gear, anything that you're going to get really sweaty in, I probably wouldn't buy, I would buy new." So, it is not surprising that one popular retro-fashion purchase by vintage fashion enthusiasts is reproduction lingerie – lingerie that is made ne, but resembles vintage undergarments. As Iris explained,

> before the sixties, it was all natural fabrics, so silk, wool, cotton . . . there was no stretch in vintage clothing so [contemporary] people find it hard to find vintage clothes that fit them. In the 50s . . . they were wearing corsets or they were wearing girdles or they were wearing things that pulled them in. And obviously it was post-war so they didn't have a lot of food. You know, like people weren't used to eating the kind of diet that we have. So I guess yeah modern reproduction

vintage clothing has a lot of stretch in the fabric. They've got zips, it's easier to get into than vintage . . . they had hooks and eyes . . .

Even if, as Iris implied, one reason for purchasing reproduction vintage lingerie would be to provide the required silhouette to make vintage clothes "fit right," purchasers of reproduction lingerie are also avoiding having to wear used vintage lingerie that has been contaminated by its former wearer.

Given the technological difficulty of recreating many used textiles into new textiles mentioned earlier, refashioning existing textiles into new items is also a growing trend that could help reshape the take-make-waste trajectory of fashion items. For example, consider Belle (WF58), who lives in a historical fishing village in Australasia and who enjoys dressing up in early nineteenth century style and wandering around the village, speaking to tourists (she is not paid or asked to do so). In an interview, she explained how creating these dresses from old fabric found in charity shops made her feel more authentically from that time period, and more unique, compared to the people around her. Thus refashioning used textiles into new garments is also a viable use of unwanted fashion items.

Contamination and Recommerce

Acculturation can influence the degree of acceptance of contamination by prior users of a fashion item. For example, Diana (Cambodian female aged 22) told me that she accepted old things that were "kinda contaminated" and her mother did not "really like to buy an old thing [be]cause other people have used it." Diana's friend Tiara (mentioned earlier) refused to purchase and re-use clothes formerly owned by the deceased. When hearing this, Diana recounted how she purchased something from a deceased estate clothing sale and then after going to bed that night "thinking that they were there and I was like ohhh. I got really paranoid . . .". She explained that she is only able to feel comfortable with reacquired clothes whose previous owners had since passed away, because, in her words "I wash it, I always try to cleanse it, yeah wash it," and as she wore it over time it became "hers" rather than "theirs." So even if the specific prior user is unknown, the fact that they are categorized as "deceased" imbued their contamination with negative valence. Diana tried to decontaminate the deceased prior wearer's essence by cleaning the garment, and re-contaminated it with her own essence by wearing it over time.

Culture and Recommerce

The perceptions that buying used is an indicator of financial restrictions can be a social deterrent to engaging in recommerce, or, at least, in admitting to doing so. The idea that people only purchase used because they cannot afford to buy new was rather more universal in the past then it is today. However, this perception still persists in countries as diverse as Taiwan (Karatzas et. al. 2019) and in Italy (Gazzola et al. 2020). Prior research with respect to sustainable luxury and contamination has mainly focused on research within Western cultural contexts (Athwal et al. 2019). Similarly, past work on consumer contamination has been largely Eurocentric (Nemeroff and Rozin 2018), with the exception of an examination of contamination in Hindu weddings (Fernandez, Veer, and Lastovicka 2011). Since culture influences how universal beliefs are expressed (Nemeroff and Rozin 2018), future research with non-Western consumers to examine how culture influences the acceptance of recommerce is needed. For example, observations at Malaysian garage sales revealed to me that although Asian (Chinese, Indian, and Malay) consumers often wear clothes used by, or shared with, family members, they reject used clothes worn by strangers. In other words, contamination by the in-group of interpersonal networks is acceptable, but contamination by unknown strangers is not. Yet Cervellon et al. (2012) report that Chinese consumers, despite disliking wearing used clothes, enthusiastically purchase vintage fashion. Research is needed to understand how consumers, particularly Asian consumers, are able to negotiate the tensions inherent in rejecting used clothes contaminated by unknown others, and wearing used luxury fashion, also contaminated by unknown others. Cervellon et al. (2012) describe the trend of the most aristocratic Chinese families handing down original couture (i.e. vintage luxury fashion) to successive generations. This resembles the value placed on positively contaminated gold jewellery that is handed down through generations of Hindu women (Fernandez et al. 2011) because it signals the insider status of the new wearer. Inherited vintage luxury fashion may have imbued vintage with status and distinction sufficient that purchased vintage items are viewed as positively contaminated with the essence of positively regarded prior users, even if their specific identity is unknown.

Implications

The makers and marketers of luxury fashion can certainly cash in on the opportunity to frame the purchase of smaller amounts of their quality fashion products (as opposed to greater quantities of lower quality fast-fashion products) as shopping responsibly and ethically (Mohr et al. 2022). This framing is likely to appeal to consumers since it foregrounds one of the key appeals of luxury fashion items, their exclusivity borne of their scarcity, and addresses one of its barriers to acquisition – the high cost. Since the allure of luxury fashion has trickled down to motivate purchases of fast fashion (Mohr et al. 2022), it is also possible that promoting "responsible shopping" as an important attribute of luxury fashion may lead to this value trickling down to those who would otherwise purchase fast fashion.

Influencers can significantly impact the sustainability of people's fashion choices, by endorsing either specific brands, or sustainability, or even the idea of re-acquiring used fashion. For example, British celebrity actor Emma Watson has popularized sustainable fashion choices by wearing them casually and at red-carpet events (Mohr et al. 2022). Catherine, the Duchess of Cambridge, often referred to as "Kate," is a proponent of British fashion labels, but in an attempt to appear more egalitarian often dons more affordable brands. Blog-preneurs and their fans have spawned the trend of "replikate," whereby they try to secure items that are replicas of, or which otherwise iconically resemble, items the Duchess wears (McFarlane et al. 2022). However, since the Duchess purchases from fast-fashion brands like TopShop and Zara, those clothes sell out as soon as she is seen in them, contributing to the purchase of unsustainable fast fashion.

Rent the Runway (www.renttherunway.com) was first established to offer designer dresses to women for special events but later evolved to offering everyday clothing via a subscription model. When Rent the Runway's new board member, celebrity actor Gwynth Paltrow, was asked if she would rent fashion from the company, she replied that "in my own way, I've been renting the runway for years . . . Borrowing a dress from a designer for a single moment at a premiere or an awards show, then giving it back afterward. Now I guess everyone is doing it . . ." (Paton and Maheshwari 2021). Ms. Paltrow likened renting to the common celebrity practice of borrowing fashion for use at major events, helping reshape clothing rentals as "something celebrities do." Given that celebrities are not likely to be perceived as using rented clothing to due economic constraints, this helps reframe renting luxury or other fashion items as being sustainable, away from the stigmatized notion of it being economical. Similarly, celebrity supermodels wearing vintage to red-carpet events have helped combat the notion that used clothing is only for those with limited financial means (Cassidy and Bennett 2015). Clearly, fashion influencers, whether luxury brand owners, celebrity actors and supermodels, royalty or blog-preneurs, have incredible potential (for good or bad) to influence sustainable fashion choices – these influencers have to carefully consider the implications of their fashion choices, and could also popularize wearing more ordinary used clothing (besides luxury and vintage) and help make the fashion reacquisition mode of swapping as as popular as renting. I would also suggest that unless items being offered for resale, rent or swapping were previously owned by a person attractive to potential purchasers, utilizing a commercial intermediary to facilitate monetary or non-monetary exchanges will make the contamination of used products by their prior owners less salient. Not only that, potential buyers are more likely to trust that a commercial intermediary has sanitized the products to remove biological contamination.

It is clear that although we cannot all only buy luxury, vintage or natural fashion, we cannot continue to thoughtlessly dispose of unwanted fashion items either. Circular fashion consumption can reduce waste and reduce the demand for, and production of, new garments. But, reusing materials and refurbishing existing garments also consume resources and result in carbon emissions. For example, a recent refurbishing of my vintage Hard Rock denim jacket cost me as much as the jacket originally retailed for! Consumers need to demand clarity regarding how collected old clothing is disposed of – some are even burned. Unfortunately, circularity is not a sufficient panacea for the global consequences of negative fashion. More has to be done, to facilitate the circular consumption of fashion, to collectively shape a sustainable future.

References

Argo, Jennifer J., Darren W. Dahl, and Andrea C. Morales (2006), "Consumer Contamination: How Consumers React to Products Touched by Others," *Journal of Marketing* 70 (2), 81–94.

Argo, Jennifer J., Darren W. Dahl, and Andrea C. Morales (2008), "Positive Consumer Contagion: Responses to Attractive Others in a Retail Context," *Journal of Marketing Research* 45 (6), 690–701.

Athwal, Navdeep, Victoria K. Wells, Marylyn Carrigan, and Claudia E. Henninger (2019), "Sustainable Luxury Marketing: A Synthesis and Research Agenda," *International Journal of Management Reviews* 21, 405–26.

Beckham, Daisy, and Benjamin G. Voyer (2014), "Can Sustainability be Luxurious? A Mixed-Method Investigation of Implicit and Explicity Attitudes towards Sustainabile Luxury Consumption," *NA-Advances in Consumer Research* 42, ed. June Cotte and Staey Wood, Duluth MN: Association for Consumer Research, 245–50.

Belk, Russell W., Melanie Wallendorf, and John F. Sherry Jr. (1989), "The Sacred and the Profane in Consumer Behavior: Theodicy on the Odyssey," *Journal of Consumer Research* 16 (1), 1–38.

Brydges, Taylor (2021), "Closing the Loop on Take, Make, Waste: Investigating circular Economy Practices in the Swedish Fashion Industry," *Journal of Cleaner Production* 293, 126245.

Brown, Stephen, Robert V. Kozinets, and John F. Sherry Jr. (2003), "Teaching Old Brands New Tricks: Retro Branding and the Revival of Brand Meaning," *Journal of Marketing* 67 (3), 19–33.

Cairns, Hannah M., Elaine L. Ritch, and Claire Bereziat (2021), "Think Eco, be Eco? The Tension between Attitudes and Behaviours of Millenial Fashion Consumers," *Journal of International Consumer Studies* 126201277.

Cassidy, Tracy D., and Hannah R. Bennett (2012), "The Rise of Vintage Fashion and the Vintage Consumer," *Fashion Practice* 4 (2), 239–62.

Cervellon, Marie-Cécile, Lindsay Carey, and Trine Harms (2012), "Something Old, something Used: Determinants of Women's Purchase of Vintage Fashion vs Second-Hand Fashion," *International Journal of Retail & Distribution Management* 40 (12), 956–74.

Danziger, Pamela N. (2022a), "Luxury Resale Market is on Fire and RealReal Lit the Fuse," *Forbes*, February 5, https://www.forbes.com/sites/pamdanziger/2022/02/05/luxury-resale-is-on-fire-and–therealreal-lit-the-fuse/?sh=643e59f213c1, accessed July 15, 2022.

Danziger, Pamela N. (2022b), "The Tribe of Fashion Thrifters Is Growing. ThredUp Invites Brands To Get On Board," *Forbes*, July 5, https://www.forbes.com/sites/pamdanziger/2022/07/05/the-tribe-of-fashion-thrifters-is-growing-thredup-invites-brands-to-get-on-board/?sh=1fc99a372ae0, accessed July 15, 2022.

D'Arpizio, Claudia, Federica Levato, Constance Gault, Joëlle de Montgolfier, and Lyne Jaroudi (2021), "From Surging Recovery to Elegant Advance: The Evolving Future of Luxury," *Bain and Company Luxury Study*, https://www.bain.com/insights/from-surging-recovery-to-elegant-advance-the-evolving-future-of-luxury/, accessed July 15, 2022.

Douglas, Mary (1966), "Purity and Danger: An Analysis of Concepts of Pollution and Taboo," London: Routledge & Kegan Paul.

Ellen MacArthur Foundation (2017), *A New Textiles Economy: Redesigning Fashion's Future*, https://ellenmacarthurfoundation.org/publications, accessed July 15, 2022.

Ellen MacArthur Foundation (2020), *Vision of a Circular Economy for Fashion*, https://ellenmacarthurfoundation.org/publications, accessed July 15, 2022.

Fernandez, Karen V. (2015), "Of Gates and Doors: A Critical Reflection on Agency," *Research in Consumer Behaviour* 17, ed. Rusell.W. Belk, Jeff B. Murray, and Anastasia Thyroff, 155–70, Bingley, UK: Emerald.

Fernandez, Karen V. (2022), "The "fake it till we make it" path to a shared, sustainable society," in *Anti-Consumption: Exploring the Opposition to Consumer Culture*, ed. Hélène Cherrier and Michael S.W. Lee. Routledge. Forthcoming.

Fernandez, Karen V., and John L. Lastovicka (2011), "Making Magic: Fetishes in Contemporary Consumption," *Journal of Consumer Research* 38 (2), 278–99.

Fernandez, Karen V., Ekant Veer, and John L. Lastovicka (2011), "Golden Ties that Bind: Crossing Boundaries in Diasporic Hindu Wedding Ritual," *Consumption, Markets and Culture* 14 (3), 245–65.

Fashion United (2016), *Global fashion industry statistics – International apparel*, https://fashionunited.com/global-fashion-industry-statistics, accessed July 19, 2022.

Gazzola, Patrizia, Enrica Pavionne, Roberta Pezzetti, and Daniele Grechi (2020), "Trends in the Fashion Industry. The Perception of Sustainability and Circular Economy: A Gender/Generation Quantitative Approach," *Sustainability* 12, 289.

Henninger, Claudia Elisabeth, Nina Bürklin, and Kirsi Niinimäki (2019), "The Clothes Swapping Phenomenon–When Consumers become Suppliers," *Journal of Fashion Marketing and Management: An International Journal* 23 (3), 327–344.

Joy, Annamma, John F. Sherry Jr, Alladi Venkatesh, Jeff Wang, and Ricky Chan (2012), "Fast fashion, Sustainability, and the Ethical Appeal of Luxury Bbrands," *Fashion Theory* 16 (3), 273–95.

Karatzas, Stelios, Alexandros Kapoulas, and Constantinos Vasilios Priporas (2019), "Consumers' Perceptions on Complexity and Prospects of Ethical Luxury: Qualitative Insights from Taiwan," *Australasian Marketing Journal* 27 (4), 224–32.

Lang, Chunmin, and Cosette M. Joyner Armstrong (2018), "Collaborative Consumption: The Influence of Fashion Leadership, Need for Uniqueness, and Materialism on Female Consumers' Adoption of Clothing Renting and Swapping," *Sustainable Production and Consumption* 13, 37–47.

Lee, Michael S.W., Miriam Seifert, and Helene Cherrier (2017), "Anti-Consumption and Governance in the Global Fashion Industry: Transparency is Key," *Governing Corporate Social Responsibility in the Apparel Industry after Rana Plaza*, ed. Anil Hira & Maureen Benson-Rea, 147–74, New York: Palgrave Macmillan.

Manshoven, Saskia, Maarten Christis, An Vercalsteren, Mona Arnold, Mariana Nicolau, Evelyn Lafond, L. Mortensen, and L. Coscieme (2019), "Textiles and the Environment in a Circular Economy," *European Topic Centre on Waste and Materials in a Green Economy*, 1–60.

McFarlane, Asheigh, Kathy Hamilton, and Paul Hewer (2022), "Putting Passion to Work: Passionate Labour in the Fashion Blogosphere," *European Journal of Marketing* 56 (4), 1210–31.

Mochaelidou, Nina, George Chritodoulides, and Caterina Presi (2022), "Ultra-high-net-wokth Individuals: Self-presentation and Luxury Consumption on Instagram," *European Journal of Marketing* 56 (4), 949–67.

Mohr, Iris, Leonora Fuxman, and Ali B. Mahmoud (2022), "A Triple-Trickle Theory for Sustainable Fashion Adoption: the Rise of a Luxury Trend," *Journal of Fashion Marketing and Management* 26 (4), 640–60.

Nemeroff, Carol, and Paul Rozin (1994), "The Contagion Concept in Adult Thinking in the United States: Transmission of Germs and of Interpersonal Influence," *Ethos* 22 (2), 158–86.

Nemeroff, Carol, and Paul Rozin (2018), "Back in Touch with Contagion: Some Essential Issues," *Journal of the Association for Consumer Research* 3 (4), 612–24.

O'Reilly, Lynn, Margaret Rucker, Rhonda Hughes, Marge Gorang, and Susan Hand (1984), "The Relationship of Psychological and Situational Variables to Usage of a Second-Order Marketing System," *Journal of the Academy of Marketing Science* 12 (3): 53–76.

Paton, Elizabeth, and Sapna Maheshswari (2021), "Ready to Return: Fashion Rental is Back," *New York Times*, May 25, https://www.nytimes.com/2021/05/25/business/rent-the-runway-clothing-covid.html, accessed July 1" https://www.nytimes.com/2021/05/25/business/rent-the-runway-clothing-covid.html, accessed July 1, 2022.

Rozin, Paul, Linda Millman, and Carol Nemeroff (1986), "Operation of the Laws of Sympathetic Magic in Disgust and Other Domains," *Journal of Personality and Social Psychology* 50 (4), 703–12.

Taunton, Esther (2021), "Allbirds, Icebreaker Team up to Support Climate-Friendly Regenerative Wool," *Stuff*, February 12, https://www.stuff.co.nz/business/farming/124213717/allbirds-icebreaker-team-up-to-support-climatefriendly-regenerative-wool, accessed July 1" https://www.stuff.co.nz/business/farm ing/124213717/allbirds-icebreaker-team-up-to-support-climatefriendly-regenerative-wool, accessed July 1, 2022.

Thredup (2022), *2022 Resale Report*, https://www.thredup.com/resale/, accessed July 1, 2022.

Meri-Maaria Frig, Pia Polsa, and Finola Kerrigan

9 Shifting Towards a More Sustainable Fashion Future

The fashion industry is one of the most harmful industries in the world and continues to grow despite widespread awareness of its environmental and social impacts (Boström and Micheletti 2016; Hvass 2013; Niinimäki et al. 2020; Indvik 2020). It functions mostly in a linear way, contributing to a take-make-waste economy (Ellen MacArthur Foundation 2017). Drawing together the extensive research on aspects of this topic, this chapter establishes how fashion is unsustainable and identifies different ways the unsustainability of fashion could be reduced and the key stakeholders who can instigate such change.

Introduction

> Buy less, choose well, make it last
>   -Vivienne Westwood

As it stands now, fashion is not sustainable. The fashion industry is one of the most polluting industries in the world: it is estimated to be responsible for 8–10% of annual global carbon emissions (Hvass 2013; Niinimäki et al. 2020; Indvik 2020). Waste, microplastics (Heikkilä et al. 2021), microfibers (European Parliament 2020), and harmful chemicals (Dahlbo et al. 2015) from clothing pollute waters and threaten our health. Significant amounts of fresh water (79 trillion liters annually) and land are used in fashion production (Boström and Micheletti 2016; Dahlbo et al. 2021; European Parliament 2020; Niinimäki et al. 2020). Many of the garments are wasted as they are either never or rarely worn: it is estimated that the fashion industry produces 92 million tons of textile waste annually (Degenstein, McQueen, and Krogman 2021; Joy and Peña 2017; Morgan and Birtwistle 2009; Niinimäki et al. 2020). Fast fashion has also led to low-quality materials that do not last (Fletcher 2010) and seasonal thinking in fashion has led to discarded products even if the garments would last (Jang et al. 2012).

Aside from the negative environmental impact, social issues in the fashion industry are widely known. For example, the industry can be seen as a leading industry of child and forced labor (thefashionact.org). The human rights impact of the garment industry is traced back to the complex global supply chains that characterize the field (Joy and Peña 2017).

Acknowledgments: we are grateful for Master's and Bachelor's students at Hanken school of Economics whose theses inspired this chapter: Emma Ranne, Ellen Huhtamies, Annika Rönnblad, Ida Havunta, and Ida Åstrand.

https://doi.org/10.1515/9783110783933-009

Different solutions have been suggested to address the problems in the fashion industry: these include, for example, the 3R initiatives (reuse, repair, recycle) (Armstrong et al. 2016; Dahlbo et al. 2021; Gorge et al. 2015). However, these initiatives do not change the logic of fashion and the dominant paradigm of fashion (Mukendi et al. 2020) and they largely attribute responsibility to the consumers, ignoring the other forces of influence such as whole system designs from materials to services (De los Rios and Charnley 2017; Ekström and Salomonson 2014). In this chapter, we will discuss this dominant paradigm of fashion, power relationships in fashion, and how that logic could be reversed, in line with sustaincentrism that seeks to avoid or mitigate social and environmental harm (Joy 2022; Joy and Peña 2017) and earth logic for fashion that calls for radical and systemic efforts to rethink fashion outside the growth logic and put the earth first in decision making (Fletcher and Tham 2019).

This chapter draws on the wealth of research into fashion consumption and sustainability and, in so doing, establishes the ways in which fashion is environmentally and socially unsustainable. It presents insights from past research into how fashion can be more sustainable and where the responsibility lies for this.

Sustainable Fashion

Fashion can be defined as "a culturally endorsed form of expression, in a particular material or non-material phenomenon, which is discernible at any given time and changes over time within a social system or group of associated individuals" (Sproles 1974, 463–472). Hence, fashion is socially and culturally constructed and exposed to use of power over individual decisions (Mikkonen et al. 2014). For some, the idea of "sustainable fashion" is an oxymoron (see Henninger et al. 2016; Clark 2008) but for others, sustainability itself can be fashionable. Following Atik et al. (2022, 8), we understand sustainable fashion as a form of expression that responds to the voices of the more silent stakeholders, such as the employees in the supply chains and the natural environment, and not only to the voices of fashion consumers.

Several different solutions for unsustainable fashion have been suggested. In this chapter we cover them by defining these solutions, exploring consumer actions in support of them, discussing the ways in which they are related to sustainability, and finally providing some suggestions as to how sustainability in fashion can be enhanced further. What is apparent from the coming sections is that many of the "new" business models harness traditional modes of production and consumption and may require an unlearning rather than a sense of progressing to new production and consumption modalities: many of the solutions put responsibility over individual consumers, instead of contributing to a system change.

Recycle

Recycling is not a novel act: "textile recycling originated in the West Riding of York-shire about 200 years ago when the 'rag and bone' men went door-to-door to collect rags, metal and any other household articles" (Birtwistle and Moore 2017, 212) and in some countries, unusable clothes have traditionally been cut into strips to make them to rag rugs. When clothes are recycled, they can be sold as such, repaired to be resold as clothes, or reused for purposes other than clothing (Abraham 2011). Environmental and economic concerns drive more ecological disposal options, such as resale, dona-tion, and reusing (Joung and Park-Poaps 2013; Turunen 2022). As consumers are in-creasingly aware of the ecological impact of fashion consumption, recycling – the processing of materials for use as raw materials in new products (Heikkilä et al. 2021) – has evolved into a core tenet of sustainability. With the circular economy sug-gested as a solution to current sustainability problems, recycling is increasingly both embraced and enhanced in fashion production and consumption.

However, the sheer number of textiles being produced and purchased has been rapidly increasing (Chakraborty et al. 2022; Indvik 2020). Research continuously shows that consumers often do not know what to do with the clothes that they no longer want (Arangdad et al. 2019; Ekström and Salomonson 2014; Joung 2014; Mu-kendi et al. 2020). While in some studies consumers have reported that higher aware-ness of the social and environmental impact of fashion can affect their clothing disposal behavior (Joung 2014), fashion-oriented consumers generally continue to throw away garments rapidly and with little ethical reflection (McNeill et al. 2020). Still, although the second-hand phenomenon is currently a major trend (Turunen 2022), many consumers hold negative attitudes toward used garments (Heikkilä et al. 2021; Mukendi et al. 2020). Motivation for second-hand shopping in general terms seems to be other than sustainability as second-hand consumers look for uniqueness, nostalgia, and frugality (Guiot and Roux 2010) or fashionability (Ferraro, Sands, and Brace-Govan 2016).

Due to consumer demand and changing regulations, fashion companies are inves-ting in recycling and take-back schemes (Chakraborty et al. 2022). While fast-fashion giants such as H&M and Zara have garment collection services in their stores, their real sustainability credentials have been questioned (Heikkilä et al. 2021; Stål and Corvellec 2022; see also Figure 9.1). The green marketing of fast-fashion brands only perpetuates increasing consumption by promoting the purchase of new products (Turunen 2022). Recycling programs have also been criticized for their lack of transparency, as informa-tion about what happens to the donated clothes after disposal largely remains a secret. Researchers as well as investigative journalists have followed the path of donated clothes via recycling centers to countries in the Global South, where a large proportion of the clothes are burned or thrown away (Hawley 2009; Knus-Gálan 2021).

In addition to encouraging post-use recycling, fashion companies can support cir-cularity by using deadstock materials in their designs and endorsing upcycling (using

Figure 9.1: Bloggers and social media activists can raise awareness of greenwashing and put pressure on firms to act responsibly.
Source: https://outilespyy.com/hm-is-the-donald-trump-of-recycle-week/.

used textiles as materials) and zero waste design that aims to minimise waste already in the production stage (Heikkilä et al. 2021). For example, several fashion brands have recently introduced products that are made from collected PET plastic bottles (Heikkilä et al. 2021). While the upcycled collections can increase environmental awareness, they can often be criticized for accentuating the true sustainability credentials of the products and obscuring the responsibility of the production and supply chain systems in fashion.

Recycling is more efficient in the production stage when the composition of the material is known (Ho and Choi 2012). Recycling technologies are being rapidly developed to enable fibre quality restoration and textile-to-textile recycling (Heikkilä et al. 2021). Currently, the sorting of textiles is mainly done by hand (Heikkilä et al. 2021). While there are clearly positive developments in terms of recycling capability, a lack of product information can impede efficient recycling in the supply chain. Acknowledging the need for policymakers to play a role in tackling sustainability issues in the fashion industry, European regulators have proposed an ambitious textiles strategy to kill fast fashion (Chakraborty et al. 2022).

Even if recycling at first glance seems like a perfect solution for overconsumption, there are further impediments to mass recycling of garments. The quality of clothes and fabrics does not always enable recycling and garments can be too complicated to be recycled (Andersen 2007). Consumers also perceive recycling as not convenient enough to be a realistic alternative (Dahlbo et al. 2015). Therefore, recycling can contribute to more sustainable practices through actions from industry, policymakers, and consumers, but additional actions need to be introduced alongside this.

Reuse and Rewear

Eco-conscious consumers have adopted various ways to extend the life of once purchased fashion items (Dobscha et al. 2012). Reusing refers to ways to extend the use of items (or their components) to make them last longer (Ho and Choi 2012). Reusing can also refer to transferring a product to a new user (Heikkilä et al. 2021), for example by donation to family and friends or charity (Bianchi and Birtwistle 2012). In case the old clothes cannot be used or repaired, they can be reused for purposes other than clothing (Abraham 2011).

Modern consumers tend to have a myriad of unused or forgotten items in their wardrobes. For example, nearly two-thirds of the products sold on second-hand luxury platforms are almost never worn (Turunen 2022). Sustainability-minded consumers have established that the most sustainable items are the ones that you already have, purchasing high-quality clothing that can be worn for a long time or sometimes passed along in the family or swapped with others (Bianchi and Birtwistle 2012). Furthermore, they restyle clothes in new and various ways, pairing items with different alternatives to create a new look and increase the versatility and use of one garment. Media articles on sustainable fashion increasingly cover stories on outfit repeating (rewearing the same outfit repeatedly) (Atik et al. 2022). With sustainability becoming fashionable, environmental activists and conscious consumers present counterarguments as to what constitutes sustainable fashion. That is, the environmental advantages of purchasing new items can be questioned.

While there has been a focus on sustainable production modes, the idea of sustainable clothes as those which are long lasting in terms of quality and style needs to be considered (Jung and Jin 2016; Nurmi 2021). For example, the "little black dress" by Coco Chanel has been regarded as revolutionary in terms of functional, long-lasting design (Atik et al. 2022). The reuse potential of a garment is heavily affected by the design (Heikkilä et al. 2021). 80% of the environmental impact of the product is determined by the design stage (Ho and Choi 2012). It is here that we see some tension between the concepts of "sustainability" linked to longevity of use and the idea of fashion as "so closely allied with changing trends and premature product replacement" (Fletcher and Williams 2013, 81). The fashion industry exercises power over seemingly free individuals by changing trends and thereby reducing the longevity of clothing.

Some fashion brands have also adopted resell/reuse platforms such as swap events (Dobscha et al. 2012; Hvass, 2013; Turunen, 2022). Swapping used clothes has been seen as a good way to prolong the service life of clothes and provide consumers the thrill of getting new items. Swapping is particularly supported by consumers that appreciate fashion (Weber, Lynes, and Young 2017). It nevertheless remains a rare activity. Organizations such as Global Fashion Exchange (https://www.globalfashionx change.org/) are committed to mainstreaming swapping through facilitating large scale swapping events.

Despite the efforts made to incentivise and facilitate more sustainable practices such as swapping, in reality, resource consumption in the textiles industry is estimated to triple between 2015 and 2050 (Ellen MacArthur Foundation 2017; Nurmi 2021). Recent reports have also revealed systematic practices of the retail sector to destroy and throw away items, such as customer returns and products that have minor faults. Brands like Burberry, Amazon, Nike, Victoria's Secret, and H&M have been reported to destroy unsold clothes (Atik et al. 2022; Mayo 2021).

It is apparent that consumer communities play a particularly important role by educating and advising others and popularizing sustainable behaviors (Joy and Peña 2017; Mukendi et al. 2020). Those consumers who generally recycle and are environmentally aware are also the ones who demonstrate the same behavior when it comes to clothing (Bianchi and Birtwistle 2012). Consumers tend to think that current materials are not durable enough or high quality enough to be reused or re-worn (Dahlbo et al. 2015). Further research is warranted to study how more sustainable practices can be scaled for the masses (Mukendi et al. 2020) and make such practices fashionable. Studies indicate the need to take a collective, social approach rather than one which focuses on individual responsibility by for example questioning the concept of fashion as changing trends, investigating the role of capitalism, and the social dominant paradigm of growth as drivers of fashion, and seeing the role of individuals as more than consumers.

Reduce/Refuse

Many consumers have chosen to reduce or refuse mindless consumption (Joy et al. 2015). Concepts including anti- and non-consumption, sufficiency, consumer resistance, countercultural movements, and boycotting characterize efforts to reject consumer capitalism (e.g., Gorge et al. 2015; Joy et al. 2015). These sustainable lifestyles could be supported by policies and regulations that would restrict the neoliberal "freedom" of fashion creators to govern consumers and limit self-expression to unsustainable options (see also Mikkonen et al. 2014).

Essentially, these movements have been born from a need to oppose current exploitative practices and to redefine what makes a "good life" (Joy et al. 2015). Whereas fashion consumption is primarily driven by the short-term gratification that consumers feel when buying new clothes, critical consumers can seek gratification by objecting to that or finding gratification in what they already have (Joy and Peña 2017).

While consumption and consumerism are so deeply ingrained in our societies and identities that questioning them is considered radical, harmful fashion consumption also faces resistance (Aja Barber in Nurmi 2021). For example, sustainable lifestyles may be reflected in appreciation for artisanship (Joy et al. 2015) and minimalism, which is meant to help declutter and simplify life (Chayka 2020). The minimalist trend has been seen as a response to increasing dissatisfaction with materialism and commodification but has also been criticized for promoting the consumerist values it purports to critique by promoting a specific minimalist fashion style (Chayka 2020).

Advocates of strong sustainable consumption (Lorek and Fuchs 2013) call for reduced consumption (Armstrong et al. 2016). This is reflected in the "fashion-detox" phenomenon, voluntary abstinence of clothing acquisition, for a chosen period of time (Armstrong et al. 2016; Mukendi et al. 2020). The environmental benefits of these short-term experiments can be countered by their rebound effects, as consumers can feel compelled to consume as usual afterward (Mukendi et al. 2020). In consequence, not even voluntary consumer actions necessarily lead to sustainability and therefore actions on other societal levels are needed so that not all the responsibility for sustainable actions rests on the consumer level.

Fashion firms have also noted the escalating resistance to fast fashion and overconsumption. For example, on Black Friday in 2011, the apparel brand Patagonia famously ran a "Don't Buy This Jacket" ad in the New York Times (Armstrong et al. 2016). With the ad, the brand urged people to consume less – or to think twice about what they buy (Patagonia 2022).

Slow fashion has been suggested as a solution to the problems in the fashion industry (Clark 2008; Fletcher 2010; Watson and Yan 2013). It is defined as a philosophy, design approach, and consumption style that is underpinned by reduced production and consumption, lessened planetary impact, and ethical practices (Mukendi et al. 2020; Joy and Peña 2017). Slow fashion, inspired by the slow food movement (see Clark 2008), is thus positioned as an alternative to growth-based fast fashion.

The voluntary initiatives to shift the fashion industry towards sustainability have nevertheless been understood to have failed (Pucker 2022). It has been suggested that more stringent regulation is needed to force the industry to address climate change and other societal crises (Pucker 2022), moving away from neoliberalism. The growth imperative is increasingly understood to be at the core of the harmful planetary impact of the fashion industry (Fletcher 2010; Pucker 2022). Furthermore, intergovernmental regulation has been called for to monitor the global fashion industry (Laudal 2010).

Care and Repair

While materials, quality and design contribute to the longevity of a garment, another key aspect of sustainable fashion is concerned with care and repair. Repairing and taking care of fashion garments, as well as refraining from over-cleaning (Dombek-Keith and Loker 2011), are regarded as essential clothing life cycle extension behaviors (McNeill et al. 2020). While researchers have noted a societal capability gap in taking care of and mending clothing (Mukendi et al. 2020), commercial repair is available in care and mending services as well as in some fashion retail shops. Environmentally conscious consumer communities have also organized clothing repair workshops to endorse a mindful connection to fashion and to influence change (Mukendi et al. 2020). Linked to this is the idea of "visible mending" (McGovern and Barnes 2022) where craft skill in terms of repair is left on display in clothing to demonstrate the commitment to and skill involved in prolonging the life of a garment. From crafting communities to established brands such as Patagonia or Barbour, this not new but rebranded practice has gained some momentum. Again, collective or social responses to sustainability challenges are necessary to support the possibilities of individuals to govern, or "structure the possible field of action" to make fashion sustainable (Foucault 1982, 790).

At the same time, fast fashion clothes are estimated to last for ten washes (Joy et al. 2015). It is often cheaper, and more convenient, to buy a new product than to have it repaired – which was not always the case. Figure 9.2 shows a more than 60 years old piece of transgenerational clothing that brands itself as "the life time product," not a lifestyle product. Unsustainable clothing disposal is driven by the fashionability and condition of items as well as changes in personal taste (McNeill et al. 2020) but that personal taste is also governed by the fashion industry and influencers. Mc-

Figure 9.2: "The life time product".

Neill and colleagues found that garment maintenance, such as repairing, can be increased by emphasizing the personal emotional connection between the wearer and the garment (2020), like transgenerational clothing could do. For example, slow fashion consumers often describe their clothing as art and feel an emotional connection to what they wear (Watson, Zarley, and Yan 2013). Accordingly, care and mending services highlight not only the ecological benefits of taking care of your garments, but also the personal and style benefits of knowing the garments that we wear (Kiuru, Manninen, and Valkola 2020). Repair services are also an essential part of sustainable brands. Repair and upgrade services also create important opportunities for luxury brands (Joy et al. 2015). As self-repair and community repair events remain as subculture activities (Mukendi et al. 2020), circular business models that provide maintenance and mending services are of key importance.

Rent

When renting clothing, consumers can use fashion items instead of purchasing new garments or owning them themselves (Arrigo 2022; Jain et al. 2021). Fashion rentals are becoming increasingly common for example because of their perceived sustainability potential and the present macro-trends such as the sharing economy (Jain et al. 2021; Lang et al. 2020). Literature on fashion rentals has examined business-to-consumer as well as peer-to-peer fashion rentals (Arrigo 2022; Iran and Schrader 2017; Jain et al. 2021). In addition, some fashion brands have also enabled an option to rent their garments (Arrigo 2022).

The new innovative business models have been praised for their sustainability credentials, such as for reducing waste, emissions, and raw material consumption, extending the use and lifecycle of garments, and opposing overconsumption (Arrigo 2022; Jain et al. 2021; Lang et al. 2020). Renting is understood to contribute to a reduction in the production of new clothes (Arrigo 2022). However, research shows that environmental reasons are not the primary motives for consumers to engage in fashion rental. Instead, consumers most often seek to try new styles, express their identity, try luxury fashion items, or to meet a specific dress code for a special occasion (Arrigo 2022; Jain et al. 2021). If these motivations generally apply for fashion consumption, then renting provides a solution for the need for change and novelty.

The environmental benefits of clothing rentals have also been critically examined (Johnson and Plepys 2021; Levänen et al. 2021). For example, Johnson and Plepys (2021) found that the environmental savings depend on how often consumers wear the rented items and how they travel to rental stores, and to what extent renting substitutes other forms of consumption. Some consumers are also likely to consume as usual after participating in the practice (Arrigo 2022). The environmental impact of renting is further affected by washing and ironing, as well as transportation and delivery (Arrigo 2022;

Levänen et al. 2021). Due to these externalities, the environmental burden of sharing garments can in fact be larger than consumption as usual (Levänen et al. 2021).

Fashion renting can nevertheless challenge the consumption culture and the dominant social paradigm to shift away from the disposable culture (Arrigo 2022). For fashion rental businesses, the main barriers include the reservations many consumers have against collaborative consumption (Jain et al. 2021). Nevertheless, fashion rentals are expected to become a future trend (Lang et al. 2020). For this innovative business model to demonstrate its full sustainability potential, renting should be combined with other ecological practices that have a low climate impact (Levänen et al. 2021).

Social Sustainability in Fashion

While much of this chapter has been devoted to environmental sustainability considerations, we now turn to the related concept of social sustainability. The current fashion system is characterized by the race to the bottom, as fashion firms from fast fashion to luxury brands typically seek to procure the lowest prices globally (Kennedy et al. 2017). Consequently, within the present system, companies may gain a competitive advantage by sourcing from countries with the weakest regulations and infrastructure (thefashionact.org). This leads not only to lower prices but also to environmental damage, longer supply chains, weak worker rights, and unsafe working conditions.

The Rana Plaza factory collapse in Bangladesh in 2013 caused widespread concern about the working conditions of garment workers and led to some improvements in labour rights (Kennedy et al. 2017). For example, several fashion brands have now signed the International Accord, which ensures that garment factories are made safe. However, multiple fashion brands are yet to sign the Accord agreement. Watchdog groups such as the Clean Clothes Campaign (cleanclothes.org) keep track of which brands have committed to improving worker safety.

Yet, despite the widespread calls to improve the rights of garment workers, the problems are deep-rooted in the fashion system and clothing brands continue to find themselves in scandals concerning their sourcing practices. Several well-known fashion brands have been connected to forced labour by Uyghurs in Xinjiang, China (see for example Friedman 2022b; Kelly 2020). It is estimated that cotton produced in the Xinjiang region can be found in one-fifth of cotton garments in the global apparel market (Friedman 2022b).

Research on sustainable fashion consumption has shown significant growth in ethical concern about social issues, such as sweatshop labor (Lundblad and Davies 2016; Niinimäki 2010). Slow fashion brands respond to these ethical concerns by producing items locally and knowing their entire supply chain. Some widely known consumer movements such as Fashion Revolution (fashionrevolution.org) aim to incite change in fashion consumption and production through research, education, and advocacy. It is becoming increasingly clear, however, that consumer movements as well as voluntary business initiatives are not sufficient to tackle the social issues in the fashion industry, and regulation is needed to hold fashion brands accountable for their environmental and social impact (Friedman 2022a).

Ecosystem for Fashion

What is evident from our overview of the existing literature is that a systems-based approach is required to progress the sustainable fashion agenda and to move away from the neoliberal and growth-based fashion paradigm. Such an approach will see the burden for change largely resting with industry actors, regulators, and, to a much smaller extent, the consumer. None of the above solutions are possible if the fashion industry from material production to distribution systems will not address this. If fabrics are not durable or recyclable then reuse, recycle, and repair are not possible. If the production of fabrics and clothes is not toxic-free and clean as well as socially sustainable then whatever consumer efforts are done, the environmental and social change will not happen. Therefore, actions are also needed from fashion producers such as The Jeans Redesign Guidelines that call for durable and healthy materials, recyclable clothes, and traceable production and distribution or circular business models (Ellen MacArthur Foundation 2021). Kering's development of an environmental profit and loss account (https://www.kering.com/en/sustainability/measuring-our-impact/our-ep-l/) is also a step towards this aim. To make circularity possible several barriers need to be overcome at many levels of society (Grafström and Aasma 2021). Shifting towards a more sustainable fashion future requires a clear shift away from individual responsibility, and a holistic examination of the responsibility of all actors such as producers, influencers, marketers, governments, logistic firms, and retailers. Drawing on the presented extant research on sustainable fashion, we suggest some key actions for producers, policymakers, and consumers (Table 9.1).

Along with this systems-based approach, we support Gupta et al.'s (2019) assertion that a shift from fashion to style may be required to pursue the sustainability agenda. The somewhat inevitable centrality of the market and extractive capitalist logic within the contemporary fashion system seems to preclude the fashion industry and fashionable consumers from making progress towards sustainable aims. However, a focus on style, rooted in caretaking, valuing longevity, swapping and renting, as a status symbol and building an ecosystem around this to allow these practices to be rediscovered may be a way forward. Such a redirection from the fashion market to a marketplace supported by the education system, support for small and local industries, investment in new technologies in terms of sustainable materials, sustainable manufacturing, and improved washing practices are necessary to make such a shift, coupled with laws and regulations when voluntary change is not sufficient.

Table 9.1: Actions for producers, policy makers, and consumers to support a shift towards sustainability in fashion.

Initiatives	Actors and Actions
Recycle	– Producers: Consider the possibility for textiles to be recycled already in the design/production stage; Offer information to consumers as to how to recycle – Policymakers: Develop policy to incentivize production of recyclable and sustainable materials; Improve facilities for recycling; Support innovation in recycling technology; Introduce binding requirements for the reusability and reparability of textiles and introduce regulation to stop the destruction of unsold or recycled textiles – Consumers: Consume less; Check labels; Consider potential to recycle at end of life: reuse or facilitate reuse, when possible
Reuse and Rewear	– Producers: Invest in quality; Consider design properties that allow for multiple use; Offer repair services and facilitate reselling; Normalize reusing and restyling in marketing; In online retail: offer clear descriptions of products and streamlined, slower returns – Policymakers: Incentivize and facilitate community reuse activities; Support circular business models; Promote creative consumption practices among consumers through advertising campaigns focused on developing consumer creativity through reimagining, repurposing, and reusing garments rather than replacing – Consumers: Favor garments that are long-lasting in terms of quality and style; Restyle clothes you already have
Reduce/ Refuse	– Producers: Enable on-demand manufacturing; Improve production quality and, when possible, reduce production quantities – Policymakers: Support social marketing campaigns aimed at reducing consumption; Help tackle greenwashing in fashion; Push for improved disclosure and transparency in global supply chains – Consumers: Develop closer connections with garments and creative consumption practices; Encourage sufficiency practices and questioning what do we really need
Care and Repair	– Producers: Use labels and offer advice to promote conscious garment care; Offer repair services and high-quality garments; Consider prioritizing fabrics requiring less laundering – Policymakers: Invest in upskilling consumers in repair; Social marketing campaigns aimed at reducing unnecessary laundering; Incentives for companies providing repair services – Consumers: Develop conscious care practices around garments such as laundering less and learning how to repair; Support community activities such as clothing repair workshops
Rent	– Producers: Produce high quality garments; Allow ease of rental; Develop sophisticated sizing to allow more consumers to rent confidently; Develop distribution practices that minimize garment travel – Policy makers: Support circular business models; Share information about the sustainability aspects of different business models and consumption practices – Consumers: Consider rental services for special occasions

References

Abraham, Nandita (2011). "The apparel aftermarket in India – a case study focusing on reverse logistics." *Journal of fashion marketing and management* 15, no. 2: 211–227.

Andersen, Mikael Skou (2007). "An introductory note on the environmental economics of the circular economy." *Sustainability Science* 2: 133–140.

Arangdad, Shaghayegh Rezaei, Kristin Thoney-Barletta, Jeff Joines, and Lori Rothenberg (2019). "Influence of demographics and motivational factors on US consumer clothing and shoes disposal behavior." *Research Journal of Textile and Apparel* 23, no. 3: 170–187.

Armstrong, Cosette M., Kirsi Niinimäki, Chunmin Lang, and Sari Kujala (2016). "A user-oriented clothing economy? Preliminary Affirmation for Sustainable Clothing Consumption Alternatives." *Sustainable development* 24: 18–31.

Arrigo, Elisa (2022). "Digital platforms in fashion rental: a business model analysis." *Journal of Fashion Marketing and Management* 26, no. 1: 1–20.

Atik, Deniz, Lena Cavusoglu, Zeynep Ozdamar Ertekin, and A. Fuat Firat (2022). "Fashion, consumer markets, and democratization." *Journal of Consumer Behaviour* 21, no: 5: 1135–1148.

Bianchi, Constanza, and Grete Birtwistle (2012). "Consumer clothing disposal behaviour: a comparative study." *International Journal of Consumer Studies* 36: 335–341.

Birtwistle, Grete, and C.M. Moore (2007). "Fashion clothing – where does it all end up?" *International Journal of Retail & Distribution Management* 35: 210–216.

Boström, Magnus, and Michele Micheletti (2016). "Introducing the Sustainability Challenge of Textiles and Clothing." *Journal of Consumer Policy* 39: 367–375.

Chakraborty, Sayan, Pak Yiu, and Lien Hoang (2022). "From China to India, Asia braces for EU plan to kill fast fashion." *Nikkei Asia*, June 10, 2022.

Chayka, Kyle (2020). *The Longing for Less: Living with Minimalism*. New York: Bloomsbury Publishing.

Cherrier, Hélène, and Jeff B. Murray (2004). "The sociology of consumption: The hidden facet of marketing." *Journal of marketing management* 20, no: 5–6:509–525.

Clark, Hazel (2008). "SLOW+ FASHION – an Oxymoron – or a Promise for the Future . . .?" *Fashion Theory* 12, no. 4: 427–446

Dahlbo, Helena, Kristiina Aalto, Hanna Salmenperä, Hanna Eskelinen, Jaana Pennanen, Kirsi Sippola, and Minja Huopalainen (2015). "Tekstiilien uudelleenkäytön ja tekstiilijätteen kierrätyksen tehostaminen Suomessa [More efficient re-use of textiles and recycling of textile waste in Finland]." The Finnish Environment.

Dahlbo, Helena, Aija Rautiainen, Hannu Savolainen, Pauliina Oksanen, Piia Nurmi, Marketta Virta, and Oskari Pokela (2021). "Textile flows in Finland 2019." Reports from Turku University of Applied Sciences 276.

De los Rios, Irel Carolina, and Fiona J.S. Charney (2017). "Skills and Capabilities for a Sustainable and Circular Economy: The Changing Role of Design." *Journal of Cleaner Production* 160: 109–122.

Degenstein, Lauren M., Rachel H. McQueen, and Naomi T. Krogman (2021). "'What goes where'? Characterizing Edmonton's municipal clothing waste stream and consumer clothing disposal." *Journal of Cleaner Production* 296: 1–11.

Dobscha, Susan, Andy Prothero, and Pierre McDonagh (2012). "(Re)Thinking Distribution Strategy: Principles from Sustainability." In *Marketing Management: A Cultural Perspective*, edited by Lisa Penaloza, Nil Toulouse and Luca Visconti, 461–74. New York: Routledge.

Dombek-Keith, Kathleen, and Suzanne Loker (2011). "Sustainable Clothing Care by Design". In *Shaping Sustainable Fashion*, edited by Alison Gwilt and Timo Rissanen, 101–118. London, UK: Earthscan.

Ekström, Karin M., and Nicklas Salomonson (2014). "Reuse and recycling of clothing and textiles – A network approach." *Journal of Macromarketing* 34, no. 3: 383–399.

Ellen MacArthur Foundation (2017). A new textiles economy: Redesigning fashion's future. Available at: https://archive.ellenmacarthurfoundation.org/assets/downloads/A-New-Textiles-Economy.pdf (last accessed July 18, 2023).

Ellen MacArthur Foundation (2021). The Jeans Redesign. Available at: https://ellenmacarthurfoundation. org/the-jeans-redesign (last accessed July 18, 2023).

European Parliament (2020). The impact of textile production and waste on the environment. Available at: https://www.europarl.europa.eu/news/en/headlines/society/20201208STO93327/the-impact-of-textile-production-and-waste-on-the-environment-infographic (last accessed October 19, 2022).

Ferraro, Carla, Sean Sands, and Jan Brace-Govan (2016). "The role of fashionability in second-hand shopping motivations." *Journal of retailing and consumer services* 32: 262–268.

Fletcher, Kate (2008). *Sustainable Fashion and Textiles: Design Journeys*. Routledge: London.

Fletcher, Kate (2010). "Slow fashion: an invitation for systems change." *Fashion Practice* 2, no. 2: 259–266.

Fletcher, Kate, and Dilys Williams (2013). "Fashion education in sustainability in practice." *Research Journal of Textile and Apparel* 17, no. 2: 81–88.

Fletcher, Kate, and Mathilda Tham (2019). EARTH LOGIC. Fashion Action Research Plan. Available at: https://katefletcher.com/wp-content/uploads/2019/10/Earth-Logic-plan-FINAL.pdf (last accessed July 18, 2023).

Foucault, Michael (1982). "The Subject and Power." In *Beyond Structuralism and Hermeneutics*, edited by Hubert L. Dreyfus and Paul Rabinow, 777–795. London: Harvester Wheatsheaf.

Friedman, Vanessa (2022a). "New York Could Make History With a Fashion Sustainability Act." *The New York Times*, January 7, 2022.

Friedman, Vanessa (2022b). "U.S. Effort to Combat Forced Labor Targets Corporate China Ties." *The New York Times*, January 5, 2022.

Gorge, Hélène, Maud Herbert, Nil Özçağlar-Toulouse, and Isabelle Robert (2015), "What do we really need? Questioning consumption through sufficiency," *Journal of Macromarketing* 35, no: 1: 11–22.

Grafström, Jonas, and Siri Aasma (2021). "Breaking circular economy barriers." *Journal of Cleaner Production* 292: 1–14.

Guiot, Denis, and Dominique Roux (2010). "A second-hand shoppers' motivations scale: antecedents, consequences and implications for retailers." *Journal of Retailing* 86: 355–371.

Gupta, Shipra, Wencke Gwozdz, and James Gentry (2019). "The Role of Style Versus Fashion Orientation on Sustainable Apparel Consumption." *Journal of Macromarketing* 39, no. 2: 188–207.

Hawley, Jana (2009). "Understanding and improving textile recycling: a system perspective." In *Sustainable textiles: Life cycle and environmental impact*, edited by R.S. Blackburn, 179–199. Woodhead, New York, NY.

Heikkilä, Pirjo, Minna Cheung, Kirsti Cura, Ilona Engblom, Jouko Heikkilä, Vafa Järnefelt, Taina Kamppuri, Minna Kulju, Inka Mäkiö, Piia Nurmi, Rosa Palmgren, Päivi Petänen, Niko Rintala, Annariina Ruokamo, Eetta Saarimäki, Kaisa Vehmas, and Marketta Virta (2021). "Telaketju – Business from Circularity of Textiles." VTT Technical Research Centre of Finland. VTT Research Report No. VTT-R-00269-21.

Henninger, Claudia E., Panayiota J. Alevizou, and Caroline J. Oates (2016). "What is sustainable fashion?" *Journal of Fashion Marketing and Management: An International Journal* 20, no. 4: 400–416.

Ho, Holly Pui-Yan, and Tsan-Ming Choi (2012). "A Five-R analysis for sustainable fashion supply chain management in Hong Kong: a case analysis." *Journal of fashion marketing & management* 16, no. 2: 161–175.

Hvass, Kerli Kant (2013). "Post-retail responsibility of garments – a fashion industry perspective." *Journal of fashion marketing and management* 18, no. 4: 413–430.

Indvik, Lauren (2020). "Sustainable fashion? There's no such thing." *Financial Times*, November 13, 2020.

Iran, Samira, and Ulf Schrader (2017). "Collaborative Fashion Consumption and its Environmental Effects." *Journal of Fashion Marketing and Management: An International Journal* 21, no. 4: 468–482.

Jacobs, Kathleen, Lars Petersen, Jacob Hörisch, and Dirk Battenfeld (2018). "Green thinking but thoughtless buying? An empirical extension of the value-attitude-behaviour hierarchy in sustainable clothing." *Journal of Cleaner Production* 203: 1155–1169.

Jain, Ritu, Kokil Jain, Abhishek Behl, Vijay Pereira, Manlio Giudice, and Demetris Vrontis. (2021). "Mainstreaming fashion rental consumption: A systematic and thematic review of literature." *Journal of Business Research* 139: 1525–1539.

Jang, Junghyun, Eunju Ko, Eunha Chun, and Euntaik Lee (2012). "A study of a social content model for sustainable development in the fast fashion industry." *Journal of global fashion market* 3, no. 2: 61–69.

Johnson, Emma, and Andrius Plepys (2021). "Product-Service Systems and Sustainability: Analysing the Environmental Impacts of Rental Clothing." *Sustainability* 13, no. 4: 2118.

Joung, Hyun-Mee (2014). "Fast-fashion consumers' post-purchase behaviours." *International journal of retail & distribution management* 42, no. 8: 688–697.

Joung, Hyun-Mee, and Haesun Park-Poaps (2013). "Factors motivating and influencing clothing disposal behaviours." *International Journal of Consumers Studies* 37: 105–111.

Joy, Annamma (2022). "Artification and Sustainability: Foundational Pillars of the Luxury Worlds of Art, Fashion, and Wine." In *The Future of Luxury Brands: Artification and Sustainability*, edited by Annamma Joy, 1–32. Berlin, Boston: De Gruyter.

Joy, Annamma, John F. Sherry, Jr., Alladi Venkatesh, Jeff Wang, and Ricky Chan (2015). "Fast Fashion, Sustainability, and the Ethical Appeal of Luxury Brands." *Fashion Theory* 16, no. 3: 273–296.

Joy, Annamma, and Camilo Peña (2017). "Sustainability and the Fashion Industry: Conceptualizing Nature and Traceability." In *Sustainability in Fashion: A Cradle to Upcycle Approach*, edited by Claudia Heninger, Panayiota Alevizou, Helen Goworek, and Daniella Ryding, 31–54. Cham, SE: Palgrave Macmillan.

Jung, Sojin, and Byoungho Jin (2016). "From Quantity to Quality: Understanding Slow Fashion Consumers for Sustainability and Consumer Education." *International Journal of Consumer Studies* 40: 410–421.

Kelly, Annie (2020). "'Virtually entire' fashion industry complicit in Uighur forced labour, say rights groups." *The Guardian*, July 23, 2020.

Kennedy, Ann-Marie, Sommer Kapitan, Neha Bajaj, Angelina Bakonyi, and Sean Sands (2017). "Uncovering Wicked Problem's system structure: seeing the forest for the trees." *Journal of Social Marketing* 7, no. 1: 51–73.

Kiuru, Jenni, Maria Manninen, and Johanna Valkola (2020). *Maintain*. Helsinki: Gummerus Kustannus Oy.

Knus-Gálan, Minna (2021). "How we investigated the global billion business of used clothes – with trackers." *Dataharvest – The European Investigative Journalism Conference*, October 8, 2020.

Laitala, Kirsi (2014). "Consumers' clothing disposal behavior – a synthesis of research results." *International Journal of Consumer Studies* 38: 444–457.

Lang, Chunmin, Muzhen Li, and Li Zhao (2020). "Understanding consumers' online fashion renting experiences: A text-mining approach." *Sustainable Production and Consumption* 21: 132–144.

Laudal, Thomas (2010). "An Attempt to Determine the CSR Potential of the International Clothing Business." *Journal of Business Ethics* 96: 63–77.

Levänen, Jarkko, Ville Uusitalo, Anna Härri, Elisa Kareinen, and Lassi Linnanen (2021). "Innovative recycling or extended use? Comparing the global warming potential of different ownership and end-of-life scenarios for textiles." *Environmental Research Letters* 16, no. 5: 1–11.

Lorek, Sylvia, and Doris Fuchs (2013). "Strong Sustainable Consumption Governance – Precondition for a Degrowth Path?" *Journal of Cleaner Production* 38: 36–43.

Lundblad, Louise, and Iain A. Davies (2016). "Motivations behind sustainable fashion consumption." *Journal of Consumer Behavior* 15: 149–162.

Markkula, Annu, and Johanna Moisander (2012). "Discursive Confusion over Sustainable Consumption: A Discursive Perspective on the Perplexity of Marketplace Knowledge." *Journal of Consumer Policy* 35, no. 1: 105–125.

Mayo, Aleeya (2021). "Amazon isn't alone in reportedly destroying unsold goods. Nike, Burberry, H&M and others have also come under fire for torching their own products." *Insider*, June 22, 2021.

McGovern, Alyce, and Clementine Barnes (2022). "Visible mending, street stitching and embroidered handkerchiefs: How craftivism is being used to challenge the fashion industry." *International Journal for Crime, Justice and Social Democracy* 11, no. 2: 87–101.

McNeill, Lisa S., Robert P. Hamlin, Rachel H. McQueen, Lauren Degenstein, Tony C. Garett, Linda Dunn, and Sarah Wakes (2020). "Fashion sensitive young consumers and fashion garment repair: Emotional connections to garments as a sustainability strategy." *International Journal of Consumer Studies* 44: 361–368.

McNeill, Lisa S., and Rebecca Moore (2015). "Sustainable fashion consumption and the fast fashion conundrum: fashionable consumers and attitudes to sustainability in clothing choice." *International Journal of Consumer Studies* 39, no. 3: 212–222.

Mikkonen, Ilona, Handan Vicdan, and Annu Markkula (2014). "What not to wear? Op- positional ideology, fashion, and governmentality in wardrobe self-help." *Consumption Markets & Culture* 17, no. 3: 254–273.

Morgan, Louise R., and Grete Birtwistle (2009). "An investigation of young fashion consumers' disposal habits." *International Journal of Consumer Studies* 33: 190–198.

Mosbech, Anne-Marie (2012). "Goodbye, Fast Fashion." *Focus Denmark*, December 3, 2012.

Mukendi, Amira, Iain Davies, Sarah Glozer, and Pierre McDonagh (2020). "Sustainable fashion: current and future research directions." *European Journal of Marketing* 54, no. 11: 2873–2909.

Niinimäki, Kirsi (2010). Eco-clothing, consumer identity and ideology. Sustainable Development 18: 150–162.

Niinimäki, Kirsi, Greg Peters, Helena Dahlbo, Patsy Perry, Timo Rissanen, and Alison Gwilt (2020). "The environmental price of fast fashion." *Nature Review; Earth and Environment* 1: 189–200.

Nurmi, Anniina (2021). Rakastan ja vihaan vaatteita [I love and hate clothes]. Painotalo: Otavan Kirjapaino Oy.

Patagonia (2022). Don't Buy This Jacket, Black Friday and the New York Times. Available at: https://www.patagonia.com/stories/dont-buy-this-jacket-black-friday-and-the-new-york-times/story-18615.html (last accessed October 19, 2022).

Pucker, Kenneth, P. (2022). The Myth of Sustainable Fashion. *Harvard Business Review*, January 13, 2022.

Sproles, George B. (1974). "Fashion theory: A conceptual framework." *Advances in Consumer Research* 1: 463–472.

Stål, Herman, I., and Corvellec, Hervé (2022). "Organizing Means–Ends Decoupling: Core–Compartment Separations in Fast Fashion." *Business & Society* 61, no. 4: 857–885.

Thompson, Craig J., and Gokcen Coskuner-Balli (2007). "Enchanting Ethical Consumerism: The Case of Community Supported Agriculture." *Journal of Consumer Culture* 7, no. 3: 275–303.

Turunen, Linda Lisa Maria. (2022). "Luxury Resale Shaping the Future of Fashion." In *The Future of Luxury Brands: Artification and Sustainability*, edited by Annamma Joy, 185–202. Berlin, Boston: De Gruyter.

Watson, Maegan Zarley, and Ruoh-Nan Yan (2013). "An exploratory study of the decision processes of fast versus slow fashion consumers." *Journal of Fashion Marketing and Management* 17, no. 2: 141–159.

Weber, Sabine, Jennifer Lynes, and Steven B. Young (2017). "Fashion Interest as a Driver for Consumer Textile Waste Management: Reuse, Recycle or Disposal." *International Journal of Consumer Studies* 41: 207–215.

Deniz Atik and Zeynep Ozdamar Ertekin

10 The Illusion of Democracy in Fashion Industry

Introduction

Democratization of fashion has been a topic of interest both in academia and popular media. The popular discourses suggest that fast fashion – simultaneously emulating high fashion designs and making them available for the masses at affordable prices – has democratized fashion (e.g., Pous 2013; Scott 2005). For instance, one of the biggest fast fashion brands, Zara, presents itself as an important agent in democratizing the latest clothing styles for consumers (Bowman and McCammon 2019). Similar arguments have been made for democratization of luxury. Buying counterfeit products of luxury fashion, according to some, can benefit both consumers and the companies whose brands are being copied. It is good for consumers because knock-offs enable them to take part of fashion and enjoy latest trends at affordable prices; it is good for companies because counterfeit increases the brand awareness and prestige of luxury brands (Nia and Zaichkowsky 2000; Raustiala and Sprigman 2012). Collaborations between designer luxury brands and fast fashion brands, such as H&M and Karl Lagerfeld, H&M and Balmain, or Missoni and Target, also enable consumers from different social classes to have access to luxury labels, benefiting co-partner brands in terms of brand loyalty and increased market share (Mrad, Farah, and Haddad 2019). Thus, it has been assumed that the democratization of luxury increases the level of awareness and popularity of the brand and provides access to luxury for the masses.

Conversely, democratization of luxury also leads to brand equity erosion and impairs a luxury brand's uniqueness value and image (Shukla et al. 2022), and in none of these practices the main aim is to democratize fashion or make it more inclusive. Recent scholarly research showed that, at consumer level, the diffusion of fashion to larger consumer segments does not necessarily indicate that fashion is democratized, due to persistent problems that hamper inclusivity and sustainability goals (Atik et al. 2022), as the speed and trend driven "fast fashion" business model has high environmental and social costs (Bowman and McCammon 2019). We will discuss this in more detail in the next section. Furthermore, recent research also uncovered links and overlaps between the broadening of the markets and marketing and the neoliberal ideology that emphasizes expansion of markets at any cost beyond the economic realm through the marketization of every aspect of social experiences – which has led to the rise in inequality and economic crises (Dholakia et al. 2020; Ozgun et al. 2017). Atik et al. (2022) suggests that the cycle of fashion becoming a principle of economic interest (for maximizing corporate profits) is the underlying reason for retarding democratization. According to Dholakia et al. (2020, 868), "[T]o reorient away from serv-

https://doi.org/10.1515/9783110783933-010

ing only the interests of centralized capital and to serve the needs of people the world over, marketing thought and practice need to reorient to innovative ideas that transcend the broadened and generic marketing concepts."

Democratization has been conceptualized in different domains. The conceptualizations of democratization within the management and the marketing areas mainly focus on consumers' broader freedom of choice and access to markets/goods; some also highlight consumer participation and co-creation (Shukla et al. 2022). In this chapter, we explore "democratization of fashion" from a more holistic perspective, at institutional level, to see if the practices of the multiple constituents of the fashion system are democratizing for everyone involved in the making and consumption of fashion. For such an assessment, we investigate the power structures and the labor dynamics of the industry and its societal and environmental impact.

The Palgrave Macmillan Dictionary of Political Thought defines democracy as "government by the people as a whole (Greek: demos) rather than by any section, class or interest within it" (Scruton 2007). This definition serves well the purpose of this chapter for understanding how democratic the fashion industry is and seeing if everyone is attended equitably from the creation of fashion to its dismissal. In the case of fashion, "the further the equality of conditions advances, the more fashion is democratized, in the sense that ever-wider sectors of society become, actually or potentially, initiators (models) and followers (imitators) of fashions" (Rosa 2013, 85). Here, it becomes critical to question if it is enough to call fashion democratic when fashion becomes more accessible and more people have the chance to become initiators and followers.

Since the discourses of democratization have been mainly concerned with the diffusion of fashion to larger consumer segments (e.g., Joy et al. 2012; Pous 2013; Scott 2005), we start our discussion by taking a glance at the potentials of democratization at consumer level. Then, we extend our discussion to seek for traces of democracy from the creation of a fashion product to its production and disposal. To conclude, we offer suggestions for a more democratic fashion system.

Lack of Democracy Where Fashion is Consumed

Fast fashion that adapts catwalk designs to be sold simultaneously and affordably in mass markets offers potentials for democratization, according to some scholarly and popular discourses, allowing people, regardless of their socio-economic status, to participate in fashion (e.g., Joy et al. 2012; Pous 2013; Scott 2005). Such participation would also allow them to gratify their artistic and aesthetic needs through fashion as "wearable art" (Venkatesh et al. 2010). However, the recent historical analysis of Atik et al. (2022) shows that the diffusion of (cheap versions of) latest fashion trends to larger number of consumers does not necessarily award democratization in fashion market.

This is rather ". . . a mass delusion that is a democratic right for everyone to purchase cheap clothing that looks luxe", as Jordan Phillips in her book about the lure of luxe (cited in Kissa 2015) defies against "McFashion," a concept used to refer to fast fashion to reflect the "speed with which gratification is provided" (Joy et al. 2012, 276). The fashion industry still endorses a distinction between superior high-end fashion and the lower-end mass market (Atik et al. 2022). Rose (2020a), who writes for *Mochni*, which is an international publication for raising global awareness for a fairer, cleaner and slower world, summarizes this illusion of democracy very concisely:

> Consumers aren't any better off with fast fashion. In fact, my opinion is they are worse off. Prior to fast fashion, you may not have owned the latest trends, but the quality of the garments you did own was integral. Clothes were well made, and you could tell. Now, anyone can have the latest fashion but they are guaranteed to have to replace those garments after a few wears, as the cheap dye fades or the stitching comes undone or they acknowledge the poor cut of a garment that never looked how it should. Fast fashion has not guaranteed unfettered and equal access to the elite fashion synonymous with quality and style (Rose 2020a).

Rose (2020b) and Atik et al. (2022) emphasize that social class differences are still prominent in fashion market. Fast fashion is being replaced by ultra-fast fashion by giants such as Zara, H&M, and Shein that are launching extraordinary volumes of new clothes into the market (Sharpe, Retamal, and Brydges 2022). As the industry constantly encourages perceived obsolescence by changing trends and offering new designs to promote consumption (Cooper 2005; Kennedy et al. 2017; Joy at al. 2012), even the social classes who can afford these new styles are not fulfilled due to insatiable desire for newness that fashion constantly fuels (Atik and Ozdamar Ertekin 2022). Consequently, both literary discussions and experience of fashion shift from the liberatory and celebratory ideals to normative expectations that the system triggers (Venkatesh et al. 2010). The consumers, irrespective of the social class they belong to, feel pressured to follow the trends and guidelines and become subject to the demands of aesthetic economy and body culture (Postrel 2003; Venkatesh et al. 2010), instead of enjoying the artistic notion of fashion.

Furthermore, the majority of people is underrepresented and underserved in fashion industry that idealizes whiteness, thinness, and youth. Digitalization of fashion, through the widespread use of social media, presents potentials for democratization by facilitating consumer activism and collective movements of underrepresented consumers (Atik et al. 2022; Cavusoglu and Atik 2019, 2021). However, "despite the potentials of democratization facilitated by social media platforms, markets tend to absorb consumers' creative activities, institutionalize them, and offer them back as new products to broader consumer segments. The corporatization of such creative consumer activities hinders consumer empowerment in decisions made regarding the final product" (Atik et al. 2022, 1142), and such consumer movements are still marginal. Therefore, considering the definition of democracy we stipulated above, the industry is not inclusive and the different consumer segments are not served equitably in the fashion market.

Rose (2020a) states very rightfully: "The hardest thing to swallow about the 'fast fashion = democracy' argument is that the democratic ideal stops with the consumer." The people who are making fast fashion not only cannot even afford the cheap fast fashion they produce but more importantly lack the rights and privileges of the consumers of fashion (Atik et al. 2022; Rose 2020a). The true cost of the cheap and affordable fashion for the masses in the West reveals itself brutally in less developed parts of the world where fashion is produced: "For those working to manufacture and produce fast fashion, the system is more Hunger Games than Utopian Fashion Wonderland" (Rose 2020a).

Lack of Democracy Where Fashion is Produced

The industry, dominated by big fast-fashion retailers, is designed to maximize profit at any cost. This is once more in line with the neoliberal ideology that enshrines the market as an ideal around the notion of competition. Through a Foucauldian analysis, Dholakia et al. (2020) affirm:

> within the liberal tradition itself, the concept of 'market' has been transformed into something else by the neoliberal intervention, and the 'freedom' inscribed in the 'free market' has been disfigured to a signify an ethos of "Every Man for Himself and God Against All" rather than a set of inalienable democratic rights (p. 886)

Selling large quantities of clothing at cheap prices and making latest styles of fashion available to all social classes under the promise of "democratization of fashion" bears environmental and social costs (Bick, Halsey, and Ekenga 2018). As strikingly depicted in the documentary movie *The True Cost* by Andrew Morgan, the human and environmental costs of the ever-expanding fashion industry is extremely severe (Ozdamar Ertekin 2017). Exposed to extremely low wages and devastating working conditions, factory workers in less developed parts of the world such as Bangladesh and Cambodia have no voice for improving their conditions; even if they try, they face unjust, even violent treatments (Ozdamar Ertekin 2017). Accordingly, the astonishing popularity of fast fashion retailers such as Zara, H&M, and Shein comes at the expense of deprived social and environmental demeanor in less developed parts of the world where environmental and labor regulations are lax. As a result, garment manufacturing countries such as Cambodia, Bangladesh, and Vietnam are facing an "extreme risk" for modern slavery. Labor rights abuses of workers in the supply chain such as child labor, discrimination, and forced labor have gotten worst globally over the years (Sharpe, Retamal and Brydges 2022).

Since democracy is not the first word (if not the last) that comes to mind in fashion industry, recent academic studies have been pressingly calling for a more sustainable fashion system (Bick, Halsey, and Ekenga 2018; Clark 2008; Fletcher 2010; Ozdamar Ertekin and Atik 2015, 2020; Ozdamar Ertekin et al. 2020). Human health and human rights are constantly violated at each step along the supply chain. Respiratory hazards due to poor ventilation, lung disease and cancer, accidental injuries, and even death due to lack of safety standards are among the occupational hazards, to name a few. Periodic reports of international disasters, such as the 2013 Rana Plaza factory collapse, which killed 1,134 Bangladeshi workers (Ozdamar Ertekin 2017), and various other sweatshop scandals signify these unsafe working conditions. Low wages, excessive overtime to meet unreasonable deadlines with temporary and subcontracted workers, and the use of child labor further intensify the exploitation of workers in the fashion industry (Cataldi, Dickson, and Grover 2010; Cline 2012, Fletcher 2007; McRobbie 1997; Ozdamar Ertekin and Atik 2015).

Furthermore, fast fashion industry is known to be the second highest polluting industry after oil. The industry accounts for around 20% of the world's water pollution (The World Bank 2019). Around 8,000 different types of hazardous chemicals are used in the production of textiles (Elle MacArthur Foundation 2017). Consequently, from the growth of cotton that requires excessive water and pesticides to the release of untreated dyes, heavy metals, and other toxicants into local water sources, the environmental costs involved in textile manufacturing are prevalent, adversely affecting the health of animals, plants, and local residents (Bick, Halsey, and Ekenga 2018). Even sustainability initiatives and efforts such as switching to more sustainable materials and fibers and offering ethically and environmentally conscious alternatives have not been able to resolve the industry's increasing use of resources and generation of waste (Sharpe, Retamal and Brydges 2022).

As the environmental and social costs of the industry show more and more warning signals, fast fashion retailers have begun to make promises to become more sustainable. For instance, Zara announced that by 2025 90% of the raw materials the company uses will be organic, sustainable or recycled; 80% of the energy will come from renewable sources, and it aims for zero waste transition. These are important steps in becoming greener and sets a good example to other supply chain partners and manufacturers. However, as Elizabeth L. Cline argues, as long as the business model is based on speed and fast turnover of styles, making and sourcing those products in a more environmental way still does not solve the problem (Bowman and McCammon 2019). Furthermore, these promises and changes mostly address environmental issues. Ethical issues that prohibit the system to become democratic are still not addressed. Regrettably, lack of democracy in fashion industry does not stop where fashion is produced and consumed but stretches to the extreme ends of the continuum from where it is created to where it is discarded.

Lack of Democracy where Fashion is Created

> The purpose of artistic creativity is not to satisfy the needs of a mass market. Artistic creativity is above all the means through which artists express themselves. Commercial creativity, on the other hand, does not have this freedom of expression. This is because its purpose is to achieve another subject's objective, the firm. The firm's reason for existence lies in its ability to satisfy market needs (Saviolo and Testa 2002, p. 23).

Earlier studies have long recognized that the creation of fashion is not purely an artistic one but also a relentlessly commercial one to allure the mass market. Research shows that designers' artistic freedom is compelled by forces both within and outside the company – such as the brand image the company wants to sustain and the production and competitive constraints – but mainly compelled by profit driven aims (Atik and Fırat 2013). Nowadays such constraints on the freedom of creativity reveal themselves even more strikingly. Dilys Williams, the director of the Centre for Sustainable Fashion at the London College of Fashion, suggests that today "The designer is obsolete and, instead, engineers and sophisticated software allow the production of clothes that are fit for the screen, designed for obsolescence, destined for landfill" (Williams 2022). Shein, which is a giant Chinese fast fashion retailer as big as Zara and H&M combined, is the vanguard of this business model. Shein offers constant and timely mark-downs of prices at the expense of designers' creativity and product quality, constantly fueling consumers' desire for the new for corporate profitability (Williams 2022). The company is also known for its controversial practices, stealing designs from small labels and artists (Das 2020; Williams 2022).

The catwalk images, designs, and trends are copied with few modifications by fast fashion retailers at an accelerating speed and offered at low prices, which undermines the value of fashion and design. Raustiala and Sprigman (2012) suggest a provocative relationship between imitation and innovation. They propose that high fashion created knockoffs, and the freedom to imitate luxury designs enabled the fashion cycle to run faster and forced the industry to become even more creative. However, our discussion in previous sections shows that the speed of the fashion cycles has devastating social and environmental consequences, and not everyone shares their views in terms of artistic creation in fashion industry.

Due to the speed of superficial change, there are no big fashion statements anymore. Cline (2012) and Biehl-Missal (2013) address the "painfully simple designs" and "self-degrading styling" while Korica and Bazin (2019, p. 1484) underline that "there is so much sameness and that everything is homogenized." Consequently, the homogenization of design and artificial newness have replaced creativity and originality (Ozdamar Ertekin et al. 2020), leading to lack of diversity and diminishing cultural value of clothing. As the designers are constantly remixing and refashioning to keep up with the speed of the system, timelessness and aesthetic quality of fashion is compromised. Appadurai (1996, 85) refers to this conflict as the tension between the aesthetics of ephemerality and the aesthetics of duration. Therefore, it becomes crucial to consider new product development and creation from an aesthetic perspective (Venkatesh et al. 2010).

Nowadays, based on the corporate agenda, even the lifespans of creative directors of luxury fashion brands is short-lived. Commercial priorities supersede the artistic voice of the creative agents and the aesthetic authenticity of the brand, leading to an unsustainable flow of creativity and impairment of artisanal craftsmanship. In the pursuit of growth and profit margins, supposedly "democratizing" fashion has diminished creativity and craftsmanship (Wingco 2021). Therefore, we find it safe to acknowledge that there is also a lack of democracy at the creation stage of fashion, and the power rests in the hands of commercially driven fashion corporations rather than the creative constituents of the fashion system such as designers or artists.

Lack of Democracy Where Fashion is Discarded

Looking at the other extreme end of the continuum, although getting products to the consumers in the West is seen to be the end point of the fashion supply chain, environmental injustices do not stop there (Bick, Halsey, and Ekenga 2018). Fast fashion has changed the way people buy and dispose of clothing, encouraging consumers to view fashion products as disposable. By offering the latest trends at extremely low prices, this throw-away fashion model has caused consumption to go up through the ceiling, which in turn has produced tons of textile waste to end up in landfills or second-hand clothing markets in poorer countries.

A recent ABC News article with an impactful title, "Dead white man's clothes" (Besser 2021), discloses that West African countries such as Ghana have become the dumping grounds of millions of unwanted used clothing items from Europe, North America, and Australia for resale and reuse. However, almost half of these products are in such bad conditions that they end up in landfills, not only causing an environmental catastrophe but also damaging the health of local people through the methane gas trapped inside the old piles of synthetic textiles. Even resale does not provide a solution to overproduction and overconsumption. As many brands today offer incentives to secondhand shoppers to buy more, the fast-growing secondhand market raises more concerns about the environmental impact of throwaway fashion. Recently, fast fashion brands such as Zara and Shein have been launching their own resale platforms, which increased debates on whether these brands are trying to enhance their sustainability initiatives by offering repair services to enable consumers to extend the life of their old garments (by providing a peer-to-peer resale marketplace and an option to donate their unwanted clothes) or using resale as another tool to fuel faster consumption (Kent 2022).

Williams (2022) focuses on the fast fashion mega retailer Shein that ships to 250 countries around the world and the environmental damage the company creates not only from production and deliveries but also returns that cost more to put back in circulation than dumping as landfills. Unsold second-hand clothing in huge consumer markets such as the United States is compressed into 1,000-pound bales, exported to countries like Ghana to be categorized by low-wage workers and sold in second-hand markets (Besser 2021; Bick, Halsey, and Ekenga 2018). As said earlier, the large quantities of unsold items become solid waste, clogging rivers and polluting the environment in countries that lack healthy waste systems.

Once more, the countries of the global South, which are the textile dumping grounds of the West, are the ones who suffer the most from the lack of democracy. Unfortunately, the waste problem in the apparel industry is not only associated with fast fashion retailers. The luxury fashion companies such as Burberry are destroying and burning unsold stock so that their products will not be sold on the black market and to avoid markdown prices, in order to protect their exclusivity and preserve their brand equity (Ozdamar Ertekin 2019; Ozdamar Ertekin and Atik 2022).

Conclusion and Suggestions for a More Democratic Fashion System

As Williams (2022) precisely states: "We should be under no illusions: ultra-fast fashion has little to do with democratization and much more to do with profit and wealth for those at the top." From the creation of fashion to its demise, the power lies in the hands of giant fast fashion corporations, seeking to maximize their profit at any cost. They are the ones who bear the biggest responsibility if we want to leave behind a better world for future generations. They need to adopt a new transformative corporate logic with a sustainability mindset (Ozdamar Ertekin et al. 2020), which requires ecologically and socially conscious production processes at the design stage, in choice of materials, in fair treatment of workers, in minimizing waste, and in adoption of circular business models. Even in the case of luxury fashion, which currently focuses on enabling the middle class to have access to affordable luxury products, the gap between rich and poor has been widened while the conglomerates grew bigger and richer (Wingco 2021).

Recently, Suk (2021) identified characteristics of the democratization of fashion to include individual autonomy, diversity, and accessibility, which means that many people can access and enjoy fashion. However, as per the discussions shared in this chapter, the current fashion system enables neither true autonomy nor accessibility, and it is not fully inclusive or diverse. Suk (2021) argues that social media has shifted the balance of power to influencers and bloggers, transforming consumers to become producers and promoters of fashion, creating a new era of fashion democracy. On the other hand, even the fashion bloggers and influencers who have access to sources, tools, and knowledge do not have enough power to determine fashion, as the system is largely under the control of giant corporations (Atik et al. 2022). It is true that social media creates a platform for democratization of fashion by enabling people to express themselves and have their voices heard (Boyd 2015); however, the system still lacks empowerment of minorities, diverse groups of consumers, and people involved in production of fashion.

Atik et al. (2022) discuss the potentials for a more democratic fashion scene presented by sustainable fashion production and consumption (Ozdamar Ertekin and Atik 2020) and the potentials presented by the digitalization of fashion – especially the use of social media that helps increase the voice of underrepresented consumers (Cavusoglu and Atik 2021). However, the authors also argue that sustainable fashion is still not the dominant practice in the industry since speed and low-cost have become competitive instruments for fast fashion suppliers and retailers to grow their corporate profits (Atik et al. 2022; Atik and Firat 2013; Ozdamar Ertekin and Atik 2015). There are also barriers against sustainable, circular, and collaborative consumption practices such as second-hand clothing consumption, rentals, or swapping due to hygiene and quality concerns while the fast fashion corporations are fueling the restless desire for the new with bargain prices (Atik and Ozdamar Ertekin 2022). Furthermore, "despite the potentials of democratization facilitated by social media platforms, markets tend to absorb consumers' creative activities, institutionalize them, and offer them back as new products to broader consumer segments. The corporatization of such creative consumer activities hinders consumer empowerment in decisions made regarding the final product" (Atik et al. 2022, 1142). Mass consumers can afford only the cheap replicas of catwalk designs; White/Western dominance is still prevalent, and there are still underrepresented consumer segments (Atik et al. 2022). Consequently, fast fashion does not democratize the fashion system. On the contrary, it comes at a high cost for society, workers, and the environment. Corporations' greed for growth and profit often exceeds the need to create a more democratic and sustainable system. Therefore, democratization of fashion remains as a big challenge that the industry needs to prevail.

To end our chapter on a positive note, for the industry to change for the better and to become more democratic and less damaging, there are actions that the different institutional actors can take. Sustainable fibers and materials could be used in textile production and practices and policies that reduce environmental pollution, waste, and exploitation of natural resources can be adopted (Bick, Halsey, and Ekenga 2018; Ozdamar Ertekin and Atik 2020). Certification and Fair-Trade organizations and coalitions such as Sustainable Apparel Coalition should encourage industry-wide adoption of internationally recognized certification criteria, ethical and environmental standards, indexes, and measuring tools to promote practices that ensure health and safety across the supply chain (Bick, Halsey, and Ekenga 2018; Ozdamar Ertekin and Atik 2020). In this regard, the cooperation of governments, public policymakers, and trade organizations is also critical (Gupta, Gwozdz, and Gentry 2019).

Governments can enforce legislation and regulate the activity of markets and trade by taxing goods and services (Gupta, Gwozdz, and Gentry 2019). They can also offer incentives to support local manufacturers and initiatives (Bick, Halsey, and Ekenga 2018) and reinforce the human rights and environmental protection regulations throughout the supply chain (Atik and Ozdamar Ertekin 2022). Otherwise, lack of standards comes at a high price for the planet and people, as the exploitative practices of the corporations do not consider the additional costs incurred in pollution, emissions, waste, environmental degradation, and loss of biodiversity and human wellbeing (Williams 2022). Therefore, public policymakers and fashion associations need to enforce that pricing strategies reflect the true cost, including human and environmental cost, of production (Atik and Ozdamar Ertekin 2022).

Firms can adopt socially and environmentally responsible production processes throughout the supply chain and trade policies, regulations, certifications, and standards can be effective in changing the fashion industry to become more democratic and sustainable; however, consumers also have an important role to slow down consumption and adopt more sustainable consumption practices. In this regard, consumers can support companies and practices that minimize their negative impact on people and the planet by making more informed and sustainable consumer choices: choosing quality over quantity and classic styles over changing trends; buying less and higher quality clothing that lasts longer; buying ethical, fair trade, and organic products; demanding transparency and ethical production from fashion brands; recycling, upcycling (a term for reuse of discarded products to create a new product), and mending their clothes; and buying secondhand clothes or supporting collaborative consumption models such as sharing, swapping or renting (Bick, Halsey, and Ekenga 2018; Atik and Ozdamar Ertekin 2022).

To conclude, the fashion industry's main concern has never been democracy, sustainability nor inclusion. Instead, the system has survived on distinction, copying, economic growth, and profit opportunities. Fast fashion companies making the latest fashion trends available to mass consumers and the industry's efforts to include the underrepresented voices and segments are only illusions of democracy (Atik et al. 2022). The only way the fashion system and industry can become truly democratic is when multiple institutional actors and constituents of the fashion system collaborate together to address the injustices caused by excessive consumption and production practices, make reforms to support global environmental and social justice to advance democracy, and shift to a post-growth fashion industry.

References

Appadurai, A. (1996), *Modernity at Large*. University of Minnesota Press.

Atik, D., Cavusoglu, L., Ozdamar Ertekin, Z., and Fırat, A. F. (2022), "Fashion, Consumer Markets, and Democratization," *Journal of Consumer Behaviour*, 21 (5), 1135–1148. https://doi.org/10.1002/cb.2061

Atik, D., & Fırat, F. (2013), "Fashion Creation and Diffusion: The institution of Marketing," *Journal of Marketing Management*, 29, 836–860. https://doi.org/10.1080/0267257X.2012.729073

Atik, D., & Ozdamar Ertekin, Z. (2022), "Desire for the New versus Sustainability: Conflicting Needs in Fashion Consumption," *Journal of Social Marketing*, in press. https://doi.org/10.1108/JSOCM-02-2022-0036

Besser, L. (2021), "Dead white man's clothes," *ABC News*, available at https://www.abc.net.au/news/2021-08-12/fast-fashion-turning-parts-ghana-into-toxic-landfill/100358702 (accessed 21 March 2022).

Bick, R., Halsey, E., & Ekenga, C.C. (2018), "The global environmental injustice of fast fashion," *Environ Health* 17 (92). https://doi.org/10.1186/s12940-018-0433-7

Biehl-Missal, B. (2013), "Art, Fashion, and Anti-consumption," *Journal of Macromarketing*, 33 (3), 245–57.

Bowman, E., & McCammon, S. (2019), "Can Fast Fashion and Sustainability Be Stitched Together?" https://www.npr.org/2019/07/27/745418569/can-fast-fashion-and-sustainability-be-stitched-together (July 27, 2019).

Boyd, K. C. (2015), "Democratizing fashion: The Effects of the Evolution of Fashion Journalism from Print to Online Media," *McNair Scholars Research Journal*, 8 (4), 17–34.

Brydges, T., Hracs, B. J., & Lavanga, M. (2018), "Evolution versus Entrenchment: Debating the Impact of Digitalization, Democratization and Diffusion in the Global Fashion Industry," *International Journal of Fashion Studies*, 5 (2), 365–372. https://doi.org/10.1386/infs.5.2.365_7

Cataldi, C., Dickson, M., & Grover, C. (2010), "Slow Fashion: Tailoring a Strategic Approach towards Sustainability," thesis, Blekinge Institute of Technology, Karlskrona, Sweden.

Cavusoglu, L., & Atik, D. (2021), "Accumulating Capital through Social Media: Transformative Power of Underrepresented Fashion Consumers," *Journal of Consumer Marketing*, 38 (5). https://doi.org/10.1108/JCM-08-2020-4074

Cavusoglu, L., & Atik, D. (2019), "Diversity Delusion in Fashion Industry," in R. Bagchi, L. Block, & L. Lee (eds.), NA – *Advances in Consumer Research*, vol. 47, Duluth, MN: Association for Consumer Research, 489–490.

Clark, H. (2008), "Slow Fashion: An Oxymoron or a Promise for the Future?" *Fashion Theory: The Journal of Dress, Body & Culture*, 12 (4), 427–46.

Cline, E. L. (2012), *Overdressed: The Shockingly High Cost of Cheap Fashion*. New York, NY: Penguin Group.

Cooper, T. (2005), "Slower consumption: reflections on product life spans and the 'throwaway society,'" *Journal of Industrial Ecology*, 9 (1/2), 51–67. doi: 10.1162/1088198054084671.

Das, S. (2020), "'They took my world': fashion giant Shein accused of art theft," *The Guardian*, [Online] available at https://www.theguardian.com/artanddesign/2022/mar/06/they-took-my-world-fashion-giant-shein-accused-of-art-theft (accessed July 12, 2022).

Dholakia, N., Ozgun, A., & Atik, D. (2020), "The Unwitting Corruption of Broadening of Marketing into Neoliberalism: A Beast Unleashed?" *European Journal of Marketing*, 55 (3), 868–893. https://doi.org/10.1108/EJM-10-2018-0688

Ellen MacArthur Foundation (2017), "A New Textiles Economy: Redesigning Fashion's Future" (accessed November 4, 2019), available at: https://www.ellenmacarthurfoundation.org/assets/downloads/publications/A-New-Textiles-Economy_Full-Report.pdf.

Fletcher, K. (2010), "Slow Fashion: An Invitation for Systems Change," *Fashion Practice: The Journal of Design, Creative Process and the Fashion*, 2 (2), 259–266. https://doi.org/10.2752/175693810X12774625387594

Fletcher, K. (2007), "Slow Fashion," Ecologist (accessed November 29, 2012) [available at: http://www.theecologist.org/green_green_living/clothing/269245/slow_fashion.html].

Gupta, S., Gwozdz, W., & Gentry, J. (2019), "The Role of Style versus Fashion Orientation on Sustainable Apparel Consumption", *Journal of Macromarketing*, 39 (2), 188–207. https://doi.org/10.1177/0276146719835283

Joy, A., Sherry, J.F., Venkatesh, A., Wang, J., & Chan, R. (2012), "Fast Fashion, Sustainability, and the Ethical Appeal of Luxury Brands," *Fashion Theory*, 16 (3), 273–296. https://doi.org/10.2752/175174112X13340749707123

Kennedy, A.M., Kapitan, S., Bajaj, N., Bakonyi, A., & Sands, S. (2017), "Uncovering wicked problem's system structure: seeing the forest for the trees," *Journal of Social Marketing*, 7 (1), 51–73.

Kent, S. (2022), "Is Resale Fuelling Overconsumption?" *The Business of Fashion* [Online], available at https://www.businessoffashion.com/articles/sustainability/pretty-little-thing-secondhand-resale-boohoo-sustainability-waste-overconsumption-fast-fashion/ (September 2, 2022)

Kissa, L. (2015), "Is Sustainable Fashion A Luxury?" *NewEurope* [Online], available at https://www.neweurope.eu/article/sustainable-fashion-luxury/ (January 12, 2015).

Korica, M., & Bazin, Y. (2019), "Fashion and organization studies: Exploring conceptual paradoxes and empirical opportunities," *Organization Studies*, 40 (10), 1481–1497. https://doi.org/10.1177/0170840619831059

McRobbie, A. (1997), "A New Kind of Rag Trade," in *The Consumer Society Reader*, ed. Juliet B. Schor and Douglas B. Holt, 433–45. New York: The New Press.

Mrad, M., Farah, M.F., & Haddad, S. (2019), "From Karl Lagerfeld to Erdem: a series of collaborations between designer luxury brands and fast-fashion brands," *Journal of Brand Management*, 26 (5), 567–582.

Nia, A., & Zaichkowsky, J. L. (2000), "Do counterfeits devalue the ownership of luxury brands?" *Journal of Product and Brand Management*, 9(7),485–497.

Ozdamar Ertekin, Z. (2019), "Can luxury fashion provide a roadmap for sustainability?" *Markets, Globalization & Development Review*, 4 (1), Article 2. https://doi.org/10.23860/MGDR-2019-04-01-03

Ozdamar Ertekin, Z. (2017), "The True Cost: The Bitter Truth behind Fast Fashion," *Markets, Globalization & Development Review*, 2 (3), Article 7. https://doi.org/10.23860/MGDR-2017-02-03-07

Ozdamar Ertekin, Z., & Atik, D. (2022), "Luxury Fashion and Sustainability: Challenges, Conflicts, and Possibilities," in *New Directions in the worlds of Art, fashion and wine: Sustainability, Artification and Digitalization*, ed. Annama Joy. Maryland: Lexington Books (in press).

Ozdamar Ertekin, Z., & Atik, D. (2020), "Institutional Constituents of Change for a Sustainable Fashion System," *Journal of Macromarketing*, 40 (3). https://doi.org/10.1177/0276146720932274.

Ozdamar Ertekin, Z., & Atik, D. (2015), "Sustainable Markets: Motivating Factors, Barriers, and Remedies for Mobilization of Slow Fashion," *Journal of Macromarketing*, 35 (1), 53–69. https://doi.org/10.1177/0276146714535932

Ozdamar Ertekin, Z., Atik, D., & Murray, J. (2020), "The Logic of Sustainability: Institutional Transformation towards a New Culture of Fashion," *Journal of Marketing Management*, 36 (15–16). https://doi.org/10.1080/0267257X.2020.1795429

Ozgun, A., Dholakia, N., & Atik, D. (2017), "Marketization and Foucault," *Global Business Review*, 18 (3S), 1–12.

Pedersen, E.R.G., & Andersen, K.R. (2015), "Sustainability Innovators and Anchor Draggers: A Global Expert Study on Sustainable Fashion," *Journal of Fashion Marketing and Management*, 19 (3), 315–327. http://doi.org/10.1108/JFMM-08-2014-0059

Postrel, V. (2003), *The Substance of Style*. New York: HarperCollins.

Pous, T. (2013), "The Democratization of Fashion: A Brief History," *Time* [Online], available at https://style.time.com/2013/02/06/the-democratization-of-fashion-a-brief-history/ (accessed January 31, 2020)

Raustiala, K., & Sprigman, C. (2012), *The Knockoff Economy: How Imitation Sparks Innovation*, Oxford University Press: Oxford, UK.

Rosa, A. M. (2013), "The evolution and democratization of modern fashion: From Frederick Worth to Karl Lagerfeld's fast fashion," *Comunicação e Sociedade*, 24, 79–94.

Rose, A. (2020a), "Why Fast Fashion Is NOT Democratic Fashion," *Mochni* [Online], available at https://mochni.com/is-fast-fashion-really-democratic-fashion/ (accessed May 5, 2021).

Rose, A. (2020b), "Is Fast Fashion Racist?" *Mochni* [Online], available at https://mochni.com/is-fast-fashion-racist/ (accessed May 5, 2021)

Saviolo, S., & Testa, S. (2002), *Strategic Management in the Fashion Companies*. Milano: Etas.

Scott, L.M. (2005), *Fresh Lipstick*. New York, NY: Palgrave Macmillan.

Scruton, R. (2007), *The Palgrave Macmillan Dictionary of Political Thought*, 3rd ed. Palgrave Macmillan: New York.

Sharpe, S., Retamal, M., & Brydges, T. (2022), "To make our wardrobes sustainable, we must cut how many new clothes we buy by 75%," *The Conversation* [Online], available at https://theconversation.com/to-make-our-wardrobes-sustainable-we-must-cut-how-many-new-clothes-we-buy-by-75-179569 (April 12, 2022).

Shukla, P., Rosendo-Rios, V., & Khalifa, D. (2022), "Is luxury democratization impactful? Its moderating effect between value perceptions and consumer purchase intentions," *Journal of Business Research*, 139, 782–793. https://doi.org/10.1016/j.jbusres.2021.10.030

Suk, H. (2021), "The characteristics of democratization of fashion and fashionocracy in the global fashion industry," *The Research Journal of the Costume Culture*, 29 (4), 488–504. https://doi.org/10.29049/rjcc.2021.29.4.488

The World Bank (2019), "How Much Do Our Wardrobes Cost to the Environment?" (accessed October 23, 2019) [available at: https://www.worldbank.org/en/news/feature/2019/09/23/costo-moda-medio-ambiente].

Venkatesh, A., Joy, A., Sherry, J. F., & Deschenes, J. (2010), "The aesthetics of luxury fashion, body and identify formation," *Journal of Consumer Psychology*, 20 (4), 459–470. https://doi.org/10.1016/j.jcps.2010.06.011.

Williams, Dilys (2022), "Shein: the unacceptable face of throwaway fast fashion," *The Guardian*, [Online] available at https://www.theguardian.com/fashion/2022/apr/10/shein-the-unacceptable-face-of-throwaway-fast-fashion (accessed July 7, 2022).

Wingco, T.D. (2021), "Luxury or nothing: the 'democratisation' of luxury fashion," https://honisoit.com/2021/07/luxury-or-nothing-the-democratisation-of-luxury-fashion/ (July 16, 2021).

Binyam Zenebe Andargie, Charlene Gallery, and Claudia E Henninger

11 Textile Supply Chains and Colonialism – Insights from Ethiopia

Introduction

Although the textile industry has a long-standing history, it has changed quite dramatically over the past decades (Rauturier, 2022). Whilst in the past garments were predominantly designed for the upper class, as they were tailor made and rather expensive, this changed with the Industrial Revolution (Perkins, 2013). Garments are no longer for selected people, but rather are designed to be accessible to the masses (Bick et al., 2018). Two implications can be mentioned here; on the one hand, making garments accessible to a wider audience has reduced class systems and thus potential bias against social standing; yet, on the other hand, we have seen increased concerns and criticisms emerge related to sustainability (or the lack thereof) (Blazquez et al., 2020; Henninger and Brydges, 2022; Brydges et al., 2022).

Although making garments accessible can be positively perceived, we currently see a situation that could be described as "ad absurdum." To explain, within the Global North we increasingly see more garments being consumed and discarded, after only a couple wears. Fashion retailers are increasing their yearly lines to almost one every week, often at the cost of quality (Azevedo, 2018; Monroe, 2021). In today's society, garments have lost their value in that they are seen as disposable items, which are cheap to acquire and readily available at any point in time. Yet this comes at a cost, seeing as these cheap garments need to be produced somewhere. This "somewhere" is often in the Global South, where reports have outlined poor working conditions and the lack of living wage payments (CCC, n.d.; van Elven, 2019; LBL, 2022).

Within this chapter the focus is on Ethiopia, a country that has started to heavily invest in the textile industry and has seen a growth rate of 51% in the past decade (BSR, 2017; Maasho, 2017; FashionUnited, 2021; Alliance Experts, 2022). Even though there are investments made in the textile industry, van Elven (2019) outlines that "Ethiopian garment workers (are) paid the lowest wages in the apparel industry." According to Barrett and Baumann-Pauly (2019) the "government's eagerness to attract foreign investment led it to promote the lowest base wage in any garment-producing country – now set at the equivalent of $26 a month" (p. 1), which implies that these (often female) garment workers are unable to be self-sufficient and not only live in poverty but also in very constrained spaces that often lack sanitation facilities.

Although the outlook is rather bleak, Ethiopia does have potential to gain a unique position within the textile industry, seeing as it has a lot of heritage and culture to offer. To explain, Ethiopia has a long-standing textile weaving heritage (Atelier 55, n.d.), with the crafts described as reflecting "the cultural diversity in Ethiopia – they result

https://doi.org/10.1515/9783110783933-011

from a combination of the creativity, culture and the heritage and the environment of the craftspeople" (Dubois, 2008: 5). Ethiopian textiles are often vibrant in color and have different patterns integrated; until today the thickness of the material and also partly the decoration is used as an indicator of social standing (Purdy, 2015).

Ethiopia only briefly experienced colonization during World War II, when it was occupied by Italy, before being liberated and becoming one of the first countries to be independent and "sign the Charter of the United Nations" (Marcus, 2022). Although trade reforms have been introduced, Ethiopia remains one of the poorest among the African countries, which can have negative impacts on how it markets itself and the way its workers, especially in the fashion industry, are treated.

Within this chapter the focus is on de-colonialism, thereby outlining key issues that remain within the fashion industry to date, by drawing specifically on Ethiopia as a case study.

Background

Ethiopia

Ethiopia is situated in East Africa and bordered by Kenya, Somalia, Eritrea, Sudan, South Sudan and Djibouti, and has a population of approximately 100 million people (Mehretu, 2022). The country has embarked on an ambitious transition towards being a fast-growing state, although as of late it has received "negative attention due to a series of humanitarian violations that according to the UN, amount to war crimes and crimes against humanity" (UN HRC, 2022). This chapter takes on a historic view and reflects on its textile history, thus, the authors remain neutral in regards to the current situation in the country.

In the last decade, the vision of Ethiopia is to "to become a country where democratic rule, good governance and social justice reign upon the involvement and free will of its peoples, and once extracting itself from poverty to reach the level of a middle-income economy by 2025" (Worldbank, 2013). Although youth unemployment steadily decreased since 1999, it remains a key issue and priority as it affects people living in both urban and rural areas, with many youth not having skills and/or education (Broussar and Tekleselassie, 2012; Sisay, 2013). The government's plan to tackle this challenge was to develop policies that support the development of the manufacturing sector and encourage young people to set up their own enterprises (Sisay, 2013).

Ethiopia's textile and garment sector has received increased attention from the government with setting up policy interventions, such as the Ethiopian Industrial Development Strategy (2013–2025) (FDRE, 2013). In addition to its low labor costs, the country also used to enjoy preferential trade agreements with the European Union through the Everything but Arms Act and with the US through the Africa Growth and Opportunity

Act (AGOA) (Coulibaly et al., 2022). However, the US has removed Ethiopia from AGOA, due to "violations of internationally recognized human rights" (Thomas, 2021). The government's commitment towards the fashion and textile sector is shown by large investments in a variety of areas, including but not limited to transportation, trade logistics, and industrial park developments, all of which are essential in order to build up an infrastructure that enhances the country's competitive edge and, thus, allows the country to build into a fashion sourcing hub (Barrett and Baumann-Pauly, 2019). The investment into the fashion and textile sector has led to the creation of more than 200 factories across the country, with most of the factories exporting their products overseas. Currently, the fashion sector "is an important source of income that provides employment for over 450,000 people (2013), up more than 200% from 2010/2011" (ITC, 2016), of which 60% are female (ibid.).

Based on the statistics and information provided, Ethiopia provides an interesting case for further investigation, especially when reflecting on theoretical concepts such as colonialism and social sustainability.

Social Sustainability and Ethiopia

Countries on the African continent in very general terms have a history of textile production and design, which are well known for their vibrant colors and artisanry (Canales, 2021). As highlighted, Ethiopia has heavily invested in the fashion and textile sector, yet it could be argued this has been done at the cost of sustainability, namely social sustainability (Barrett and Baumann-Pauly, 2019). Within this chapter we follow Elkington's (2004) definition of sustainability, who has visualized the concept as a Venn diagram, whereby the three circles representing economic, social, and environmental sustainability ideally overlap. The point at which all three elements intersect is seen to represent sustainability. Although the concept can be criticized for being too simplistic, as well as the fact that sustainability may never be reached – as what we believe to be sustainable today may change in the future – it provides a basis for discussion (Henninger and Brydges, 2022; Henninger et al., 2022).

As alluded to previously, within this chapter, the focus is on social sustainability or the lack thereof. The latter is often associated with low wages and unsafe and/or poor working conditions. Even though these issues are known, they are not always immediately addressed. There are many reasons as to why these may not always be addressed; for example, suppliers often sub-contract other suppliers, which makes processes very complex and at times not fully transparent. In addition, homeworking has increased, whereby it is unclear whether all homeworking places can and/or are following general health and safety rules. Additionally, we also need to consider home and host country regulations. To explain, within the UK for example there are governmental regulations that clearly outline minimum wages (UK.gov, n.d.), whilst in other countries this may not be the case. Thus, in the past the question of what a living wage is has been posed but not answered. Although it is out of the scope of this chapter to debate these areas further, they are vital to keep in mind in order to fully comprehend what has happened in the past and how this transpires within our current working practices.

In linking back to the core of this chapter, we are taking a more historic view through revisiting colonialism and its impact on Ethiopia. In doing so, it may become apparent that social sustainability has been an issue for a long time, in that throughout history we have observed inequalities, further fostered by colonialism, in which one part of humanity has taken over another. The following section carefully defines and unpicks what colonialism implies within the fashion context.

Colonial Discourse

Colonialism or colonization can best be defined as one nation taking over another nation and/or foreign territory, predominantly overseas and often through force and violence (Osman, 2020). It can thus be defined as "the practice by which a powerful country controls another or other countries" (Oxford Dictionary, 2022). Within literature, we see the terms colonialism and imperialism often used interchangeably, as colonialism has a symbiotic relationship with imperialism (Hirson, 1991; Wolfe, 1997). Indeed, both colonialism and imperialism indicate the suppression of one country by another (Ashcroft et al., 2002); both employ force and influence often enforced through strategic military advantages (e.g., Hirson, 1991; Osman, 2020). Where the terms of colonialism and imperialism differ is indicative in the process by which each exert dominance. Imperialism refers to the direct or indirect monetary and political governance of another country, foreign control of which can be established without the need for physical or significant settlement (Galtung, 1979; Wolfe, 1997). In contrast, countries that undertake colonialism do so mainly to benefit economically from the exploitation of the valuable natural and human resources of the colonized country, which can only be executed successfully through direct and physical settlements (Lange et al., 2006; Greiner, 2021).

Throughout history there are broadly speaking two waves of colonialism, the first one starting in the fifteenth century and focusing on the "European expansion before 1763" (Magdoff, n.d.), driven by the surge for spices (Asia) and gold (National Geographic, 2022). The "discovery of lands" predominantly centered on Latin and South America, with the second wave classified as happening from 1763 (Magdoff, n.d.) and coinciding with the Industrial Revolution. The African continent was especially impacted by the second wave, whereby forced labor in the form of slavery emerged, with people being exploited on cotton fields and within textile production in order to advance industrialization in what is now known as the Global North.

To reiterate this further, colonialism, a concept advocated by Renan in *La Reforme intellectuelle et morale* in 1871, was initially presented as "the extension of civilisation," which ideologically justified the self-ascribed racial and cultural superiority of the Western World over the non-Western World (Britannica, n.d.). Colonization is based on the doctrine of cultural hierarchy and supremacy which, through colorism and a system of caste, identified the white man at the top of the social order, positioned to educate and advance the rest of world (Lange et al., 2006; Stanford Encyclopedia of Philosophy, 2017; Blakemore, 2019). Although this is a historic account of the different waves of colonization, the issues outlined from the past can still be observed in today's society, with the emergence of modern slavery (Uzogara et al., 2014; ILO, 2022). Although the meaning of colonialism has changed over time, its modern usage refers to the conservation of political, social, economic, and cultural domination over people indigenous to the colonized country by a foreign and distant power for an extended period (Bell, 1991).

In addition to the two waves of colonialism identified, within the literature colonialism is described using different terminology including, but not limited to, settler, exploitation, plantation, surrogate, and internal colonialism (Finley, 1976; Shoemaker, 2015), all of which have a negative connotation. Within the context of this chapter, which hones in on the fashion industry, there are two types of colonialism that tie in intimately: Settler and Exploitation colonialism, which will be discussed further in the following sections of this chapter.

Colonization and the Subjugation of Women

Whilst scholars continue to draw on post-colonial philosophies in the analysis of the European colonization of the Americas, Australasia, and Africa, in the attempt to gain insights into the patriarchal power dynamics of which were central to institutionalized colonial ideologies and practices, few researchers have applied feminist or gender-based theories to support this understanding (Spencer-Wood, 2016). As alluded to in the previous section, colonialism is often defined as colonizers violently taking over foreign lands, with the aim of gaining economic benefits, such as access to resources, and at the same time oppressing people indigenous to the lands, which is referred to as slavery (Silliman, 2005).

However, colonization can also be viewed as a metaphor or symbolism of female subjugation as, it can be argued, the expansion of colonialism was primarily achieved due to the suppression of women indigenous to the colonized territory (e.g., Pateman, 1988; Marini, 1990):

> Because women and men perform different social roles, they exhibit different repertoires. Gender differentiation in social roles therefore produces gender differences in behaviors, abilities and dispositional traits. (. . .) "Different" usually means unequal, since the roles filled by [women and men] do not bring the same power and privilege (Marini, 1990: 110).

Stoler (1989) was one of the first feminist anthropologists to affirm how racialized and patriarchal philosophies of gender and sexuality were foundational to colonial enterprise and expansion. Stoler (1989), whose research focuses on the bodies of women of color, demonstrates how the sexualization and the devaluation of black and brown women's bodies reinforced white male supremacy during the period of colonization. This may also have impacts on women working within the fashion industry, as stereotypes and sexualization of black women in particular remains an issue today.

Within the previous paragraph, we have outlined what colonialism implies; more recently we have also seen the emergences of decolonization, which has sparked debate surrounding institutional racism in the Global North (e.g., Moosavi, 2020). To reiterate this further, decolonization is a movement that reveals inequalities that are often deeply rooted in society's ethnic multicultural coexistence. It has also exposed the entrenched ideologies which prioritize the dominance and privilege of "whiteness" through trade and exploitation of marginalized countries, pervasive in western society (Moncrieffe, 2020). Within the fashion industry, the corporeality and brutality of colonialist dynamics are palpable (Grier et al., 2017), even today. Examples that can be listed are the extraction of raw materials (e.g., spices, precious materials) and the exploitation of resources in the competitive global race to the bottom, colonial advertising that sexualizes black females in particular within marketing communications, awash with black and brown archetypes, designed to reinforce negative, socio-cultural stereotypes, and the whitewashing of entire industries, most notably within fashion and beauty, in which underrepresented black and ethnic minority consumers are exploited and misappropriated for economic gain (Florant et al., 2020).

Fashion can be seen as a political tool, hidden behind a neoliberal globalism paradigm, the design of which suggests the Global North advances, civilizes, and dignifies the rest of the world (Pfeiffer, 2018). Fashion is also rooted in a colonialist mindset, facilitated by twenty-first century capitalism grounded in an economy of extractivism, which de-stabilizes resource-rich countries and advances the destruction of Mother Earth (Mignolo and Walsh, 2018). Here is also where the concept of modern slavery re-emerges, in that an overwhelmingly large percentage of global fashion companies have adopted principles and practices of slave-based labor primarily towards skilled BIPOC (black, indigenous, and people of color) women throughout their supply chain to generate wealth and continue an ecosystem of exploitation (e.g., Common Objective, 2018; UnSeen, 2022).

A further observation that can be made is that similar to fashion trends, which are reoccurring, history is (unfortunately) repeating itself. As alluded to, in the past fashion brands became wealthy and established through the use of slavery (pointing back to indigo and cotton farming); the same phenomenon is happening today (Busby, 2020; Paton et al., 2021).

Summary and Concluding Remarks on Section

In summary, within the previous section we have provided a brief historic account of colonialism and the impact that can still be felt to date, in terms of distribution of wealth, exploitation of resources and more importantly people, as well as power dynamics. Although Ethiopia has only been very briefly colonized in the past (Marcus, 2022), there may be some parallels that can be drawn between developments on the African continent in more general terms. Moreover, with the Ethiopian government putting a special focus on the textile and fashion industry, which has had positive economic sustainability effects, at the same time this has had negative implications for social sustainability in that Ethiopian garment workers are seen to be the lowest paid in the apparel industry (van Elven, 2019). The latter aspects will be carefully considered within this chapter, as sustainability was made a key global priority popularized by the United Nations Sustainable Development Goals (SDGs) (UN, 2022), thereby honing in on aspects of no poverty (SDG 1), gender equality (SDG 5), and responsible consumption and production (SDG 12) in particular.

Methodology

This chapter is qualitative in nature and provides insights from Ethiopia; more specifically, semi-interviews were conducted with 15 experts working within the Ethiopian fashion supply chain. For reasons of anonymity and confidentiality, all names and positions have been removed.

   As alluded to, the interviews were semi-structured, which allowed for a more conversational style interview to take place, with dialogues organically emerging. The focus of the interviews predominantly centered on sustainability, especially surrounding the social aspects, which will be carefully examined and related to decolonization within this chapter.

   Initially the researchers coded parts of the data set independently in accordance with Easterby-Smith et al.'s (2008) seven step guide of familiarization, reflection, conceptualization, cataloguing concepts, re-coding, linking, and re-evaluation. After the first round of coding any discrepancies were discussed, and a coding framework established, before the lead author performed the majority of the coding.

Findings and Discussion

As highlighted, 15 experts working within the Ethiopian fashion and textile industry, more specifically across the supply chain, were interviewed. Overall, we have seen the emergences of a variety of themes falling within the social sustainability remit, namely living conditions and general health and safety, the building of unions, gender equality, and child labor, all of which are discussed in the following.

Living Conditions

Within the introduction it was highlighted that even though the Ethiopian fashion and textile industry has seen a dramatic economic growth, garment workers in Ethiopia have been named as those being paid the least (Van Elven, 2019). This has further been confirmed by the experts, who outlined that they also believe garment workers are not paid a lot of money (Participants 1 and 3). To explain, unlike in the UK where the minimum wage is regulated by the government (UK.gov, n.d.), within Ethiopia no such regulation exists. Participants outlined that within some factories workers do not earn more than £20 per month, which can of course have an impact on living conditions, as well as raise issues surrounding health and safety standards.

To put this into perspective also, £20 per month barely covers monthly rents. Thus, concurring with what has been reported in the media and other reports (Barrett and Baumann-Pauly, 2019; Elven, 2019; LBL, 2022), findings suggest that overall social sustainability aspects concerning living arrangements remain poor. When questioning why factories are not increasing base salaries, seeing as the problem is known, experts outlined that productivity and workers efficiency are low – which may be linked to a lack of skills and education (Broussar & Tekleselassie, 2012; Sisay, 2013). Participant 5 further indicates "other sectors in the country are paying the same, we are working on projects, but we can't force our factories to decide what level of salaries to pay, etc.". This quote is particularly interesting, as it outlines key issues that can also be linked to colonialism. To explain this further, in the past forced labor was used to irrigate cotton fields and produce garments in factories in a manner to keep prices at a minimum. Forced labor (e.g., slavery) implies limited or no pay, whilst factory conditions were not much better, with female workers in particular often having to work long hours at very low wages. Yet refusing work implies that someone else may take on the job, as skill levels are low and need for paid employment is high (e.g., Kozlowski, 2019). As alluded to, however, exploitation is not an issue of the past, but rather persists in the twenty-first century, with various brands having been accused of utilizing forced labor, not only in the Global South but also in the Global North (Voss et al., 2019; Johnson, 2020; AntiSlavery, 2022).

It has to be highlighted here that it is not claimed that labor within the factories that are referred to in this chapter have forced labor, but rather that parallels can be drawn, in that it is essential to break norms and provide more support for workers within supply chains. As indicated, history is repeating itself, with exploitation of workers especially within supply chains having been brought forward as key issues in the industry. Within Ethiopia, we can see progress being made, with Ethiopia having accepted and signed international human right standards and instruments, including but not limited to the Universal Declaration of Human Rights (UDHR), which can be seen as a step in the right direction.

Health and Safety and the Link to Living Conditions

A positive finding within the data set was that experts highlight health and safety is vital across the supply chain and something that is taken very seriously. Explanations as to why this may be the case are, for example, to ensure that production can be continued, as without people on the factory floor producing items factories can no longer operate, which falls within the economic part of sustainability. Moreover, as was outlined in the introduction, the government has heavily invested in the textile and fashion sector, with the goal of creating a fashion sourcing hub that attracts foreign investors.

In recent years accusations of modern slavery have tainted the reputation of a variety of fashion retailers, some of whom have barely recovered (e.g., Voss et al., 2019; Johnson, 2020; AntiSlavery, 2022). Thus, it becomes increasingly important for, especially, foreign investors to collaborate and work with factories that not only adhere to certain standards but also provide adequate and safe working environments in order to avoid disasters, such as Rana Plaza in 2013 where thousands lost their lives (e.g., Parveen, 2014).

Within the interviews two main issues were raised and discussed, the first concerning industrial accidents and the second focusing on workers' overall well-being. Participant 6 outlines that "we work with the factories to make sure that they follow our code of compliance, but we don't leave it to annual audits to make sure that the factories are following our guidelines, we first make sure that the factory is capable of following all the safety guidelines, and continuously work with them on areas that need improvement." From the interview it is apparent that in the past key failures of compliance included blocking fire exits, using unsafe equipment, and/or malfunctioning fire alarms. Yet, due to random inspections and continuous audits, as well as improved relationships with factory owners, these issues have been addressed.

Whilst the physical surroundings are improving, from the interviews it is apparent that the experts feel more could be done for workers' well-being, in that workers often move to different parts of the country and need to accustom to their new surroundings. With youth employment being fostered as part of government initiatives, more training should be provided to ensure they can gain necessary skills and are less stressed. What needs to be outlined here is that "youth" is not equated to children, as child labor is not accepted within the supply chains. According to the experts, the Ethiopian government has outlined that children are not permitted to work within textile and garment factories and has imposed age restrictions, with "youth" classified as being 18 or older. As participant 5 observed, when it comes to children at least the government is insistent on children not being involved in supply chains. One concern that was raised by experts is that although child labor is prohibited within the garment sector, it is unclear whether this is also enforced within the raw material stages. Because supply chains are complex, full transparency might not always be possible. Moreover, experts outline that in the past children have worked to support the likes of cotton picking, especially in rural areas, which can be an issue.

What can be concluded here is that with increased focus on sustainability, including both social and economic, we can observe increased decolonization, whereby workers are increasingly moving to the forefront of concern.

Unionization and Gender Equality

An interesting finding concerns unionization, which can be seen as part of decolonization as it provides workers with a voice and outlines any inequalities that may exist. With the Ethiopian government wanting to attract foreign investment, there has also been support from the government to allow the creation of unions, and indeed has actively encouraged these. Participant 10 highlights that "as a fashion buyer whose corporate goal is to reach 100% of workers represented by labor union across its supply chain, unionization is on top of the sustainability goals, and that the challenge is not only to persuade factory owners to allow unionization, but also efforts to persuade workers to form or join unions are challenging." From the various interviews it is apparent that one of the key barriers to join a union from a worker's perspective is wages. Joining a union costs money, which is often not affordable. We may see a vicious circle emerging in that low wages can increase investment, as low labor cost countries are often preferred due to being able to sell garments at higher profits while, on the other hand, low wages implies that workers cannot join a union to represent them across the supply chain. A question that can be posed here is whether the pressure to produce at low costs can be described as colonial power display, in that workers do not have an opportunity to openly voice their concerns through the power of the masses.

A further barrier to joining a union, aside from finances, is the fact that workers do not believe their voice will be heard and, thus, joining a union will have no impact and/or benefit for them. According to the experts more needs to be done to communicate benefits of unionization and fully educate the workforce in order to make changes in the future.

Unionization can be seen as a first step towards equality, in that all parties involved gain a voice and are increasingly heard. Although there still seems to be a long way to go, progress is being made. On the other hand, an area that has seen substantial progress is within the remit of gender equality. Within Ethiopia there is an increase focus on empowering women, thus counteracting their subjugation (e.g., Pateman, 1988; Marini, 1990; Spencer-Wood, 2016) by providing them with more opportunities and fighting stereotypes.

Within the Ethiopian fashion and textile sector we see an increasing number of women employed, which may not be surprising as the fashion industry globally is dominated by a female workforce. According to the experts, increasingly creating more opportunities for females to join the workforce allows them to be self-sufficient and independent. Yet, currently, and in line with what is globally known, there is a lack of female representatives within leading positions. Participant 11 mentions that "traditional gender roles are still prevalent, and gender stereotypes need to be addressed, and the garment sector is working actively to provide all the necessary support". The participant continues by outlining that there are plans especially among the fashion actors they are working with to address this challenge.

Concluding Remarks

The aim of this chapter was to provide insights into the Ethiopian market by highlighting whether there are any parallels with colonialism that can be observed and how these can be addressed, especially when focusing on areas of sustainability.

According to the interviewees, progress is made by supporting workers to form unions and empowering females to gain more independence and self-sufficiency. Yet, the fact that Ethiopian garment workers are among those that are paid the least can be a key challenge. In reflecting on colonialism and decolonization what can be highlighted is that there remain colonialist paradigms within the fashion supply chain, which is also prevalent within Ethiopia. With buyers often possessing more power than suppliers, prices can be kept low, which results in workers being paid low wages that often restrict them within their freedom. This, however, is not solely a phenomenon that can be observed in Ethiopia but is a general issue within the fashion and textile sector.

An interesting aspect that emerged is the fact that increased sustainability strategies that are being implemented foster a decolonization approach, with workers gaining a voice, often fostered initially by the urge to increase economic sustainability. Within the chapter only the voices of experts were heard, thus it is suggested that future research should focus on workers' voices and analyze to what extent they feel their voices are heard and changes are happening.

References

Alliance Experts (2022) *The textile industry in Ethiopia and Ethiopian garment production*, Alliance Experts (online): https://www.allianceexperts.com/en/knowledge/countries/africa/trends-in-the-textile-industry-in-ethiopia/, 09/10/2022

AntiSlavery (2022) *Cotton crimes persist*, AntiSlavery (online): https://www.antislavery.org/cotton-crimes-persist/, 10/10/2022

Ashcroft, B., Griffiths, G., & Tiffin, H. (2002) *The empire writes back – theory and practice in post-colonial literatures*, 2nd edition, Routledge: Abingdon, UK

Atelier 55 (n.d.) *Textiles: Muya Ethiopia inspired by Ethiopia's rich textile heritage*, Atelier 55 (online): https://www.atelier55design.com/textiles-muya-ethiopia-inspired-by-ethiopias-rich-textile-heritage/, 09/10/2022

Azevedo, A. (2018) *The impact of the 52 micro-seasons on the environment*, Medium (online): https://medium.com/@andreaazevedo_32670/the-effects-of-the-52-micro-seasons-on-the-environment-edd87951b74f, 31/01/2022

Barrett, P.M. & Baumann-Pauly, D. (2019) *Made in Ethiopia: Challenges in the garment industry's new frontier*, WBCSD (online): https://humanrights.wbcsd.org/project/made-in-ethiopia-challenges-in-the-garment-industrys-new-frontier/, 18/07/2023

Bell, W. (1991) Colonialism and internal colonialism, in Lachmann (ed.) *The encyclopaedic dictionary of sociology*, 4th edition, Dushkin Publishing: Guilford, CT.

Benard, A.A.F. (2016) Colonizing black female bodies within patriarchal capitalism: feminist and human rights perspectives, *Sexualization, media & society*, 1–11.

Bick, R., Halsey, E., & Ekenga, C.C. (2018) The global environmental injustice of fast fashion, *Environmental Health*, 17(92): 1–4

Blakemore, E. (2019) *What is colonialism?*, National Geographic (online): https://www.nationalgeographic.com/culture/article/colonialism, 09/10/2022

Blazquez Cano, M., Henninger, C.E., Alexander, B., & Franquesa, C. (2020) Consumers' knowledge and intentions towards sustainability: A Spanish fashion perspective, *Fashion Practice*, 12(1): 34–54

Britannica (n.d.) *La Reforme intellectuelle et morale*, Britannica (online): https://www.britannica.com/topic/La-Reforme-intellectuelle-et-morale, 09/10/2022

Broussar, N.H., & Tekleselassie, T.G. (2012) *Youth unemployment, Ethiopia country study*, IGC (online): https://www.theigc.org/project/youth-unemployment-ethiopia-country-study/, 09/10/2022

Brydges, T., Henninger, C.E., & Hanlon, M. (2022) Selling sustainability: Investigating how Swedish fashion brands communicate sustainability to consumers, *Sustainability: Science, Practice, Policy*, 18(1): 357–370

BSR (2017) *Ethiopia's emerging apparel industry: options for better business and women's empowerment in a frontier market*, BSR (online): https://www.bsr.org/reports/BSR_Ethiopia_Scoping_Study_HERproject.PDF, 09/10/2022

Busby, A. (2020) *With allegations of slavery and unsafe working conditions, is Boohoo the unacceptable face of fast fashion?*, Forbes (online): https://www.forbes.com/sites/andrewbusby/2020/07/05/with-allegations-of-slavery-and-unsafe-working-conditions-is-boohoo-the-unacceptable-face-of-fast-fashion/?sh=11924fa716e9, 10/10/2022

Canales, K. (2021) *Farbic of the African diaspora*, VAM (online): https://www.vam.ac.uk/blog/museum-life/fabric-of-the-african-diaspora, 09/10/2022

CCC (Clean Clothes Campaign) (n.d.) *Poverty Wages*, CCC (online): https://cleanclothes.org/poverty-wages, 26/07/2022

Common Objective (2018) *Modern slavery and the fashion industry*, Common Objective (online): https://www.commonobjective.co/article/modern-slavery-and-the-fashion-industry, 10/10/2022

Coulibaly, S., Kassa, W., & Zeufack, A. (2022) *Re-engineering African trade with the European Union and United States: Success requires reform on both sides*, Worldbank (online): https://blogs.worldbank.org/africa

can/re-engineering-african-trade-european-union-and-united-states-success-requires-reform, 09/10/2022

Dubois, J. (2008) *Roots and flowerings of Ethiopia's traditional crafts*, UNESCO (online): https://unesdoc. unesco.org/ark:/48223/pf0000184662, 09/10/2022

Easterby-Smith, M., Thorpe, R., & Jackson, P. (2008) *Management Research*, 3rd edition, SAGE Publications: London, UK

Elkington, J. (2004) Enter the Triple Bottom Line, Chapter 1, in Henriques, A. and Richardson, J. (eds.) *The Triple Bottom Line, Does it all add up?*, Earthscan: London, UK, pp. 1–16

FashionUnited (2021) *Why fashion producers are choosing Ethiopia*, FashionUnited (online): https://fashionunited.uk/news/business/why-garment-producers-are-choosing-ethiopia /2021041454967, 09/10/2022

FDRE (2013) *Ethiopian Industrial Development Strategic Plan (2013–2025)* FDRE (online): https://www.eebcoun cil.org/images/publications/Ethiopian%20Industrial%20Development%20Strategic%20Plan%20 (2013–2025).pdf, 09/10/2022

Finley, M.I. (1976) Colonies: an attempt at a typology, *Transactions of the Royal Historical Society*, 26: 167–188

Florant, A., Julien, J.P., Stewart, S., Yancy, N., & Wright, J. (2020) *The case for accelerating financial inclusion in black communities*, McKinsey (online): https://www.mckinsey.com/industries/public-and-social-sector /our-insights/the-case-for-accelerating-financial-inclusion-in-black-communities, 11/10/2022

Galtung, J. (1979) A structural theory of imperialism, *Journal of Peace Research*, 8(2): 81–117

Greiner, P.T. (2021) *How colonialism's legacy makes it harder for countries to escape poverty and fossil fuels today*, The Conversation (online): https://theconversation.com/how-colonialisms-legacy-makes-it-harder-for-countries-to-escape-poverty-and-fossil-fuels-today-159807, 09/10/2022

Grier, S., Thomas, K., & Johnson, G. (2017). Re-imagining the marketplace: addressing race in academic marketing research, *Consumption Markets & Culture*, 22(1), 91–100.

Henninger, C.E., & Brydges, T. (2022) The Whatever Phenomenon of sustainability in the fashion industry, in Canning, C., McColl, J., & Ritch, E. (eds.), *New Perspectives in Critical Marketing and Consumer Society*, Springer: Chams

Henninger, C.E., Brydges, T., Jones, C., & Le Normand, A. (2022) That's so trashy – artification in the luxury fashion industry, in Joy, A. (ed.) *Future of luxury: sustainability and Artification*, de Gruyter, Boston, MA

Hirson, B. (1991) Colonialism and imperialism, *Searchlight South Africa*, 2(3): 7–18

ILO (2022) *50 million people worldwide in modern slavery*, ILO (online): https://www.ilo.org/global/about-the -ilo/newsroom/news/WCMS_855019/lang–en/index.htm, 10/10/2022

ITC (2016) *Ethiopia – textile and clothing value chain roadmap 2016–2020*, INTRACEN (online): https://intracen.org/sites/default/files/media/file/media_file/2022/09/22/ethiopia_tc_vcr_5-2_web. pdf, 09/10/2022

Johnson, B. (2020) *Leicester: up to 10,000 could be victims of modern slavery in textile factories*, Skey News (online): https://news.sky.com/story/leicester-up-to-10-000-could-be-victims-of-modern-slavery-in-textile-factories-12027289, 10/10/2022

Kozlowski, A (2019) *Fashion production is modern slavery: 5 things you can do to help now*, The Conversation (online): https://theconversation.com/fashion-production-is-modern-slavery-5-things-you-can-do-to-help-now-115889, 10/10/2022

Lange, M., Mahoney, J., & vom Hau, M (2006) Colonialism and development: a comparative analysis of Spanish and British colonies, *American Journal of Sociology*, 111(5): 1412–1462

LBL (Labour Behind the Label) *Living Wage*, LBL (online): https://labourbehindthelabel.org/living-wage/, 26/07/2022

Maasho, A. (2017) *Ethiopia bets on clothes to fashion industrial future*, BusinessInsider (online): https://www. businessinsider.com/r-ethiopia-bets-on-clothes-to-fashion-industrial-future-2017-11?r=US&IR=T, 09/10/2022

Magdoff, H. (n.d.) *Western colonialism*, Britannica (online): https://www.britannica.com/topic/Western-colonialism#ref25864, 09/10/2022

Marcus, H.G. (2022) *Ethiopia*, Britannica (online): https://www.britannica.com/place/Ethiopia, 09/10/2022

Marini, M.M. (1990) Sex and gender: what do we know?, *Sociological Forum*, 5: 95–120

Mehretu, A. (2022) *Ethiopia*, Britannica (online): https://www.britannica.com/place/Ethiopia, 09/10/2022

Mignolo, W.D., & Walsh, C.E. (2018) *On decoloniality, concepts, analytics, praxis*, Duke University Press: Durham, NC

Moncriffe, M.L. (2020) *Decolonising the history curriculum*, Springer: Heidelberg

Monroe, R. (2021). *Ultra-fast Fashion Is Eating the World*, The Atlantic (online):. https://www.theatlantic.com/magazine/archive/2021/03/ultra-fast-fashion-is-eating-the-world/617794/, 8/16/21

Moosavi, L. (2020) The decolonial bandwagon and the dangers of intellectual decolonialisation, *International Review of Sociology*, 30(2): 332–354

National Geographic (2022) *Motivations for colonization*, National Geographic (online): https://education.nationalgeographic.org/resource/motivations-colonization, 09/10/2022

Osman, J. (2020) *What is colonialism? A history of violence, control and exploitation*, Teen Vogue (online): https://www.teenvogue.com/story/colonialism-explained, 09/10/2022

Oxford Dictionary (2022) *Colonialism*, Oxford Dictionary (online): https://www.oxfordlearnersdictionaries.com/definition/american_english/colonialism, 09/10/2022

Parveen, S. (2014) Rana Plaza factory collapse survivors struggle one year on, BBC (online): http://www.bbc.co.uk/news/world-asia-27107860, 10/10/2022

Pateman, C. (1988) *The sexual contract*, Stanford University Press, Stanford, CA

Paton, E., Gallois, L., & Breeden, A. (2021) *Fashion retailers face inquiry over suspected ties to forced labour in China*, New York Times (online): https://www.nytimes.com/2021/07/02/fashion/xinjiang-forced-labor-Zara-Uniqlo-Sketchers.html, 10/10/2022

Perkins, S. (2013) *Clothing and textiles in the Industrial Revolution*, Blankstyle (online): https://www.blankstyle.com/articles/clothing-and-textiles-industrial-revolution, 26/07/2022

Pfeiffer, G. (2019) Balibar, citizenship and the return of right populism, *Philosophy & Social Criticism*, 46(3): 323–341

Purdy, J.M. (2015) *Made in Ethiopia?*, African Studies Student Conference (online): https://scholarworks.bgsu.edu/cgi/viewcontent.cgi?article=1040&context=africana_studies_conf, 09/10/2022

Rauturier, S. (2021) *What you need to know about fast fashion brands' 'eco' collections*, GoodOnYou (online): https://goodonyou.eco/fast-fashion-eco-collections/, 01/02/2022

Rauturier, S. (2022) *What is fast fashion and why is it so bad?*, Good on You (online): https://goodonyou.eco/what-is-fast-fashion/, 18/07/2023

Shoemaker, N. (2015) *A typology of colonialism*, Historians (online): https://www.historians.org/research-and-publications/perspectives-on-history/october-2015/a-typology-of-colonialism, 09/10/2022

Silliman, S.W. (2005) Culture contact or colonialism? Challenges in the archaeology of Native North America, *American Antiquity*, 70: 55–74.

Sisay, A. (2013) *Youth unemployment: lessons from Ethiopia*, UN (online): https://www.un.org/africarenewal/magazine/may-2013/youth-unemployment-lessons-ethiopia, 09/10/2022

Spencer-Wood. S.M. (2016) Feminist theorizing of patriarchal colonialism, power dynamics, and social agency materialized in colonial institutions, *International Journal of Historical Archaeology*, 20(3): 477–491.

Stanford Encyclopedia of Philosophy (2017) *Colonialism*, Stanford (online): https://plato.stanford.edu/entries/colonialism/, 09/10/2022

Stoler, A.L. (1989) Making empire respectable: the politics of race and sexual morality in 20th century colonial cultures, *American Ethnologist*, 16(4): 634–660.

Thomas, D. (2021) *US to suspend Ethiopia, Guinea and Mali from AGOA in 60 days* AGOA (online): https://agoa.info/news/article/15923-us-to-suspend-ethiopia-guinea-and-mali-from-agoa-in-60-days. html, 18/10/2022

UK.gov (n.d.) *National minimum wage and national living wage rates*, Gov.uk (online): https://www.gov.uk/ national-minimum-wage-rates, 09/10/2022

UN (2022) *Do you know all 17 SDGs?* UN (online): https://sdgs.un.org/goals, 10/10/2022

UN HRC (2022) *International COmmission on Human Rights Experts on Ethiopia*, UN (online): https://www. ohchr.org/en/hr-bodies/hrc/ichre-ethiopa/index, 18/10/2022

UnSeen (2022) *Modern slavery in fashion*, UnSeen (online): https://www.unseenuk.org/modern-slavery-in-fashion/, 10/10/2022

Uzogara, E.E., Lee, H., Abdou, C.M., & Jackson, J.S. (2014) A comparison of skin tone discrimination among African American men: 1995 and 2003, *Psychology for Men & Masculinity*, 15(2): 201–212.

Van Elven, M. (2019) *Ethiopian garment workers paid the lowest wages in the apparel industry*, FashionUnited (online): https://fashionunited.uk/news/business/ethiopian-garment-workers-paid-the-lowest-wages-in-the-apparel-industry/2019050743039, 18/07/2023

Voss, H., Davis, M., Sumner, M., Waite, L., Ras, I.A., Singhal, D., & Jog, D. (2019) *Journal of the British Academy*, 7(s1): 61–76.

Wolfe, P. (1997) History and imperialism: a century of theory, from Marx to Postcolonialism, *The American Historical Review*, 102(2): 388–420.

Worldbank (2013) *Ethiopia economic update: laying the foundations for achieving middle income status*, Worldbank (online): https://www.worldbank.org/en/country/ethiopia/publication/ethiopia-economic-update-laying-the-foundation-for-achieving-middle-income-status, 09/10/2022

Samira Iran, Hanieh Choopani, and Nikoo Mirzapoor

12 Exploring the Intersection of Minimalism, Luxury, and Sustainability in Fashion Consumption

Introduction

Minimalism has been enjoying a growing trend in the past few decades, especially in the Global North context, which encourages people to purchase and own fewer garments. In this regard, many practical guidebooks and tutorials have been recently published, promoting the idea of moving toward a minimalist lifestyle by applying different decluttering methods for minimalism. The most famous one is the book written by Marie Kondo, introducing the KonMari-method, which motivates consumers to only keep the possessions that bring them joy (Kondo, 2014). Besides, great emphasis is given to the organization of the remaining goods and the tidiness of the space after decluttering (Kondo, 2014).

The environmental benefits of minimalism in the fashion context are still unclear. On the one hand, reducing the number of possessed goods can potentially lead to a more sustainable lifestyle in terms of material consumption (Muster et al., 2022; Chamberlin and Callmer, 2021). On the other hand, the reduction of some products in the context of a minimalist lifestyle might lead to an increase in other resource-intensive practices such as intercontinental flights or living in large spaces (due to the saved financial means).

Besides, minimalism can promote a rather luxurious lifestyle, where one is motivated to reduce the number of goods consumed but chooses selected, exclusive goods (e.g., exclusive watches or bags, etc.). The two concepts of luxury and sustainability have previously been described as a paradox (Athwal et al., 2019). This might be because luxury is often associated with products made from expensive materials and/or exotic skins, which in the past has created an outcry for animal welfare, whilst sustainability focuses on social, environmental, and economic harmony. Still, the concept of luxury has been commonly applied to describe products or services with high quality and a rich heritage that often come at a premium price. Besides, this concept is associated with rarity, exclusivity, and uniqueness (e.g., Okonkwo, 2007; Turunen, 2018). Due to the durability of luxury goods, these products can lead to more sustainability in the fashion context. In this regard, Francois-Henri Pinault, chief executive officer of Kering (2019), claims that "luxury and sustainability are the same."

The interconnection between luxury fashion and sustainability (e.g., Joy et al., 2012) or minimalism and sustainable fashion consumption (e.g., Muster et al., 2022) have previously been subjects of academic research. Still, to the knowledge of the authors, the interrelationship between minimalism, luxury fashion, and sustainable consumption

https://doi.org/10.1515/9783110783933-012

has not been extensively researched yet. Hence, in this conceptual book chapter, the authors are going to explore the potential outcomes of minimal but luxury fashion for sustainable consumption. The main question to be answered is whether and how minimalist and luxury fashion are connected to sustainable consumption.

Literature Review

Before discussing the existence of interconnection between the three concepts of minimalism, luxury fashion, and sustainable fashion consumption in section 3, these concepts are introduced in this section.

Sustainable Fashion Consumption

The so-called fast fashion trend (meaning: producing and consuming inexpensive, low-quality garments in ever-faster cycles) has led to social as well as environmental impacts (Ellen MacArthur Foundation, 2017). For example, the fashion industry is becoming increasingly wasteful, as about 30% of the produced items are incinerated or landfilled without ever being sold or used (SITRA Studies, 2015). Besides, the consumption side of the industry in Europe (including consumption of clothing, footwear, and household textiles) is ranked as the fourth-highest contributor to greenhouse gas emissions (EEA, 2019). In the Global North, the prices of garments have decreased during the last three decades. For example, the prices of fashion items have dropped by more than 30% between 1996 and 2018 (EEA, 2019). Such a decrease in clothing prices has led to an increase in per-person sales of garments and the number of purchased garments per person increased by 40% between 1996 and 2012 in Europe (Šajn, 2019). While buying more garments and spending less on them, the active usage of garments decreased globally by 36% from 2005 to 2017 (Ellen MacArthur Foundation, 2017).

Against this background, the concept of sustainable fashion has emerged. Sustainable fashion refers to garments and footwear, which are designed, produced, (re-)used, and disposed of in a way that is aligned with the concept of sustainable development (Stanszus and Iran, 2014). Thus, sustainable fashion does not only mean reducing the environmental as well as socio-economic impacts of the production side of garments but also their usage and post-usage phase.

To achieve sustainability in fashion consumption, various ideas (such as purchasing organic and fair-trade garments or upcycling) have been developed. Most of such alternative practices emphasize efficiency strategies, which can be achieved by increasing the frequency and/or intensity of using fashion items. However, it is recently highlighted that an absolute reduction of material use is necessary to achieve sustainability goals (e.g., Schneidewind and Palzkill-Vorbeck, 2011). Hence, sufficiency-based approaches need to be more promoted (e.g., Spangenberg and Lorek, 2019). Sufficiency is defined as "avoidance of over- and underconsumption which implies a reduction of material consumption levels in absolute terms in affluent societies" (Gossen et al., 2019, p. 1). This calls for fundamental alteration in the current consumption patterns (e.g., Spangenberg and Lorek, 2019), for example, towards a minimalistic approach.

Minimalism in the Fashion Industry

In everyday language, the word minimalist is commonly used to describe something that has been reduced to its most basic and essential elements (VanEenoo, 2011). The term minimalism became widely used in the late twentieth century, but it was originally coined by David Burlyuk in 1929 for a catalog of an exhibition at the Dudensing Gallery featuring John Graham's paintings. Minimalism as an art movement emerged primarily during the 1960s and could have been summed up by the motto "make it pure and simple" (Strickland, 2000; VanEenoo, 2011). This concise phrase encapsulates the guiding principle behind minimalism. In the fashion industry, a popular trend towards minimalism and decluttering has recently emerged, particularly in the Global North countries (Meissner, 2019). This trend is similar to what researchers called voluntary simplicity in the 1970s. Voluntary simplicity can be regarded as a concept against overconsumption of material resources and overwork. It promotes the idea of reducing working time and material consumption and instead focusing on increasing the well-being of individuals. Voluntary simplicity is defined as: "the choice out of free will . . . to limit expenditure on consumer goods and services and to cultivate non-materialistic sources of satisfaction and meaning" (Etzioni, 1998, p. 620). Concepts such as minimalists, frugalists, low materialists, or downshifters are often associated with Voluntary Simplicity (Rebouças and Soares, 2020). In particular, downshifting and voluntary simplicity have sometimes been applied as interchangeable terms (Hamilton and Mail, 2003). However, Aidar and Daniels (2020) distinguish these concepts from each other (p. 3). They mention that downshifting is more related to deciding to reduce income and consumption to improve quality of life while voluntary simplicity usually implies broader lifestyle changes that involve inner or spiritual growth and the pursuit of strong environmental values. Hence, the process of decluttering (or downshifting) can be seen as an act toward voluntary simplicity (Chhetri et al., 2009; Tan, 2000; McDonald et al., 2006). By using less clothing, participants become more comfortable with less and are happier as a result (Vladimirova, 2021).

Since the publication of the book *The Life-Changing Magic of Tidying* (Kondo, 2014), the decluttering trend has enjoyed an increasing interest among consumers. Kondo invites individuals to reduce their material possessions and only keep those goods that bring them joy (Kondo, 2014). She also emphasizes the importance of tidiness and organization of the goods in the living space and suggests specific folding and organization techniques (Kondo, 2014). This is aligned with the main aim of minimalism: "to get rid of too much noise and focus on the essence" (VanEenoo, 2011, p. 11). Although many other publications around the idea of decluttering usually address the topic for different areas (e.g., fashion, furniture, books, etc.), most of them start the process of downshifting by focusing on fashion items (Münsch et al., 2022). It seems that practicing minimalism in the fashion context can be an entering gate to a holistic minimalist lifestyle.

Luxury Fashion Consumption

Luxury consumption is highly relevant to its psychological value (Vickers and Renand, 2003), status symbol (Chadha and Husband, 2006), and the individual's self-concept (Vigneron and Johnson, 1999). Therefore, it can particularly be explained in terms of having a symbolic rather than a utilization function. From a product perspective, luxury items can be defined by their higher quality and exclusiveness, and by satisfying desires rather than needs (e.g., Athwal et al., 2019). They often require extensive material and skill resources and are durable (Atwal and Williams, 2009; Kapferer and Bastien, 2009). Some of the luxury products focus on wealth (e.g., classic and traditional luxury goods) and some of them are based on competencies related to workmanship, society, and culture's tales that are made by someone who is an expert and also has aesthetic knowledge (Wang, 2021). Luxury fashion brands do not follow the pace of fast fashion and still only offer a few collections per year. They mostly select a rather timeless design for their products.

Consumers are currently criticizing the luxury industry for its lack of effort for integrating sustainability ideas into its processes (e.g., lack of supply-chain transparency or exploiting animals and workers) (Dekhili and Achabou, 2016; Kapferer and Michaut-Denizeau, 2014). Joy et al. (2012, p. 290) argue that "since luxury brands create desire through innovative design, and influence consumption processes, they can become leaders in sustainability." Against this background, luxury brands (e.g., Gucci, Saint Laurent, Prada) are slowly changing their strategies to integrate sustainability ideas in their sourcing, manufacturing, and marketing. For example, they started to implement sustainable strategies such as using energy-efficient light resources or being committed to becoming fur-free. Still the meaning of sustainability in the luxury context is not clear (Dean, 2018). In this paper, similar to the paper by Athwal et al. (2019), sustainable luxury refers to luxury that is environmentally and/or ethically conscious in all the processes from production to consumption and is "oriented toward correcting various perceived wrongs within the luxury industry, including animal cruelty, environmental damage, and human exploitation" (Athwal et al., 2019, p. 406; Lundblad and Davies, 2015). As examples of sustainable fashion luxury, one can mention eco-conscious fashion items, fair-trade pieces of jewelry, and innovative textiles or materials.

The Connection between Luxury, Minimalism, and Sustainable Consumption

To provide a more detailed picture, the interconnection between the three concepts of minimalism, luxury, and sustainable consumption in fashion is discussed from two different aspects in this section.

Minimalism and Luxury as a Trend Toward More Sustainable Fashion

Engaging mainstream consumers with sustainable fashion consumption has been a challenge (Chamberlin and Callmer, 2021). But Chamberlin and Callmer (2021) suggest that "the recent growth in popularity of decluttering and well-being movements, exemplified by Marie Kondo's globally successful method for tidying up, may help" (p. 1). This could be because minimalism involves achieving a desired outcome by utilizing a restricted amount of material, as implied by its name (VanEenoo, 2011). Vladimirova (2021) claims that Marie Kondo's decluttering method emerged "at the perfect moment when clutter from overconsumption, including from fast fashion, reached a new peak" (p. 112). Therefore, it seems that today's consumers are somehow exhausted from the act of collecting and storing more and more fashion items. This might be a window of opportunity for motivating them toward a more sufficient clothing consumption by reducing the number of their possessed goods.

Besides, minimalism allows individuals to eliminate excessive distractions and concentrate on the core essence (VanEenoo, 2011). Minimalism and decluttering value the concept of having less and encourage consumers to release themselves from the stress and burden of owning unnecessary goods and therefore increase their well-being. As well-being is associated with decreasing workload and consumption (e.g., Jackson, 2009), concepts such as decluttering and minimalism "may have significant consequences for environmental as well as social sustainability" (Chamberlin and Callmer, 2021, p. 2). VanEenoo (2011) also argues whether it would be more satisfying and cost-effective in terms of time and energy to incorporate simplicity into our routine.

Moreover, downshifting and having a reduced selection of items in consumers' wardrobes can help them keep an overview of what they have and finally decrease the idling capacity of their wardrobes and increase the utilization of the existing items (e.g., Iran and Geiger, 2018). This might lead to decreasing the environmental burden of the fashion industry. However, the management of wardrobes requires an intensive analysis of emotions (Mellander and Mcintyre, 2020) since garments cannot be seen as isolated goods and the memories or the dreams associated with them make the act of "letting go" very challenging. Sometimes, it might even be like a message of letting dreams and future life go (Gregson et al., 2007a; 2007b). Detaching oneself from the garments depends on many factors such as "norms of gender, bodies, and social life" (Mellander and Mcintyre, 2020, p. 11). But still, even though positive emotions can be attached to each garment, the contents of the closet as an undifferentiated mass are often a source of anxiety and guilt because they serve as reminders of past bad decisions and investments (Mellander and Mcintyre, 2020). Therefore, to motivate consumers to make a long-term shift towards sustainable fashion consumption, ways should be found that allow them to explore their relationship with not only each possessed fashion item but also with their wardrobes as a whole (e.g., Callmer, 2019; Mellander and Mcintyre, 2020) and to reduce their possessions. Besides, detachment and attachment patterns are intertwined with normative notions of wrong and right in life (Mellander and Mcintyre, 2020, p. 4). The point of dealing with sustainability here is to examine how trends toward sustainable lifestyles are shaping up and how these claims clash with everyday practices (Mellander and Mcintyre, 2020, p. 4). In addition, decluttering wardrobes can be seen as a challenge in which consumers need to ask themselves "what they wear and why" (Vladimirova, 2021, p. 115). In this regard, they are invited to explore their needs and separate them from their dreams and desires (Vladimirova, 2021). It seems that minimalism has the potential to motivate consumers to satisfy their physical and psychological needs as well as desires for more well-being in their life while contributing to sustainability in the fashion industry (Lloyd and Pennington, 2020).

Not only is decreasing the number of possessed fashion items effective, but other aspects are also playing crucial roles in promoting sustainable consumption in the fashion industry. For example, it is claimed that decreasing purchases of new clothing pieces together with increasing the usage time of each garment have large emission reduction effects (Coscieme et al., 2022). Hence, durability as an important dimension of sustainable consumption (Haws et al., 2014; White et al., 2019) should be considered in the selection of items for a reduced wardrobe. A product can be defined "as durable if it provides extended functional benefits (e.g., it does not deteriorate after a few washes in the case of apparel goods), as well as stylistic benefits (e.g., it does not quickly go out of style, reflecting its timelessness)" (Sun et al., 2021, p. 29). This is true about luxury products which offer consumers both high status and rarity and a longer lifetime and durability (Kapferer, 2010; Wiedmann et al., 2007).

The central point of durability in the definition of luxury products is both function and style (Amatulli et al., 2017; Athwal et al., 2019). The longstanding interest in quality and craftsmanship allows luxury brands to effectively address some of the fast fashion issues and play a leading role in sustainability (Joy et al., 2012). Joy et al. (2012) argue that luxury brands can lead a role in sustainability since they emphasize aesthetics and artisanal quality in their products. Aesthetics in luxury items can influence consumers' desire to value artisanal quality. This means that a luxury product is complete only when it becomes an element of the consumer's self-image and its appearance reflects and reinforces the consumer's aesthetics (Joy et al., 2012). When these aesthetic are mixed with high-quality art crafts of artisans, the product becomes timeless and will last longer in consumers' hands. Thus, by emphasizing the overlap between sustainable consumption and luxury on the aspect of product durability, Sun et al. (2021) argue that (due to the longer lifetime and more environmentally friendly disposal ways) luxury goods have the potential to be more sustainable than conventional ones. Still, by ignoring the importance of durability, many consumers currently prefer to purchase multiple fast fashion items rather than fewer luxury products (Sun et al., 2021). But, in the past years, ideas such as sustainable luxury consumption (Amatulli et al., 2017), "buy less, buy better" (Cline, 2016), and the new trend of celebrities showing up with the same outfit on different occasions (Cantor, 2020) have been suggested and promoted to achieve sustainability in the fashion industry through luxury and higher quality products. It seems that purchasing fewer high-quality fashion items could allow consumers to not only be more sustainable but also make strategic financial resource management (Sun et al., 2021).

Furthermore, "because luxury fashion is concerned with longevity, durability and quality" (Ozdamar-Ertekin, 2019, p. 8), it can promote a sharing economy. For example, Village Luxe and Designerex, two luxury rental companies and platforms, are enabling access to expensive luxury items with "affordable rental prices" (Ozdamar-Ertekin, 2019, p. 10). By renting higher quality items through sharing platforms, people value access instead of ownership (Lewittes, 2019), which can support sustainability. Above all, heritage and quality do not cause pollution, depletion of natural resources, and global warming since they are mostly related to the petroleum and transportation industries. Most of the ateliers are affiliated with major fashion houses in major fashion cities such as Paris and Milan, so there is little exploitation of the labor force (Joy et al., 2012), but outsourcing to other countries can cause all the issues related to fast fashion brands.

Besides, luxury fashion brands are now more than acting on consumers' awareness about sustainability. For example, Kering and Stella McCartney integrated rental service and the second-hand market respectively as sustainability ideas (Campos Franco et al., 2020). Also, luxury brands might have more power to support sustainability ideas by "managing their suppliers to comply with and improve social and environmental conditions, fulfilling the triple-bottom lines and consumer demands for transparency" (Ozdamar-Ertekin, 2019, 14) and persuading consumers to pay more for durable products (Godart, 2015). For example, Armani and Gucci have started integrating corporate social responsibility and ethical codes of conduct into their organizations. Another example is Louis Vuitton, which recently published a report on its energy and water consumption by implementing a "green supply chain initiative" to become more transparent (Ozdamar-Ertekin, 2019).

Therefore, a combination of a minimalist wardrobe including a reduced number of durable luxury products or shared luxury items seems to be a viable strategy for sustainable fashion consumption. By this, consumers can not only satisfy their needs and desires but also move towards a more sustainable lifestyle.

Minimalism and Luxury as a Threat to Sustainable Fashion

We discussed that through the process of downshifting or decluttering consumers decrease the number of their possessed fashion items (sometimes radically) and make a reduced version of their wardrobes (Chamberlin and Callmer, 2021). Owning and consuming fewer fashion items can lead to more sufficient fashion consumption (see previous section). However, what comes after decluttering is still ambiguous. For example, it is important to know how consumers dispose of their unwanted garments. Depending on if they resell them, put them in a garbage bin, give them as gifts to others locally, or put them in recycle bins, the environmental as well as social impact of their decluttering might differ. Besides, if decluttering and having more space in the wardrobe encourage consumers on their future purchases (Lang et al., 2013), the sustainable benefits of decluttering can be overrun by new material consumption. Therefore, fashion minimalism and living with a selected number of clothing items does not necessarily mean that individuals do not purchase new products, but it might only result In the faster replacement of older items with newer ones (Muster et al., 2022). Hence, minimalism does not necessarily result in consumers taking a sustainable fashion consumption approach and minimalism could be like a threat to sustainable fashion if individuals do not consider all aspects of sustainability such as how they throw away their clothes or if they buy more after decluttering.

Furthermore, fashion minimalism might encourage consumers to purchase fewer but higher-quality products (Sun et al., 2021). It means that an individual might decide to have only one bag in the wardrobe but then purchase this from a non-sustainable luxury brand. This can per se be less problematic for environmental sustainability if individuals benefit from the durability aspect of the luxury product (Atwal and Williams, 2009) and use it for a long time before disposing of it. Hence, as sustainable consumption and luxury both focus on product durability, the consumption of fewer, high-quality items can encourage engaging in sustainability (Sun et al., 2021). But it can also have negative effects if the individuals engage in a fast replacement of the non-sustainable luxury products with other similar products (Lang et al., 2013) since luxury products usually demand more material resources for production.

Besides, previous studies on sustainable fashion consumption have shown that when talking about sustainable fashion, consumers have a rather unpretty image of the products in their minds. Consumers were usually referring to sustainable fashion items as not stylish (Joergens, 2006; Joy et al., 2012). It seems that the phrase "eco-fashion" evokes memories of the environmental and hippie movements from the 1960s and 1970s, where environmentally conscious fashion often comprised of shapeless, reused garments (Welters, 2008). Winge (2008, 520) further differentiates between eco-dress and eco-fashion. Eco-dress is linked to the hippie era, whereas eco-fashion now implies luxury and sophistication. Van Nes and Cramer (2005) suggest that when consumers were asked about their expectations for eco-fashion in the future, they prioritized durability, quality, and style. Interestingly, durability, quality, and style are also key features that overlap with luxury brands, along with a sense of personal accomplishment (Joy et al., 2012). At the same time, when looking at images of minimalist lifestyles (especially in social media), a rather luxurious image of clean empty spaces with a few high-quality products can be seen (e.g., Martin-Woodhead, 2022). This idea could be supported by the motto of minimalism as an art movement that emphasizes simplicity and pureness (Strickland, 2000). Such perceived luxurious images can motivate consumers towards more sustainable fashion consumption (Oz-damar-Ertekin, 2019) since, unlike classic sustainability strategies such as sufficient consumption, it delivers a positive stylish message about sustainability. However, a luxurious image of a sustainable minimalist wardrobe can also deliver a message that a minimalist lifestyle is targeting a specific group of consumers, particularly more wealthy individuals (Liu et al., 2018; Currid-Halkett, 2017). Hence, minimalist luxury is defined as affluent individuals who choose to "stand out from mainstream consumer" by using limited luxury products (Wilson and Bellezza, 2022, p. 8) and these people usually spend a vast amount of money to take a simplistic approach (Chayka, 2020). Additionally, if luxury represents consuming for individual" pleasure and buying un-necessary purchases, it will be against sustainable fashion consumption (Kapferer and Michaut-Denizeau, 2014; Ozdamar-Ertekin, 2019).

It seems that the idea of minimalist luxury fashion consumption can have several environmental benefits, however, the backlashes and possible negative impacts of this idea cannot be overlooked and requires more careful consideration in terms of how consumers throw away their garments after decluttering, if they are encouraged to replace faster and buy more after a while when they take a minimalist approach and have more space, or whether minimalist and luxury fashion consumption is lim-ited to a specific community of society.

Strengths, Limitations, and Future Research

A particular strength of this conceptual article is that it attempted to make a connec-tion between the three concepts of luxury, minimalism, and sustainable fashion con-sumption, which is an under-researched topic. However, there is a need for empirical research (including life cycle assessments) on this topic to evaluate the environmental as well as social sustainability of a minimalist wardrobe with luxury fashion items. Furthermore, it is suggested to research if consumers keep on taking a minimalist ap-proach to their fashion wardrobes and do not replace new items after a while or to study if the wardrobe consisting of luxury fashion items is accessible to all people in society. Thus, future research should represent a deeper understanding of how mini-malist luxury can be accessible to all people and achieve more insight into how these concepts can impact sustainable fashion consumption.

Conclusion

The wardrobes cannot function well if they are overfilled with fashion items that cannot be seen or are not being used. Like other ecosystems, wardrobes require strategies to manage their waste. For this, the current paper discusses minimalism and decluttering as a method to decrease the idling capacities of wardrobes. Through reduced wardrobes, individuals can have an overview of their possessed fashion items and put them to use. This might lead to less need for a new production of fashion items and as a result to more sustainability in the fashion industry. Besides, if the selected items for the capsule wardrobe are luxury products and high-quality art crafts which emphasize heritage and aesthetics and are durable and artisanal, they can be used for a longer time while satisfying the psychological needs of individuals such as uniqueness, status, and social norms. Therefore, having a minimalist wardrobe consisting of luxury products might have the potential for promoting more sustainable fashion consumption.

However, minimalism can only be sustainable if individuals do not engage themselves in purchasing new products right after decluttering when they create more space. Moreover, minimalist wardrobes should attract more consumer groups and not only focus on a niche market of wealthy individuals. If only a group of rich individuals are able to engage in minimalist and luxury fashion consumption, these two concepts cannot contribute enough to promote sustainable fashion consumption.

References

Aidar, L., and Daniels, P. (2020). A critical review of voluntary simplicity: Definitional inconsistencies, movement identity and direction for future research. *The Social Science Journal*. https://doi.org/10.1080/03623319.2020.1791785

Amatulli, C., De Angelis, M., Costabile, M., and Guido, G. (2017). *Sustainable luxury brands: evidence from research and implications for managers*. London: Palgrave Macmillan.

Athwal, N., Wells, V.K., Carrigan, M., and Henninger, C.E. (2019). Sustainable luxury marketing: a synthesis and research agenda. *International Journal of Management Reviews*, *21*(4), 405–426. https://doi.org/10.1111/ijmr.12195

Atwal, G., and Williams, A. (2009). Luxury brand marketing-the experience is everything! *Journal of Brand Management*, *16*, 338–346. https://doi.org/10.1057/bm.2008.48

Callmer, Å. (2019). *Making sense of sufficiency: entries, practices and politics*. [Doctoral dissertation, KTH Royal Institute of Technology, Sweden: Stockholm]. http://kth.diva-portal.org/smash/get/diva2:1380175/FULLTEXT02.pdf. Accessed November 9, 2022.

Campos Franco, J., Hussain, D., and McColl, R. (2020). Luxury fashion and sustainability: looking good together. *Journal of Business Strategy*, *41*(4), 55–61. https://doi.org/10.1108/JBS-05-2019-0089

Cantor, C. (2020, February 7). *A greener red carpet. Columbia News*. https://blogs.ei.columbia.edu/2020/02/07/red-carpet-sustainable-fashion/. Accessed November 12, 2022.

Chadha, R., and Husband, P. (2006). *The cult of the luxury brand: inside Asia's love affair with luxury*. Nicholas Brealey.

Chamberlin, L., and Callmer, Å. (2021). Spark joy and slow consumption: an empirical study of the impact of the KonMari method on acquisition and wellbeing. *Journal of Sustainability Research, 3*(1). https://doi.org/10.20900/jsr20210007

Chayka, K. (2020). *The Longing for Less: Living with Minimalism*. Bloomsbury Publishing.

Chhetri, P., Stimson, R.J., and Western, J. (2009). Understanding the downshifting phenomenon: a case of south east Queensland, Australia. *Australian Journal of Social Issues, 44*(4), 345–362. https://doi.org/10.1002/j.1839-4655.2009.tb00152.x

Cline, E. (2016). The power of buying less by buying better. The Atlantic. https://www.theatlantic.com/business/archive/2016/02/buying-less-by-buying-better/462639/. Accessed November 9, 2022.

Coscieme, L., Akenji, L., Latva-Hakuni, E., Vladimirova, K., Niinimäki, K., Henninger, C., Joyner-Martinez, C., Nielsen, K., Iran, S., and D´Itria, E. (2022). *Unfit, Unfair, Unfashionable: Resizing Fashion for a Fair Consumption Space*. Hot or Cool Institute, Berlin.

Currid-Halkett, E. (2017). *The Sum of Small Things: A Theory of the Aspirational Class*. Princeton, NJ: Princeton University Press.

Dean, A. (2018, September 18). Everything is wrong: a search for order in the ethnometaphysical chaos of sustainable luxury fashion. *The Fashion Studies Journal*. https://www.fashionstudiesjournal.org/longform/2018/2/25/everything-is-wrong-a-search-for-order-in-the-ethnometaphysical-chaos-of-sustainable-luxury-fashion-4h33n. Accessed November 9, 2022.

Dekhili, S., and Achabou, M.A. (2016). Is it beneficial for luxury brands to embrace CSR practices?. In *Celebrating America's Pastimes: Baseball, Hot Dogs, Apple Pie and Marketing?*, 3–18. Springer International Publishing. https://doi.org/10.1007/978-3-319-26647-3_1

EEA. (2019, November 19). *Textiles in Europe's circular economy*. https://www.eea.europa.eu/publications/textiles-in-europes-circular-economy. Accessed November 1, 2022.

Ellen MacArthur Foundation. (2017, November, 28). *A new textiles economy: redesigning fashion's future*. https://ellenmacarthurfoundation.org/a-new-textiles-economy. Accessed November 1, 2022.

Etzioni, A. (1998). Voluntary simplicity: Characterization, select psychological implications, and societal consequences. *Journal of Economic Psychology, 19*, 619–643. https://doi.org/10.1007/978-3-662-10347-0_17

Godart, F. (2015), "Three Ways Luxury Fashion Can Be Sustainable," Insead, https://knowledge.insead.edu/responsibility/three-ways-luxuryfashion-can-be-sustainable-4067 Accessed January 20, 2023.

Gossen, M., Ziesemer, F., and Schrader, U. (2019). Why and how commercial marketing should promote sufficient consumption: a systematic literature review. *Journal of Macromarketing, 39*(3), 252–269. https://doi.org/10.1177/0276146719866238

Gregson, N., Metcalfe, A., and Crewe, L. (2007a). Identity, mobility, and the throwaway society. *Environment and Planning D: Society and Space, 25*(4), 682–700. https://doi.org/10.1068/d418t

Gregson, N., Metcalfe, A., and Crewe, L. (2007b). Moving things along: the conduits and practices of divestment in consumption. *Transactions of the Institute of British Geographers, 32*(2), 187–200. https://doi.org/10.1111/j.1475-5661.2007.00253.x

Hamilton, C., and Mail, E. (2003). Downshifting in Australia: a sea-change in the pursuit of happiness [Electronic resource]. *The Australia Institute*. https://www.tai.org.au/documents/downloads/DP50.pdf

Haws, K., Page Winterich, K., and Walker Naylor, R. (2014). Seeing the world through green-tinted glasses: how green consumers' use motivated reasoning to refer environmentally friendly products. *Journal of Consumer Psychology, 24*(3), 336–354. https://doi.org/10.1016/j.jcps.2013.11.002

Iran, S., and Geiger, S.M. (2018). To wear or to own? influences of values on the attitudes toward and the engagement in collaborative fashion consumption. In Heuer, M., and BeckerLeifhold, C. (Eds.), *Eco friendly and Fair: fast fashion and consumer behavior*, 153–162. Routledge, New York, USA.

Jackson T. (2009). Prosperity without growth: Economics for a finite planet. London: Earthscan.

Joergens, C. (2006). Ethical fashion: myth or future trend? *Journal of Fashion Marketing and Management, 10*(3), 360–371. https://doi.org/10.1108/13612020610679321

Joy, A., Sherry, J.F., Venkatesh, A., Wang, J.J., and Chan, R.Y. (2012). Fast fashion, sustainability, and the ethical appeal of luxury brands. *Fashion Theory, 16*, 273–295. https://doi.org/10.2752/175174112X13340749707123

Kapferer, J. (2010). All that glitters is not green: the challenge of sustainable luxury. *European Business Review*, 40–45.

Kapferer, J.N., and Bastien, V. (2009). *The luxury strategy: break the rules of marketing to build luxury brands.* London: Kogan Page.

Kapferer, J.N., and Michaut-Denizeau, A. (2014). Is luxury compatible with sustainability? luxury consumers' viewpoint. *Journal of Brand Management, 21*, 1–22.

Kering. (2019). https://www.kering.com/en/sustainability/. Accessed December 1, 2022.

Kondo, M. (2014). *The life-changing magic of tidying up: the Japanese art of decluttering and organizing.* Berkeley, CA: Ten Speed Press.

Lang, C., Armstrong, C.M., and Brannon, L.A. (2013). Drivers of clothing disposal in the US: an exploration of the role of personal attributes and behaviors in frequent disposal. *International Journal of Consumer Studies, 37*(6), 706–714. https://doi.org/10.1111/ijcs.12060

Lewittes, E. (2019, February 1). How fashion brands can create a more sustainable end-to-end retail economy. Fashionista. https://fashionista.com/2019/02/sustainable-fashion-brands-end-to-end-retail-economy. Accessed January 4, 2023.

Liu, Z., Yildirim, P., and Zhang, Z.J. (2018). *Less is more: the case of minimalist luxury.* https://ssrn.com/abstract=3246729. http://dx.doi.org/10.2139/ssrn.3246729

Lloyd, K., and Pennington, W. (2020). Towards a theory of minimalism and wellbeing. *International Journal of Applied Positive Psychology, 5*, 121–136. https://doi.org/10.1007/s41042-020-00030-y

Lundblad, L., and Davies, I.A. (2015). The values and motivations behind sustainable fashion consumption. *Journal of Consumer Behaviour, 44*, 309–323. https://doi.org/10.1002/cb.1559

Martin-Woodhead, A. (2022). Limited, considered and sustainable consumption: The (non)consumption practices of UK minimalists. *Journal of Consumer Culture, 22*(4), 1012–1031. https://doi.org/10.1177/14695405211039608

McDonald, S., Oates, C.J., Young, C.W., and Hwang, K. (2006). Toward sustainable consumption: researching voluntary simplifiers. *Psychology and Marketing, 23*(6), 515–534. https://doi.org/10.1002/mar.20132

Meissner, M. (2019). Against accumulation: lifestyle minimalism, de-growth and the present post-ecological condition. *Journal of Cultural Economy, 12*, 185–200. https://doi.org/10.1080/17530350.2019.1570962

Mellander, E., and Petersson McIntyre, M. (2020). Fashionable detachments: wardrobes, bodies and the desire to let go. *Consumption Markets and Culture, 24*(4), 343–356. https://doi.org/10.1080/10253866.2020.1802258

Muster, V., Iran, S., and Münsch, M. (2022). The cultural practice of decluttering as household work and its potentials for sustainable consumption. *Frontiers in Sustainability, 3*, 1–18. https://doi.org/10.3389/frsus.2022.958538

Okonkwo, U. (2007). *Luxury Fashion Branding: Trends, Tactics, Techniques.* London: Palgrave Macmillan.

Ozdamar-Ertekin, Z. (2019). *Can Luxury Fashion Provide a Roadmap for Sustainability?.* Markets, Globalization & Development Review, 4(1), Article 3. https://doi.org/10.23860/MGDR-2019-04-01-03

Rebouças, R., and Soares, A.M. (2020). Voluntary simplicity: a literature review and research agenda. *International Journal of Consumer Studies, 45*(3), 303–319. https://doi.org/10.1111/ijcs.12621

Šajn, N. (2019). Environmental impact of the textile and clothing industry. *EPRS | European Parliamentary Research Service.* https://www.europarl.europa.eu/RegData/etudes/BRIE/2019/633143/EPRS_BRI(2019)633143_EN.pdf. Accessed November 1, 2022.

Schneidewind, U., and Palzkill-Vorbeck, A. (2011). Suffizienz als business case: nachhaltiges ressourcenmanagement als gegenstand einer transdisziplinären betriebswirtschaftslehre. https://doi.org/10.1007/978-3-8349-3746-9_4

SITRA Studies (2015, October). The opportunities of a circular economy for Finland. *A publication series*. https://media.sitra.fi/2017/02/28142449/Selvityksia100.pdf. Accessed November 1, 2022.

Spangenberg, J.H., and Lorek, S. (2019). Sufficiency and consumer behaviour: from theory to policy. *Energy Policy*, *129*, 1070–1079. https://doi.org/10.1016/j.enpol.2019.03.013

Stanszus, L., and Iran, S. (2014). Sustainable fashion. In Idowu, S.O., Capaldi, N., Fifka, M., Zu, L., and Schmidpeter, R. (Eds.), *Dictionary of corporate social responsibility*, 154–155. Springer. https://doi.org/10.1007/978-3-319-74367-7_13

Strickland, E. (2000). *Minimalism – Origins*. Bloomington, IN: Indiana University Press.

Sun, J.J., Bellezza, S., and Paharia, N. (2021). Buy less, buy luxury: understanding and overcoming product durability neglect for sustainable consumption. *Journal of Marketing*, *85*(3), 28–43. https://doi.org/10.1177/0022242921993172

Tan, P. (2000). *Leaving the rat race to get a life: a study of midlife career downshifting* [Doctorate thesis, Swinburne University, Hawthorn, Australia].

Turunen, L.L.M. (2018). Concept of luxury through the lens of history. In *Interpretations of luxury.* Palgrave advances in Luxury, 13–29. London (UK): Palgrave Macmillan, Cham. https://doi.org/10.1007/978-3-319-60870-9_2

VanEenoo, C. (2011). Minimalism in art and design: concept, influences, implications and perspectives. *Journal of Fine and Studio Art*, *2*(1), 7–12. http://dx.doi.org/10.29228/SOBIDER.32562

Van Nes, N., and Cramer, J. (2005). Influencing Product Lifetime through Product Design. *Business Strategy and the Environment*, *14*(5), 286–99.

Vickers, J.S., and Renand, F. (2003). The marketing of luxury goods. *The Marketing Review*, *3*, 459–478. https://doi.org/10.1362/146934703771910071

Vigneron, F., and Johnson, L.W. (1999). Review and a conceptual framework of prestige-seeking consumer behavior. *Academy of Marketing Science Review*, *1*. http://www.amsreview.org/articles/vigneron01-1999.pdf. Accessed November 3, 2022.

Vladimirova, K. (2021). Consumption corridors in fashion: deliberations on upper consumption limits in minimalist fashion challenges. *Sustainability: Science, Practice and Policy*, *17*(1), 103–117. https://doi.org/10.1080/15487733.2021.1891673

Vladislava, N., and Valentina, G. (2021). Purchasing patterns in luxury consumption: transitional transaction categories. *Procedia Computer Science*, *193*, 351–360. https://doi.org/10.1016/j.procs.2021.10.036

Wang, Y. (2021). A conceptual framework of contemporary luxury consumption. *International Journal of Research in Marketing*, *39*(3), 778–803. https://doi.org/10.1016/j.ijresmar.2021.10.010

Welters, L. (2008). The Natural Look: American Style in the 1970s. *Fashion Theory*, *12*(4): 489–510.

White, K., Habib, H., and Hardisty, D.J. (2019). How to SHIFT consumer behaviors to be more sustainable: a literature review and guiding framework. *Journal of Marketing*, *83*(3), 22–49. https://doi.org/10.1177/0022242919825649

Wiedmann, K.P., Hennigs, H., and Siebels, S. (2007). Measuring consumers' luxury value perception: a crosscultural framework. *Academy of Marketing Science Review*, *7*(7), 1–21. https://doi.org/10.1007/978-3-8349-4399-6_5

Wilson, A.V., and Bellezza, S. (2022). Consumer Minimalism. *Journal of Consumer Research*, *48*(5), 796–816. https://doi.org/10.1093/jcr/ucab038

Winge, T. M. (2008). Green is the New Black: Celebrity Chic and the 'Green' Commodity Fetish. *Fashion Theory*, *12*(4), 511–24.

Bianca Grohmann and Annamma Joy

13 From Conscious Capitalism to Philanthro-Capitalism: Framing the Sustainability Paradox Facing Patagonia

Introduction

A growing number of organizations shift towards more sustainable practices, due to either societal pressure or genuine interest. This shift is particularly noticeable in highly pollutant industries, such as the fashion industry. At the same time, Gen Z and Millennial consumers are increasingly concerned about the environmental and social impact of fashion labels and consider sustainability when purchasing clothing items (*Global Powers of Luxury Goods 2020*, 2020). Because sustainable brands attract more consumers and generate increasing sales, their production and consumption increase. This poses a threat to the environmental and social advances made by sustainable brands. If the loop of circularity is not fully closed, an increase in production and consumption likely leads to more waste, emissions, and pressure on supply chain partners. This chapter explores this paradox in the fashion industry. It examines the case of Patagonia, a premium outdoor clothing label that is considered by many as a pioneer in the realms of sustainable fashion.

Patagonia: History, Sustainability Goals, and Programs

From Socio-Capitalism to Philanthro-Capitalism

Patagonia is an outdoor clothing brand that is based on the premise of "saving our home planet," as stated by its mission statement. The brand's core values include creating the best product while causing no unnecessary damage, as well as using business to "protect nature," while not being restricted by convention. Patagonia's mission statement and core values suggest that this sustainability is one of the clothing brand's pillars.

Acknowledgements: We thank Maria de paz Marengo for her assistance in the literature review and preparation of the first draft of this book chapter.

https://doi.org/10.1515/9783110783933-013

Patagonia was a leader in what Mackey and Sisodia (2014) call conscious capitalism. Shortly after its creation, the organization started to show its commitment to socio-environmental causes. One year after its founding, Patagonia supported its first environmental cause, a protest against development plans in the Ventura River region. In the following years, the brand started launching its own environmental campaigns and increased the economic resources given to sustainable initiatives. Thirteen years after the creation of the brand, Patagonia started donating a portion of its sales to environmental groups. While this may seem counterproductive in terms of profit maximization, campaigns like these can generate goodwill and increase sales, potentially resulting in a larger net profit. For example, in 2016 the brand vowed to donate all Black Friday sales to environmental groups in an effort to combat consumerism. Prior to the announcement, Patagonia forecasted a total of $2 million in sales but generated $10 million, showing that the initiative attracted more consumers than expected (Addady, 2016). Overall, building brand image as a socially responsible, sustainability-driven brand has positively impacted Patagonia's brand loyalty (especially among Millennials) and sales growth, with a fourfold growth in revenue over the past ten years (Fox, 2019).

Moreover, Patagonia strives to create a high-quality, healthy workspace for its employees. Good working conditions have the potential to positively affect employee performance, which can result in major economic benefits for companies. Between 1996 and 2011, more than half of the companies identified as conscious outperformed the S&P 500 index (Schwartz, 2013). Schwartz (2013) attributes this to healthier relationships with suppliers and communities, motivated employees with higher productivity levels, and stronger brand loyalty from consumers.

Regardless of it being genuine care for the triple bottom line or a result from greenwashing, consumers have certainly responded favorably to the brand's sustainable practices. In recent years, Patagonia has experienced increased demand for its products, some of it attributable to its reputation as a sustainable company. Consequently, the aim of this analysis is to determine whether the increased demand due to the brand's "sustainable" status and its circular practices damage or strengthen its progress towards its sustainability goals.

Patagonia's founder, Yvon Chouinard, recognized that while Patagonia can take important steps toward sustainable business performance, consumers must also reduce their consumption. Although consumers have begun to rent, repair, and recycle, it is not clear whether they are willing to consume less. In addition, the investor-owned business model—in which profits for stakeholders is paramount—is not compatible with long-term sustainability. Due to the inherent trade-off between profits and social and environmental engagement, a different business model was considered more appropriate to support sustainability goals. As a result, Patagonia adopted a philanthro-capitalism philosophy in 2022. Yvon Chouinard dedicated the family-owned company to the fight against climate change, such that, moving forward, 100 million dollars of the company's yearly profits are directed towards this cause. The funds are managed by the Holdfast Collective that is dedicated to climate action. Because it is classified as a social welfare organization, it can directly lobby on US climate policy (Auld & Grabs, 2022). In this business model, there is a split between the voting stock held by the Patagonia Purpose Trust and non-voting stock held by the Holdfast Collective (Auld & Grabs, 2022). The Purpose Trust was designated for business purposes in order to ensure that the needs of consumers, the community, and employees are met (Erskine, 2022).

Philanthro-capitalism is associated with a variety of challenges because it relies on a market-based approach to philanthropy and includes a goal of profit maximization (Berkeley Economic Review, 2019). One prominent feature of this form of capitalism is that philanthropy is integrated into the business model. Because of this the charity becomes the site for selling goods and services, eventually leading to capital accumulation (Burns, 2019). Consumers are made to believe that their consumption will benefit others, by saving lives for instance. Their socio-political influence increases, leading to what Buffett (2013) named the charitable-industrial complex. This ensures consistent support of causes and increases the level of organizational accountability to the supported causes. But it also makes money; Tom's shoes, for example, was valued at $625 million in 2014 before the proliferation of copy-cat brands led to its take-over by creditors in 2019 (Kim, 2020). Philanthro-capitalism can be criticized on several grounds. First, it seeks to address social and environmental concerns that business activities helped create in the first place. Second, it may not be appropriate for a company to solve social and environmental issues that require fundamental and large-scale social and institutional change. Third, foundations operating for profits (such as the Chan-Zuckerberg Initiative) are associated with limited transparency and entail tax benefits—which may engender attributions of self-serving (rather than altruistic or strategic) motives for the support of social and environmental causes.

How Patagonia Portrays Itself: A Look at Patagonia's Website

The first step in this analysis is identifying how the company communicates its sustainable endeavors. One key towards making its commitment to sustainability known to the public is through the brand's website. This is especially crucial in an environment in which e-commerce is rapidly gaining traction among consumers. An overview of Patagonia's sustainable initiatives is available on its homepage, and therefore easily accessible to consumers. At the bottom of this page there are four hyperlinks related to sustainability, along with short descriptions of each initiative (*Patagonia Homepage*, n. d.). These four hyperlinks provide more information on Patagonia's Ironclad Guarantee, Footprint, the Worn Wear program, and the 1% for the Planet initiative.

Patagonia's Ironclad Guarantee promises repair, replacements or refunds for customers who are unhappy with the product's performance, as well as inexpensive repairs for damaged (wear and tear) goods (*Ironclad Guarantee*, n.d.). This guarantee is designed to extend the product's life and avoid unnecessary disposal. If no returns were allowed and no solutions were offered for wear and tear, customers would likely dispose of the items.

The Footprint section provides details regarding Patagonia's environmental and social impact. It describes Materials and Environmental Programs, Social Responsibility Programs, Why Regenerative Organic, and Where We Do Business (*Environmental & Social Footprint*, n.d.). There is a section dedicated to sharing Patagonia's recent progress towards its sustainability goals, providing multiple concise, measurable results in regard to various aspects of sustainability. Some of these sections will be revisited in this chapter. One unique feature of Patagonia's website is the inclusion of 102 articles on supply chain and sustainability issues affecting the company (*Environmental & Social Footprint*, n.d.). The aim of these articles is to educate consumers not only on environmental and social impacts of the clothing industry but also to raise awareness of the steps Patagonia has taken to combat these problems.

The Worn Wear program is a truly innovative solution to the waste created by harmful disposal. It provides an alternative to consumers who want to get rid of their old Patagonia items without sending them to the landfill. As opposed to other safe forms of disposal, the Worn Wear program offers store credit in exchange for used clothing in good condition (*Worn Wear*, n.d.). Therefore, in addition to the satisfaction created by helping save the planet, the program provides a monetary incentive to consumers. After receiving and inspecting returned items, Patagonia cleans and prepares them for resale (*Worn Wear*, n.d.). Worn Wear customers then get the chance to purchase these goods for less than the original price, effectively extending the products' life and promoting circularity. Like conventional Patagonia products, all items sold through this program are covered by the Ironclad Guarantee. Apart from second hand goods and unsold warehouse items (e.g., clothing with minor defects), the Worn Wear site also offers a Recrafted collection, made from recycled scraps from no longer usable clothing that is sent back to Patagonia (*Worn Wear*, n.d.). Since the sources for the scraps vary a lot, the resulting pieces are unique, meaning that no two pieces from this collection are identical.

The 1% for the Planet initiative consists of Patagonia pledging 1% of its sale revenues to repair ecological damage and preserve the environment (*Model – 1% for the Planet*, n.d.). Since 1985, Patagonia has donated over 140 million USD to environmental groups (*1% for the Planet*, n.d.). Given the success of the pledge, Patagonia founded a non-profit organization that clusters businesses that have joined the pledge. Moreover, the non-profit organization has recently allowed individuals to join the program and donate 1% of their annual salary (*Model – 1% for the Planet*, n.d.). By joining the program, members establish relationships with the charitable organizations and other donors, which results in valuable networking and a boost to their reputation, as all donations are certified.

Transparency is becoming increasingly important for fashion brands, as a large portion of their socio-environmental impact affects external stakeholders. In an attempt to become more transparent, some brands engage in increasing disclosure of information about their entire supply chains. Consistent with this practice, Patagonia's "Where Do We Do Business" section includes information on the impacts of Patagonia owned and operated stores, as well as those external to the organization (*Where We Do Business*, n.d.). Moreover, it features a detailed map including farms, mills, and facilities across the globe with detailed location information, as well as details on their supplier screening process (*Factories, Farms and Mills*, n.d.). Furthermore, consumers can discover where products were manufactured by looking at the product description, which improves product traceability and brand transparency (*Patagonia Men's Diamond Quilted Bomber Hoody*, n.d.).

Patagonia also provides educational resources for consumers to guide their shopping practices, thus promoting responsible sustainable consumer behaviour. First, Patagonia's website presents a guide for responsible, sustainable consumer behaviour, which consists of ten tips to make informed purchase decisions and contribute to the circular economy. From helping consumers spot greenwashing to encouraging consumers to demand action against unsustainable practices, the guide provides the consumer with the steps on how to become a responsible, sustainable consumer (*A Guide to More Responsible Shopping*, n.d.). Instead of presenting the brand as a solution to sustainability issues, the content's only aim seems to be to raise awareness of environmental and social issues and to inform consumers how to deal with them. Additionally, Patagonia published a glossary of terms relevant to responsible, sustainable consumer behavior, aimed at further educating the consumer on informed purchase decisions (*Shop Informed*, n.d.). Once again, most of the points are not directly tied to Patagonia, touch on a variety of topics, such as animal welfare and circular economy, and apply to any shopping experience. However, there are a few references to their own sustainable initiatives (e.g., the Worn Wear program) and concepts that indirectly relate to the brand due to their sustainable commitments (e.g., Fair Trade Certified labels). Although this section is also highly informative, the content implies that Patagonia contributes to the solution of some of these issues.

The "Don't Buy this Jacket" Campaign

In 2011, Patagonia bought ad space in the New York Times right before Black Friday to make a statement on the waves of consumerism occurring on that specific date (Thangavelu, 2020). The purpose of this ad was to make people question their purchasing decisions and to incite a conversation on consumerism, especially on the effects of these practices. Moreover, this campaign was aimed at differentiating Patagonia from its competitors. While businesses benefit from higher sales volume and creating more revenues, Patagonia sought to position itself as a brand that does not aspire to higher sales volume. Rather, it seeks to sell products that last longer and minimize environmental and social damage. Furthermore, as Patagonia embraces the circular economy, it attempts to positively influence post-consumption behaviour and disposal, which differentiates it from many other companies in the fashion industry.

Materials and Environmental Responsibility Programs

In 2019, Patagonia reported that virgin petroleum-based products represented the largest percentage of materials used by volume, making up 48% of total materials (*Annual Benefit Corporation Report*, 2020). Recycled materials also constituted a large portion, standing at 31% of the total materials (*Annual Benefit Corporation Report*, 2020). Lastly, cotton and other plant-based materials and wool and other animal products made up the remaining 16% and 5%, respectively (*Annual Benefit Corporation Report*, 2020). Table 13.1 describes the socio-environmental impact of most of the materials used by Patagonia.

Table 13.1: Patagonia's materials and their impact (Patagonia.com, n.d.).

Material	Impact
Regenerative Organic Certified Pilot Cotton	Organic practices restore the soil's natural health, improve the living conditions of farmers, and uphold animal welfare (*Regenerative Organic Certification Pilot Cotton*, n.d.).
NetPlus® Recycled Fishing Nets	Recycling fish nets reduces the amount of plastic in the ocean, which gravely affects sea life. Moreover, the program provides an additional income to surrounding communities. It also cuts down the amount of virgin plastic needed for production (*NetPlus® Recycled Fishing Nets*, n.d.).
PrimaLoft® P.U.R.E (Produced Using Reduced Emissions)	This technology eliminates the need for heat used to melt fibers to manufacture insulation by altering the chemical structure of polyester. Thus, it decreases carbon emissions and energy use (*Patagonia® PrimaLoft® P.U.R.E.*, n.d.).
Recycled Spandex	Reduces the need for virgin spandex, which uses petroleum (a highly pollutant resource and big contributor to global warming) (*Recycled Spandex*, n.d.). Recycling results in waste reduction and improves circularity.
Organic Cotton	As opposed to conventional cotton, it avoids the use of chemicals. In turn, this practice promotes healthy natural environments and strengthens biodiversity. There is a 45% decrease in carbon dioxide emissions and a 90% reduction in water use (when compared to conventional growing practices) (*Organic Cotton Fabric*, n.d.).

Table 13.1 (continued)

Material	Impact
Recycled Cotton	Recycling scraps reduces waste, extends the life cycle of the fibers, and promotes circularity. It avoids the harmful effects of conventional cotton growing and diminishes the number of resources needed to manufacture cotton. There is an 80% decrease in carbon dioxide emissions (when compared to conventional growing practices) (*Recycled Cotton Fabric*, n.d.).
Cotton in Conversion	Buys organic cotton from farms that are yet to be certified but on track to do so (*Cotton in Conversion*, n.d.). Consequently, it encourages farmers to convert from conventional to organic cotton.
Polyester	Virgin polyester uses petroleum, which is highly pollutant. Though the volume used at Patagonia is not as high as recycled polyester, some smaller quantities are still used (*Polyester Fabric*, n.d.).
Recycled Polyester	84% of polyester based fabrics used at Patagonia was recycled (*Recycled Polyester*, n.d.). Recycling reduces the need for virgin petroleum-based fibers, such as virgin polyester, as well as the amount of waste produced and carbon emissions.
Nylon	Like virgin polyester, it uses petroleum and causes the same harmful effects as the former fiber. The volume of virgin nylon used this season is 2% and it is quickly being replaced by recycled alternatives (*Nylon Fabric*, n.d.).
Recycled Nylon	Reduces need for virgin petroleum-based materials and the effects arising from their manufacture/extraction. Recycling post-consumer waste (e.g., plastic bottles) and pre-consumer nylon (e.g., factory scraps) also reduces waste and promotes circular practices. Recycled nylon represents 90% of the nylon used by Patagonia (*Recycled Nylon Fabric*, n.d.).
Recycled Down	Recycling feathers from bedding, cushions, and other goods which are no longer resaleable reduces the amount of waste going to the landfill and extends the life span of the material. Moreover, there was a 31% decrease per kg. of material in carbon dioxide emissions from using recycled down as insulation (*Recycled Down*, n.d.).
Wool	Virgin wool is grown following rigorous animal welfare and land management standards. Even though Patagonia's programs massively reduce the harms, there is still some environmental impact derived from wool production as some small amount of chemicals are allowed if necessary (*Wool Fabric*, n.d.).

Table 13.1 (continued)

Material	Impact
Recycled Wool	Recycled wool represents 12% of wool materials used. Recycling extends the life of the wool fibers and reduces waste. It avoids the environmental effects of producing virgin wool (e.g., damage to the land, water usage, chemicals to treat the fiber). There was a decrease of 83% in carbon dioxide emissions as a result of using recycled instead of virgin wool (*Recycled Wool Fabric*, n.d.).
Nonfluorinated DWR (Durable Water Repellent)	A DWR is a chemical coating used to waterproof fabrics. This type of fabric does not contain fluorine, a toxic chemical which persists in the environment after bonding with carbon. The issue with this innovative solution is that the fluorine-free coating is not as durable as the conventional one, so certain items still require fluorinated DWRs (e.g., a long-wear raincoat) (*Nonfluorinated DWR Finish*, n.d.).
Recycled Cashmere	Used to combat the decrease in quality and overgrazing of cashmere goats in Mongolia produced by the higher demand for the material. Patagonia uses cashmere scraps and blends them with 5% virgin wool to create a durable fiber (*Recycled Cashmere Fabric*, n.d.).
Yulex® Natural Rubber	Functions as a replacement for neoprene and limestone, thus reducing the harmful effects of producing these elements. This natural rubber is extracted for hevea trees, which absorb carbon. As a result, there is an 80% decrease in carbon dioxide emissions caused per wetsuits (when compared to standard neoprene ones) (*Yulex® Natural Rubber*, n.d.).
Advanced Denim	Uses sulfur dyes that bond to the fabric more easily, reducing water usage, energy consumption, and carbon dioxide emissions (*Advanced Denim*, n.d.).
Spandex	Since it is petroleum based, its manufacture has similar effects to other materials like virgin polyester. The quantities used are minimal, so Patagonia prioritizes conversion to non-petroleum materials of other more widely used materials, such as nylon and polyester (*Spandex*, n.d.).
REFIBRA® Lyocell	Combines sustainably sourced wood pulp and recycled cotton scraps. Reduces waste and extends the life span of the cotton. Given its closed-loop production, nearly all of the solvent used is recovered and reused and the water is recycled (*REFIBRA® Lyocell*, n.d.).
TENCEL® Lyocell	Like REFIBRA® lyocell, though it is not blended with recycled cotton. It also uses a closed-loop production, so most of the solvents are recovered and the water is recycled (*TENCEL® Lyocell Fabric*, n.d.).

Table 13.1 (continued)

Material	Impact
Hemp	Uses very little water and no synthetic fertilizers. Contributes to good soil health. Patagonia's suppliers minimize waste by using a holistic approach (i.e., using every part of the plant to avoid waste and create solutions to other pollutants such as plastics) (*Hemp Fabric*, n.d.).
Polyurethane	It consumes less resources for production in comparison to PVC and causes less harm to the environment and human health (*Polyurethane*, n.d.). The goal is to use only recycled yarns and bio-based fibres in the future, to minimize carbon dioxide emissions.
PTFE (Polytetrafluoroethylene)	It needs vast amounts of energy and chemicals to be produced. Therefore, Patagonia chooses to employ this material only in combination with recycled fibers and only when it is absolutely needed for higher performance (*PTFE (Polytetrafluoroethylene)*, n.d.).
Fluorinated DWR	Fluorine is not biodegradable, so this material has a high environmental cost. Even though Patagonia is moving towards fluorine-free alternatives, fluorinated DWRs are still needed for some higher performance pieces (*Fluorinated DWR (Durable Water Repellent) Finish*, n.d.).
UPF (Ultraviolet Protection Factor) Design	Protects the consumer from the damaging effects of ultraviolet radiation. There are two methods: by using special yarns and construction, or by adding titanium dioxide (reef-safe, similar to the active ingredient in sunscreen) to the materials (*UPF Fabric for Sun Protection*, n.d.).

Patagonia established multiple programs aimed at diminishing the environmental impact caused by the fashion industry and at preserving the environment. Table 13.2 summarizes these programs, which support Patagonia's main environmental goals for the next five to ten years (*Environmental Responsibility Programs*, n.d.). These goals consist of

1. 100% carbon neutrality by 2025.
2. All products made from "recycled, reclaimed, or renewable" materials by 2025.
3. All packaging being "100% reusable, home compostable, renewable, or easily recyclable" by 2025.
4. All hemp and cotton being 100% regenerative organic certified by 2030.

The Patagonia website suggests that some progress has been made towards fulfilling these goals. For example, in 2022, 64% of the textiles used were made from recycled resources (*Environmental Responsibility*, n.d.), 100% of virgin cotton is grown using organic processes, and 100% of virgin down is Advanced Global Traceable Down Standard certified (*Environmental Responsibility*, n.d.).

There are some challenges, however. Patagonia claims that the number of recycled items has decreased for two reasons (*Annual Benefit Corporation Report*, 2020). First, Patagonia was able to put items back on the market, thus extending the life span of the items without using additional resources to bring them back to good condition. Second, many items were no longer usable and impossible to recycle, which negatively impacted resale opportunities. To avoid waste generation, Patagonia stored these items until a viable recycling stream emerged (*Annual Benefit Corporation Report*, 2020).

Moreover, increasing sales augmented Patagonia's ecological footprint (*Annual Benefit Corporation Report*, 2020). This reveals the trade-off facing brands committed to sustainability and circularity. Profit growth is often achieved by increasing sales, yet growth frequently entails environmental damage. According to supporters of conscious capitalism, sales growth and sustainable development are nonetheless not mutually exclusive.

Social Responsibility Programs

In addition to environmental issues, corporate social responsibility also encompasses social concerns. Because of the lower costs of garment manufacturing in some regions of the world, many apparel brands, like Patagonia, choose to outsource their manufacturing. However, the downside to this practice consists of extremely low wages paid to apparel workers. According to the Clean Clothes Campaign, these workers are paid, on average, two to five times less than the living wage (*Poverty Wages*, 2019). As a result, workers struggle to provide enough food, shelter, education, and healthcare for their families, and are not able to accumulate any kind of savings (*Poverty Wages*, 2019). Earnings below the living wage therefore seriously affect the well-being of workers and their families.

Patagonia claims to be committed to providing a living wage to workers across the entire supply chain. Since many supply chain partners are external to Patagonia, it uses industry tools and standards to measure supply chain members' compliance. In doing so, Patagonia aims at minimizing social inequities and stimulating net positive benefits for workers and surrounding communities. As a result, Patagonia participates in multiple programs aimed at promoting social responsibility. Table 13.2 summarizes these programs.

Currently available information does not suggest that increased consumption of Patagonia's products is associated with social drawbacks. This is likely because social concerns are generally considered in the context of production. However, a significant increase in demand could change production operations, requiring the company to expand its supply chain in order to meet demand. If this necessitates the inclusion

Table 13.2: Patagonia's environmental and social programs (Patagonia.com, n.d.).

Program	Summary
Fair Trade	Program that helps workers in developing countries improve their working and living conditions while encouraging good environmental practices. By paying a premium to acquire Fair Trade certified products, Patagonia has impacted more than 72,000 workers (*Fair Trade Certified*^{TM}, n.d.).
$H_2No^®$ Performance Standard	Is the standard Patagonia upheld for three key categories: breathability, durability, and waterproofness. The aim is for all H_2No materials to avoid petroleum-based inputs and rely on recycled inputs. Moreover, the objective is to extend the life span of the fabrics (and of the finished goods) (*$H_2No^®$ Performance Standard*, n.d.).
Supply Chain Environmental Responsibility Program	Program that ensures that all Patagonia suppliers across the globe are complying certain environmental standards. These span over many areas, such as: "environmental management systems, chemicals, water use, water emissions, energy use, greenhouse gases, other air emissions and waste" (*Supply Chain Environmental Responsibility Program*, n.d.).
Global Traceable Down Standard	Certification guaranteeing that all virgin down follows high animal welfare standards (e.g., avoid live plucking and force feeding). It also allows full traceability from the farm where it is extracted to the final manufacturing facility (*Advanced Traceable Down Standard*, n.d.).
Responsible Wool Standard (RWS)	Certification guaranteeing that all virgin wool follows high animal welfare and land management standards. Since all suppliers are RWS certified, the virgin wool is not blended with any non-RWS fibers (*Responsible Wool Standard*, n.d.).
Forest Stewardship Council	NGO dedicated to the protection of forests. Patagonia sources FSC-certified materials (e.g., natural rubber, paper) (*Forest Stewardship Council*, n.d.). By doing so, materials are obtained in an environmental and socially responsible manner, without creating harm for the forests or the communities surrounding them.
Regenerative Organic Certified Pilot Programs	Program aimed at producing food and fibers following "the highest organic standards" (*Regenerative Organic Certification*, n.d.). These practices target an improvement in farmers' lives, promotion of animal welfare, soil restoration, and greenhouse gas reductions.
Living Wage	Program that encourages all Patagonia partners, especially apparel assembly ones, to pay wages according to the Fair Labour Association's standards and the Anker methodology (*Living Wage*, n.d.).

Table 13.2 (continued)

Program	Summary
Material Traceability	Program aimed at making all materials traceable, from raw material extraction to the finished good (*Material Traceability*, n.d.). This certifies that the materials being used in manufacture are truly sustainable and that no chain-of-custody problems occurred in-between.
Bluesign®	External organization evaluating every step of Patagonia's supply chain to decrease the resources being used and help manage chemical processes along the chain (e.g., dyeing) (*bluesign®*, n.d.). It promotes healthy environmental and social standards.
Fair Labour Association® (FLA)	Patagonia is one of the founders of the FLA. This non-profit organization pursues the highest levels of accountability from businesses regarding "responsible labour practices." The FLA randomly audits its members to analyze how their supply chains measure up against their standards and to identify areas of weaknesses and/or improvement (*Fair Labor Association®*, n.d.).
Migrant Workers	Program that supports the high-quality employment of migrant workers (i.e., upholding responsible recruitment and avoiding exploitation) without asking for any payments from the employees. This is relevant in a context where migrant workers have to pay brokers to obtain a job in a foreign country like Taiwan, where some of Patagonia's suppliers operate (*Migrant Workers*, n.d.).

of less socially responsible suppliers offering lower wages or worse work conditions, supply chain expansion may give rise to a trade-off between incorporating new suppliers who do not meet social responsibility standards and risking product shortages in order to meet sustainability goals.

Patagonia's Circularity Model

Although Patagonia pursues sustainable practices, does it apply circular economy principles? According to the Ellen MacArthur Foundation (2020), the circular economy is based on "the principles of designing out waste and pollution, keeping products and materials in use, and regenerating natural systems." For fashion brands, this model implies three stages (*Vision of a Circular Economy for Fashion*, 2020): first, the designers conceive products with ethically sourced materials; then, companies transport these products via eco-friendly (i.e., low to no pollution) modes. Apart from selling to end consumers, these products could also be leased; finally, if the product reaches the end of its life cycle, it should be disposed in a way that does not damage the environment. If possible, the product should be recycled to create a new product, thus "closing the circle." Given its contribution to every stage of the product life cycle, this model can be a good predictor of the level of involvement in sustainable practices.

First, it becomes apparent that Patagonia is very concerned with creating products from ethically sourced materials. While its materials are not entirely impact-free, it reflects progress with regard to material sourcing. Patagonia has multiple programs aimed at reducing virgin animal and petroleum-based materials and promoting the use of recycled materials. Moreover, these recycled materials are not necessarily sourced from clothing, as they are derived from plastic bottles or fishing nets, which suggests that the brand also tackles sustainability issues external to its own operations. Additionally, Patagonia holds suppliers to certain sustainability standards to ensure that their impact is diminished. Furthermore, the Worn Wear program functions as a sourcing tool for recyclable textiles (if items are not fit to be resold).

This leads to another step in the circular model that Patagonia addresses—the reduction of waste. Worn Wear extends the life span of clothing items which consumers might have disposed of incorrectly (i.e., to a landfill). Patagonia deconstructs items that are not in good condition, and uses these textiles to create new pieces of clothing. Items that are in good condition, on the other hand, are cleaned and resold by Patagonia, thus extending the life span of items, before they are disposed of, ideally in a sustainable manner (e.g., through recycling).

The application of the circularity model in Patagonia's operations is also reflected in its commitment to reducing pollution created by transportation methods and its retail stores. Although it is far from being carbon neutral, Patagonia has made big steps towards lowering carbon emissions. Currently, 76% of its stores use renewable energy (*Owned and Operated Facilities*, n.d.). Patagonia has also made sustainable investments in the communities surrounding its buildings to promote the use of renewable energy, especially on a residential level (*Owned and Operated Facilities*, n.d.). Another big portion of the organization's greenhouse gas emissions stem from transportation along the supply chain, representing approximately 8% of total emissions (*Owned and Operated Facilities*, n.d.). Most emissions result from the increased use of air transportation methods that, although fast and convenient, are highly pollutant to the environment. To address this issue, Patagonia is shifting inbound operations from traditional air freight to drop-shipping, and discouraging express shipping (i.e., two-day shipping) to consumers to avoid an increased number of flights (*Owned and Operated Facilities*, n.d.). Furthermore, the organization generates very little water waste, most of which originates in its bathrooms. To counteract this, one of Patagonia's Californian facilities uses a system based on condensation from AC units to water plants, and another one that filters out rainwater and sends it back to the ocean (*Owned and Operated Facilities*, n.d.). Lastly, Patagonia also has programs to reduce waste at its facilities (e.g., factories, distribution centers, stores). These include the gradual reduction of single-use plastics, training of employees on waste reduction practices, digitalization of some business processes, and promotion of recycling and composting through clear signage and education (*Owned and Operated Facilities*, n.d.). Some of these programs have positive implications for the surrounding community, as Patagonia employees might take their learnings, apply them to their personal lives, and pass on this knowledge to other community members.

Overall, these practices reflect a strong commitment to the application of the circularity model to Patagonia's operations. Patagonia has established circularity programs for almost every step of the supply chain, from the extraction of the raw materials to the disposal of the final product. While it is far from being "perfectly circular" due to it not being entirely pollution-free, it is increasingly becoming more circular. The main obstacles toward full circularity consist of the pollution generated by raw material extraction and the emissions caused by transportation and facilities. Although Patagonia increased its use of recycled materials, several virgin and highly pollutant materials, such as fluorinated DWR, seem to be difficult to phase out due to a lack of sustainable alternatives. Moreover, even though Patagonia's standards are helpful in improving traceability and encourage fair practices in the supply chain, some suppliers are not entirely compliant and negatively affect animals and the environment. For example, PETA discovered that some of Patagonia's wool suppliers were not upholding the Responsible Wool Standard (RWS) because they did not follow guidelines for proper shearing of sheep and mistreated wounds caused by poor extraction techniques (*PETA Calls Out Patagonia for Secrecy Around New Wool Source*, 2018). Third parties observed and reported several other RWS violations at Patagonia suppliers' facilities, which led Patagonia to distance itself from the suppliers, although RWS violations reoccurred (Schillmann, 2020). This suggests a weakness in the brand's assessment of suppliers, especially in the wool sector, and raises the question of how closely Patagonia should monitor supply chain partners to preclude similar transgressions.

Similarly, emissions resulting from transportation might be harder to tackle than that originating from facilities. Patagonia converted its US facilities to 100% renewable energy sources, proving that it is possible to do it outside the country too (*Owned and Operated Facilities*, n.d.). However, the choice between air freight and less polluting transportation modes implies trade-offs for the company. While Patagonia can restructure parts of its processes to accommodate longer shipping times from the suppliers to distribution centers, consumers tends to prefer shorter shipping times and are unlikely to adjust to longer shipping times. Many factors contribute to this behaviour, such as items' trendiness or consumers' immediate need for items. Whereas some consumers might adapt to not receiving their items within a few business days, others may decide that the benefits of receiving their order quickly outweigh the costs of air shipping, or may consider switching to an alternative brand selling similar products and offering faster shipping.

The Social Impact of the Circular Model

While the relationship between the circular economy (CE) and its social effects might not be as clear as the nexus between the CE and its environmental outcomes, some positive social consequences arise. Some of these effects are directly related to programs and people inside the organization, and relate to improvements in employment, workers' health and safety, and participation in business decision making (Padilla-Rivera et al., 2020). Meanwhile, other social effects are more indirect and have a wider impact on the community, such as the eradication of poverty, gender equity, and food security (Padilla-Rivera et al., 2020). For example, the Living Wage program targets the employees' health and safety while ensuring that their families' basic needs are met (i.e., above the poverty line with full food security). In line with this, the partnership with Fair Trade encourages participation from small business owners while supporting local economies and communities surrounding them. Such effects manifest in the form of increased investment in quality education and job creation, among others.

The challenge in assessing the social impact of the CE relates to its measurement and in establishing how much of it is attributable to a specific circular initiative. Some aspects of measuring the environmental effect of a circular initiative are relatively easily quantifiable and directly correlated with a program, such as the number of recycled plastic bottles used to craft a certain amount of a new fabric. However, the number of lives affected by the recycling program and the level of impact might not be as clear, since other external factors and stakeholders are involved. Therefore, although existing frameworks can help organizations like Patagonia quantify part of their social impact, the qualitative effects of the CE are harder to measure and thus harder to attribute to a specific initiative (Padilla-Rivera et al., 2020).

External Evaluations of Patagonia's Sustainability Performance

Since the Sustainability Paradox arises from increased production brought about by growing consumption of sustainable brands, an understanding of external stakeholders' assessment of Patagonia's sustainability is critical. Consumer perceptions of a brand's sustainability impact its reputation, and subsequently affect consumer demand and brand loyalty. Consumers' perceptions of a brand's sustainability is frequently influenced by indexes and certifications that gauge an organization's sustainability performance and are often well-recognized by consumers. Several indices compare Patagonia's sustainability performance to its competitors' and serve as indicators of consumers' perception of the brand's sustainable actions.

Benefit Corporation Certification

A clear indication of Patagonia's inclination toward conscious capitalism is its status as a benefit corporation. This kind of corporation "legally protects an entrepreneur's social goals by mandating considerations other than just profit" (Bend & King, 2014). Patagonia was the first organization in California to obtain this status in December 2011 through B Lab, the non-profit organization that created and confers the B Corp certification, which is a type of benefit corporation (*About B Lab*, n.d.). Given the recognition of this certification, obtaining it can build legitimacy regarding a company's sustainable practices. According to Stammer (2016), this type of certification can mitigate consumers' skepticism regarding organizational intentions, as publicizing sustainable commitments through social media can be perceived as disingenuous if not accompanied with relevant actions. As a third-party certification, the B Corp certification fosters consumer trust, which in turn can affect the sales, profitability, and overall value of the organization. To become B Corp certified, an organization must achieve a score of 80 in the B Impact Assessment, which measures performance in terms of governance, workers, community, environment, and customers (*Patagonia Works*, n.d.). Table 13.3 displays Patagonia's scores following its certification.

Table 13.3: Patagonia's B impact assessment scores (Annual Benefit Corporation Report, 2020).

Dimension	2012	2014	2016	2019
Governance	14.7	17.1	17.3	16.9
Workers	25.0	24.0	24.9	20.8
Community	19.9	30.9	58.7	63.8
Environment	47.5	34.7	44.8	43.5
Customers	–	7.1	5.8	6.3
Overall	107.3	113.9	151.5	151.4

Patagonia's environmental and social performance has grown steadily from 2012 until 2016. This increase reflects a commitment to continuous improvement of sustainable practices. Thereafter, the brand's score has stagnated, which may reflect the fact that progress becomes progressively harder. Patagonia's scores are more easily evaluated in the context of other organizations. Patagonia's 2019 score almost doubles the one required to obtain certification, and nearly triples the median score obtained by other organizations. This indicates superior sustainability performance compared to other organizations.

In examining Patagonia's scores by dimension, it becomes apparent that the community dimension drives the growth in overall score. The community score has grown consistently over time, whereas scores on other dimensions have fluctuated throughout the years. When comparing the first to the latest assessment, the only other category showing an improvement is governance, although the 2019 score is still the second lowest Patagonia obtained. The customer dimension was not measured in 2012, and its introduction likely explains the rise in scores from 2012 to 2014, despite a major decrease on the environment dimension. The workers' category seems to show the greatest decline, from 25 points in 2012 to 20.8 in 2019. It must be noted that these fluctuations are not necessarily a reflection of a change in the company's performance, as the assessment standards are updated every three years to adapt to the ever-changing business landscape and the rise of new environmental and social issues (B The Change, 2019). As a result, assessment standard changes affect scores (either positively or negatively) even if there is no change in an organization's performance.

There are no detailed indications as to the median or average scores for each dimension. B Lab nonetheless publishes a list of top scoring companies for each dimension. In 2021, B Lab declared Patagonia as "Best for the World" in both the community and environment impact areas for scoring in the ninety-fifth percentile on these dimensions among similarly sized organizations (> 250 employees) (*Best For The World 2021: Community List*, 2022; *Best For The World: Environmental List 2021*, 2022). Patagonia is thus a leader in community and environment-related actions, at least among the 100,000 companies that B Lab assessed. Since Patagonia is not featured in the other Best for the World lists, its performance in terms of the governance, workers, and customers dimensions it not as strong relative to other companies being assessed. Nonetheless, the lack of comparative statistics precludes any conclusions related to these impact areas.

Fashion Transparency Index

The Fashion Transparency Index was developed by the Fashion Revolution activism movement to analyze the public disclosure of human rights and environmental policies of 250 fashion brands and retailers in terms of five dimensions (Ditty et al., 2021):
– Policy and commitments: this dimension captures environmental and social policies for workers throughout the supply chain, and their application and goals attached to these policies. The weight of this dimension in the total score is 13.2% (Ditty et al., 2021).
– Governance: this dimension reflects social and environmental performance responsibilities are distributed among executive board members, as well as the connections between these responsibilities and employee, CEO, and supplier performance. The weight of this dimension in the total score is 5.2% (Ditty et al., 2021).
– Traceability: this dimension relates to the level of details published about three stages of the supply chain: raw materials, facilities and mills, and manufacturers. The weight of this dimension in the total score is 29.6% (Ditty et al., 2021).

–   Know, show, and fix: this dimension examines disclosure and results of due dili-
    gence processes and audits for members of the supply chain. It considers conflict
    resolution when issues arise, as well as processes workers must follow to file a
    complaint and how those are addressed. The weight of this dimension in the total
    score is 18.8% (Ditty et al., 2021).
–   Spotlight Issues: this dimension captures disclosure regarding urgent issues, such
    as living wages, racial and gender equality, and sustainable practices. The weight
    of this dimension in the total score is 33.2% (Ditty et al., 2021).

One of the main advantages of using this index to assess Patagonia's performance is
that it comprises a relatively large number of companies of similar size, and provides
a detailed breakdown of each brand's performance, whereas such details are lacking
from the B Impact Assessment. It is nonetheless important to acknowledge that—compared to the B Impact Assessment—the Fashion Transparency Index focuses on public
disclosure instead of measuring policy impact. Moreover, the veracity of the brands'
claims and publicly disclosed information is not verified (Ditty et al., 2021). Finally,
although the Fashion Transparency Index scores comprise aspects beyond an organization's sustainability performance, Patagonia's scores on sustainability related dimensions allows for an evaluation of its level of public disclosure in comparison to
other organizations. Table 13.4 displays Patagonia's 2021 scores and rank for each dimension, as well as average and maximum scores across all fashion brands and
retailers.

Table 13.4: Patagonia's Fashion Transparency Index scores (Ditty et al., 2021).

Dimension	Patagonia's Score	Average	Maximum	Rank
Policy and commitments	78%	53%	94%	60th
Governance	54%	31%	85%	54th
Traceability	68%	19%	97%	17th
Know, show, and fix	47%	19%	55%	19th
Spotlight issues	41%	15%	72%	26th
Overall	56%	23%	78%	16th

In 2021, Patagonia was ranked 16th with a score of 56%. The highest score obtained
was 78% and the mean score was 23%. It is important to note that the overall score is
not an average of the scores on each dimension, due to heterogeneous weights. As a
result, Patagonia ranked 16th due to high performances on the two dimensions with
the largest weights (i.e., traceability and spotlight issues), although it failed to rank
above 17th on any one dimension. This suggests that Patagonia is perceived as a brand
with high levels of disclosure overall.

Good on You

Good on You is an Australian "social impact business" that rates fashion brands' sustainable practices (*About Good on You,* n.d.). The rating measures the brands' performance on three dimensions—planet, people, and animals. An advantage of this rating system is the disaggregation of environmental and social aspects of sustainability performance. Its disadvantage lies in the fact that it is based on information obtained in 2020, and does not reflect organizational performance following the Covid-19 pandemic.

In 2020, Good on You awarded Patagonia a "good" rating (4/5 stars) (*Patagonia— Sustainability Rating,* 2020). Patagonia scored highest on the planet dimension, with a 4/5 rating, due to the brand's use of environmentally friendly materials, as well as its commitment to greenhouse gas reduction across the entire supply chain (Wolfe, 2020). The score reflects the lack of programs to prevent deforestation (Wolfe, 2020) in light of Patagonia's use of cellulose and natural rubber-based materials. Patagonia's use of Forest Stewardship Council certified paper and raw materials does not directly address deforestation concerns, but is a step in the right direction.

Patagonia received a 3/5 rating on the people dimension. Despite a relatively high level of disclosure, especially regarding the final stages of production (Wolfe, 2020), there is little information available on initial supply chain stages, which also resulted in Patagonia's Fashion Transparency rating of 51–60% (Wolfe, 2020). Moreover, even though Patagonia is committed to providing a living wage to all workers (including those of external supply chain partners), most of the apparel workers are still underpaid, with only 35% of the apparel assembly workers receiving a living wage (*Living Wage,* n.d.). Nonetheless, there is a commitment to providing living wage and good working conditions, as evidenced by Patagonia's involvement with the Fair Labor Association, the Migrant Workers Program, and Living Wage.

Lastly, Patagonia scored a 3/5 on the animals dimension. The brand declared a commitment to "minimizing animal suffering," but does not have a formal animal welfare policy (Wolfe, 2020). Animal-based materials (e.g. wool, down feathers) can be traced back to the first stages of production, which shows Patagonia's commitment to traceability. Despite its commitment to eliminate all virgin animal-based fibers, the list of materials provided on the sustainability section of Patagonia's website suggests that the brand uses virgin wool. The brand nonetheless increasingly relies on recycled wool and recycled down. Good on You states that Patagonia also uses leather in some of their products, such as the Wild Idea Work Boots (*Patagonia Men's Wild Idea Workwear Boots,* 2021). Patagonia failed to include this material in the materials list shown on its website. Given the extensive amount of information on the impact of other materials used (even if they entail a net negative impact), this omission raises concerns about the brand's transparency. Relatedly, the product description for the leather boots does not make reference to the material's social and environmental impact, whereas the impact of other materials is included in product descriptions.

Patagonia's Sustainability Performance

Taken together, multiple indices provide a holistic assessment of stakeholder percep-tions of Patagonia's social and environmental performance. Despite the drawbacks of individual indices, all examine organizational performance on similar and comple-mentary dimensions, and reveal similar evaluations at different levels of granularity. Overall, the indices suggest that Patagonia is relatively more sustainable and trans-parent than most companies in the fashion industry. It performs above average on all dimensions measured by these indexes, and is on the B list (Best for the world). Fur-thermore, Patagonia is associated with relatively high levels of disclosure, as evi-denced by its ranking in the Fashion Transparency Index. Transparency translates into more information available in the calculation of organizational performance in-dices, and potentially results in greater accuracy of any measurements of Patagonia's social and environmental performance. Transparency also increases the accessibility of Patagonia's sustainable practices to consumers, and allow consumers to derive their own judgment of the brand's sustainability more easily.

Across all three indices, Patagonia's strongest performance dimension relates to its environmental practices. This is consistent with the brand's own reporting of sus-tainability efforts and goals, which centers around environmental actions, such as the introduction of sustainable materials and the reduction of waste. The performance dimension that provides most room for improvement relates to the treatment of workers. Both Good on You and the Fashion Transparency Index reveal that there is little disclosure regarding initial supply chain stages, and that workers in these supply chain stages struggle to maintain a living wage. With an increased focus on traceabil-ity, these issues are more likely to be addressed, due to better and more information regarding supply chain partners, which ultimately facilitates the identification of problems and supply chain partner accountability.

Overall, Patagonia's relative strong performance on all indices supports that stakeholders—including consumers—perceive it as a sustainable brand. This percep-tion coincides with mounting environmental awareness of younger generations. As such, the correlation between Patagonia's sustainability reputation and consumer choice is likely positive. Although this implies that the brand can rely on a stable or even expanding consumer base, the social and environmental impact of growing de-mand generates challenges for Patagonia's future status as a sustainable brand.

Conclusion

The Sustainability Paradox is a contemporary phenomenon in the fashion industry that captures the ultimately negative environmental and social impact of growing consumer demand for sustainable brands. Although relatively less damaging than fast fashion, the increase in sustainable brands' production to meet demand is associated with a rise in material use, emissions, and creation of waste, effectively leading to rising environmental as well as social costs.

Is it possible to overcome the Sustainability Paradox? If so, how? On the production side, a scalable, net-zero set of operations would ensure that changes in production quantity do not adversely affect the environment. A circular model could be the way to achieve this, as it would eliminate waste, extend materials' life cycle, and regenerate natural environments. Yet, despite its long history and favorable reputation as a sustainable brand, Patagonia demonstrates that circularity is extremely difficult to achieve, as it depends on technological progress, which is to some extent external to the company. An example of this is Patagonia's failure to replace non-sustainable materials (e.g., fluorinated DWR) with sustainable alternatives, due to losses in performance, which are critical to the life of the product, especially in the outdoor clothing sector.

Hence, it is essential to consider the consequences of rising demand for and consumption of sustainable brands. The Patagonia case reveals that a rise in consumption entails a pressure to increase production. If production is not fully climate neutral, for instance, a rise in production will likely increase the total polluting effects (e.g., more waste and emissions). If rising demand cannot be met by existing supply chain partners, pressure to extend material sourcing and the supply chain may also engender social costs. In addition, growing demand relates directly to an increase in shipping of items or consumer displacement toward stores, both of which negatively impact the environment. Since the purchase decision is made by consumers, much of the environmental and social damages caused by the consumption side are outside of brand's control, especially those related to product disposal. For example, Patagonia is not able to directly influence how long consumers keep products or how they are going to dispose of them (e.g., by recycling, donating, or disposing them as waste). Nevertheless, the company can create more durable products to extend their life cycle, and educate consumers on proper disposal. Like Patagonia, businesses can also incentivize customers to dispose of their products in environmentally friendly ways through circular initiatives, such as the Worn Wear initiative.

In conclusion, both producers and consumers need to make changes to overcome the sustainability paradox. A possible solution is full circularity, as the net-zero effect would eliminate potential damage caused by an increase in product demand. Nonetheless, this does not signify that initiatives other than full circularity are useless. On the contrary, even though increasing consumer demand for sustainable products may augment pollution created by environmentally conscious organizations, the net effect on the environment is likely positive due to the shift in consumption from non-sustainable to an environmentally friendly organization. Similar incremental contributions to the solution of social inequities may occur as consumers increasingly shift toward socially responsible organizations. Nevertheless, social and environmental cost at the organizational and macro levels can only be reduced if all fashion brands strive to achieve full circularity. Patagonia's move from social capitalism to philanthro-capitalism demonstrates that the politics of social and institutional change might be better addressed if organizations focused on purposes (e.g., climate change, social equity) instead of emphasizing the primacy of shareholder profits, as proposed in traditional business models.

References

1% for the Planet. (n.d.). Patagonia. Retrieved July 16, 2021, from https://www.patagonia.ca/one-percent-for-the-planet.html

A Guide to More Responsible Shopping. (n.d.). Patagonia. Retrieved July 18, 2021, from https://www.patagonia.com/consumer-guide/responsible-shopping.html

About B Lab. (n.d.). Retrieved April 25, 2022, from https://www.bcorporation.net/en-us/movement/about-b-lab

About Good on You. (n.d.). *Good On You*. Retrieved April 25, 2022, from https://goodonyou.eco/faqs/

Addady, M. (2016, November 29). *Patagonia's Donating All $10 Million of Its Black Friday Sales to Charity*. Fortune, November 29, 2016. https://fortune.com/2016/11/29/black-friday-2016-patagonia/

Advanced Denim. (n.d.). Patagonia. Retrieved July 18, 2021, from https://www.patagonia.com/our-footprint/advanced-denim.html

Advanced Traceable Down Standard. (n.d.). Patagonia. Retrieved July 18, 2021, from https://www.patagonia.com/our-footprint/traceable-down-standard.html

Annual Benefit Corporation Report. (2020). Patagonia Works. https://www.patagonia.com/on/demandware.static/-/Library-Sites-PatagoniaShared/default/dwf14ad70c/PDF-US/PAT_2019_BCorp_Report.pdf

Auld, G., & Grabs, J. (2022). Has Patagonia defined a new gold standard for business responsibility? *The Conversation*, October 5, 2022. Retrieved December 19, 2022 from https://theconversation.com/has-patagonia-defined-a-new-gold-standard-for-business-responsibility-191250

B The Change. (2019, January 15). *3 Things We've Improved in the B Impact Assessment (and How It Can Help Your Business)*. Medium. https://bthechange.com/3-things-weve-improved-in-the-b-impact-assessment-and-how-it-can-help-your-business-9df15bf62096

Bend, D., & King, A. (2014). Council Post: Why Consider a Benefit Corporation? *Forbes*, May 30, 2014. https://www.forbes.com/sites/theyec/2014/05/30/why-consider-a-benefit-corporation/

Berkeley Economic Review. (2019). The Merits and Drawbacks of Philanthrocapitalism. Retrieved December 19, 2022 from https://econreview.berkeley.edu/the-merits-and-drawbacks-of-philanthrocapitalism/

Best For the World™ 2021: Community List. (2022). https://www.bcorporation.net/en-us/best-for-the-world-2021-community

Best For the World™ 2021: Environment List. (2022). https://www.bcorporation.net/en-us/best-for-the-world-2021-environment

Bluesign®. (n.d.). Patagonia. Retrieved July 18, 2021 from https://www.patagonia.com/our-footprint/bluesign.html

Burns R. (2019). New Frontiers of Philanthro-Capitalism: Digital Technologies and Humanitarianism. Antipode, *vol. 51*: 4, 1101–1122.

Cotton in Conversion. (n.d.). Patagonia. Retrieved July 18, 2021, from https://www.patagonia.com/our-footprint/cotton-conversion.html

Ditty, S., Simpliciano, L., Barry, C., & Williot, D. (2021). *Fashion Transparency Index 2021*. Fashion Revolution. https://www.fashionrevolution.org/about/transparency/

Environmental & Social Footprint. (n.d.). Patagonia. Retrieved July 16, 2021, from https://www.patagonia.ca/our-footprint/

Environmental Responsibility. (n.d.). Patagonia. Retrieved July 18, 2021, from https://www.patagonia.com/environmental-responsibility-materials/

Environmental Responsibility Programs. (n.d.). Patagonia. Retrieved July 18, 2021, from https://www.patagonia.com/our-responsibility-programs.html

Erskine, M. (2022). Yvon Chouinard and the Patagonia Purpose Trust: What is it and will it work? *Forbes*, September 16, 2022. Retrieved January 2, 2023, from \ https://www.forbes.com/sites/matthewerskine/2022/09/16/yvon-chouinard-and-the-patagonia-purpose-trust-what-is-it-and-will-it-work/?sh=199c3eb12deb

Factories, Farms and Mills. (n.d.). Patagonia. Retrieved July 18, 2021, from https://www.patagonia.com/factories-farms-mills/

Fair Labor Association®. (n.d.). Patagonia. Retrieved July 18, 2021, from https://www.patagonia.com/our-footprint/fair-labor-association.html

Fair Trade Certified^{TM}. (n.d.). Patagonia. Retrieved July 18, 2021, from https://www.patagonia.com/our-footprint/fair-trade.html

Fluorinated DWR (Durable Water Repellent) Finish. (n.d.). Patagonia. Retrieved July 18, 2021, from https://www.patagonia.com/our-footprint/dwr-durable-water-repellent.html

Forest Stewardship Council. (n.d.). Patagonia. Retrieved July 18, 2021, from https://www.patagonia.com/our-footprint/forest-stewardship-council.html

Fox, G. (2019, March 26). *The Rise of Conscious Capitalism*. Forbes. https://www.forbes.com/sites/gretchenfox/2019/03/26/the-rise-of-conscious-capitalism/

Global Powers of Luxury Goods 2020. (2020). Deloitte.

Kim, A. I. (2020). How Toms Went From a $625 Million Company to Being Taken over by its Creditors. *Business Insider* December 27, 2020. Retrieved July 19, 2023, from https://www.businessinsider.com/rise-and-fall-of-toms-shoes-blake-mycoskie-bain-capital-2020-3

H₂No® Performance Standard. (n.d.). Patagonia. Retrieved July 18, 2021, from https://www.patagonia.com/our-footprint/h2no-performance-standard.html

Hemp Fabric. (n.d.). Patagonia. Retrieved July 18, 2021, from https://www.patagonia.com/our-footprint/hemp.html

Ironclad Guarantee. (n.d.). Patagonia. Retrieved July 16, 2021, from https://help.patagonia.com/s/article/Ironclad-Guarantee

Living Wage. (n.d.). Patagonia. Retrieved July 18, 2021, from https://www.patagonia.com/our-footprint/living-wage.html

Mackey, John, and Rajendra Sisodia (2014), Conscious Capitalism: Liberating the Heroic Spirit of Business. Harvard Business Review Press, Boston.

Material Traceability. (n.d.). Patagonia. Retrieved July 18, 2021, from https://www.patagonia.com/our-footprint/material-traceability.html

Migrant Workers. (n.d.). Patagonia. Retrieved July 18, 2021, from https://www.patagonia.com/our-footprint/migrant-workers.html

Model—1% for the Planet. (n.d.). 1% for the Planet. Retrieved July 16, 2021, from https://www.onepercentfortheplanet.org/model

NetPlus® Recycled Fishing Nets. (n.d.). Patagonia. Retrieved July 18, 2021, from https://www.patagonia.com/our-footprint/netplus-recycled-fishing-nets.html

Nonfluorinated DWR Finish. (n.d.). Patagonia. Retrieved July 18, 2021, from https://www.patagonia.com/our-footprint/nonfluorinated-dwr-durable-water-repellent.html

Nylon Fabric. (n.d.). Patagonia. Retrieved July 18, 2021, from https://www.patagonia.com/our-footprint/nylon.html

Organic Cotton Fabric. (n.d.). Patagonia. Retrieved July 18, 2021, from https://www.patagonia.com/our-footprint/organic-cotton.html

Owned and Operated Facilities. (n.d.). Patagonia. Retrieved July 18, 2021, from https://www.patagonia.ca/where-we-do-business/owned-and-operated.html

Padilla-Rivera, A., Russo-Garrido, S., & Merveille, N. (2020). Addressing the Social Aspects of a Circular Economy: A Systematic Literature Review. *Sustainability, 12*(19), 7912. https://doi.org/10.3390/su12197912

Patagonia® PrimaLoft® P.U.R.E. (n.d.). Patagonia. Retrieved July 18, 2021, from https://www.patagonia.com/our-footprint/primaloft-pure.html

Patagonia Homepage. (n.d.). Patagonia. Retrieved July 16, 2021, from https://www.patagonia.ca/home/

Patagonia Men's Diamond Quilted Bomber Hoody. (n.d.). Patagonia. Retrieved July 18, 2021, from https://www.patagonia.com/product/mens-diamond-quilted-bomber-hoody/27610.html

Patagonia Men's Wild Idea Workwear Boots. (2021). Patagonia. https://www.patagonia.com/product/mens-wild-idea-workwear-boots/79385.html

Patagonia Works. (n.d.). B Corporation. Retrieved April 25, 2022, from https://www.bcorporation.net/en-us/find-a-b-corp/company/patagonia-inc

Patagonia—Sustainability Rating. (2020, August). Good On You. https://directory.goodonyou.eco/brand/patagonia

PETA Calls Out Patagonia for Secrecy Around New Wool Source. (2018, September 13). PETA. https://www.peta.org/blog/peta-responds-patagonias-lack-concern-new-sheep-cruelty-expose/

Polyester Fabric. (n.d.). Patagonia. Retrieved July 18, 2021, from https://www.patagonia.com/our-footprint/polyester.html

Polyurethane. (n.d.). Patagonia. Retrieved July 18, 2021, from https://www.patagonia.com/our-footprint/polyurethane.html

Poverty wages. (2019). [Folder]. Clean Clothes Campaign. https://cleanclothes.org/poverty-wages

PTFE (Polytetrafluoroethylene). (n.d.). Patagonia. Retrieved July 18, 2021, from https://www.patagonia.com/our-footprint/ptfe-polytetrafluoroethylene.html

Recycled Cashmere Fabric. (n.d.). Patagonia. Retrieved July 18, 2021, from https://www.patagonia.com/our-footprint/recycled-cashmere.html

Recycled Cotton Fabric. (n.d.). Patagonia. Retrieved July 18, 2021, from https://www.patagonia.com/our-footprint/recycled-cotton.html

Recycled Down. (n.d.). Patagonia. Retrieved July 18, 2021, from https://www.patagonia.com/our-footprint/recycled-down.html

Recycled Nylon Fabric. (n.d.). Patagonia. Retrieved July 18, 2021, from https://www.patagonia.com/our-footprint/recycled-nylon.html

Recycled Polyester. (n.d.). Patagonia. Retrieved July 18, 2021, from https://www.patagonia.com/our-footprint/recycled-polyester.html

Recycled Spandex. (n.d.). Patagonia. Retrieved July 18, 2021, from https://www.patagonia.com/our-footprint/recycled-spandex.html

Recycled Wool Fabric. (n.d.). Patagonia. Retrieved July 18, 2021, from https://www.patagonia.com/our-footprint/recycled-wool.html

REFIBRA® Lyocell. (n.d.). Patagonia. Retrieved July 18, 2021, from https://www.patagonia.com/our-footprint/refibra.html

Regenerative Organic Certification. (n.d.). Patagonia. Retrieved July 18, 2021, from https://www.patagonia.com/our-footprint/regenerative-organic-certification.html

Regenerative Organic Certification Pilot Cotton. (n.d.). Patagonia. Retrieved July 18, 2021, from https://www.patagonia.com/our-footprint/regenerative-organic-certification-pilot-cotton.html

Responsible Wool Standard. (n.d.). Patagonia. Retrieved July 18, 2021, from https://www.patagonia.com/our-footprint/responsible-wool-standard.html

Schillmann, C. (2020). *Patagonia Inc. Under a sustainability perspective.*

Schwartz, T. (2013, April 4). Companies that Practice "Conscious Capitalism" Perform 10x Better. *Harvard Business Review.* https://hbr.org/2013/04/companies-that-practice-conscious-capitalism-perform

Shop Informed. (n.d.). Patagonia. Retrieved July 18, 2021, from https://www.patagonia.com/consumer-guide/shop-informed.html

Spandex. (n.d.). Patagonia. Retrieved July 18, 2021, from https://www.patagonia.com/our-footprint/spandex.html

Stammer, R. (2016, December 6). *It Pays to Become a B Corporation.* Harvard Business Review. https://hbr.org/2016/12/it-pays-to-become-a-b-corporation

Supply Chain Environmental Responsibility Program. (n.d.). Patagonia. Retrieved July 18, 2021, from https://www.patagonia.com/our-footprint/supply-chain-environmental-responsibility-program.html

TENCEL® Lyocell Fabric. (n.d.). Patagonia. Retrieved July 18, 2021, from https://www.patagonia.com/our-footprint/tencel-lyocell.html

Thangavelu, P. (2020, February 3). *The Success of Patagonia's Marketing Strategy.* Investopedia. https://www.investopedia.com/articles/personal-finance/070715/success-patagonias-marketing-strategy.asp

UPF Fabric for Sun Protection. (n.d.). Patagonia. Retrieved July 18, 2021, from https://www.patagonia.com/our-footprint/upf-fabric.html

Vision of a Circular Economy for Fashion. (2020). Ellen MacArthur Foundation.

Where We Do Business. (n.d.). Patagonia. Retrieved July 18, 2021, from https://www.patagonia.com/where-we-do-business/

Wolfe, I. (2020, November 24). *How Ethical Is Patagonia?* Good On You. https://goodonyou.eco/how-ethical-is-patagonia/

Wool Fabric. (n.d.). Patagonia. Retrieved July 18, 2021, from https://www.patagonia.com/our-footprint/wool.html

Worn Wear. (n.d.). Worn Wear. Retrieved July 16, 2021, from https://wornwear.patagonia.com

Yulex® Natural Rubber. (n.d.). Patagonia. Retrieved July 18, 2021, from https://www.patagonia.com/our-footprint/yulex.html

Part 4: **The World of Wine**

Camilo Peña

14 A Sustainability Comparison and Critique of Conventional, Organic, and Natural Wine Making Approaches

Introduction

There is still debate around the concept of sustainability with varying definitions and multiple concepts connected to it (Vittersø and Tangeland 2015). This chapter will contribute to the elucidation of what sustainability means in the particular case of the wine industry by providing a comparison between three different wine making approaches. Additionally, the chapter will present a critical discussion on what is missing and what should be incorporated in the framing of sustainable wine making approaches.

Sustainability in wine has been recently framed on the basis of five main elements of a program or framework: the type of program or main goal; the scale or territorial scope; the governance or primary responsibility for planning and implementation; the depth of the program; and the learning potential resulting from the sustainability program (Flores 2018; Navarini and Domaneschi 2022). While sustainability in the wine world might have differences depending on national or institutional frameworks (Flores 2018; Szolnoki 2013), there are some common characteristics that are transversal to regions and institutions and that fall under particular winemaking approaches. These approaches inform views on what sustainability is and how it is implemented by wineries (Berghoef and Dodds 2013). The following chapter will present differences in key socio-environmental areas between three wine making approaches: conventional, organic, and natural. While the chapter will mention and consider certain biodynamic practices, it will focus on the organic approach given the number of similarities between both approaches and that some consider biodynamic viticulture to be a more extreme form of organic viticulture but without support of conclusive scientific explanations (Robinson and Harding 2015). The main differences between organic and biodynamic approaches will be explained in this chapter, when describing the organic approach.

Some wine experts (e.g., Goode and Harrop 2011) would argue that an authentic, interesting, and good quality wine should incorporate elements such as sustainable viticultural practices, good quality grapes and reduced number of additives, a good representation of terroir or sense of place, a vigilant eye for fault and damaging of the wines through the production process, and an appropriate level of ripeness (achieved through a proper timing of grape picking). This chapter will focus on the sustainability and socio-environmental aspects of the complete wine making process, from viticulture to cellaring.

https://doi.org/10.1515/9783110783933-014

Some sustainability topics that are perhaps not part of the direct wine growing or wine making process, but that form part of the process to achieve a bottle of wine, include the choice of bottle (e.g., bottle weight and its environmental impacts), use of cork or screw cap (each with different environmental considerations), the choice of bottling wines on-site versus bulk shipping, and the use of recycled materials, among others. These are business decisions and marketing aspects that are not usually included in the way that conventional, organic, and natural wines differentiate themselves. Nonetheless, these are sustainability aspects that should be incorporated in a sustainable wine making operation. These aspects will not be within the scope of this chapter, which will focus on the more direct elements of wine growing and making, but should be acknowledged when assessing and critiquing the way sustainability is implemented by wineries.

While conventional, organic, and natural winemaking are not the only approaches to wine making and also not the only ways to incorporate sustainability (with most contemporary wine making approaches incorporating some form of sustainability), the three will be compared as main, relevant, and growing approaches to wine making. The descriptions and details provided for each approach will be informed by both primary data from the author's experiences in Canadian wineries in British Columbia (from 2013 to 2020) and by secondary data in the form of scholarly articles and industry reports and guidelines.

Wine and Sustainability

Consumers interested in sustainability demand certain characteristics of the products they purchase, e.g. when choosing clothing, coffee, chocolate, or other types of food (Thompson and Arsel 2004). The wine industry has a particular niche of products that are marketed towards these more pro-social and environmentally conscious consumers. For instance, while some winemakers are incorporating organic and/or biodynamic techniques into their wine making (Legeron 2014), some others have decided to approach winemaking from a less interventionist perspective such as with the natural wine making movement (Goode and Harrop 2011; Legeron 2014). These winemaking approaches have a common interest to reduce the environmental impacts of winemaking while reducing the number of inputs that go into both wine growing and cellaring processes. But sustainable initiatives are not limited to organic, biodynamic, and natural wine making, with many conventional wine making approaches incorporating initiatives and practices that seek to reduce the environmental impacts of wine production.

The following sections will focus on describing and comparing organic and natural wine making approaches in relation to conventional wine making. Key differences (and similarities) will be detailed, using conventional wine making as the baseline and main point of comparison.

Organic versus Conventional Approach

The organic approach to wine making mostly focuses on the grape growing and viticultural practices of the process. Organic viticulture centers in avoiding the use of human-made compounds including fertilizers, herbicides, fungicides, and insecticides by instead using preventive methods and organic/biodynamic preparations to fertilize the soil and control pests. Biodynamic and organic approaches have many similarities, as will be detailed here. Beside these multiple similarities, there are three main areas of difference between organic and biodynamic viticulture: the biodynamic approach seeks to convert the vineyard into a self-sustaining system; the biodynamic vineyard should be treated regularly with nine mineral and herb based biodynamic preparations; and when following biodynamics, key wine making tasks (e.g., pruning, picking, and bottling) should embrace certain spiritual aspects such as following moon calendars to harness beneficial formative forces from the earth, the sky, the sun, and the moon (Robinson and Harding 2015).

While conventional viticulture might rely mostly on handling pests and diseases as they occur, the organic approach focuses on preventive measures such as canopy management – techniques that aim to improve yield and quality and to control vine diseases addressing canopy microclimate by improving the sun exposure of leaves and grapes – to reduce the reliance on inputs that go into the vineyard.

Other preventive methods include: mechanical weeding, a more labour intensive approach to controlling weeds and preventing them from growing to a volume that gets overwhelming and thus requires use of herbicides or other methods for weed control; mulching, i.e., using recycled trees, brush, and grass clippings over vines to prevent weeds growing and to act as natural fertilizers (when broken down by earth worms); preventive leaf removal for various purposes, including to increase air circulation, reduce humidity, and thus help prevent botrytis bunch rot. Most of these approaches take more work and time and are usually justified by producers through their commitment to organic and natural wine making approaches and sometimes framed as a labour of commitment to the environment.

When inputs are required in the vineyard, the organic approach usually relies on organic materials such as organic compost, manure, organic sprays, and biodynamic preparations. These inputs are sometimes required to stimulate and maintain a healthy population of various soil microorganisms. This is particularly relevant for viticulture given that these are perennial crops that do not allow for crop rotation. While commercial fertilizers usually feed the vine itself, organic fertilizers like compost aim to improve the quality and biological properties of the soil. Through this process, a slower release of mineral nutrients is possible via living organisms such as earthworms and beneficial bacteria and fungi. Commercial fertilizers offer a faster and more direct path to nutrient provision but do not promote or enhance the soil biota – the population of organisms living in the soil – such as is the case with most organic and biodynamic viticultural practices.

One of the main reasons for why many conventional wineries prefer not to switch to organic viticulture, despite the reported benefits to the environment, a growing consumer interest, and long-term improvements to vineyard yield and pest risk (Robinson and Harding 2015), is the uncertainty of what happens when switching from one approach to the other, especially during the second and third years of transition. During these years, there is a risk for vineyards to produce lower yields (perhaps not enough for a winery to cover their costs) and for higher disease pressure. These conditions are correlated and could occur given the change in how nutrients are now provided in a slower form (from the soil, as described earlier) compared to the quick form provided by commercial fertilizers.

One mechanism to deal with this is preparing vineyards ahead of time and maintaining a preventive, rather than reactive, vineyard management approach. This means a wine grower would first put in place mechanisms to create and protect the soil biota needed for a successful organic/biodynamic viticulture transition. For instance, using compost and cover crops can help create and protect the soil biota. This preparation can bring with it a soil that is more likely to hold water and nutrients than other less microbiologically diverse soils.

With a more prepared and microbiologically diverse soil, benefits directly associated with the wine's quality can emerge. Some argue that in these organic and biodynamic vineyards, the soil's nutrient and water composition promotes mycorrhiza – the symbiotic relationship between a fungus and a plant such as the vine. The mycorrhizal fungi will aid the vine's roots in penetrating deeper into the soil and increasing the surface area of the roots, allowing the vine to better access and use nutrients in the soil. This at the same time is said to contribute to making wines more terroir-driven and complex (Robinson and Harding 2015).

Altogether, organic and biodynamic wineries have a more ecosystemic take to vineyard management by considering the multiple (micro)organisms that live and interact in their vineyards. For these wineries, it is about trying to get a balanced ecosystem with as little human-made input as possible. This includes microorganisms such as the aforementioned fungi and also organisms such as tapeworms and birds. For instance, it is not uncommon for organic, biodynamic, and natural wineries to have chickens roaming in their vineyards acting as bug and insect control as well as walking fertilizers; or pigs and sheep acting as lawnmowers.

Two additional areas that are of importance when considering the sustainability of wine making operations are water and energy management. For the latter, there are no clear differences or standards set for conventional versus organic/biodynamic (or natural) wineries. Some conventional wineries might have LEED certified buildings, while others might not. Improvements towards sustainable energy sources such as solar and wind technology might be pursued in relation to funding capabilities and owner priorities, but nothing associated with the standards or regulations related with conventional/organic/natural wine making approaches.

In terms of water management, another area not strictly regulated under the organic (or natural) wine making approach, there are two key areas that will be discussed here: irrigation (vineyard use) and hygiene and temperature control (winery/

cellar use). Most wineries typically have systems in place to know and control how much water is used for vines with irrigation systems, usually drip systems, that allow for more control and less water usage. These drip irrigation systems make up for water needs not satisfied by natural rainfall. Nonetheless, there are certain types of soils that can store more water than others and thus need less irrigation. These are usually deep loamy or silt soils and are found in valley floors (e.g., in certain locations of the Okanagan and Napa valleys). Still, next to these soils there might be other (shallower) soils that require more irrigation. The understanding of each particular soil, as related to the ecosystemic management approach, might be more usual in certain organic/natural vineyards but can still be seen in many conventional wineries that are becoming aware of how they use their irrigation systems.

The water used for hygiene and temperature control is very standard across wine making approaches. Hygiene in the cellar is regarded as a vital practice in modern wine making, in order to control bacteria and wild yeasts. The need for cleanliness of the cellar involves, among other things, a significant amount of water usage. It is not clear whether the fact that certain organic/biodynamic and natural wineries might decide to work with wild yeasts implies a reduced amount of water used for cellar cleaning purposes. Finally, for temperature control purposes, despite the use of glycol temperature regulating tanks, many wineries still rely on the use of water to cool down tanks when needed. This is seen as a small price to pay compared to the possibility of spoilage of the wine stored in these tanks.

Within the cellar/winery, organic wine usually allows for similar inputs compared to conventional wine making approaches, with the caveat of sulfur dioxide and the need to use organic inputs when possible. The allowed quantity of sulfur dioxide used in organic wineries varies depending on wine color, sweetness, and style but are usually 25%–35% lower than what is allowed for a conventional winery (Robinson and Harding 2015). When possible, any additives, agents, and aids such as egg whites or sugar should be organic. Altogether, organic wineries follow an additional number of standards, usually aligned with organic accreditations, that go beyond the regular standards followed by conventional wineries (e.g., Canadian Food Inspection Agency standards).

Finally, for social impacts, both organic and conventional (as well natural) wineries work by the rules with regards to employment and security requirements. In some cases, there is an established process for communicating with neighbors about new processes or other activities that might be disruptive to the community. While both types of wineries have an educational component, where customers are taught about their wine making processes, organic and biodynamic wineries add the organic/biodynamic component to their teaching. This usually includes additional considerations for the environment and health as framing for why they do things different than conventional wineries. Natural wineries also add some additional educational components around their cellaring practices.

Natural versus Conventional Approach

Given that many of the differences between organic and conventional wine making are also applicable to natural wine making (as detailed in the previous paragraphs), this section will focus on the additional differences that make the natural wine making approach different to both conventional and organic. Most of these differences are evidenced in cellaring/winery practices.

Natural wines are usually associated with small, independent producers that hand-pick their grapes and employ sustainable, organic, and biodynamic practices in their vineyards. Natural wine makers will usually rely more on an artisanal approach to wine making and will prefer not to use chemical interventions in the winery, relying more on physical interventions and naturally occurring process. Following this, natural wine makers will not use additives in the making of wines and will minimize or remove altogether the use of sulfur dioxide, sometimes kept only for the final bottling process, to ensure stability. Indeed, some natural wine makers will critique the permitted use of sulfur dioxide in wine made from organically grown grapes. Nonetheless, with not much guidance on natural wine making procedures until recently, natural wine movements are still developing a more clear identity and specific guidelines (Peña-Moreno 2022).

Overall, a key overarching element that characterizes natural wines, and differentiates the approach from the organic and the conventional, is the removal of as many human interventions from the wine making process as possible. Natural wine making is a wine movement that emerges from the opposition to over-extracted and over-oaked wines that were so popular around the turn of the twentieth century and in some instances a movement that promotes more transparency in the labelling of wines to really reflect what is being added to the wines, e.g., processing aids, agents, and other additives commonly used in conventional and organic wine making (Robinson and Harding 2015). All these ideas revolve around the objective to achieve a wine that is more pure, reflective of terroir, and *vivant* (alive). The latter relates to the number of micro-organisms, such as yeast and bacteria, that are still present in many natural wines, even many years after bottling, compared to conventional wines (Legeron 2014).

The natural wine movement has received criticism from some in the wine world due to a number of reasons. A first reason relates to the use of the word "natural," since many wine makers will argue that their wines, although not labelled as natural wines, are still natural; in other cases, some might also argue that there is no such thing as a natural wine, since all wine requires some level of human (and chemical) intervention to prevent spoilage. Others will argue that the result of minimal use of sulfur dioxide and clarification processes leads to natural wines being prone to instability and spoilage because of unwanted bacteria and yeast. Moreover, this argument is taken to the shipping aspect of wine, where some would argue that shipping natural wines will either ruin the wine or will require energy-intensive temperature control measures to protect it. Finally, while some natural wine advocates say that reduced exposure to sul-

fur dioxide in wine helps with reducing hangovers, headaches, allergies, and intoleran-
ces, others will argue this is yet to be scientifically proven and that the levels of sulfur
dioxide used in wine are minimal and should cause no issues for wine drinkers.

The main differences between natural and other wine making approaches are
seen in the cellar/winery. Natural wine makers will follow the tenet of minimal intervention by reducing or altogether removing any additives being used in the winery.
The major exception to this rule is the occasional and minimal use of sulfur dioxide
(usually at bottling). With this in mind, many natural wine makers will rely almost
exclusively on the naturally occurring yeasts on grape skins and in the winery environment. As with these naturally occurring yeasts, some sulfur dioxide is produced
during the fermentation process, so a little can be present in all wines. Regardless,
some natural wine makers will specialize or be known for their extreme *vins sans
souffre* approach, i.e., making wines without any added sulfur dioxide at all.

This reliance on natural and indigenous yeasts provides the argument for some
natural wine makers to position their wines as true reflections of their terroir. But to
be able to rely on only indigenous yeasts and not have trouble with other unwanted
bacteria or yeast, natural wine makers must have knowledge and attention to detail
about what happens in the winery. For instance, a hygienic environment is needed in
order to prevent further use of sulfur dioxide. In some cases, a natural wine maker
might have to decide between having Brettanomyces take over the profile of a wine
or using sulfur dioxide to get rid of the "Brett" yeast (as some call the Brettanomyces).
Some natural wine makers will argue that having dominant levels of Brett will inhibit
terroir, as it would make all wines taste the same. In this case, these wine makers will
justify the use of sulfur dioxide to control the levels of Brett and thus protect the wine
from becoming overpowered by it.

So, while most natural wine makers will follow similar viticultural practices as
those seen in organic viticulture, the main differences are evidenced on how the wine
is processed and fermented in the cellar/winery. Nonetheless, there is still debate
even between some natural wine makers, especially around the use of sulfur dioxide.
On the one hand, "purists" natural wine makers will argue that wine should be free
of all additives, including sulfur dioxide, in order to allow for indigenous yeasts to
occur and give character and complexity to the wine. They argue that wine making
with no sulfur dioxide is possible by having a very hands on and controlled cellar
environment. On the other hand, natural wine makers that still rely on sulfur dioxide
will argue that letting wine be controlled by whatever bacteria or yeast that ends up
in the wine making process will be counterproductive to the idea of having a wine
reflective of terroir. They say that this disconnects from the efforts that were taken in
the vineyard to preserve a quality and terroir-driven grape.

This debate will continue and while some differences might be evident within the
natural wine making world, it is clear that it is the approach that goes farthest away
from conventional wine making approaches. While organic wine making will focus
on vineyard practices, with some considerations in cellar practices, the natural wine

making approach embraces organic/biodynamic vineyard practices while extending the critique to overuse of chemicals and human-made inputs to the cellar. A summary of the main differences between all three approaches discussed in the previous paragraphs is presented in Table 14.1.

Table 14.1: Three different sustainability approaches in wine making.

Element	Sub-element	Conventional approach	Organic approach	Natural approach
Ecosystem Management		Focus in the vineyard without much consideration of the external and underlying ecosystem.	Try to get a balanced ecosystem with little intervention.	Try to get a balanced ecosystem with little intervention. Working with plants and animals as to get no dominant aspect of the land, but a balanced relationship between all.
Soil and Nutrition Management		Focused on playing it safe as with pesticide management: commercial and conventional fertilizers are used to improve soil and nutrition.	Use cover crops and manures to help improve soils. Consider ecosystemic aspects in how soils and nutrition are affected.	
Viticultural and Pest Management	**Fertilizers**	Synthetic fertilizers, non-organic compost	Organic compost, manure, cover crop, fish-fertilizer, biodynamic preparations / preventive methods, e.g., canopy management	
	Weed control	Commercial Herbicides	Mechanical weeding, mulching, flame weeding	
	Powdery mildew	Commercial fungicides	Organic sprays, aerated compost tea, biodynamic preparations	
	Botrytis	Commercial fungicides	Preventive leaf removal	
	Leaf hoppers	Commercial insecticides	Promoting biodiversity in areas surrounding vineyards, attracting natural predators, sticky tape, manual pick one by one	
	Cutworms	Commercial insecticides	Leave extra buds, chickens grazing under vines, sticky tape	
	Rodents	Baits (usually poisonous)	Traps, sulfur bombs (in extreme cases)	

Table 14.1 (continued)

Element	Sub-element	Conventional approach	Organic approach	Natural approach
Water Management		Amount of water used by vines is known and controlled; irrigation systems are usually drip systems that allow for more control and less water usage. Water use for hygiene and temperature control as needed	Overall, especially for bigger wineries, the same approach as conventional. For smaller wineries, there is a learning phase in which each soil is studied to learn about its water capacities and needs.	
Energy Management		No clear rule or standard. Working on reducing energy consumption; this element is very heterogeneous. Improvements towards sustainable energy sources such as solar and wind technology (this represents a big investment so the smaller wineries usually do not have the funds for this).		
Wine making	**Allowed wine additives**	Yeasts, yeast nutrient, milk derivatives, tannins, sugar, enzymes, tartaric acid, malic acid, citric acid, various fining agents, and sulfur dioxide in quantities under 350 parts per million	Natural yeast and yeast nutrients, organic milk derivatives, bentonite as fining agent, sulfur dioxide under 100 parts per million. When possible, inputs should be organic.	No regulations, but natural wines usually have none of the additives found in the other categories; wild/indigenous yeast is used for fermentation; no sulfite or less than 10 parts per million added. Still, some debate exists around the use of sulfur dioxide.
	Sanitizers	Caustic soda, phosphoric acid	Ozone, steam, citric sulfite	
	Standards	Follow Canadian Food Inspection Agency (CFIA) standards, other accreditations and inspections are voluntary	Mandatory third-party inspections, organic accreditations, trace back to all ingredients and wines, CFIA standards	CFIA unless certified organic, in which case they would follow same as organic

Table 14.1 (continued)

Element	Sub-element	Conventional approach	Organic approach	Natural approach
Social: Employees, Neighbors, and Community		They work by the rules with regards to employment and security requirements. There is an established process for communicating with neighbors about new processes or other activities that might be disruptive (e.g. noise, smells).	Similar to conventional, with an additional factor of communicating and teaching customers about organic and/or biodynamic processes	Similar to organic, with the added educational aspect of testing and learning about natural farming methods and then sharing this knowledge with industry and customers

Conclusion, Discussion, and Critique of Sustainability in Wine

Much of the contemporary discourse on sustainability relies on categorizations that present different approaches to particular socio-environmental topics. In this chapter, the case of sustainable wine making has been summarized by presenting three distinct approaches to sustainable practices in a comparative form. Each approach has specific areas of focus with the overarching concept of sustainability as transversal to all. With each sustainability approach implementing different methods for every wine making process (see Table 14.1), the associated socio-environmental benefits could be quantified and compared to create differential sustainability performance and sustainability rankings that could be legitimated through certifying bodies that operate through labels, indicators, and overall certification schemes.

The first consideration missing in many conventional, organic, biodynamic, and natural wine making guidelines and certifications is the need to incorporate clear standards for other areas of wine making that have clear environmental impacts such as water and energy use. While some industry guidelines might incorporate recommendations on these areas, current certifications focus on particular areas (e.g., LEED-certified buildings) and do not incorporate all aspects of sustainability into an encompassing approach that considers and acknowledges the interrelationship between all aspects of wine making. One problem with this individual approach to standards and certifications is that there is a lack of context and nuance into how to incorporate specific improvements given the particular situation of each winery – e.g., whether it is following a conventional, organic, or natural wine making approach. While consultation and third-party assessments might help wineries in addressing their specific situations, there is currently no clear rationale as to why and how a winery should approach a particular energy or water efficiency program given their overall wine making approach.

While marketing and communications around sustainability can be identified for at least parts of most wineries' websites or labels, organic and natural wineries seem to use sustainability as part of their brand identity more than conventional wineries. This still needs to be further explored but a first evidence for such wider and more institutionalized marketing can be seen in the use of logos that communicate the wines have been produced under particular organic, biodynamic, and natural approaches.

Furthermore, for wineries to be able to legally label their wines as "organic" (and in a few places to label them as "natural") and to use logos demonstrating their wines have been produced under certified processes (or to be able to certify their installations are built under particular green standards, such as LEED), they need to incur the costs of certification. This will vary by location (some wineries might receive subsidies for switching to organic wine making and in some regions smaller wineries might not need to be certified to name their products "organic"), but in cases where smaller wineries must follow the same certification process as larger wineries the cost might be too high for some. The cost for certification could include a one-time application fee and subsequent renewal and inspection fees. This is a financial area that should be considered alongside winery size and revenue, when comparing and critiquing sustainability approaches in wine.

Moreover, other areas of impact (e.g., social) are not clearly defined and regulated. Thus, and as reflected in the literature on wine sustainability, there is a significant lack of understanding of the social impacts of wine making. While Table 14.1 mentions one very summarized view of the main social elements under consideration when assessing a winery's sustainability, these elements need further research and understanding. Moreover, these social impacts focus on immediate stakeholders, such as employees, neighbors, and customers, but there needs to be a deeper understanding of other (perhaps less obvious) social impacts of growing and selling wine. For instance, what are the considerations for a product that has taken land space to grow an alcoholic beverage instead of food staples? Given that wine is an alcoholic beverage, what additional socio-cultural considerations should be considered when assessing a winery's sustainability that are perhaps not applicable to agricultural food products? How does the growth in the number of wineries and volume of wine sold per capita relate to concerns around alcohol consumption?

Following this line of future research, the wine industry has been historically associated with a White and Western society. What are the implications of the push for a more diverse, equitable, inclusive, and just society for the wine industry? Is the industry diverse enough? Is it equitable? The author recalls attending one particular event hosted by the one of the biggest wine growers associations in a North American wine growing region. The association was proud to present what would be their new two-minute long video promotion of the local wine region. Perhaps a reflection of this need to better understand the need for diversity in the industry, the video included only white people, mostly (presumably) upper and middle class, playing golf, drinking wines, and having fun. Not even one person of color was included. At the moment, the author thought that the uncomfortable feeling was perhaps his own fault, but then realized that the person next to him, a White woman, had also noticed this unfortunate omission.

How to acknowledge and reconcile the fact that most of these wineries (particularly in what is known as the New World of wine) are located in unceded traditional territory of Indigenous populations? For all the talk about opposing the mainstream wine paradigms (Peña 2022), the connection of wine to its provenance and history (Joy et al. 2021), and the importance and use of terroir as rooted in authenticity, history, and tradition (Cappeliez 2017), little has been considered about how wine fits into the contemporary post-colonial world where much of what was considered the mainstream and accepted history is being critically reviewed to incorporate the Indigenous perspective.

Some of these ideas might not be as easy to quantify as quantity of water used or percentage of sulfur added, but still need acknowledgement and incorporation into the sustainability agenda of wine research. In the meantime, even those categories that are easier to quantify and assess need a more strategic and holistic consideration; one that goes beyond the sometimes polarizing and individual views of how things are supposed to be done in the industry.

Despite the benefits of sustainability categorizations, there is a risk for organizations to focus too much on certifications and on the competition that could emerge from these comparative and differential spaces. Although this could promote an ongoing sense of competitiveness and efforts on continuous improvements, it is not entirely clear what the consequences of this competitive and contested way to frame sustainability are (Navarini and Domaneschi 2022). One possibility would be to move from a place of categorization and differentiation into one of integrated sustainability views. This could involve the incorporation of sustainable practices from all wine making approaches within an overarching frame of sustainability. For instance, this framing could incorporate and embrace post-colonial understandings of land and nature that go beyond anthropocentric views on value as binary: valuable for humans or unvaluable for humans.

Changing this binary understanding, and embracing a holistic view of nature as intrinsically valuable, would imply a move away from the dichotomies that are common in western views of sustainability (e.g., rational/irrational, chaos/order, good/bad). Therefore, perhaps the need for a better understanding and for the incorporation of the Indigenous perspective in the wine world is more pressing than ever.

References

Berghoef, Naomi and Rachel Dodds (2013), "Determinants of Interest in Eco-Labelling in the Ontario Wine Industry," *Journal of Cleaner Production*, 52, 263–71.

Cappeliez, Sarah (2017), "How Well Does Terroir Travel? Illuminating Cultural Translation Using a Comparative Wine Case Study," *Poetics*, 65(January), 24–36.

Flores, Shana Sabbado (2018), "What Is Sustainability in the Wine World? A Cross-Country Analysis of Wine Sustainability Frameworks," *Journal of Cleaner Production*, 172, 2301–12.

Goode, Jaime, and Sam Harrop (2011), *Authentic Wine: Toward Natural and Sustainable Winemaking*, Berkeley and Los Angeles, California: University of California Press.

Joy, Annamma, Kathryn A. LaTour, Steve John Charters, Bianca Grohmann, and Camilo Peña-Moreno (2021), "The Artification of Wine: Lessons from the Fine Wines of Bordeaux and Burgundy," *Arts and the Market*, 11(1), 24–39.

Legeron, Isabelle (2014), *Natural Wine: An Introduction to Organic and Biodynamic Wines Made Naturally*, London and New York: Cico Books.

Navarini, Gianmarco, and Lorenzo Domaneschi (2022), "Sustainable Wine: The Discursive Production of Sustainability in the Wine Field," in *The Routledge Handbook of Wine and Culture*, ed. Steve Charters, Marion Demossier, Jacqueline Dutton, Graham Harding, Jennifer Smith Maguire, Denton Marks, and Tim Unwin, Routledge, 331–41.

Peña, Camilo (2022), "Wines and Subversive Art: A Conceptual Definition of Natural Wines," in *The Future of Luxury Brands: Artification and Sustainability*, ed. Annamma Joy, De Gruyter, 251–64.

Peña-Moreno, Camilo (2022), "Expanding Conceptualizations of Sustainability through Artification, Sensoriality, and Ideology: The Case of the Okanagan Valley Wine Industry," https://open.library.ubc.ca/collections/24/items/1.0413016.

Robinson, Jancis, and Julia Harding (2015), *The Oxford Companion to Wine*, 4th ed., ed. Jancis Robinson, Oxford: Oxford University Press.

Szolnoki, Gergely (2013), "A Cross-National Comparison of Sustainability in the Wine Industry," *Journal of Cleaner Production*, 53, 243–51.

Thompson, Craig J., and Zeynep Arsel (2004), "The Starbucks Brandscape and Consumers' (Anticorporate) Experiences of Glocalization," *Journal of Consumer Research*, 31(December), 631–42.

Vittersø, Gunnar, and Torvald Tangeland (2015), "The Role of Consumers in Transitions towards Sustainable Food Consumption. The Case of Organic Food in Norway," *Journal of Cleaner Production*, 92, 91–99.

Anna-Mari Almila and David Inglis

15 The Gendered Dynamics of the Artifying of Wine

Introduction: Artifying Wine

In recent years an interdisciplinary research field has arisen concerning the "artifica-tion" of objects not intrinsically possessed of art-like qualities (Naukkarinen and Saito 2012; Naukkarinen 2012; Saito 2012; Shiner 2012; Vihma 2012). An artification process may be said to be characterized by "a series of *crossings*, sometimes tentative, of the boundaries between art and non-art, performed by numerous social actors on pre-existing objects" (Proust 2019: 339, emphasis in original).

Shapiro and Heinich (2012: 9) recognize four possible permutations when non-artistic entities become "art": 1) "durable" cases, where an entire category of thing is widely understood to retain its art-like qualities over time; 2) "partial" cases, where a category of thing is only partly seen as art, or where only sub-types of that thing are widely understood to be art; 3) "ongoing" cases, where the becoming-art process is ongoing, in flux, and headed in as yet uncertain directions; and 4) "unattainable" cases, where a type of entity proved to be difficult or impossible to subject to redefini-tion as art.

While rendering non-artistic objects as "artistic" may make them seem more eco-nomically valuable and culturally legitimate, artification is nonetheless irreducible to legitimation issues alone (Shapiro and Heinich 2012). Following the inspiration of the historical sociologist Norbert Elias (Inglis 2021), as advocated by Shapiro (2019), we can distinguish two major sorts of processes: a) artification, involving longer-term and largely unconscious social processes not directed by any specific group of people; and b) more conscious, explicit, and shorter-term strategies of artifying objects, car-ried out by specific sorts of more-or-less self-interested actors, especially those con-cerned with selling things for profit by adding perceived value to them.

One type of artifying strategy concerns instances of the marketing of luxury goods, where the strategic and self-conscious emphasizing of their allegedly "artistic" nature by producers and sellers seeks to reinforce a sense amongst potential buyers of their prestige and relative scarcity (Kapferer 2014; Passebois-Ducros et al. 2015; De Angelis et al. 2020; Massi and Turrini 2020; Grohmann 2022; Marin et al. 2022). Artify-ing modes of marketing seek to strengthen "associations of rarity, exclusivity, sophis-tication, and luxury in consumers' minds" (Grohmann 2022: 206). Such artifying strategies involve the blurring of the boundaries between "art" and commodities for sale (Joy 2022).

Strictly speaking, as wine has only very recently been presented explicitly in art-like ways, it has not undergone a long-term process of artification as such (Shapiro

https://doi.org/10.1515/9783110783933-015

2004), and therefore does not (yet) count as a "durable" case of artification. Premium wine thus currently figures as, at most, an instance of "partial" and/or "ongoing" artification. No-one can deny that institutionalized wine language and talk have historically drawn upon words and images from the domain of art appreciation. According to Tomasi (2012: n.p.) "the language of wine tasting is rich in words stemming from the jargon of aesthetics and art criticism. Words such as 'harmonic,' 'balanced,' 'elegant,' 'subtle,' 'flat,' 'dynamic,' 'complex' can be used not only to describe art objects such as paintings, musical works, sculptures or buildings, but also to refer to certain qualities of a wine." However, the use of artistic terms to describe wine is not necessarily an indication of artification, but rather just an instance of actors in one field borrowing terms from another, in this case a highly culturally legitimate one, so as not to have to completely invent new terminology (Shapiro and Heinich 2012).

Moreover, higher-end wine constitutes a case in some ways unlike those cultural objects and fields of cultural production typically studied by sociologists of artification (Shapiro and Heinich 2012). Wine was already strongly legitimated, intellectualized, and institutionalized, including in terms of powerful legal scaffoldings affording protection to producers from unscrupulous rivals and imitators (e.g. Charters 2012; Demossier 2020; Almila 2023), by the time anyone thought to render certain wines more "artistic" than they had been hitherto.

But especially over the last 50 years, some higher-end wine has certainly been subjected to artifying strategies. Those engaged in producing and selling higher-end and premium wines sometimes relate them to art in one way or another. The "art of winemaking" and "art of fine wine" are widely claimed categories today (Negrin 2015: 426). Two main sorts of claims can be made when marketing and related discourses try to artify a specific wine: a) weaker, more modest, and more metaphorical claims, indicating that a wine is simply like or akin to art (it is "art-like"); and b) stronger, bolder, and more literal claims stating that a wine is a form of art in and of itself (it is "artistic").

Central to both sorts of claims is the rhetorical and discursive positioning of the maker of the wine. Winemakers self-presenting, or represented by others, as "artists," or at least as artist-like, must not seem to be fully bound by the terrain of the vineyard or by the winemaking tradition of their region. Instead, they must seem to be actively fulfilling an individualized and singular vision of what the wine should be like, just as "artists" (are widely assumed to) pursue unique visions in and through what they make (Passebois-Ducros et al. 2015).

It is important for any artifying strategy to distance the "art" from objects or practices of low cultural status (Jones 2019). Thus, when artifying a specific wine, it may be necessary to underline its distance from lower-end, mass market wines, by calling it "fine wine" (Joy et al 2021), recalling conventional phrases of art worlds such as "fine art." It is also easier to achieve successful artifying if the "art" in question can be directly related to an established art field (Hughson 2019), such as artifying graffiti by comparing it to already established visual arts. But as there is no established artistic field that would be directly relevant for making comparisons to winemaking, other means must be employed.

This chapter considers the hitherto very under-researched issue of the gendered factors at work when wine is subjected to artifying strategies and thus created by some people as being, or being like, "art." We reflect upon these through a sociological lens. Therefore, we do not seek to adjudicate about whether any specific wine is, or is like, "art," in the manner that some philosophers might want to do (Tomasi 2012). We merely register the fact that some people either believe and/or seek to convince others that a given wine is art-like or artistic in some sense defined by those persons (Joy et al. 2021).

Our point is that many such beliefs and activities have gendered elements. When the domains of wine and (Western or Western-influenced) art come together, some long-standing gendered, and sometimes deeply patriarchal,[1] phenomena meet and mingle with others, in turn creating emergent phenomena that bear the marks of the histories of their respective sources. No oenological or artistic phenomenon can ever be wholly gender neutral. When wine becomes subject to certain types of artifying process, such that certain wine phenomena become "art-like" or "artistic" in some way, the resulting situation will always be gendered, whether more obviously or more implicitly so, and whether in more explicitly patriarchal ways or not.

After looking at the gendered, and often patriarchal, nature of both wine and art worlds and institutions, we consider matters to do with the artifying of wine in relation to two focal points: artifying the makers of wine, and artifying the labels of wine. These areas indicate profound instances of the gendered nature of the wine/art nexus. We conclude that, given the very long-standing gendered nature of the social institutions of both "wine" and "art," a potential danger involved in the artifying of wine is that gendered norms are imported from the world of art, such that wine is made even more gendered than it was before. Rendering wine as "art" is unlikely to undo patriarchal norms of, and masculinist thinking about, wine, but it is instead potentially capable of reinforcing them.

We must note at the outset that we will mostly consider only higher grade and relatively more expensive wines, as it is these that are much more likely to be subjected to, or otherwise involved in, artifying processes than mass-market wines. The latter are often bound up with forms of patriarchal cultural forms, such as obviously

---

1 Patriarchies can be defined as social orders in which, overall, men's interests are prioritized over women's, social relations and institutions involve the subjugation of women in various inter-related ways, and cultural imaginaries present the female as inferior in multiple manners. Patriarchal social orders are rooted in powerful cultural orientations concerning appropriate and inappropriate male and female behaviours, these assumptions animating multiple social spheres which often reinforce each other. Patriarchal notions and practices concerning (supposedly inferior) female biology, psychology, sexuality, fertility, and motherhood, medical and psychological vulnerabilities, domesticity, and (non-) participation in public spheres, are all inter-related (Walby 1991).

sexist and sexualized packaging and advertising (Almila 2019). Generally, the gendered and patriarchal elements of artifying processes are less blatant and crude than that, precisely because they are associated with, and are part of the symbolic creation of, more "classy" wine products, in the universe of which a certain level of apparent aesthetic refinement is conventionally expected. That means that the gendered elements in higher-end, so-called "fine" wines tend to be more sophisticated, and thereby possibly more discreet or insidious, than those in the world of mass market offerings.

On the Gendering of Art and of Wine

Wine and art, as long-standing institutions of the Western world, have at least two major features in common. First, both have gone through organisational and institutional forms of change, structural differentiation, legal consolidation, and intellectualisation (Shapiro and Heinich 2012; Shapiro 2019). Second, the social worlds of wine and of art have over many centuries been deeply marked and shaped by gendered, often patriarchal, social relations and cultural assumptions.

Across the world, the history of the production of symbolic and aesthetic objects is marked by highly gendered dynamics and practices. This is certainly true of the social institutions of production, appreciation, and consumption of those special kinds of objects that in the modern West came to be understood from the late medieval period onwards as constituting the domain of "art" (Inglis and Hughson 2005). Women have generally occupied less privileged positions than men within contexts of artistic production and commentary, while being represented in visual and plastic arts in often reductive and stereotypical manners, especially as regards matters of sexuality and sexualized embodiment. The very category of "artist" itself is historically associated with masculine traits, and women have accordingly struggled to gain appreciation as socially legitimated "artists" (Wolff 2000).

Since at least the 1970s, there have been trends towards the various domains of art becoming less patriarchal and more diverse in gender and other terms (Krull 1989). Still, one could argue that strong traces of earlier patriarchal thinking remain at a deep level, most notably in terms of the ongoing, although contested, assumptions, that an "artist" is a male figure, and that his artworks are more prestigious than cultural objects created by craftworkers, who are coded as more feminine figures (Callen 1985).

Like art, wine has always been gendered in multiple ways, and it continues to be so today. For the whole time that humans have made wine from grapes – some 8,000 years – wine has been profoundly gendered in many ways, encompassing both how it has been made and how it has been drunk or otherwise put to use. Historically and cross-culturally, there have been far more social restrictions on women than there have been on men in terms of who may legitimately make and partake of wine, and wine has been bound up with broader patriarchal social relations and cultural formations over its entire history (Almila and Inglis 2022).

In terms of production, wine-related labour has been very gendered historically, with men by and large in control of vineyards, wineries, and the means of distributing the final product to consumers in locations both near and far from the site of production (Almila 2019; Matasar 2006). As an agricultural product, wine making has reflected both broader patriarchal norms as to the proper place of women in rural households and agricultural enterprises, and also patriarchal myths about the potentially polluting nature of women's presence in wine making locales (Almila 2021). Once wine making became organized according to capitalist demands of profit maximisation, in a geographically uneven set of developments stretching from the seventeenth century CE onwards (Colman 2010), older patriarchal norms were usually reproduced rather than strongly challenged or fundamentally altered. In this sense, wine making today is still underpinned by a nexus of long-standing agricultural and capitalist forms of patriarchy (Almila and Inglis 2022).

In terms of its appreciation and consumption, wine has also been deeply gendered for millennia. There has been a long-standing and strong association between wine and heterosexual seduction (Almila 2021). Wine's presumed tendency to provoke sexual licentiousness in women is known to have been commented upon already in ancient Greece (Matasar 2006). Champagne has been considered an aphrodisiac for several centuries (Guy 2003). Moreover, connoisseurship has implied a mastery of the subject matter, a hyper-masculine understanding of the possession and deployment of wine-related knowledge (Almila 2019).

Wine language has historically been very gendered. As recently as the 1980s, expressions such as "voluptuous," "racy," or "like an old lady" were standard and acceptable in wine tasting circles (Inglis 2019a). Wine has often been likened to women, in ways that rely on sexist stereotypes, or considered to be best consumed by men at the same time as they enjoy the sexual favours of females (Almila and Inglis 2022). In such thinking, women exist not to make their own informed choices, for they are assumed to be in possession of much less knowledge about wine than men, but merely to be impressed with male *savoir faire* (Almila 2021). Such widespread cultural assumptions have profoundly impacted on women's self-understandings and behaviours as wine drinkers (Atkin et al 2007a; 2007b; Barber and Almanza 2006; Barber et al 2006; 2007; Thach 2012). Well into the twentieth and twenty-first centuries, women have been generally much less confident in their wine selections than their male counterparts, and they have been much more reliant on the opinions of "experts," who themselves were almost exclusively men until the last few decades (Johnson and Bastian 2007; Ritchie 2009).

Contemporary research indicates that today, while women buy most of the wine drunk in households on an everyday basis, they may well externalise the buying of special occasion wine to male family members (Ritchie 2009). They may be under more pressure to justify their wine-drinking than men (Almila 2022). Women also regularly estimate their own wine knowledge lower than do men (Johnson and Bastian 2007).

Women often rely on intermediaries, whether human or non-human, such as wine shop personnel or stickers on bottles informing the buyer that the wine has won a prize, when making wine-buying decisions (Atkin et al. 2007a). Female wine consumers often feel more easily intimidated by male wine professionals than men, and some male professionals may indeed seek to intimidate women customers (Almila 2019).

However, wine may also, under specific circumstances and through particular modes of action, be de-gendered and re-gendered in certain ways that challenge previously dominant patriarchal norms (Almila 2021). Given that wine has been greatly gendered for thousands of years, any shorter-term tendencies to de-gender it – which have substantially existed only over the last 40 years or less – have so far only been partial, although not without some more recent gains for women (Almila and Inglis 2022). Thus, female wine consumption today is less restricted than it has been historically (e.g. Remus 2014), but it remains quite gendered in certain ways, with women tending to drink wine marketed to them as compatible with conventional notions of femininity (Almila 2019; Almila and Inglis 2022).

In some senses the threshold to participating in higher-level wine appreciation, whether as a professional or an amateur, is lower than ever, although access to wine varies from one social group to another (Inglis and Ho 2022). Women have both benefitted from, and been key contributors to, wider processes of the democratisation of wine, even if rendering wine worlds more equitable has been a very patchy process (Howland 2013).

One important feature of the artifying of a non-artistic set of cultural objects is the intellectualisation of them by various interested parties, rendering them into the sophisticated and formal vocabularies of aesthetic appreciation (Shapiro 2019). But wine had already been subjected to its own distinctive language of appreciation for centuries, so intellectualisation was a long-standing feature of wine worlds well before any explicit attempts to artify wine. In the late twentieth century trends began towards the replacement of the elaborate vocabularies of qualitative wine tasting with points systems, rating wines out of 100 points, or five stars, and so on. The first and most influential such system, which was widely copied, was created by the American wine critic Robert Parker (McCoy 2006). Joy et al. (2021) indicate the influence of Parker in enlarging the role of critics in the bestowing of prestige to a vintner's reputation.

We can also note the de-intellectualizing thrust of Parker's and others' points systems. A consumer can judge the quality of a wine simply with reference to how many points it has been awarded by an influential critic or judging panel, apparently taking away any need for deep wine knowledge. Such systems are simultaneously reductive, simplifying, and open to question by Parker's adversaries on the one hand (Nossiter 2010), and a means of opening up wine in a democratizing manner to hitherto excluded groups on the other. Thus, de-intellectualizing tendencies, which are in one way the opposite of artification processes, may lead to greater levels of inclusion of women into the world(s) of wine. That raises the issue of how artifying strategies may, wittingly or not, reinstate, reinforce, or create new gendered dynamics in wine.

Over the last 40 years market and professional relations have been slowly and unevenly restructured such that some opportunities for women to be regarded as legitimate makers, sellers, and promoters of wine have opened up. This has partly occurred through new educational opportunities for women vis-à-vis wine, with wine education nowadays being less obviously patriarchal in nature than it has been in preceding centuries (Matasar 2006). An important component here is the global standardisation of wine language, embodied in professional courses and programs, such as those offered by the London-based organisation called the Wine & Spirit Educational Trust (WSET), that are available to take in many countries and which use uniform terminology to describe the properties of wines.[2] The construction of a global *lingua franca* of wine (Robinson 2021) has allowed women to participate more fully in wine discourse, and its professional applications, than was the case before, especially as this language is apparently devoid of gendered elements.

An interesting part of this development is wine writing, in which women have often been more successful than in other fields of wine professionalism; we can think of the pioneering wine taster and writer Pamela Vandyke-Price (1923–2014) or, much more famously, Jancis Robinson (1950–), widely considered one of the most influential wine critics in the world today. Many women have indeed chosen to focus on wine writing as it has provided more flexible working conditions than, say, grape-growing and wine making, which are bound by the seasons and sometimes unpredictable climatic and weather conditions. Flexibility is an important consideration for a woman with caring duties (Matasar 2006; Brenner 2007). Writing about wine also involves operating in a less stressful working environment than a sommelier might face in a restaurant, dealing with the sometimes sexist, even obnoxious, male clientele (Almila 2019; 2021).

Artifying the Winemaker

Today, wine is centrally about marketing, and thus also how it is framed and presented by makers and sellers to different sorts of potential buyers. In mass-market,

---

2 This language in question is certainly not guilty of misogyny or sexism. However, some argue that the language is remarkably Eurocentric, based as it is upon flavours that people from certain parts of western Europe are likely to have tasted, when these flavours are not common elsewhere, and therefore the description may not make sense to people from other parts of the world (see e.g. Robinson 2021). WSET (2016: 2, our emphasis) assures the candidate of the level 3 wine exam (the last level before diploma) that while "you are not restricted to the terms [recommended by WSET to describe aroma and flavour characteristics . . .] You are, however, *strongly encouraged* to use" them in your tasting exam.

standardized wines, the figure of the "winemaker" does not feature nearly as much as it does in the universe of premium wines. The exceptional qualities of such wines can be attributed not only to the bounties of Nature and the unique location of the vineyard, but also to the capacities of the person who is singled out as the wine's creator (Karpik 2010). Historically, it has been men who have overwhelmingly been winemakers, or who have been the public face of wineries, with women's labor being much less publicly recognized (Matasar 2006).

The creative skills of the winemaker today can be constructed and presented along various lines. They may be construed as a "scientist," equipped with new technologies like stainless steel tanks for fermentation. Such a presentation trades upon wider masculinist stereotypes of the male scientist. Alternatively, the winemaker may be presented as an "artist," someone who imposes their creative vision on vines, grapes, soil, and so on (Inglis 2019a).

In the Western tradition, "art" is made by a certain type of person, an "artist." This is a person who has for long stretches of time been understood to be characteristically male. To be a real artist is not merely to be a skilled craftsman (Joy 2022), another stereotypically male figure, nor is virtuosity enough in itself for the realisation of true "art" (Sizorn 2019). In the medieval world, a craftsman worked for a guild, while the "artist" became an independent cultural producer through multiple processes of artification stretching across the early modern period and into the nineteenth century (Shapiro and Heinich 2012). The artist carries with him a kind of singularity of creative vision (Bajard 2019), while the craftsman remains loyal to the conventions and traditions of the craft (Kapferer 2014). To claim the status of an artist is to claim the right to autonomous creative freedom, historically the privilege of men.[3]

So, when a winemaker is referred to as an "artist," their winemaking work defined as artistic labour, and the end-products presented as works of art (or at least as being somehow art-like), longstanding gendered ideas of art and artists are projected onto wine, a world which was already strongly gendered.[4] This double gendering of wine has ramifications for women in that world.

---

3 Yet the demands of commerce might conflict with this claim and must be managed accordingly (Crane 2019). The role of the artist involves managing the paradoxical nature of art in the modern world: "[w]hile art has become increasingly commodified through its use as a promotional tool, its value rests on the disavowal of its commodity status" (Negrin 2015: 427).

4 Yet the projection of the categories "art" and "artist" onto wine faces many resistances. The ways in which wine is institutionalized, especially in Europe, contradict the very idea of the free "artist." Legal protection within the EU is dependent on rules governing the extent of geographical areas, the types of grape varietals, and legitimated production techniques (Inglis 2019b). Especially in the most prestigious areas of France, those usually associated with the finest of "fine wines" such as Bordeaux and Bourgogne, *terroir*, grapes, and specific winemaking techniques are at the heart of how the wine will taste and develop. Although there is great skill involved in winemaking, it is a minority position to say that there is an artist involved, and not much marketing tries to go down that rhetorical path. Such a

Over the last 40 years, more women have developed viable careers as winemakers, partly through taking up opportunities afforded to them by university degrees in oenology and wine management. As a result, some women have excelled in making high quality, high prestige wines (Matasar 2006; Brenner 2007). But when the role and persona of winemaker is subjected to artifying strategies, rendering it equivalent to "artist," it is more likely that such a situation will benefit male winemakers, because they fit more easily into the category of "artistic genius" than do their female counterparts. Women typically have to work extremely hard, and harder than men, to gain any kind of recognition in the wine world (Matasar 2006; Brenner 2007; Almila 2019). Adding to that already existing disadvantage, they are also likely to struggle to claim the elevated status of singular creative talent and to bask in the glow of an artistic aura (Buurman 2017). As women struggle to win some status and legitimation as winemakers anyway, they are likely doubly to struggle to win recognition as artist winemakers, in part because of the masculinist bias built into that category over several centuries.

A central conventional feature of post-Renaissance Western art, especially painting, is that the (male) artist puts their name in the form of a signature somewhere on the artwork, thus proving its authenticity with a stamp of (self-)approval. The signature on the canvas implies a singularity of artistic vision and expresses that individual's charisma (Passebois-Ducros et al. 2015). In marketing terms, especially regarding products that can be eaten or drunk, the signature on the label or packaging may also stand as a guarantee of quality. This is not a wholly new development in wine terms, for the family name of producers or merchants was a marker of quality placed on labels (for how this worked in, for example, Champagne, see Guy 2003). Such a "signature" was not very much akin to an artist's moniker written on a canvas.

An artifying innovation of the last quarter of the twentieth century was the deployment of the signatures of individual wine professionals on labels as if they were, or at least were like, artists' signatures (Negrin 2015). The wine is therefore identified as the result of a creative endeavor, while the person signing the bottle was singularized by being presented as akin to an artist, the kind of person who signs the results of their creative labour. This is certainly the case if the signatory is a winemaker. But if they are a consultant who advises winemakers how to create wines – the most famous instance being that of the globally-recognized French consultant Michel Rolland – the signature on the bottle is less a claim to artistic merit and more a traditional assertion of quality level, the wine being made in a legitimated "signature style" combining craftsmanship together with scientific knowhow. In such a case, the older notion of the merchant's signature blends with the persona of winemaker as scientist. In both this and the case of the signature of the winemaker-as-artist, the writing of the name implies

---

positioning is probably more likely in the less regulated and less tradition-bound countries of the so-called New World, such as Australia and Chile (Beverland and Luxton 2005).

masculine notions of mastery. This is probably why female winemakers rarely deploy signatures as part of their marketing armamentarium.[5]

The scientist and the artist are not the only ways winemakers can self-present or be presented by others. Another possible framing is that of the "peasant," strongly rooted symbolically in the earth of the vineyard, and a custodian of long-standing winemaking traditions (Inglis 2019a).

There are (at least) two branches in this way of thinking. On the one hand, the peasant can be presented as a patriarch, exercising traditionalistic lordship over the land. On the other hand, they can be formulated as a midwife to the fecund earth, a caring and sympathetic aide to Nature. The feminized, empathetic role of midwife stands in contrast to the masculinist persona of the artist: midwives do not make art, they facilitate the emergence of new life. Winemaking as midwifery also implies that the winemaker is subservient to the greatest artist of all, Nature, which is sometimes presented in feminized form, as Mother Nature (Inglis 2019a). The midwife symbolism suggests a non-patriarchal way of understanding oenological creation, devoid of the masculinist biases of the artist imaginary. And yet, given that the midwife is also a role that both male and female winemakers can take on, the taking up of it has gendered imbalances too. While females may struggle to be accepted as artists, no such stigma seems to attach to male winemakers taking on the guise of the midwife.

Artifying Wine Labels

If winemakers can be subject to artifying strategies that are gendered, so too can be the labels on the bottles that winemakers labour to fill.

A wine label is a device for facilitating communication between two realms, that of wine producers and sellers, and that of consumers (Eden 2011). It may simplify some types of information while retaining the complexity of others. It offers multiple cues and hints meant to channel a consumer's choice, such as displaying awards won by the wine, verbal descriptions of provenance and taste, and visual imagery meant to connote certain ideas, such as luxury, tradition, or fun (Allen and Germov 2010).

A wine label thus can be a relatively complex text that can transform the "quotidian need" for a glass of wine "into imagined extravagances" (Finkelstein and Quiazon 2007: 20). Labels – especially the more aesthetically ambitious varieties – can transfer their own aesthetic qualities onto the wine in the bottle, suggesting many different

---

5 There are of course exceptions to this tendency. For example, winemaker Gina Gallo's name and signature appear on the labels of her family company's "Signature" series of wines. As a member of one of the world's most powerful winemaking families, hitherto dominated by male members, she presumably possesses the inherited capitals – social, cultural, and professional – to be confident enough to lend her signature to wines, as male winemakers more typically do.

sensibilities such as sublimity, superiority, earthiness, or subtlety (Finkelstein and Quiazon 2007). If the label has gendered elements, these are projected onto, and in some senses into, the wine.

One of the most basic elements on a label are the names, variously of the winery, or the winemaker, or of the specific wine. Naming strategies are intended to connote certain ideas – ranging from tradition to edginess – and are often deeply gendered. Neethling's (2017) review of names in the South African wine industry reflects patterns to be found across the world in terms of nomenclature. Wines, wineries, and brands may be named in terms of, for example, estate owners and winemakers ("Kosie du Toit"); patriarchs, matriarchs, and other ancestors deemed worthy of commemoration ("The Eleanor Chardonnay"); relationships ("The Grandfather"); hagiographical names (real or fictional, such as "St. James" or "The Saint"); names of gods and goddesses ("Juno," "Jupiter"); and fictional characters, often female and sexualized ("Party Girl," "Wild Girl," "Lady in Red").

While some types of names are liable to be fitted together with classical and modernist art visual imagery, sexualized female names are more likely to be illustrated with pin-up pictures or illustrations akin to the style of graphic novels. Sexualized male names are practically non-existent in the world of labels. A notable and non-heterosexual exception is Californian wine currently marketed in some countries with the artist[6] Tom of Finland's erotic illustrations of male bodies on the labels.

What has been conventionally understood in the West as "art" has been used to advertise and market wine since the mid-nineteenth century. But "starting in 1944, renowned French vintner Philippe, Baron de Rothschild was the first to commission artists to design his wine labels [. . .]. Rothschild's partnerships with artists featured such luminaries as Cocteau, Chagall, Picasso and Dali [. . .]. Such branding situated Rothschild wines as daring, elegant, sensual and high value – much as the arrestingly modernist images on the bottles were" (Joy et al 2021: 25).

John Berger (1972) famously spoke of how, historically, Western visual and plastic arts express and embody ways of looking and seeing that are deeply gendered and have had a profound effect on wider forms of consciousness, including in terms of how gender is constructed. Importantly, the woman in art is constantly observing herself and conscious of this – she is both surveyor and surveyed: "Men act and women

---

6 Tom of Finland (Touko Valio Laaksonen, 1920–1991) is famous for creating highly sexualized drawn images of gay men in active, suggestive poses. Initially considered as a pornographer, sexual deviant, and criminal by mainstream Finnish society, in his later years he was consecrated as a internationally known bona fide artist, and his images were eventually legitimized as proper art, if still somewhat controversial. Less sexually explicit instances of his imagery are today used for gay-friendly marketing purposes on a range of goods, such as bedsheets. Some critics regard this sequestered imagery as redolent of cultural appropriation of queer culture, taking the edge out of Tom of Finland's work (Lehtonen n.d.). Tom of Finland-branded wine draws upon the tamed marketing imagery while residually implying that the wine carries an artist's seal of approval.

appear. Men look at women. Women watch themselves being looked at" (Berger 1972: 47). This is particularly obvious in the history of nude portraits, where the woman is the key category, existing for the male observer, for his desire and his possession: "She is not naked as she is. She is naked as the spectator sees her" (Berger 1972: 50). She is a sexually desirable object, but not sexually active herself. Given this history, uses of Western classical and modernist artistic imagery on wine labels would tend to reproduce the gender biases of that history, while extending them into an already gendered domain.

But such a situation did not play out uniformly across the world's major winemaking areas. From the 1980s onwards, the countries of the so-called New World of wine – regions outside of the "Old World" of southern and western European winemaking, most notably the Americas and Australia – became legitimated sources of higher-end wine (Inglis and Almila 2019). Some differences in the artifying strategies of wine labels could be observed between Old and New Worlds. While "the European vineyards tend [ed] to associate their product with venerated masterpieces of European art, New World vineyards embrace[d] emerging artists, often from their own countries, rather than relying solely on artists with established reputations, perhaps reflecting a desire to appeal to those with a capacity to appreciate the new" (Negrin 2015: 425).[7] As a result, artified European labels tended to draw upon the sexist imagery of the Western artistic tradition more than New World labels did. But the latter were certainly not free of gendered imagery; it just tended to be expressed in less traditionalistic aesthetic ways.

Some such visual images used on wine labels today are – depending on interpretation – either risqué or outright sexist.[8] Pin-up style drawings of attractive and enticing women on the front label may be used to target male customers, representing the supposed sexual sensuousness of the wine (Le Bel 2005). It is not just mass-market wines that contain contentious images of women, for the world of "natural" wines and hipster-ish appreciation of them are also full of these: "Adorning the high shelves

7 In Europe today, contemporary artists are collaborating with winemakers, such as in the case of Feudi di San Gregorio winery in the Italian region of Campania, whose "art expressions" feature presents the designers who create the wine labels, as well as the architects who designed the winery buildings, and visual artists, many with local backgrounds, whose work has been exhibited in the winery. Along with the artists, two "vine whisperers" are presented, but their connection to anything artistic remains unclear, focused as they are on landscape and vine heritage. By presenting such different categories of people under the label of "art," connections between heritage and artistic innovation are made, while the differences between the two realms are blurred. This sort of connection is also evoked in the rhetoric used: "Winemaking is art and this is why art is so important at Feudi di San Gregorio." See https://www.feudi.it/en (accessed February 17, 2023).
8 Not all images of women on labels have been or are sexist. In late nineteenth century Champagne, strong female icon figures, such as Queen Victoria and Jeanne d'Arc, were presented on labels for marketing purposes. In the wake of the international success of the *Veuve Clicquot* brand, the word "veuve" (widow) was used to evoke certain feminine connotations for the wine, whether the winery had anything to do with widows or not (Guy 2003; also Almila 2023).

of the world's natural wine bars are two sorts of empty bottles. There are rarities from the likes of Clos Rougeard and Pierre Overnoy. Then there are wine labels with boobs on them" (Ayscough 2020, n.p.).

The latter sorts of labels have been favoured especially by male (often French or other European) "natural" wine makers, who consider the imagery to very much belong in the realm of legitimate art, and merely express aesthetic appreciation of the female form. In the US, on the other hand, some imagery used on labels is highly sexualized, but more in line with pin-up posters than "legitimate" art traditions (see e.g. Shaw 2021; Baker 2019).

The responses of women professionals and amateurs to such labels may often be less than positive. Jas Swan of Katla Wines, a young female natural winemaker in the Mosel valley, has noted of them: "If I go to a restaurant to enjoy a bottle of wine, I'm there to have fun. I don't want to be reminded of the misogyny I encounter in the wine world" (in Ayscough 2020, n.p.).

Conclusion

When wine and art are brought together by artifying strategies, it seems that everyone wins. Winemakers have their status and prestige elevated by being compared with and likened to artists; artists whose work is used on labels, or by some other means to promote a wine, gain new kinds of visibility and recognition; the buyers and drinkers of wine can engage in pleasant aesthetic experiences. And yet the artifying of wine has all sorts of gendered elements, some more apparent and some less so. Both wine and (Western) art have been gendered for centuries, and oftentimes have been outright patriarchal in nature. While limited reconstructions of them in more egalitarian directions have occurred in recent decades, the profoundly sexist histories of both domains still inform endeavors to make wine seem to be like art. The category of artist is a longstanding masculinist one, as is the idea of his signature expressing the nature of his singular genius. Deploying visual art on labels often brings with it the history of sexism in Western art. Not all artifying mechanisms are patriarchal, but many of them are, at least implicitly. Those engaged in such activities would do well to be mindful of this fact, especially if they are otherwise committed to the creation of more egalitarian and diverse social relations in the realms of their own professional practice.

References

Allen, M.P. and Germov, J. (2010). Judging taste and creating value: The cultural consecration of Australian wines. *Journal of Sociology* 47(1): 35–51.
Almila, A. 2019. Wine, Women and Globalization: The Case of Female Sommeliers. In *The Globalization of Wine*, edited by D. Inglis and A. Almila. London: Bloomsbury.

Almila, A. 2021. A Wine Flight of Gendered Sociologies: Vignettes of (Apparent) Trivialities. *Journal of Cultural Analysis and Social Change* 6(2): 11.

Almila, A. 2022. Wine and the Gendered Self-Gift: Conceptual Considerations. In *Wine and the Gift*, edited by P. Howland. London: Routledge.

Almila, A. 2023. Paris and Champagne, or 'fashion' and 'champagne' – Parallels, Connections, Comparisons. In *Drinks in Vogue: Exploring the Changing Worlds of Fashions and Beverages*, edited by D. Inglis and H.K. Ho. London: Routledge.

Almila, A. and Inglis, D. 2022. Threats of Pleasure and Chaos: Wine and Gendered Social Order. In *The Routledge Handbook of Wine and Culture*, edited by S. Charters, M. Demossier, J. Dutton, G. Harding, J. Smith Maguire, D. Marks, and T. Unwin. London: Routledge.

Atkin, T., Nowak, L. and Garcia, R. 2007a. Women Wine Consumers: Information Search and Retailing Implications. *International Journal of Wine Business Research* 19(4): 327–339.

Atkin, T.S., Garcia, R. and Lockshin, L.S. 2007b. A multidimensional study of the diffusion of a discontinuous innovation. *Australasian Marketing Journal* 14(2): 17–33.

Ayscough, A. 2020. Natural wine labels on the borderline. *Wine Business International*, December 16. Accessed February 17, 2023. https://www.wine-business-international.com/wine/general/natural-wine-labels-borderline

Bajard, F. 2019. The Unfinished Artification of Ceramics in France: Reversing Stigma and Creating a New Artistic Norm. *Cultural Sociology* 13(3): 276–292.

Baker, J. 2019. Silly Wines & Sexist Labels. *Bloom Magazine*, March 18. Accessed February 17, 2023. https://www.magbloom.com/2019/03/silly-wines-sexist-labels/

Barber, N. and Almanza, B.A. 2006. Influence of wine packaging on consumers' decision to purchase. *Journal of Foodservice Business Research* 9(4): 83–98.

Barber, N., Almanza, B.A. and Donovan, J.R. 2006. Motivational Factors of Gender, Income and Age on Selecting a Bottle of Wine. *International Journal of Wine Marketing* 18(3): 218–232.

Barber, N., Ismail, J. and Taylor, D.C. 2007. Label fluency and consumer self-confidence. *Journal of Wine Research* 18(2): 73–85.

Berger, J. 1972. *Ways of Seeing*. London: Penguin.

Beverland, M. and Luxton, S. 2005. Managing integrated marketing communication (IMC) through strategic decoupling: How luxury wine firms retain brand leadership while appearing to be wedded to the past. *Journal of Advertising* 34(4): 103–116.

Brenner, D. 2007. *Women of the Vine: Inside the World of Women Who Make, Taste, and Enjoy Wine*. Hoboken NJ: Wiley.

Bryant, L. and Garnham, B. 2014. The Embodiment of Women in Wine: Gender Inequality and Gendered Inscriptions of the Working Body in a Corporate Wine Organization. *Gender, Work and Organization* 21 (5): 411–426.

Buurman, N. 2017. Engendering Exhibitions: The Politics of Gender in Negotiating Curatorial Authorship. *Journal of Curatorial Studies* 6(1): 115–138.

Callen, A. 1985. Sexual Division of Labor in the Arts and Crafts Movement. *Woman's Art Journal* 5(2): 1–6.

Charters, S. 2012. The Organisation of Champagne: A Historical and Structural Introduction. In *The Business of Champagne: A Delicate Balance*, edited by S. Charters. Abingdon: Routledge.

Colman, T. 2010. *Wine Politics: How Governments, Environmentalists, Mobsters, and Critics Influence the Wines We Drink*. Berkeley: University of California Press.

Crane, D. 2019. Fashion and Artification in the French Luxury Fashion Industry. *Cultural Sociology* 13(3): 293–304.

De Angelis, M., Amatulli, C. and Zaretti, M. 2020. The Artification of Luxury: How Art Can Affect Perceived Durability and Purchase Intention of Luxury Products. In *Sustainable Luxury and Craftsmanship*, edited by M.Á. Gardetti and I. Coste-Manière. Berlin: Springer.

Demossier, M. 2020. *Burgundy: The Global Story of Terroir*. Oxford: Berghahn.

Eden, S. 2011. Food labels as boundary objects: How consumers make sense of organic and functional foods. *Public Understanding of Science* 20(2): 179–194.

Finkelstein, J. and Quiazon, R. 2007. Liquid images: Viewing the wine label. *Journal of Hospitality and Tourism Management* 14(1): 17–23.

Grohmann, B. 2022. Artification and Social Responsibility in the Context of Fine Wine: Opus One The Future of Luxury Brands. In *Artification and Sustainability*, edited by A. Joy. Berlin: De Gruyter.

Guy, C.M. 2003. *When Champagne Became French: Wine and the Making of a National Identity*. London: Johns Hopkins University Press.

Howland, P.J. 2013. Distinction by proxy: The democratization of fine wine. *Journal of Sociology* 49(2–3): 325–340.

Hughson, J. 2019. The Artification of Football: A Sociological Reconsideration of the 'Beautiful Game'. *Cultural Sociology* 13(3): 305–320.

Inglis, D. 2019a. Mutating and Contested Languages of Wine: Heard on the Grapevine. In *Handbook of the Changing World Language Map*, edited by S.D. Brunn and R. Kehrein. Berlin: Springer.

Inglis, D. 2019b. Wine Globalization: Longer-Term Dynamics and Contemporary Patterns. In *The Globalization of Wine*, edited by D. Inglis and A. Almila. London: Bloomsbury.

Inglis, D. 2021. Brexit barbarization? The UK leaving the EU as de-civilizing trend. *Journal of Sociology* 57(1): 59–76.

Inglis, D. and Almila, A. (eds) 2019. *The Globalization of Wine*. London: Bloomsbury.

Inglis, D. and Ho, H.K. 2022. Beyond white: On wine and ethnicity. In *The Routledge Handbook of Wine and Culture*, edited by S. Charters, M. Demossier, J. Dutton, G. Harding, J. Smith Maguire, D. Marks and T. Unwin. London: Routledge.

Inglis, D. and Hughson, J. 2005. *The Sociology of Art: Ways of Seeing*. Basingstoke: Palgrave Macmillan.

Jones, G.M. 2019. New Magic as an Artification Movement: From Speech Event to Change Process. *Cultural Sociology* 13(3): 321–337.

Johnson, T.E. and Bastian, S.E.P. 2007. A Preliminary Study of the Relationship between Australian Wine Consumers' Wine Expertise and Their Wine Purchasing and Consumption Behaviour. *Australian Journal of Grape and Wine Research* 13: 186–197.

Joy, A. 2022. Artification and Sustainability: Foundational Pillars of the Luxury Worlds of Art, Fashion, and Wine. In *The Future of Luxury Brands: Artification and Sustainability*, edited by A. Joy. Berlin: De Gruyter.

Joy, A., LaTour, K., Charters, S., Grohmann, B. and Peña, C. 2021. The Artification of Wine: Lessons from the Fines Wines of Bordeaux and Burgundy. *Arts and the Market* 11(1): 24–39.

Kapferer, J.-N. 2014. The Artification of Luxury: From Artisans to Artists. *Business Horizons* 57: 371–380.

Karpik, L. 2010. *Valuing the Unique: The Economics of Singularities*. Princeton: Princeton University Press.

Kosut, M. 2014. The Artification of Tattoo: Transformations within a Cultural Field. *Cultural Sociology* 8(2): 142–158.

Krull, E. 1989. *Women in Art*. London: Studio Vista.

Le Bel, J.L. 2005. Sensory, snob, and sex appeals in wine advertising. *International Journal of Wine Marketing* 17(3): 67–78.

Lehtonen, E. n.d. Antti Kauppinen from Tom of Finland Society: "Vanilla patriarchy has squeezed the edge out of Tom of Finland". *Finnish Institute UK + Ireland*. Accessed July 26, 2023. https://www.fininst.uk/events/antti-kauppinen-from-tom-of-finland-society-vanilla-patriarchy-has-squeezed-the-edge-out-of-tom-of-finland/

Marin, V., Barra, C. and Noyano, J. 2022. Artification strategies to improve luxury perceptions: the role of adding an artist name. *Journal of Product & Brand Management* 31(3): 496–505.

Massi, M. and Turrini, A. 2020. When Fashion Meets Art: The Artification of Luxury Fashion Brands. In *The Artification of Luxury Fashion Brands Synergies, Contaminations, and Hybridizations*, edited by M. Massi and A. Turrini. Basingstoke: Palgrave MacMillan.

Matasar, A.B. 2006. *Women of Wine: The Rise of Women in the Global Wine Industry*. Berkeley: University of California Press.

McCoy, E. 2006. *The Emperor of Wine: The Rise of Robert M. Parker, Jr., and the Reign of American Taste*. New York: Harper Collins.

Naukkarinen, O. 2012. Variations on Artification. *Contemporary Aesthetics* 4(Special): Article 2.

Naukkarinen, O. and Saito, Y. 2012. Introduction. *Contemporary Aesthetics* 4(Special): Article 1.

Neethling, B. 2017. The Role of Anthroponymic Commemoration on Wine Labels in South Africa. *Names: A Journal of Onomastics* 65(2): 65–77.

Negrin, L. 2015. Art and Fine Wine: A Case Study in the Aestheticization of Consumption. *Continuum* 29(3): 419–433.

Nossiter, J. 2010. *Liquid Memory: Why Wine Matters*. London: Atlantic Books.

Passebois-Ducros, J., Trinquecoste, J.-F. and Pichon, F. 2015. Stratégies d'artification dans le domaine du luxe Le cas des vins de prestige. *Décisions Marketing* 80(spécial): 109–124.

Proust, S. 2019. Portrait of the Theatre Director as an Artist. *Cultural Sociology* 13(3): 338–353.

Remus, E.A. 2014. Tippling Ladies and the Making of Consumer Culture: Gender and Public Space in 'Finde-Siècle' Chicago. *The Journal of American History* 101(3): 751–777.

Ritchie, C. 2009. The Culture of Wine Buying in the UK off-Trade. *International Journal of Wine Business Research* 21(3): 194–211.

Robinson, J. 2021. The Evolving Language of Wine. *JancisRobinson.com*, June 5. Accessed February 17, 2023. https://www.jancisrobinson.com/articles/evolving-language-wine

Saito, Y. 2012. Everyday Aesthetics and Artification. *Contemporary Aesthetics* 4(Special): Article 5.

Saladino, E. 2021. What Do We Mean When We Say 'Fine Wine'? *Wine Enthusiast*, August 12. Accessed February 16, 2023. https://www.winemag.com/2021/12/08/fine-wine-meaning/

Shapiro, R. 2004. The Aesthetics of Institutionalization: Breakdancing in France. *The Journal of Arts Management, Law, and Society* 33(4): 316–335.

Shapiro, R. 2019. Artification as Process. *Cultural Sociology* 13(3) 265–275.

Shapiro, R. and Heinich, N. 2012. When is Artification? *Contemporary Aesthetics* 4(Special): Article 8.

Shaw, L. 2021. ICP upholds decision over sexist wine label. *The Drink Business*, May 10. Accessed February 17, 2023. https://www.thedrinksbusiness.com/2021/05/icp-upholds-decision-over-sexist-wine-label/

Shiner, L. 2012. Artification, Fine Art, and the Myth of 'the Artist'. *Contemporary Aesthetics* 4(Special): Article 4.

Sizorn, M. 2019. The Artification of Trapeze Acts: A New Paradigm for Circus Arts. *Cultural Sociology* 13(3): 354–370.

Teil, G. 2012. No Such Thing as Terroir?: Objectivities and the Regimes of Existence of Objects. *Science, Technology and Human Values* 37: 478–505.

Thach, L. 2009. Wine 2.0 – The next phase of wine marketing? Exploring US winery adoption of wine 2.0 components. *Journal of Wine Research* 20(2): 143–157.

Thach, L. 2012. Time for wine? Identifying differences in wine-drinking occasions for male and female wine consumers. *Journal of Wine Research* 23(2): 134–154.

Tomasi, G. 2012. On Wines as Works of Art. *Wineworld: New Essays on Wine, Taste, Philosophy and Aesthetics* 51: 155–174.

Vihma, S. 2012. Artification for Well-Being: Institutional Living as a Special Case. *Contemporary Aesthetics* 4 (Special): Article 13.

Walby, S. 1991. *Theorizing Patriarchy*. Oxford: Blackwell.

Wolff, J. 2000. The Feminine in Modern Art. *Theory, Culture and Society* 17(6): 33–53.

WSET. 2016. *Understanding Wines: Explaining Style and Quality*. An accompaniment to WSET Level 3 Award in Wines. London: Wine & Spirit Education Trust.

Pierre Ly and Cynthia Howson

16 The Rise of Chinese Fine Wine Through Institutional Innovation: Foreign Partnerships, Domestic Entrepreneurs, and Sustainability Constraints

Introduction

In China, winemakers, farmers, entrepreneurs, and a host of connected stakeholders have to innovate to overcome a variety of constraints. First, the global wine industry continues to favor European roots, not only in the origin of grapes and wines, but among the most visible producers, corporate executives, sommeliers, wine writers, scholars, and even consumers. Second, regulatory challenges include inconsistent and unpredictable implementation of rules around intellectual property, water access, and, separately, food safety. This is a two-pronged challenge because producers have to innovate to secure key inputs and protect their wines from counterfeiting, but they also face the uphill battle of overcoming international prejudice against Chinese products. Quite simply, any scandal in any industry in China can spur questions about the legitimacy of a specific wine. Finally, although wine demands less water than coal or competing agricultural products, any large-scale investment represents a significant demand on a dangerously scarce resource. We use Frances Cleaver's (2001) notion of institutional bricolage to demonstrate the ways in which Chinese wineries innovate, adapt, and overcome often overwhelming social and regulatory constraints. Our research is informed by a total of approximately six months of multi-method fieldwork between 2013 and 2018 in eight Chinese wine regions (see Howson and Ly 2020) as well as periodic ongoing communication with interlocutors on social media.

We begin this chapter with an overview of the Chinese wine industry, paying particular attention to the discrepancy between Chinese wine history and China's reputation in the international wine community. Next, we show how Chinese partnerships with multinational corporations have facilitated opportunities for local producers and employees through coopetition, ensuring that the majority of production, ownership, and, in many ways, technical expertise, remained and were increasingly Chinese. For small producers, a relative lack of capital makes it especially difficult to build and maintain credibility in the face of real institutional constraints as well as anti-Chinese prejudice. In section four, we show that even under-resourced homegrown producers are able to build credibility through institutional bricolage, by build-

Pierre Ly, University of Puget Sound
Cynthia Howson, University of Washington Tacoma

https://doi.org/10.1515/9783110783933-016

ing regional agreements, leveraging trusted vendors in the online marketplace, and developing personal relationships with personalized branding. Section five highlights the role of artification as a key element of institutional scaffolding in the development of a trusted Chinese wine brand. Unfortunately, the exponential growth of a new industry is rarely ecologically sustainable. Although wine requires less water than competing industries, it thrives with irrigation in often extremely dry regions, where the tradeoff is between much needed economic development and a simply unsustainable demand for water. Here again, producers use institutional bricolage, combining regulatory solutions with informal workarounds to maintain capacity.

China Became a Major Producer in Ways that were Long Ignored by the Wine Industry

At the beginning of our research in 2013, China was already a top-ten wine producing country by volume (OIV 2021) and several premium wines had secured international awards, yet most foreigners in the industry were dismissive or entirely unaware of its existence. Long before international attention was paid to Chinese wine, investors were keenly aware of China's growing consumer market and of the role of extremely high-end luxury goods in signaling wealth and social status. Since 2013, this conspicuous consumption of luxury wine (often in the form of gifts from government officials) dropped significantly following Xi Jinping's anti-corruption efforts (Kjellgren 2019; Mustacich 2015). Over the last decade, the Chinese wine market normalized, helped by the increasing availability of wines from around the world at competitive prices, and the rise of consumers seeking good taste and value, rather than luxury.

> Despite this rising interest in wine and an optimistic discourse by wine importers and merchants, one big challenge for the industry is that wine remains a tiny fraction of alcoholic beverage consumption in China. Wine has not put a dent into the long standing domination of beer, by far the most widely consumed, and baijiu (grain spirit) (Li 2015a). This is not only true by volume, but also by revenue. Indeed, the wine segment represents a very small part of revenue in the alcoholic drinks market, compared to beer and spirits (Statista 2022). According to winemaker, professor, and writer Li Demei, for Chinese people, wine has never been a necessity, and has struggled to develop, even despite government encouragement as it sought to preserve grain for food (Li 2015a). Still, in spite of these challenges, China's wine market has seen impressive growth and there is ample room for more.

Meanwhile, lesser known to the rest of the world, China has been a wine producing country since the now-giant state-owned winery, Changyu, was founded in 1892. Chinese universities have engaged in grape breeding and wine-related research in universities for many decades. But it was not until the late 1990s that investments started to pick up in wine regions around the country and policies to regulate quality began to develop (Li and Bardají 2017). This is crucial for an emerging region because the climates, cultures, and economic environments of China's wine-growing regions are as diverse as the country itself and several promising wine regions are home to historically marginalized ethnic minority communities. While Shandong is wealthy and humid on the East coast, Ningxia is an economically isolated province with a significant Muslim minority and a desert climate. It would be easy to obscure what is distinctive about Ningxia if there were a single image of "Chinese" wine. For this reason, individual wineries and their surrounding communities have sought to ensure that the particularities of their environment are reflected in the stories of their wines though informal as well as regulatory innovation.

Production was long dominated by a few large, state-owned brands, like Changyu, Great Wall, and Dynasty, who were better known for quantity than quality. But over the past decade, a wide diversity of producers has entered the market, expanding not only the number of premium wines but a wide array of quality wines at varied price points and in diverse styles. When a Chinese red wine won Best Bordeaux Varietal over 10 Pounds at the 2011 Decanter World Wine Award, the international wine world began to take notice. Since then, many more Chinese wines have earned international awards and praise from critics, although award-winning producers continued to fight mistrust and even accusations of fraud due to their country of origin.

Within China, the development of the wine industry beyond large enterprises has been inextricably linked to economic development efforts in economically isolated western regions (Mustacich 2015; Howson and Ly 2020). China's export-led economic growth has long been biased in favor of the east coast, but starting in 2000, the government launched a Western Development Program to address regional inequality and promote growth in the west (Lai 2002). In western wine regions, such as Ningxia, the wine industry has been leveraged to bring jobs not only in agriculture and wine production, but also in tourism. Certainly, international awards have boosted the reputation of individual winners and the surrounding wine region. But it is important to note that most Chinese wine is not produced for the international community at all. The majority of Chinese wine is not only consumed domestically,[1] but reflects yet another important assumption in the global wine industry: most foreigners we encountered in wine asked about the success of exports, explicitly equating success and quality with a winery's sales in Europe, the US, or Australia. This (unconsciously or otherwise) perpetuates the notion that non-Chinese or even white consumers are the arbiters of quality.

---

[1] For discussions of economic, political, and historical aspects of the Chinese wine industry, see Mustacich (2015), N. Wang (2019), and Howson and Ly (2020).

Foreign Wine Multinationals in China: Branding, Coopetition and Building the Idea of Fine Chinese Wine

Multinational corporations (MNCs) and foreign investors have long flocked to China in hopes of accessing its rapidly growing market, so it is not surprising that they wield influence in the burgeoning local wine industry. As in other industries, until 2004, China protected Chinese ownership and industrial development in wine by requiring foreign companies to work in joint partnership with Chinese (especially state-owned) companies. This way, behemoth luxury brands like LVMH (Moet Hennessy Louis Vuitton) gained an early foothold in the Chinese wine consumer market, but also contributed to the development of the local wine industry in several key ways: name recognition, reputation for quality, and technical expertise all contribute to the development and recognition of fine wine made in China.

As the Chinese wine market grew, foreign wineries began to invest in making their own wine in China. The benefits of such projects are many. Although restrictions on foreign ownership were lifted in 2004, every major winery has continued to engage in some form of joint partnership. In each case, partnership with a state-owned firm has provided crucial access to grapes (including help coordinating agricultural labor) as well as key political resources to negotiate with local authorities. The famous Moet project in Yunnan is co-owned with a 20% share by local state-owned winery Shangri-la, a relatively absent partner that was necessary for LVMH to lease the land it needed. In Shandong province, Lafite partnered with China's CITIC International Investment Group, a state-owned construction company. Here, Lafite gained crucial access to local bureaucracy (government support for land, permits, etc.), without having any ties to a winery. In 2018, CITIC sold its 30% stake and Lafite was set to become the sole owner. By then, the needed benefits of the partnership had been achieved (J. Z. Wang 2019). By making its own wine in China, Lafite further cements its own reigning status among Chinese consumers as the best, most famous wine in the world. Meanwhile, Lafite's Domaine de Long Dai helps to continue establishing the idea of world class Chinese fine wine.

In a luxury market, the most opulent and distinctive product must be expensive and otherwise flashy. Since its first release, Ao Yun, Moet's top shelf red wine from Yunnan, the company has been quick to market it next to the world's finest wines. It has been the fine wine trading platform Liv Ex since 2016, and the 2018 vintage became the first Chinese wine to be released via the Place de Bordeaux. In professional reviews by The Wine Advocate or James Suckling, Ao Yun achieved scores and praise usually reserved for the world's finest wines (Liv-ex 2022; Suckling 2022). By investing in China and creating Ao Yun, LVMH has been able to use its branding and distribution power to place a Chinese wine as part of the global fine wine elite. Lafite's own

Chinese wine, Domaine de Long Dai, released in 2019, was also well received by critics and ambitiously priced at well over 300 US dollars a bottle (Qin 2019).

A concern here is that if premium wine were perceived as dependent on not only foreigners but globally influential power brokers and the consistent presence of foreign expertise, this could fundamentally undermine the reputation of legitimately Chinese wine. It has therefore been crucial that collaboration with foreign companies and experts represents only one component of a developing sector in an emerging region. Over the past 10 to 20 years, foreign wineries have made significant profit in various Chinese regions, but local communities, governments, and researchers have retained or expanded the role of Chinese entrepreneurship, ownership, and influence in Chinese wine.

While both LVMH and Lafite send a few key foreign experts from their group who work full time on-site for extended periods, most of the staff is Chinese. During its first year, Lafite's project in Shandong had a French winemaker and a French intern working on disease prevention, but the majority of work was undertaken by Chinese colleagues. Lafite's current head winemaker in Shandong, Denise Cosentino, is Italian, but has a long experience living and making wine in China with Chinese colleagues, including in contexts where little English is spoken. In Yunnan, LVMH's winery is run by a French manager, with a few guest foreign experts. But they work with a team of Chinese winemakers, in addition to vineyard managers who play a key role to supervise local farmers. In sum, while these projects are under the name of big French names, their products are wines made by Chinese people, and grown on China's land. These are genuinely new, fully Chinese fine wines, and not mere replicas of French wines.

What locals learn on the job benefits the Chinese wine industry more broadly, as employees often move on to other wineries, or wine jobs like marketing and distribution, with highly marketable skills. Beyond this direct development of human capital, villagers also communicate, with some continuing to produce grapes directly for sale to the local state owned winery, and sharing information with growers from other villages who make their own wines for a market of bars and restaurants for tourists. Farmers with short-term grape contracts use these broader economic changes to demand higher prices or simply work with other buyers. Of course, farmers have far less bargaining power in a saturated market like Shandong than in a rapidly changing region like Ningxia or one where the winery depends more on direct relationships with farmers, as we saw in Shaanxi.

As they enter the Chinese market, foreign wine MNCs do not primarily displace locally made products in the way that, say, a well-respected foreign car manufacturer takes market share away from less experienced local makers. Instead, wine MNCs in China engage in coopetition with local producers, thereby contributing to a group effort to build the idea and perceived legitimacy of fine Chinese wine. In many industries, coopetition can play a key role in global industrial upgrading, as competing firms benefit from cooperating in the pursuit of a common goal (Luo 2007). But it is particularly salient in the wine industry, where marketing is often tied to the perceived quality of a given region (Dana et al. 2013). Equally important, for developing wine regions, "catching up" is directly bound up with information sharing, access to foreign expertise, and access to "social technologies" (Cusmano, Morrison, and Rabellotti 2010). For foreign firms, such transfers are inherently costly, so research that seeks to identify the limits of industrial cooperation notes the temporary nature of most joint ventures, emphasizing the point at which technology transfer is more costly than the benefits of partnership (Bontempi and Prodi 2009; Brandt and Thun 2010). Indeed, if MNCs end up strengthening their local competitors to the point that they are no longer needed, the strategy may have gone too far. The ways in which China has strongly incentivized foreign companies to share technology in exchange for market access is well known and sometimes controversial.

In the case of wine, corporate collaboration can more easily remain mutually beneficial for the simple reason that technical know-how involves virtually no true industry secrets (Howson and Ly 2018). While some wineries do not disclose all their practices to consumers (especially the use of controversial additives or technologies), how wine is made, and what sets fine wine producers apart, is largely public knowledge. The exact blend of the Chandon sparkling wine may not be disclosed, but the process of how fine sparkling wine is made is no secret to anyone. Moreover, any Chinese winemaker who spends time working in winemaking at Chandon Ningxia learns not only from details about quality sparkling wine production, but also from management and marketing approaches used by LVMH. This is a common way that foreign direct investment benefits recipient economies by transferring technology, knowledge, and skills that spill over to emerging home-grown producers. Indeed, the vast majority of fine wines are produced by small and medium wineries whose reputations and credibility must be established from scratch.

How Homegrown Producers Build Credibility Despite International Prejudice and Inconsistent Regulation at Home

A major challenge for Chinese fine wine producers has been to build credibility, given the prior poor or inexistent reputation of wine made in China. While foreign-invested partnerships benefit from the foreign brand's existing name recognition and reputation for quality, local wine entrepreneurs must start from scratch, with creativity, trust, and more direct relationships with potential consumers. That said, individual stories can be powerful. Communication between individual experts and direct communication with the media have facilitated a dramatic shift in the production and public perception of quality Chinese wine. Chinese firms often struggle to overcome the reputational effects of inadequate regulation and law enforcement, particularly in the areas of food safety and intellectual property. Chinese fine wine producers have struggled to signal quality and authenticity, not only because China is an as-yet-untrusted emerging wine region but because wine is both a luxury good (subject to counterfeit trade) and an agricultural product (subject to food safety standards). Yet, fine wine has developed and gained the recognition of experts and trade publications both in China and abroad. Again, despite limitations in formal institutions and inconsistent regulatory enforcement (Allen, Qian, and Qian 2005; Yao and Yueh 2009), homegrown producers have used institutional bricolage, combining individual workarounds, the development of informal norms, and collaboration, as well as advocating for (and often receiving) changes in policy that follow a rapidly changing sector.

In fine wine production, a key issue for producers is to signal quality, and the problem is especially acute in a new production area that consumers have not yet learned to associate with high quality. This has been a long-standing challenge for Chinese wineries (Robinson 2017). There is a common stereotype about terrible mass market state-owned wines in supermarkets. But in the international wine market, even premium Chinese wine is suspect due to stereotype as well as real limits in regulation. Serious wine consumers worry about fake labels or inferior quality wine being sold in high-end foreign bottles (Muhammad et al. 2014). Wine counterfeiting is a global issue, but a significant number of the technological advancements aimed at tackling it have been developed in response to the inadequacies of China's regulations regarding intellectual property (Kehoe 2013). While the cases that make headlines are those affecting imported wines, domestic fine wine producers have also faced intellectual property issues (Boyce 2015) and several producers we met have encountered copycat versions of their labels or other threats to their brands. With regular media coverage of these issues, Chinese wine lovers may be afraid of losing face in the event that they buy fraudulent or poor quality wine, leading them to question the credibility of wine in China.

The image of Chinese wine can even be affected by the country's food safety issues, even when those are completely unrelated. A few months after a 2008 Grace Vineyard became the first Chinese wine served on a major airline, China made global news for a case of contaminated powdered milk that caused hundreds of food poisoning cases and even some infant deaths. As a result, the airline almost canceled the wine deal, prompting winery CEO Judy Chan to convince them that the winery had no connection to milk, and even offer to send samples to Europe for testing. Here, it is worth imagining a similar case in a different country. This is equivalent to canceling a contract with an American wine during the swine flu outbreak or a contract with a British product at the height of the Mad Cow Disease. In another example, a report found exceedingly high pesticide residues in the wines of state-owned Changyu winery, causing its stock to plummet overnight (China Daily 2012). Consumers mocked the winery's reponse that one would have to drink implausibly large quantities of wine for any harm to occur from pesticide residue (G. Yang 2013, 15). But the notion that excess pesticide use in one winery or region reflects poorly on all producers in a country the size of Europe is quite remarkable.

While there have been efforts to close loopholes to existing regulations of wine production, apply food safety measures to wine, and better regulate quality (C. Yang et al. 2022), Chinese wineries had to find their own ways to signal quality in an environment of low consumer trust. Here, we will focus on three types of successful strategies: working with trusted online retail shops, collaboration with reputed distributors, and public relations campaigns including personal stories and expert endorsements. Each of these is an informal solution to a partly regulatory problem, but they also require both formal and informal rules, agreements, and even technologies.

First, Chinese wineries have used authenticated online marketplaces and direct-to-consumer sales to reduce the number of intermediaries and increase consumer trust. Thanks to efforts by online retail platforms that grappled with credibility at first, Chinese consumers have come to trust online retail (Kumar 2018). Despite having been sued more than once for participating in the trade of counterfeit luxury products (Raymond 2015), Alibaba (the umbrella corporation for Taobao and TMall) became the largest retailer in the world (Goenka 2016). By 2018, China represented 42% of the global e-commerce market (Smith 2018). China's e-commerce infrastructure is incredibly efficient. It is even accessible to very small businesses, whose owners can set up stores on WeChat and sell much of their inventory through personal contacts and referrals. Bigger companies can afford to pay for higher levels of security, with each platform offering their own methods for monitoring and dealing with complaints.

TMall provides a verified outlet for premium wineries to sell their products and benefit from exclusivity. The costly registration and annual deposits required to participate serve as deterrents to most scammers. Moreover, only companies that have a physical presence and follow a multi-tiered insurance and consumer protection system can open a TMall store. However, many wineries still choose to sell on Taobao, a less trustworthy and less technologically advanced platform, despite the availability of some intellectual property protection measures. While Taobao allows both consumer-to-consumer and business-to-customer business, TMall is only for the latter, which offers more guarantee of authenticity.

Second, to gain consumers' trust, Chinese fine wine producers seek partnerships with reputable wine distributors (some with foreign ownership) whose legitimacy for sales of premium imported wine is not in question. Credible major distributors like Torres, Summergate, and East Meets West each took on just one or two Chinese wineries in their large portfolio that otherwise mostly includes imported wine. They sell their small number of Chinese wines to the same hospitality and retail clients that already buy their imported wines. While wineries could decide to sell directly to consumers (and many do); they benefit from the established good reputation of their distributors, whose portfolios are known for their quality and authenticity. Chinese fine wine gets sold in spaces where wine enthusiasts are used to buying fine wines of the world.

Finally, the most successful Chinese producers of fine wine make effective use of personal stories, combined with and relayed by expert endorsements. In his study of South African wine in the UK market, Ponte and Ewert (2009) showed that the personal story is a key verification mechanism through which consumers come to recognize a wine as belonging in the top tier. With doubts about the adequacy of regulation and difficulties to gain consumers' confidence, personal stories are even more important in China than in other previously emerging wine regions. Three of China's most critically acclaimed wineries, Grace Vineyard, Silver Heights, and Kanaan, are owned and run by women whose stories have been told in countless articles and interviews. All three wineries were founded by fathers with strong relationships in industry and government, but the younger women leaders are the ones who brought the wines to national and global fame. Here, we see crucial examples of institutional bricolage, where wineries leverage sources of power and influence without being dominated by them. Each winery leveraged and benefited from: 1) some access to local government and capital; 2) foreign networks and diverse international relationships; and 3) the charismatic personality, ingenuity, and distinct femininity of their owners.

These personal stories are also relayed in the articles and reviews of global wine expert publications. Chinese wines are regularly featured as medal winners at the annual Decanter World Wine Awards, and the Wine Advocate has a dedicated reviewer for Chinese wine, Beijing-based Master of Wine Edward Ragg (N. Wang 2019). In addition, James Suckling (2021) has published regular glowing reviews of Chinese wines, including a comprehensive tasting report of his "Top 100 wines of China 2021," which features several personal stories of winemakers and entrepreneurs. This is a classic component of wine branding, but it also speaks to the distinct role of artification as a source of legitimacy throughout the wine industry.

Artification and Innovation in Fine Wine

For a Chinese winery, being accepted in a category for which consumers are willing to pay high prices is not only a substantial achievement but also a useful tool of survival. The wine world is already full of well-established cheap and value-wine producers (many of which, notably from Chile, are imported in China). The increasing costs of labor, including that needed for burying the vines after harvest to protect them from brutally cold winters, means Chinese wine production costs are high. Combined with severe water constraints in the country's key wine regions, it is hard to imagine cheap Chinese wine labels taking over the world's supermarkets' bottom shelves. Moreover, large scale production that results in the kind of basic wines ubiquitous in Chinese supermarkets and convenience stores was largely responsible for domestic wines' low quality reputation. Thus, recognition for fine wine production, which doesn't rely on volumes and low margins, may be a more economically viable route.

Artification is an important component of wine culture, from the vineyard to the glass. Multinational corporations have skillfully incorporated passion in the stories, magic in the vineyard, and original art on the labels. But we find that artification is most impactful among small and even individually run producers. Because of the constraints discussed above, a small winery or even an individual winemaker without significant resources has little choice but to build trust through art, passion, a connection to the land where grapes are grown, and a personal connection to the brand.

The first quality Chinese wines that caught the world's attention were often inspired by red Bordeaux, and it resulted in the dominance of Cabernet Sauvignon plantings and red wines aged in new oak. Some producers have begun to embrace new trends in the wine world, including organic and biodynamic, and even low-intervention or natural wine. Silver Heights, one of Ningxia's most critically acclaimed boutique wineries, has moved beyond just talking up its combination of local roots with Bordeaux expertise. The owner, Emma Gao, studied winemaking in Bordeaux, where she met her husband, before coming home and becoming a leader in the Chinese fine wine revolution. The winery was first known (and praised) for Bordeaux blend type, oak-aged red wines. The small family story has been central since the beginning. A distribution partnership with Spanish firm Torres, which sells a lot of imported wine in China, helped place the wines in big cities like Beijing, including through Torres's own shop, Everwines. More recently, the winery has developed more independence from the Bordeaux inspiration, and more communication around sustainability and minimal intervention in the winemaking. For example, the winery's social media (including Instagram, in English, targeted at an international audience) regularly features Emma Gao talking about nature, sustainability, and doing Tai Chi in the vines. One of the latest wines is quite a departure from red Bordeaux, and embraces the natural wine trend. An orange wine named Sand Lake, made of a blend of Chardonnay, Sauvignon Blanc, and Gewurztraminer, is described as being from a "a pristine wetland" in "a renowned habitat for abundant wildlife with more than 1 million birds living in the area" (Silver Heights Vineyard 2022). The winery's biodynamic Pinot Noir also plays to the sustainability trend in premium wine, adding diversity to the portfolio and allowing Silver Heights to project quality to different ideas of fine wine, from more traditional oak-aged red Bordeaux to biodynamic and even quirky orange wine.

A similar direction can be seen in the work of an independent winemaker, Jianjun Liu, who started his career at Silver Heights. By independent, we mean he doesn't own any winery nor vineyard, but makes his wines by buying grapes from suppliers, carrying around his minimal equipment and finding space at other wineries. Interestingly, Liu learned winemaking by working at Silver Heights, and like most Ningxia (and more generally, China) wineries, early on, his independent winemaking projects focused on Cabernet Sauvignon blends. But his labels, instead of trying to look like traditional French wine, already spoke to his fondness for art and literature. His social media content blends wine, music, art, and classic films he likes. And over the last few years, he, too, has started making natural wines from grape varieties less common in China. This includes a Viognier, a Pinot Noir, and a Pét-Nat Riesling, all marketed and labeled as natural wine.

A recent article in The World of Fine Wine magazine argued that like craft brewing for beer, natural wine may generate a new interest in fine wine among younger drinkers (Schildknecht 2022). Meanwhile, in China, the natural wine scene is growing (Boyce 2019; 2020), and wine writer Jane Anson raved about Domaine des Arômes, a tiny Ningixa winery run by a young couple trained in Burgundy, practicing biodynamics in the vineyard and making low intervention wine (Anson 2017). Such an evolution is promising, as these productions do not rely on large volumes; they tell unique personal stories of the winemakers and capture rising trends in wine to expand on and diversify the emerging Chinese wine story.

In sum, despite early image problems associated with the made-in-China label, and an insufficient institutional environment to resolve them, Chinese wine entrepreneurs have begun to gain credibility in the world of fine wine, even when they are not in partnerships with foreign luxury brands. A major challenge for the continued development of this emerging industry is environmental sustainability, and in particular water scarcity, an issue that already affects large parts of the wine world. In the next section, we place wine in the context of China's water crisis.

"Not as Thirsty as Coal," but Water Scarcity Threatens Wineries and Poor Farmers Alike

Water issues are well known and increasingly salient in many established wine regions of the world, often requiring restrictions and policies to improve water management. The Ningxia Hui Autonomous Region, one of China's most promising wine regions, and the source of many award-winning wines, had appeared in the literature on China's water crisis long before the region had a wine industry. Ningxia has an arid climate and agriculture would be impossible without irrigation from the Yellow River. The dry climate and availability of irrigation are assets for wine production, but one may raise questions about the future as competing uses of the river keep growing. Moreover, in addition to extreme summer heat, another major issue is brutally cold winters, with temperatures dropping to minus 30 degrees Celsius. This requires a costly and labor intensive process of burying the vines after harvest for winter protection, as Vitis Vinifera (the subspecies of the grapevine that makes most of the world's wines), would otherwise not survive. Winters are not just cold but also very dry, which requires more watering of the vines before burying. Further, vines may be damaged in the process, especially those with more age, making it difficult to keep old vines (Li 2015b).

Ningxia is one of China's poorest provinces, and local policymakers see wine as one of the tools for poverty alleviation. As early as 2000, a report on China's Western Development strategy emphasized the potential of wine production in Ningxia to create wealth and jobs in an environmentally friendly way (White 2000). Wine was selected as one of the region's key agricultural sectors due to suitable conditions for wine grapes, in great part thanks to irrigation provided by the Yellow River. While the latter is rightly touted as an asset to the region's wines, water shortages are a major threat to the development of the industry (Hao, Li, and Cao 2015). Ningxia's farmers have long seen their livelihoods challenged by climate variability and drought (Li et al. 2013), and it doesn't help that the region is also one of China's locations for significant investments in coal, creating even more competition over water resources for other industries and agriculture (J. Li 2012; Shang et al. 2017). Further, the problem is compounded by groundwater overexploitation and pollution (Wang et al. 2019).

When the development of Ningxia wine began to accelerate, entrepreneurs were attracted by what is to this day considered prime location, large tracts of unused land at the foot of the Helan Mountain. Much of it was desert landscapes, parts of which have since been gradually reclaimed to plant vineyards. While local wineries and promotional materials often tout the benefits of irrigation from the Yellow River, at the very beginning, wineries' water use wasn't as regulated as it is today in all areas. One wine entrepreneur described the changing institutional environment that determined their access to water. Early on, the area where they started was mostly desert land, and without infrastructure connecting them to the city water system or the Yellow River, wineries each dug their own well to access groundwater, with little oversight from local authorities. It was unclear how legal the practices were, but given the local government's enthusiasm for the local wine industry, it worked like this for about a decade. Eventually, as the number of wineries and volume of wines grew exponentially larger, the government began to crack down on unregulated wells. The winery was issued a warning and inspectors started monitoring their commercial and residential water usage. The winery owner's clout and good relationships with the government helped them avoid immediate trouble. The well was still allowed, but subject to yearly re-authorization and stricter controls. Indeed, with more and more wineries in the area, unrestricted drawing on groundwater through privately dug wells is not sustainable in the long term. The owner emphasized this point, noting the need for responsible water use in an agricultural region in the middle of the desert.

These increased constraints of water use by wineries reflect a broader effort on the part of local authorities to invest in water conservation and wine is a central part of this effort. Wine grapes, along with other crops like red dates and goji berries, are seen as both higher value added and less water intensive than corn and wheat (Tan 2017). One interesting initiative is the Ningxia Irrigated Agriculture and Water Conservation Demonstration Project. Backed by a $70 million loan from the Asian Development Bank, it focuses specifically on wine grapes and dates (Asian Development Bank 2013). The project includes the installation of drip irrigation systems, which are more efficient than the traditional flood irrigation method. But its scope doesn't stop at the vineyard. To demonstrate economic viability and effectiveness, the project documents and loan agreement emphasize Ningxia's wine quality potential, the growing demand for wine in China. The project required that the local government develop a detailed marketing plan for wine, including market positioning, sales, and distribution (Asian Development Bank 2013; 2022).

The link between economic development, wine, and water is especially evident in Hongsibu, a district in the south of Ningxia where the government once relocated tens of thousands of people, notably from the Hui ethnic minority, who used to live in poor conditions in remote mountains further south. The district is known as the largest site of ecological resettlement in the country. While Hongsibu suffers from an arid climate and serious water shortage, the wide availability of yet uncultivated land was regarded as an opportunity to lift farmers out of poverty, through a major irrigation project that diverted water from the Yellow River for irrigation (Tan 2017). The wine industry is a key part of this project, and the more established wine route in the north of Ningxia has been extended south along the G110 national highway. Zhang and co-authors (2021) argue that for Hongsibu the development of wine production has had not only economic benefits by generating income for resettled farmers, but also ecological benefits, with vineyards acting as a tool to fight desertification, and wine grapes as a more water-efficient crop than alternatives, especially when using drip irrigation. For example, the authors estimate that water use by wine grapes amounts to 3,900 tons per hectare, compared to 5,400 tons per hectare for corn and wheat. On the one hand, this represents a crucial opportunity for poor farmers who had (and have) very little access to reliable agricultural income. On the other hand, new economic opportunity means new demands on a dwindling resource.

While these projects are all signs that the local authorities take water constraints seriously and have taken steps to address the issue, time will tell whether investments deliver the expected results. One expert who had conducted several site visits in the region expressed concern that while the government had subsidized the installation of drip irrigation, the equipment seemed to be there mostly for show at times. A winemaker explained that his winery had been pressured to adopt drip irrigation, but that the budget only allowed him to opt for cheap equipment, which he had not used since it was installed. This is also a form of institutional innovation, as producers have to balance compliance with their own capacity, but in this case the environment was not only unsupportive but counterproductive to the point of being both ecologically and financially unsustainable.

Beyond Ningxia, water scarcity is a problem faced by many parts of China, including other important wine regions like those in the areas around Beijing and Hebei where urbanization has long been putting pressure on water resources (W. Li et al. 2020). More generally, beyond the wine industry, despite important policy reforms, China's management of its water crisis has drawn criticism for focusing too much on supply management and insufficient regulation on demand (Zhao et al. 2015). Thus, since water has become an increasingly important issue in the wine world, the continued development of fine wine in China will depend on the sustainability of broader national and regional policies.

Conclusion

A story of innovation is rarely one of unfettered growth and unproblematic investment. From farmers to winemakers and executives, the people who make Chinese wine possible face an uphill battle, including: prejudice and anti-Chinese sentiment; inconsistent regulation of water, intellectual property, and more; and powerful social constraints around class, gender, ethnicity, and social capital. Those who have thrived have found, created, and combined alternative workarounds, otherwise known as "institutional bricolage." Like in any industry, access to networks in government or among foreign powerbrokers facilitates much more profitable investments and a much smoother road. However, we have also witnessed legitimate wealth creation among producers and farmers who began with extremely limited resources and thrived with ingenuity, cooperation, and combining varied strategies of institutional innovation.

Although our research is largely optimistic, the future of access to water is much more concerning. It is difficult to imagine continued rapid economic growth without significant control of the growing demand for water. Moreover, the global pandemic and China's evolving international relationships during the same years have been associated with significantly more volatility and unpredictability in the institutions affecting the wine industry. The sector has been challenged by the pandemic, along with the entire restaurant industry on which many wineries depend. Coincidentally, a significant wine education group had its services further interrupted by a shift in enforcement of a regulation around its status. And any trade war that impacts a specific industry (like Australian wine in China) can cause significant volatility in ways that may have ripple effects throughout the industry.

The most successful Chinese producers, regardless of size, are still thriving, but challenges have been significant and while the nature of anti-Chinese sentiment has shifted away from economic prejudice, it has also intensified during the pandemic. Only time will tell how temporary these challenges will be and whether there will be a space for productive and healthy forms of institutional bricolage.

References

Allen, F, J Qian, and M Qian. 2005. "Law, Finance, and Economic Growth in China." *Journal of Financial Economics* 77 (1): 57–116.

Anson, Jane. 2017. "Ningxia Wine: The Chinese Producers Going Biodynamic – Decanter." Decanter. October 26, 2017. https://www.decanter.com/wine-news/opinion/news-blogs-anson/ningxia-wine-biodynamic-winemaking-378680/.

Asian Development Bank. 2013. "Project Agreement for Ningxia Irrigated Agriculture and Water Conservation Demonstration Project." Text. https://www.adb.org/projects/documents/project-agreement-ningxia-irrigated-agriculture-and-water-conservation-demonstrat.

Asian Development Bank. 2022. "Ningxia Irrigated Agriculture and Water Conservation Demonstration Project." Project/Program Completion Reports, May, 73.

Bontempi, Maria Elena, and Giorgio Prodi. 2009. "Entry Strategies into China: The Choice between Joint Ventures and Wholly Foreign-Owned Enterprises: An Application to the Italian Manufacturing Sector." *International Review of Economics & Finance* 18 (1): 11–19.

Boyce, Jim. 2015. "New Wine, Old Bottle? Jia Bei Lan vs Jia Bei Lan Raises IPR and Status Issues in China's Wine Scene – Grape Wall of China." Grape Wall of China. July 27, 2015. https://www.grapewallofchina.com/2015/07/27/just-asking-say-do-these-two-wine-labels-look-similar/.

Boyce, Jim. 2019. "The Natural Wine Craze Hits China." Meiningers Wine Business International. October 8, 2019. https://www.wine-business-international.com/wine/news-events/natural-wine-craze-hits-china.

Boyce, Jim. 2020. "'You Need to Have This' | Natural Wine in China – Grape Wall of China." Grape Wall of China. August 26, 2020. https://www.grapewallofchina.com/2020/08/26/you-need-to-have-this-natural-wine-in-china/.

Brandt, Loren, and Eric Thun. 2010. "The Fight for the Middle: Upgrading, Competition, and Industrial Development in China." *World Development* 38 (11): 1555–74.

China Daily. 2012. "Gov't Researcher Responds to Chinese Wine Contamination Allegations – Lifestyle – Chinadaily.Com.Cn." China Daily. August 14, 2012. https://www.chinadaily.com.cn/food/2012-08/14/content_15674843.htm.

Cleaver, Frances. 2001. "Institutional Bricolage, Conflict and Cooperation in Usangu, Tanzania." *IDS Bulletin* 32 (4): 26–35.

Cusmano, Lucia, Andrea Morrison, and Roberta Rabellotti. 2010. "Catching up Trajectories in the Wine Sector: A Comparative Study of Chile, Italy, and South Africa." *World Development* 38 (11): 1588–1602.

Dana, Léo-Paul, Julien Granata, Frank Lasch, and Alan Carnaby. 2013. "The Evolution of Co-Opetition in the Waipara Wine Cluster of New Zealand." *Wine Economics and Policy* 2 (1): 42–49.

Goenka, Himanshu. 2016. "Alibaba (BABA) Overtakes Walmart (WMT) As Largest Retailer By Gross Volume." *International Business Times*. April 6, 2016. http://www.ibtimes.com/alibaba-baba-overtakes-walmart-wmt-largest-retailer-gross-volume-2349025.

Hao, Linhai, Xueming Li, and Kailong Cao. 2015. "Toward Sustainability: Development of the Ningxia Wine Industry." Edited by Jean-Marie Aurand. *BIO Web of Conferences* 5: 01021. https://doi.org/10.1051/bioconf/20150501021.

Howson, Cynthia, and Pierre Ly. 2018. "How China's Winemakers Succeeded (without Stealing)." The Conversation. 2018. http://theconversation.com/how-chinas-winemakers-succeeded-without-stealing-94604.

Howson, Cynthia, and Pierre Ly. 2020. *Adventures on the China Wine Trail: How Farmers, Local Governments, Teachers, and Entrepreneurs Are Rocking the Wine World*. Rowman & Littlefield Publishers.

Kehoe, Emily. 2013. "Combating the Counterfeiting Woes of the Wine Seller in China." *IDEA* 53: 257.

Kjellgren, Björn. 2019. "Fluid Modernity: Wine in China." In *The Globalization of Wine*, edited by David Inglis and Anna-Mari Almila, 115–32. Bloomsbury Publishing.

Kumar, Preeti. 2018. "How China Got Consumers to Trust E-Commerce." LinkedIn. May 9, 2018. https://www.linkedin.com/pulse/how-china-got-consumers-trust-e-commerce-preeti-kumar/.

Lai, Hongyi Harry. 2002. "China's Western Development Program: Its Rationale, Implementation, and Prospects." *Modern China* 28 (4): 432–66.

Li, Demei. 2015a. "Why It's Difficult to Sell Wine in China (Part I)." Decanter China. 2015. https://www.decanterchina.com/en/columns/demeis-view-wine-communication-from-a-chinese-winemaker/why-it-s-difficult-to-sell-wine-in-china-part-i.

Li, Demei. 2015b. "The Vines in the Chinese Vineyards Have Been Dug out of the Ground." Decanter China. April 28, 2015. https://www.decanterchina.com/en/columns/demeis-view-wine-communication-from-a-chinese-winemaker/the-vines-in-the-chinese-vineyards-have-been-dug-out-of-the-ground.

Li, Jing. 2012. "Ningxia's Coal and Farm Projects Pose Critical Threat to Water Supplies." *South China Morning Post*. September 12, 2012. https://www.scmp.com/news/china/article/1034472/ningxias-coal-and-farm-projects-pose-critical-threat-water-supplies.

Li, Weifeng, Xia Hai, Lijian Han, Jingqiao Mao, and Mingming Tian. 2020. "Does Urbanization Intensify Regional Water Scarcity? Evidence and Implications from a Megaregion of China." *Journal of Cleaner Production* 244 (January): 118592. https://doi.org/10.1016/j.jclepro.2019.118592.

Li, Yuanbo, and Isabel Bardají. 2017. "A New Wine Superpower? An Analysis of the Chinese Wine Industry." *Cahiers Agricultures* 26 (6): 65002. https://doi.org/10.1051/cagri/2017051.

Li, Yue, D. Conway, Yanjuan Wu, Qingzhu Gao, S. Rothausen, Wei Xiong, Hui Ju, and Erda Lin. 2013. "Rural Livelihoods and Climate Variability in Ningxia, Northwest China." *Climatic Change* 119 (3): 891–904.

Liv-ex. 2022. "Ao Yun 2018 Analysis Ahead of Release." *Liv-Ex* (blog). March 2, 2022. https://www.liv-ex.com/2022/03/ao-yun-2018-analysis-ahead-release/.

Luo, Yadong. 2007. "A Coopetition Perspective of Global Competition." *Journal of World Business* 42 (2): 129–44. https://doi.org/10.1016/j.jwb.2006.08.007.

Muhammad, Andrew, Amanda M. Leister, Lihong McPhail, and Wei Chen. 2014. "The Evolution of Foreign Wine Demand in China." *Australian Journal of Agricultural and Resource Economics* 58 (3): 392–408.

Mustacich, Suzanne. 2015. *Thirsty Dragon: China's Lust for Bordeaux and the Threat to the World's Best Wines.* Macmillan.

OIV. 2021. "State of the World Vitivinicultural Sector in 2020." International Organisation of Vine and Wine. April 2021. https://www.oiv.int/public/medias/7909/oiv-state-of-the-world-vitivinicultural-sector-in-2020.pdf.

Ponte, Stefano, and Joachim Ewert. 2009. "Which Way Is 'up' in Upgrading? Trajectories of Change in the Value Chain for South African Wine." *World Development* 37 (10): 1637–50.

Qin, Amy. 2019. "A French Wine From China? This $300 Bottle Is the Real Thing." *The New York Times*. October 24, 2019, sec. Business. https://www.nytimes.com/2019/10/24/business/china-wine-long-dai-lafite.html.

Raymond, Nate. 2015. "Alibaba Sued in U.S. by Luxury Brands over Counterfeit Goods." *Reuters*. May 18, 2015. http://www.reuters.com/article/us-alibaba-lawsuit-fake-idUSKBN0O02E120150518.

Robinson, Jancis. 2017. "Chinese Wine Drinkers Turn to Imports." JancisRobinson.Com. April 21, 2017. https://www.jancisrobinson.com/articles/chinese-wine-drinkers-turn-to-imports.

Schildknecht, David. 2022. "Natural Wine: Fine Wine's Funky Future?" World Of Fine Wine (blog). November 18, 2022. https://worldoffinewine.com/homepage-featured-articles/natural-wine-fine-wines-funky-future.

Shang, Yizi, Shibao Lu, Xiaofei Li, Pengfei Hei, Xiaohui Lei, Jiaguo Gong, Jiahong Liu, Jiaqi Zhai, and Hao Wang. 2017. "Balancing Development of Major Coal Bases with Available Water Resources in China through 2020." *Applied Energy* 194: 735–50.

Silver Heights Vineyard. 2022. "Silver Heights Vineyard on Instagram: 'Watch Emma in the Video to Learn Why We Named Our First-Ever Orange Wine Sand Lake Moon Like All of Our Wines, It Is a Tribute to Our Homeland Ningxia. Sand Lake, a Pristine Wetland Bordered by a Desert in Ningxia Hui

Autonomous Region, Is a Renowned Habitat for Abundant Wildlife with More than 1 Million Birds Living in the Area. It Is Therefore Honored as "the Best Place for Bird-Watching in China".'" Instagram. April 18, 2022. https://www.instagram.com/tv/CcfRpQxjYx5/.

Smith, Rob. 2018. "42% of Global E-Commerce Is Happening in China. Here's Why." World Economic Forum. April 10, 2018. https://www.weforum.org/agenda/2018/04/42-of-global-e-commerce-is-happening-in-china-heres-why/.

Statista. 2022. "Alcoholic Drinks – China." Statista Market Forcasts. 2022. https://www.statista.com/out look/cmo/alcoholic-drinks/china.

Suckling, James. 2021. "Top 100 Wines of China 2021." *JamesSuckling.Com* (blog). December 28, 2021. https://www.jamessuckling.com/wine-tasting-reports/top-100-wines-china-2021/.

Suckling, James. 2022. "James Suckling Puts Ao Yun Shangri-La 2018 to Test." *JamesSuckling.Com* (blog). February 14, 2022. https://www.jamessuckling.com/wine-tasting-reports/chinas-best-wine-ever-ao-yun-shangri-la-2018-put-to-test/.

Tan, Yan. 2017. "Resettlement and Climate Impact: Addressing Migration Intention of Resettled People in West China." *Australian Geographer* 48 (1): 97–119.

Wang, Janet Z. 2019. *The Chinese Wine Renaissance: A Wine Lover's Companion*. Ebury Press.

Wang, Natalie. 2019. "Wine Advocate Names Edward Ragg MW as New Chinese Wine Reviewer." Vino Joy News. November 4, 2019. http://vino-joy.com/2019/11/04/wine-advocate-names-edward-ragg-mw-as-new-chinese-wine-reviewer/.

Wang, Zeyu, Juqin Shen, Fuhua Sun, Zhaofang Zhang, Dandan Zhang, Yizhen Jia, and Kaize Zhang. 2019. "A Pricing Model for Groundwater Rights in Ningxia, China Based on the Fuzzy Mathematical Model." *International Journal of Environmental Research and Public Health* 16 (12): 2176.

White, Paul. 2000. "Ningxia Spearheads Western Development Strategy." China Internet Information Center (China.Org.Cn). October 9, 2000. http://www.china.org.cn/english/DO-e/2514.htm.

Yang, Chenlu, Rui Song, Yinting Ding, Liang Zhang, Hua Wang, and Hua Li. 2022. "Review on Legal Supervision System of the Chinese Wine Industry." *Horticulturae* 8 (5): 432.

Yang, Guobin. 2013. "Contesting Food Safety in the Chinese Media: Between Hegemony and Counter-Hegemony." *The China Quarterly* 214: 337–55.

Yao, Yang, and Linda Yueh. 2009. "Law, Finance, and Economic Growth in China: An Introduction." *World Development* 37 (4): 753–62. https://doi.org/10.1016/j.worlddev.2008.07.009.

Zhang, Liang, Zhilei Wang, Tingting Xue, Feifei Gao, Ruteng Wei, Ying Wang, Xing Han, Hua Li, and Hua Wang. 2021. "Combating Desertification through the Wine Industry in Hongsibu, Ningxia." *Sustainability* 13 (10): 5654. https://doi.org/10.3390/su13105654.

Zhao, Xu, Junguo Liu, Qingying Liu, Martin R. Tillotson, Dabo Guan, and Klaus Hubacek. 2015. "Physical and Virtual Water Transfers for Regional Water Stress Alleviation in China." *Proceedings of the National Academy of Sciences* 112 (4): 1031–35.

List of Contributors

Anna-Mari Almila is Senior Researcher in Cultural Sociology at the Sapienza University of Rome. She is a sociologist of fashion, wine, and other apparent trivialities. She writes in the fields of cultural, political, global, and historical sociology, and her topics include the materiality of dressed bodies and their environments; fashion globalization and the history of fashion studies; the historical/political construction of urban spaces; fashion and religion; dress in later life; and wine and gender. She loves social theory and (sociology of) wine.

Binyam Zenebe Andargie is a Digital Content Specialist at the Nike European Headquarters in Hilversum, Netherlands. He graduated from the University of Manchester with a Master of Science in International Fashion Marketing. Binyam previously worked at garment factories in Ethiopia and has interest in research about sustainability across the textile and fashion supply chain.

Deniz Atik is Associate Professor of Marketing at the University of Texas Rio Grande Valley, and founding co-editor of *Markets, Globalization & Development Review (MGDR)*. Dr. Atik's research interests focus on macromarketing, critical marketing, and transformative consumer research, especially theories of fashion, sustainability, and vulnerable consumers. She has published articles in *Marketing Theory, European Journal of Marketing, Journal of Marketing Management, Journal of Macromarketing*, and *Journal of the Association for Consumer Research*, among others. She also served as visiting professor at Bocconi University, Italy, Kyoto University, Japan, KIMEP University, Kazakhstan, Ecole de Management de Normandie, France, and as professor of marketing at Izmir University of Economics, Turkey.

Hanieh Choopani studied her master of arts in fashion and textile design with a focus on zero-waste design in apparel cutting and sewing as an integrated part of circular fashion at Alzahra University in Tehran, Iran. She is now also a DAAD scholarship holder as a Ph.D. Candidate in the field of sustainable fashion education at Freiburg University of Education and Hannover University of Applied Sciences and Arts.

Nikhilesh Dholakia is Professor Emeritus, University of Rhode Island (URI), who currently lives in Hollister, California. He is the founding co-editor of *Markets, Globalization & Development Review* (MGDR), the journal of the International Society of Markets & Development (ISMD). Dr. Dholakia's research deals with globalization, technology, innovation, market processes, and consumer culture. His current work focuses on global, social, and cultural aspects of technologies that range from human-assistive to transhuman. He also explores key global issues and processes in the marketing and management fields from critical perspectives.

Zeynep Ozdamar Ertekin is Assistant Professor of Marketing at Izmir University of Economics. She received her BA degree in Management from Bogazici University and MBA and PhD degrees in Marketing from Izmir University of Economics. Her research interests concentrate on sustainability, fashion, consumption theories, and macromarketing. She has publications in *Journal of Marketing Management, Journal of Macromarketing, International Journal of Consumer Studies, Journal of Consumer Behavior, Journal of Social Marketing, Journal of Global Fashion Marketing*, and *Markets, Globalization and Development Review* among others. She has 16 years of professional experience in the fashion apparel industry.

Karen V. Fernandez (PhD Kansas) is Associate Professor in Marketing and Director of Doctoral Studies at the University of Auckland Business School in New Zealand. Karen's research draws on Consumer Culture Theory to understand how consumption creates, shapes, and reflects identity. Her work examines how

https://doi.org/10.1515/9783110783933-017

disposal and reacquisition of used and/or discarded possessions reshapes the linear trajectory of consumption into circular consumption. Karen is an Associate Editor of *Consumption, Markets & Culture* and has published articles in the *Journal of Consumer Research*, the *Journal of Public Policy and Marketing*, the *Journal of Advertising*, the *European Journal of Marketing*, and the *Journal of Business Research*.

A. Fuat Fırat is Professor of Marketing at the University of Texas Rio Grande Valley. His research interests cover areas such as macro consumer behavior and macromarketing; postmodern culture; transmodern marketing strategies; gender and consumption; marketing and development; and interorganizational relations. He has won the *Journal of Macromarketing* Charles Slater Award for best article with co-author N. Dholakia, the *Journal of Consumer Research* best article award with co-author A. Venkatesh, and the *Corporate Communications: An International Journal* top ranked paper award with co-authors L.T. Christensen and J. Cornelissen. He has published several books including *Consuming People: From Political Economy to Theaters of Consumption*, co-authored by N. Dholakia, and is a founding editor of *Consumption, Markets & Culture*.

Meri Frig works as a postdoctoral researcher at Hanken School of Economics in Helsinki, Finland. Her research interests include CSR/sustainability communication, climate change communication, cultural intermediaries, and sustainable consumption. She has previously published her research in journals such as *Journal of Business Ethics*, *Business & Society*, and *Journal of Consumer Culture*.

Charlene Gallery is an experienced Lecturer in Fashion marketing communication, brand management and digital innovation at the University of Manchester. Her teaching practice focuses on digital innovation, social sustainability, and brand activism. Her research interests are centred around digital sustainability, curriculum decolonialisation, and creating emancipatory teaching approaches.

Bianca Grohmann, MBA, Ph.D., is Professor of Marketing, Concordia University Research Chair in Consumer Psychology and Visual Marketing, and principal investigator at the Laboratory for Sensory Research at Concordia University in Montréal, Canada. Her research interests are in consumer psychology, branding, and sensory marketing, with an emphasis on the influence of visual, olfactory, gustatory, and haptic brand elements on consumers' product and brand evaluations.

Verena Gruber is Associate Professor of Marketing at the Lifestyle Research Center at emlyon business school (France). She previously held positions at HEC Montréal and WU Vienna. Her research broadly relates to consumption and sustainability and is informed by a Transformative Consumer Research agenda that aims to benefit consumer welfare and improving quality of life. Her work has been published in journals such *Journal of Business Ethics*, *Journal of Public Policy and Marketing*, and *Psychology & Marketing*.

Claudia E Henninger is a Reader Lecturer in Fashion Marketing Management in the Department of Materials, The University of Manchester, with an interest in sustainability and the circular economy. She has been published in internationally leading journals (e.g., *EJM*, *International Journal of Management Review*) and disseminated her work at a variety of national and international conferences. Claudia is an Executive Member of the Sustainable Fashion Consumption Network, the Chair of the Academy of Marketing's SIG Sustainability, and the Research Lead for Creative MCR (University of Manchester) within the field of Creative Industries and Innovation.

Christina Holweg is Associate Professor at the Institute for Retailing & Data Science at WU Vienna University of Economics and Business (Austria). Her research focus is on retail, marketing, and topics of sustainability. Before starting her academic career, she held a senior managerial position in marketing and sales at the international consumer goods company Procter & Gamble. Her work has been published in the *Journal of Cleaner Production*, the *Journal of Public Policy and Marketing*, and the *International Journal of Retail and Distribution Management*, among others.

Cynthia Howson holds a PhD in Development Studies from the School of Oriental and African Studies. Currently a Teaching Professor of Ethnic, Gender, and Labor Studies at the University of Washington Tacoma, her research delves into the complex interplay of competing norms and identities in rural labor and entrepreneurship in developing nations. Dr. Howson's previous work encompasses a wide range of topics, including studies on women's cross-border trade in Senegal and the challenges faced by Somali refugees in accessing public services in Wisconsin. With co-author Pierre Ly, her book, *Adventures on the China Wine Trail: How Farmers, Local Governments, Teachers, and Entrepreneurs Are Rocking the Wine World* (Rowman & Littlefield, 2020) won Gourmand International's "Best in the World" award in the category of Wine and Beer Tourism.

David Inglis is Professor of Sociology at the University of Helsinki. He holds degrees in sociology from the Universities of Cambridge and York. He writes in the areas of cultural sociology, historical sociology, and social theory, applying these to contemporary social challenges. He has written and edited various books in these areas. His current research concerns globalization, cosmopolitanism, (de)civilizing processes, and the sociological analysis of wine.

Samira Iran is an expert in sustainable consumption and the sharing economy. She holds a Ph.D. in sustainable and collaborative consumption in the field of fashion and has over eight years of working experience in various multi- and transdisciplinary research projects. In addition to her current role as a project lead at Hot or Cool Institute, she is working as the lead of a citizen science project on "sufficiency and minimalism" at Technische Universität Berlin. She is also the Co-Founder of Fashion Revolution Iran and Executive Director of Sustainable Fashion Consumption Network.

Annamma Joy is Professor of Marketing at the Faculty of Management, UBC. Her research spans the domains of art, fashion, and fine wines. She has won several awards for her research, the most recent being the Louis Vuitton and Singapore management university award (second place) for best paper at the Luxury brand conference in 2018. Her work has been published in the *Journal of Consumer Research*, *Journal of Consumer Psychology*, *Journal of Business Research*, *Consumption, Markets and Culture*, *Journal of Consumer Culture*, *Cornell Hospitality Quarterly*, *Tourism Recreation Research*, *Journal of Wine Research and Arts* and *the Market*. She has written several chapters in handbooks on consumption and marketing. She has published an edited book, *The Future of Luxury Brands* (De Gruyter, 2022) and *New Directions in Art, Fashion and Wine,* published by Lexington Books in 2023.

Finola Kerrigan is Professor of Marketing at Birmingham Business School, University of Birmingham where she teaches and researches marketing and consumption. Finola has published her research in a range of international journals and edited collections and is the author of *Film Marketing* (2010/2017). Drawing on a range of qualitative and creative research methods, Finola has expertise in the areas of branding, digital identity, ethics, and the incorporation of new technologies into marketing practice and how this impacts consumers. With a specific focus on researching the cultural and creative industries, Finola centers the arts both in terms of arts-based methods and as a context for her research. As well as her academic research, which has been funded by the ESRC, EPSCR, British Academy, and a range of charitable organisations, Finola has completed a number of industry research projects in collaboration with public bodies and commercial companies.

Eva Lienbacher is Professor (FH) at the Department Business & Tourism at Salzburg University of Applied Sciences (Austria). Her research focuses on retail management and marketing as well as on the social-ecological responsibility of businesses. Her work has been published in *Industrial Marketing Management* and the *International Journal of Retail and Distribution Management*, among others.

Pierre Ly is a Professor of International Political Economy (IPE) at the University of Puget Sound. He received his PhD in Economics from the Toulouse School of Economics in France. Pierre teaches IPE courses on international trade and finance, NGOs, the Chinese economy, and a popular course called The Idea of Wine. His research interests include development, China, and the political economy of wine. His first book, co-authored with Cynthia Howson, *Adventures on the China Wine Trail: How Farmers, Local Governments, Teachers, and Entrepreneurs Are Rocking the Wine World*, published in February 2020, won Gourmand International's "Best in the World" award in the Wine and Beer Tourism books category. Prior to his focus on wine, Pierre published research on the business activities of Non-Government Organizations in Bangladesh, and online crowdfunding for microfinance institutions.

Nikoo Mirzapour studied her master of arts in fashion and textile design at Alzahra University and a bachelor of arts in design and sewing at Shariaty Technical and Vocational College in Tehran. She promotes digital design as a way to decrease fabric waste in fashion production. She is a creative and motivated digital fashion designer, skilled at 3D software such as CLO3D and Marvellous Design, and collaborated with international companies for two years as a freelance designer. In addition, she is an CAD instructor in ClO3D, Marvelous Designer, and Adobe Illustrator at various institutes in Tehran.

Chloe Preece is Associate Professor of Marketing at ESCP Business School. Her research is focused on notions of social, cultural, and economic value, primarily in the arts and creative industries. In studying these fields, Chloe takes a critical perspective to analyse the ideological assumptions which underpin markets.

Camilo Peña has a PhD in Interdisciplinary Studies (Sustainability and Marketing) and a MSc in Sustainable Development. His research interests (approached mainly through interpretivist, phenomenological, and qualitative perspectives) include sustainability, consumer culture, wine consumption and marketing, nature, market development, and social movements. He currently lives in unceded Syilx Okanagan Nation Territory and works at the University of British Columbia as a Special Research Projects Manager. He has over 10 years of academic research experience as well as nearly five years of experience in institutional and provincial research projects.

Pia Polsa is Associate Professor of Marketing at Hanken School of Economics, and has previously worked as researcher for Fudan University, Nankai University, and as a Dean for Hult International Business School in Shanghai. Her current research interests are consumer vulnerability and multi-dimensional value in cross-sector settings. She has published in journals such as *Journal of Business Ethics, Journal of Business Research, Industrial Marketing Management, Journal of Macromarketing, Journal of Services Marketing*, and *Supply Chain Management; International Journal*, among others.

Joanne Roberts is Emeritus Professor at Winchester School of Art, University of Southampton, UK. Joanne gained her PhD at the Centre for Urban and Regional Development Studies, Newcastle University, UK, and she has held academic posts at the Universities of Durham, Newcastle, Northumbria, and Southampton, UK. Her areas of expertise include creativity and innovation, luxury, knowledge management and international business. Joanne has published widely in leading international academic journals including *Journal of Management Studies, Journal of Business Ethics, Management Learning*, and *Research Policy*. She is the co-editor, with J. Armitage, of *Critical Luxury Studies: Art, Design, Media* (Edinburgh University Press, 2016) and *The Third Realm of Luxury* (Bloomsbury, 2020), and with P-Y. Donzé and V. Pouillard of *The Oxford Handbook of Luxury Business* (Oxford University Press, 2022).

Pilar Rojas-Gaviria is Associate Professor of Marketing at Birmingham Business School. Her work focuses on understanding the role of consumption in the construction of multicultural collective identities and solidarities. She draws on philosophical theories, poetry, and research on consumer behaviour.

Raneem Zaitoun is a senior undergraduate student in the Faculty of Management at the University of British Columbia-Okanagan campus. Her research interests include digital marketing and luxury brands.

Ying Zhu is an Assistant Professor of Marketing in the Faculty of Management at the University of British Columbia-Okanagan campus. She received her Ph.D. in Marketing from the Mays Business School at Texas A&M University. Her research interests include digital marketing, consumer behavior, branding, business analytics, and social networks. Her recent research focuses on investigating the impact of technology on consumers. Her research has been published in the *European Journal of Marketing, Psychology & Marketing, Journal of Brand Management, Journal of Retailing and Consumer Services*, among others.

Cristian Ziliberberg is an Early-Stage Researcher at the Aalborg University in Denmark. He works across various countries like Denmark, the US, and Moldova. His research deals with change narratives and legitimation, because he is passionate about observing and participating in individual, group, organizational, technological, and social transformations, especially under uncertainty. Empirically, he explores technological start-ups, the Metaverse, Artificial intelligence, and the leaders and innovators who build these. When doing such explorations, Cristian wears psychological, philosophical, sociological, and ideological lenses.

About the Editor

Annamma Joy is Professor of Marketing at the Faculty of Management, UBC. Her research spans the domains of art, fashion and fine wines. She has won several awards for her research, the most recent being the Louis Vuitton and Singapore management university award (second place) for best paper at the Luxury brand conference in 2018. Her work has been published in the *Journal of Consumer Research, Journal of Consumer Psychology, Journal of Business Research, Consumption, Markets and Culture, Journal of Consumer Culture, Cornell Hospitality Quarterly, Tourism Recreation Research, Journal of Wine Research* and *Arts and the Market.*

She has several chapters in handbooks on consumption and marketing. She has published two edited books, The Future of Luxury Brands, by De Gruyter in 2022 and New Directions in Art, Fashion and Wine: Sustainability, Digitalization and Artification in 2023.

https://doi.org/10.1515/9783110783933-018

List of Figures

https://doi.org/10.1515/9783110783933-019

List of Tables

https://doi.org/10.1515/9783110783933-020

Index

https://doi.org/10.1515/9783110783933-021

www.ingramcontent.com/pod-product-compliance
Lightning Source LLC
Chambersburg PA
CBHW081050220326
41598CB00038B/7049